Literacy in Early Childhood and Primary Education

Issues, challenges and solutions

Claire McLachlan
Tom Nicholson
Ruth Fielding-Barnsley
Louise Mercer
Sarah Ohi

CAMBRIDGE
UNIVERSITY PRESS

CAMBRIDGE UNIVERSITY PRESS
Cambridge, New York, Melbourne, Madrid, Cape Town,
Singapore, São Paulo, Delhi, Mexico City

Cambridge University Press
477 Williamstown Road, Port Melbourne, VIC 3207, Australia

Published in the United States of America by Cambridge University Press, New York

www.cambridge.org
Information on this title: www.cambridge.org/9781107671010

First published 2013

Cover design by Marc Martin at Lanz+Martin
Text design by Tanya De Silva-Mckay
Typeset by Newgen Publishing and Data Services
Printed in Singapore by C.O.S. Printers Pte Ltd

A catalogue record for this publication is available from the British Library

A Cataloguing-in-Publication entry is available from the catalogue of the National Library of Australia at
www.nla.gov.au

ISBN 978-1-107-67101-0 Paperback

Additional resources for this publication at www.cambridge.edu.au/academic/literacy

Literacy in Early Childhood and Primary Education

Issues, challenges and solutions

Literacy in Early Childhood and Primary Education provides a comprehensive introduction to literacy teaching and learning. The book explores the continuum of literacy learning and children's transitions from early childhood settings to junior primary classrooms, and then to senior primary and beyond.

Reader-friendly and accessible, this book equips pre-service teachers with the theoretical underpinnings and practical strategies and skills needed to teach literacy. It places the 'reading wars' firmly in the past as it examines contemporary research and practices. The book covers important topics such as literacy acquisition, family literacies and multiliteracies, foundation skills for literacy learning, reading difficulties, assessment, and supporting diverse literacy learners in early childhood and primary classrooms. It also addresses some of the challenges that teachers may face in the classroom and provides solutions to these.

Each chapter includes learning objectives, reflective questions and definitions of key terms to engage and assist readers. Further resources are also available at www.cambridge.edu.au/academic/literacy. Written by an expert author team and featuring real-world examples from literacy teachers and learners, *Literacy in Early Childhood and Primary Education* will help pre-service teachers feel confident teaching literacy to diverse age groups and abilities.

Claire McLachlan is Associate Professor, Early Years Education, at Massey University.

Tom Nicholson is Professor of Literacy Education at Massey University.

Ruth Fielding-Barnsley is Associate Professor in Literacy Education at the University of Tasmania.

Louise Mercer is Lecturer in Learning and Professional Studies at the Queensland University of Technology.

Sarah Ohi is Lecturer in Language and Literacy Education at Deakin University.

Contents

Contents

Contents

Contents

List of figures

List of tables

About the authors

Claire McLachlan is Associate Professor, Early Years Education, at Massey University in Palmerston North, New Zealand. Claire became involved with early childhood education through the Playcentre movement as a young mother of three children, and became fascinated with how young children learn. She completed her doctorate on the topic of emergent literacy in New Zealand kindergartens. She has lectured on early childhood education at the University of Wisconsin at Madison, Wisconsin; at AUT University in Auckland; and at Massey University in Palmerston North, New Zealand. As well, she has had various roles as a teacher and manager in early childhood centres. Claire has a longstanding interest in literacy and has written and edited a number of publications on teachers' beliefs and practices as they relate to literacy in the early childhood curriculum. She is the co-author of *Early Childhood Curriculum: Planning, Assessment and Implementation* and the co-editor of *Literacies in Childhood: Changing Views, Challenging Practice*. Since 2006 she has also been the co-editor of the journal *Early Education*, which is a publication aimed at early childhood practitioners.

Tom Nicholson is Professor in the School of Education at Massey University in Auckland, New Zealand, where he has been working since 2006. At Massey, he served as co-director of the Centre for Research on Children's Literacy (CERCL) from 2007 to 2010. The Minister of Education appointed him to an Expert Advisory Group of four assessment experts during 2010–11. His current research focuses on issues related to reading acquisition, reading difficulties and reading comprehension. He is also investigating whether interventions can bridge the gap between social classes in reading achievement, and stopping the summer slide in reading. Prior to coming to Massey, Tom held a personal chair in Education at The University of Auckland. His initial appointment was with the School of Education at Waikato University in Hamilton. He has been active in professional organisations, especially the Society for the Scientific Study of Reading and the International Reading Association. In 2009 Professor Nicholson won election to the Hall of Fame of the International Reading Association. He has written and co-edited several books about research and practice, including *Reading Comprehension: The What, the How, and the Why* (2012), *Dyslexia in the Workplace* (2012), *Teaching Reading Vocabulary* (2010), *Teaching Text Structures: The Key to Non-fiction Reading Success* (2007) and *At the Cutting Edge: The Importance of Phonemic Awareness in Learning to Read and Spell* (2005). He has served on the boards of educational research journals such as *Reading and Writing, Reading Research Quarterly, Scientific Studies of Reading* and *The Reading Teacher*. Professor Nicholson received his BA in English and history, and his MA in history from the University of Sydney, after which he taught high school in Sydney for several years, and then joined the Research and Planning Branch of the Department of Education in South Australia. He went on to complete his PhD in Reading Education at the University of Minnesota. He has been a Visiting Scholar at the University of Texas at Austin, Stanford University, and the University of Tasmania, Australia.

Ruth Fielding-Barnsley is Associate Professor of Literacy Education at the University of Tasmania, Australia. Prior to coming to UTAS two years ago, Ruth was lecturing in special education at Queensland University of Technology. Ruth began her interest in literacy as a primary classroom teacher in New South Wales and followed this up by completing degrees in special education and a PhD on the topic of developing a model of reading acquisition. Ruth has published several journal articles and book chapters in the area of literacy and she has also contributed to the development of the Australian Curriculum as both a writer and advisor. Her proudest achievement has been the development of a smartphone app to teach phonemic awareness, 'Profs' Phonics in 2012.

Louise Mercer is Lecturer in the School of Learning and Professional Studies at Queensland University of Technology. Prior to taking up this position in July 2007, she was a regular classroom teacher, a compensatory language teacher, a support teacher and a school psychologist (kindergarten to Year 12) in a number of school districts in Alberta and British Columbia, Canada. She was also a sessional lecturer at the University of British Columbia (Vancouver, BC) where she completed her doctorate in 2004 and at Simon Fraser University (Burnaby, BC). Louise has published several journal articles and book chapters in the area of learning difficulties, autism and reading difficulties.

Sarah Ohi is Lecturer in Language and Literacy in the School of Education, Faculty of Arts/ Education at Deakin University, Melbourne, Australia. She is passionate about improving language and literacy practices for children in their early years of life. Sarah lectures in Language and Literacy for the Early Childhood and Bachelor of Teaching programs at both undergraduate and postgraduate levels. Her doctoral research explored constructions of reading in the early childhood years and teachers' roles in the research–policy–praxis nexus. Sarah's research interests largely revolve around improving the language and literacy development of young children, improving the quality of teaching and learning in higher education through innovations and the use of technology, and strengthening the research–teaching nexus by engaging in research with practising teachers in the field. Sarah is currently engaged in further language and literacy research which will be reported in upcoming research articles.

Acknowledgements

The authors would like to thank the production team at Cambridge University Press and in particular, our Commissioning Editor, Isabella Mead. We are sincerely grateful to Isabella for her unflagging support and assistance as the team of authors for this text was assembled and negotiated and for her very helpful advice on processes and feedback on the draft chapters. This book would not have eventuated without Isabella's help and input.

Claire McLachlan would like to thank 'the Smith kids' and their families – Jessica Smith and James Edwards, Jeremy Smith, Lorraine Farrell, and Tegan and Brad Smith – for supplying photographs of her grandchildren Millie and Vaughn and great niece Amber involved with literacy activities at home. May these beautiful children have a lifelong love of literacy! Thanks to Elizabeth Henry, Massey University librarian, for her assistance in finding exemplars of early reading books. Thanks to the Ministry of Education for permission to print an extract from *The Fire Engine*. Finally, Claire would like to thank her wonderful husband, Simon Barton, for his loving support and tolerance throughout the research and writing of 'yet another little project'.

Tom Nicholson would like to thank Sara Strasser, teacher at Chavez Elementary in downtown Chicago, for allowing the use of photos of her class. Thanks to Dr Laura Tse for allowing use of the lesson plans taken from her PhD thesis. Thanks to the New Zealand Ministry of Education for permission to reprint materials from the National Standards in Reading and Writing publication; the cover page of Dot Meharry's book, *The Hole in the King's Sock*; and the images of the 'colour wheel' from the Ministry's website. Thanks to Dot Meharry, author. Thanks to Dinah Winiata for the lesson plan in Chapter 8. Thanks to Wiley publishers for permission to print the phonics scope and sequence from the *Phonics Handbook*. Thanks to Wendy Pye Publishing for allowing use of the cover of *The Watchdog Who Wouldn't*. Thanks to Ruth Fielding-Barnsley for allowing use of one of the poster images from her Sound Foundations program, and for her wise feedback on Tom's writing. Finally, but most importantly, Tom thanks his wife, Nora, who gave up precious summer holiday time so he could write chapters for the book – it was a lot to ask but really appreciated.

Ruth Fielding-Barnsley would like to thank Jo and Joel Stewart for sharing photos of their wonderful children, Alex and Clare.

Louise Mercer would like to thank all the teachers in her life, especially the pre-service teachers at the Queensland University of Technology who have so enthusiastically engaged with her in learning about how to support young people experiencing difficulties with reading and writing.

Acknowledgements

Sarah Ohi is thankful to the Lord for all things. She dearly thanks her husband Piliati Ohi and her children, Joseph, Glen and Leah, for their ongoing love, support and patience. Thanks to Piliati for his unfailing encouragement, to Glen and Leah for the inclusion of their special photo and to Joseph for his ICT support. Sarah would like to thank Claire McLachlan and Tom Nicholson for their leadership and the invitation to join the team on this project. Thanks also to the other co-authors for their collegiality. Sarah thanks her parents, Mele Tufuola and Andrew Cunningham, for introducing her to books and supporting her during her own transition to primary school. She would also like to thank her extended family for sharing photographs of their beautiful children, Alyssa, Saraya and Leanna Ohi, who are all enjoying a positive start to their literacy learning journeys.

The authors would also like to thank their employing organisations, secretarial staff and colleagues for their support while this book was written: Massey University, the University of Tasmania, the Queensland University of Technology and Deakin University.

We are grateful to the following individuals and organisations for permission to use their material in *Literacy in Early Childhood and Primary Education*. **Page 5**, **129**, **133**: Courtesy Tegan Smith; **7**, **8**: Courtesy Jessica Smith; **10**, **52**, **54**, **69**, **70**, **127**: Courtesy Lorraine Farrell; **25**: *The Fire Engine*, published by New Zealand School Publications Department, copyright © Crown, 1963; **53**: From Neuman & Dickinson *Handbook of Early Literacy Research* vol. 3, 2011. Reproduced with permission from Guildford Publications, Inc.; **74** (table 5.1): © Commonwealth of Australia 2002. Reproduced, communicated and adapted with permission of the Australian Government Department of Education, Employment and Workplace Relations, 2012; **84**, **281**: Courtesy Jo Stewart; **90**: Cartoon by Nicholson from *The Australian*, www.nicholsoncartoons.com.au. Reproduced with permission; **106** (table 7.1), **118** (table 7.3): From Justice, Block & Vukelich *Achieving Excellence in Preschool Literacy Instruction*, 2007. Reproduced with permission from Guildford Publications, Inc.; **108**, **192**, **197**, **242**, **243**: Cover of *Te Whāriki*, Image and Text from *Reading in Junior Classes*; Colour Wheel; Cover of *The Hole in the King's Sock*; Material from *National Standards Reading and Writing*. Reproduced by permission of the publishers, Learning Media Limited, PO Box 3293, Wellington, New Zealand. Copyright © MoE, 1996; 1985; no record of colour wheel first pub. date; 2001; 2009, respectively. **110**: *Belonging, Being & Becoming – The Early Years Learning Framework*, Commonwealth of Australia (2009). http://www.deewr.gov.au/EarlyChildhood/Policy_Agenda/Quality/Pages/EarlyYearsLearningFramework.aspx. Reproduced with permission; **163**, **169**, **181**, **185**:

Acknowledgements

Courtesy Sarah Ohi; **173**: Courtesy Yvette Sini; **189**, **190**: Courtesy Sara Strasser, Chavez Elementary School, Chicago; **204**: From T. Nicholson *Phonics Handbook*, pp. xv–xvi. Melbourne: Wiley. Reproduced with permission; **248** (bottom): Ruth Fielding-Barnsley; **268**: *The Watchdog Who Wouldn't*, Galaxy Kids Paperbacks, Wendy Pye Publishing Limited, 2003. © Sunshine Books. Reproduced with permission.

Every effort has been made to trace and acknowledge copyright. The publisher apologises for any accidental infringement and welcomes information that would redress this situation.

Chapter 1

Introduction

Chapter objectives

1. To explore the reasons for writing this book.
2. To identify key principles of the theoretical framework.
3. To explain key points of each chapter.
4. To provide a framework for readers to follow.

This introductory chapter provides an overview of the theoretical position adopted in this text and of the content of the chapters that follow. The chapter introduces the myths surrounding reading acquisition and the effectiveness of common pedagogies in early childhood and primary education. It also suggests ways the text can be approached by early childhood and primary pre-service teacher education students and their lecturers.

To begin, we introduce you to some scenarios which we consider are not far from the realities that teachers will face in early childhood centres and classrooms.

Scenario 1.1

You have a four-year-old boy in your early childhood classroom and you are wondering how well he will make the transition to school. Currently he spends most of his time outside in the sandpit, riding bikes or climbing things and seems to enjoy himself, but he rarely spends any time in the centre doing literacy-related activities and he wriggles constantly at mat session times and has to be told to pay attention.

Scenario 1.2

You have a five-year-old girl in your new-entrant class who can clearly already read. When asked what she likes to read at home, she names books that most children are reading at the age of 10. Recent testing reveals that not only can she read the words in the chapter books she likes, but she also has excellent comprehension of what she is reading.

Scenario 1.3

You have a six-year-old boy in your primary class who seems to be struggling with reading and is quite a long way behind the rest of the class, but the reasons why do not seem obvious. He has a large, receptive and expressive vocabulary, he knows the alphabet, his parents are both highly educated and say that he has been read to every day since he was a baby.

Scenario 1.4

There is a 10-year-old boy in your class who is well behind the other students in reading achievement and you are finding it hard to meet his needs as well as catering to the rest of the class. The boy regularly tells you that he is 'dumb at reading' and is uncooperative and frequently disruptive when it is time for reading or writing activities in the class, both of which he finds difficult. He reads slowly, struggles with word recognition and spells with difficulty, suggesting that he is having problems with hearing phonemes in words. Although he did have 'Reading Recovery' at a previous school, he doesn't seem to have made much progress. More recently, other children have started to notice that he is finding reading and writing difficult and have made comments to him such as 'it's easy' or 'you just need to follow the instructions', in response to which the boy has become both verbally and physically aggressive.

Take a moment and think about each of these scenarios. Answer the following the questions:

- What do we know about the child described in the scenario?
- Are there any issues or challenges you would face as a teacher of this child?
- What do we know about the child's context and his or her family?
- Do the issues you identified pose any potential challenges for literacy acquisition?
- What might be some solutions to the issues described in the scenario?

Part of our motivation for writing this book is to help demystify the process of learning to read and write, abilities which we see as crucial in the early years of education, as they impact on children's ability to engage fully across the curriculum areas and they provide a platform for lifelong learning. For many parents and caregivers*, the prospect of a child struggling at school is something they never want to face and finding help for a little one is the most important thing a parent can do. Similarly, teachers who face these children in the classroom will have moments of anxiety about whether the strategies they are using are the most effective to use. Allington (2010) has argued that only 25 per cent of all teachers are effective teachers of struggling readers. This text is designed to make sure that the teachers of the future will not be part of Allington's other 75 per cent, who may be effective teachers of most children but will be challenged by readers who present issues or challenges. Although we do address the issues associated with why children struggle and how to support them, our focus is effective strategies for most children, with some suggestions for those who face difficulties. Our aim is to explain how effective teachers work with families, so that they know children and their family context well and provide an appropriate range of opportunities and resources to support individual children on their journey to becoming literate. First, though, we will give you an overview of the theoretical perspective that underpins this text.

* Hereafter the term 'parent' is used to denote either a child's parent or caregiver.

Our theoretical framework

Literacy is a complex phenomenon, which could best be described as multifactorial. It involves individual, biological, social and cultural elements and, for this reason, we have based our explanations of how literacy develops on research which draws from **neuroscience** and psychology, as well as from sociology, education and anthropology. It is perhaps useful to link this explanation to Vygotsky's (1978) cultural-historical theory of child development, which has the following elements:

Neuroscience: the study of the developing brain and its influence on human learning.

- reliance on genetic or developmental analysis
- the claim that higher mental functioning in the individual derives from social life
- the claim that human action, on both the social and individual planes, is mediated by tools and signs.

Daniels (2001) indicates that in psychology two models of learning have been proposed and these serve as oppositional ends on a continuum. These two models are an 'internalisation thesis' and a 'participation antithesis', and both offer a different perspective on the relation between the individual or the psychological and the social or the collective. The internalisation model treats the individual as completely separate from the environment and there is a time lag between the time a child receives messages and their reception, assimilation and transformation in the individual. The participation model recognises a more active role for the individual and learners entering into different worlds as they learn. In this model the dualisms in inner/outer worlds and psychological/social domains are blurred.

Vygotsky's theory embraces both these models of learning, although he moved closer to a participation model in his later writing (Daniels 2001). His early writing espoused a universal pattern to development, while his later writing admitted that children's learning trajectories were social and therefore had a relativistic element. As Scott (2008, p. 84) states, 'it is the learner who is central to the process of development and has an active and intentional part to play in their learning trajectory'. This text focuses on children as active drivers of their own literacy acquisition, whose learning journey is shaped by both biology and social and cultural factors. Stahl and Yaden (2004, p. 141) similarly argue that teachers and researchers need to:

> probe more deeply into research emanating from biology and the neurosciences (see Shonkoff & Phillips 2000), children learning English as a second language (August & Hakuta 1997), learning theory (Bransford, Brown & Cocking 1999), and investigations into the causes of reading difficulty (Snow, Burns & Griffin 1998). Taken together, these findings point to the fact that all cognitive and affective learning processes are highly complex interactions between inherited and environmental factors and are selectively affected by variations in child-rearing practices, socioeconomic circumstances, family structures, adult–child interactions, educational environments, and other contextual and developmental factors.

Amber learns about books

In terms of biology, there is significant research now on how the developing brain shapes the skills and abilities that children demonstrate at different points on the continuum of literacy acquisition. The research also suggests that some children are born with conditions which will delay language development and consequently impact on literacy acquisition (see Berninger & Richards 2002 for a useful account of biological factors in literacy acquisition). Brain research has highlighted the nature–nurture factors which influence how readily children will gain literacy knowledge and skills, although the research primarily focuses on microstructure (tiny units of analysis) and macrostructure (larger units of analysis) research aspects of the brain. Microstructure research examines the involvement of chemical molecules, neurons (cells) and neural connections in literacy. Macrostructure research examines chemical activity of single molecules and neurons and the transmission and reception of electrical signals between neurons.

Berninger and Richards (2002) base their brain research on the work of a Russian neuropsychologist (Luria 1973), who introduced the notion of functional systems of the brain at work in literacy acquisition. Luria argued that multiple brain structures are involved in one function and that the same brain structures can participate in more than one functional system as part of cognitive processing. Luria, a pupil of Lev Vygotsky, rejected single-factor explanations of development and argued that higher mental processes (such as reading and writing) were functional systems and that cognitive development could not be understood without understanding both the biological and social factors that explain development (Vygotsky & Luria 1930). Vygotsky and Luria proposed that behaviour should be studied within the context of evolutionary, historical (cultural) and ontogenic (individual) development, thus explaining the essential nature–nurture components of literacy research. Berninger and Richards (2002) state that the ability of some children to gain literacy understandings is constrained by biological factors and that the degree of constraint determines how much intervention is required in the classroom or home environment to overcome the constraint. As Berninger and Richards (2002, p. 10) argue, 'Some students with biological constraints on their learning can learn but may (a) require more explicit, systematic, intense and sustained interaction than classmates; and (b) struggle more or have to work harder than classmates to learn an academic skill'. Berninger and Richards propose that nature alone seldom determines learning outcomes and that nurture – the type of teaching and learning support that children receive – is a determining factor in children's literacy achievement. Our discussions of literacy will make use of brain research where possible to explain the biological foundation of children's ability to learn.

Children's pathways or trajectories into becoming literate are significantly shaped by the social interactions and opportunities that they have; in this way, as we explain, literacy learning derives from social life. Providing children with rich literacy opportunities in early childhood and junior primary education provides a robust foundation for language development, including a rich vocabulary, knowledge of the alphabet, an awareness of sounds in the language, and an understanding of the purposes, functions and structures of print – what Marie Clay (2000a) called 'concepts about print'. There is a considerable body of research around the importance of a rich literacy environment (Neuman & Roskos 1990; Teale et al. 2009), but in addition, children need opportunities to interact with parents, teachers, other adults or other, more competent children to learn how to use the resources and make the most of the opportunities provided. Teale et al. (2009) suggest that the field of early literacy in particular has burgeoned since the early eighties, as a result of reconceptualisation about how much children understand about language and literacy through experiences without formal instruction. They argue that studies have showed how much children's understandings are shaped by a number of factors: the social processes of the home (e.g. Heath 1983), and how they become aware of print (Harste, Woodward & Burke 1984), learn through interaction with adults in read-aloud sessions (Teale 1984), begin to use invented spelling strategies as a logical and developmental solution to the language puzzle of learning about written words (Read 1975) and show metalinguistic awareness of language, words and print in English and other languages (e.g. Yaden & Templeton 1986; Ferreiro 1986). Teale et al. consider that this raft of research through the eighties legitimised 'emergent literacy', a term based on Marie Clay's (1966) notion of 'emergent reading', as a significant and important field of research and one that underpinned understandings of how to help children gain the fundamental understandings of language required for literacy acquisition. This body of research makes clear that children will not develop literacy without involvement in rich literacy environments and without support from knowledgeable adults, who understand how to sensitively support children's emerging understandings.

Vygotsky (1978) identified the twin notions of **access** and **mediation** to explain this relationship. He argued that children need both access to the resources, tools and artefacts of a culture, as well as mediation (support or guidance) by more competent adults or peers to help them to understand how to use those tools. He proposed that teachers help children to learn co-constructed knowledge within their zone of proximal development, using techniques that assist performance, such as scaffolding (Wood, Bruner &

Access and mediation: student access to learning resources and assistance provided to students using the resources by more competent adults or peers.

Ross 1976). Vygotsky (1978) argued that providing access to resources was insufficient and that if children were not given the gift of instruction, they were limited to biological maturation. He theorised that the developing mind of the child is both individual and social at the same time and is the result of a long process of developmental events. John-Steiner and Mahn (1996) consider that the primary focus of sociocultural research has been on how the social co-construction of knowledge is internalised, appropriated, transmitted or transformed in formal and informal learning settings. Gallimore and Tharp (1990) usefully define co-constructed learning within a child's zone of proximal development as follows:

- Child's performance is assisted by more competent others.
- Child shows less dependence and performance begins to internalise. Child uses directed speech for self-regulation and guidance.
- Child's performance is developed, automated and fossilised. It is smooth, integrated and automatic.
- There is sometimes a stage of deautomatisation, when performance is forgotten or rusty. The learner has to re-enter the zone of proximal development and relearn the forgotten skill.

Jessica reads to Millie

Vygotsky's (1978) definition of how children internalise and transform learning suggests that teachers use a range of strategies to promote learning. As John-Steiner and Mahn (1996, p. 197) state:

There are different modes of internalization, reflecting different teaching/interaction strategies. A continuum with direct instruction on one end to creative and collaborative learning on the other could describe the wide range of teaching/learning situations in which internalization occurs. Whether in the learning of a young child or in the activities of experienced thinkers, internalization is a fundamental part of the life-long process of the co-construction of knowledge and the creation of the new.

Vygotsky argued that the mediation provided by a more competent other person using demonstrating, modelling, questioning, feedback and task management helped the child to internalise and transform his or her understanding. We will argue that teachers play a crucial role in providing access to enriched literacy environments, including by mediating between the child's home background and cultural experiences and what Vygotsky (1998) called 'schooled concepts'. Teachers have the opportunity to open up access to new worlds for the child and through skilful and sensitive teaching support the majority of children to not only learn to read and write, but also to understand the bewildering range of new forms that literacy can take thanks to the rapid development of technology.

Vygotsky's (1978) theories have been further developed by a number of recent researchers, such as Rogoff (1990), whose cross-cultural studies identified that children also learn through being participants in the work of their families and communities. Rogoff (1990) found that even when children were not conversational partners with adults, they were involved in the adult world, for example, as participants in adult agricultural and household work. She describes the supportive engagement of Mayan

So they sent me a ...

Millie being introduced to text

mothers with their children as an example of the non-verbal guidance adults give children. Rogoff terms this **guided participation**, which takes place when creative thinkers interact with a knowledgeable person, and suggests it is practised around the world. Cultures may differ, though, in the goals of development. Many researchers have also researched Vygotsky's explanations of how learners co-construct new knowledge through their collaboration with adults and peers (Eun 2010).

> **Guided participation:** learning about social and cultural activities through participation with family members or more competent peers.

Finally, literacy acquisition does involve the understanding and use of tools and signs, as Vygotsky (1978) predicted. Eun (2010) suggests three major types of mediation in Vygotsky's theory: mediation through material tools, mediation through symbolic systems and mediation through another human being. All three are relevant to how children learn about literacy tools, the symbol system of written language, and the language associated with literacy activities. Eun further states (2010, p. 406):

> In mediating the learning process of individual students, it is important that teachers become engaged in the learning process themselves. More specifically, they need to become participant–observers (Wells 2002) in the construction of knowledge rather than assuming the role of someone who transmits already established knowledge to students. In this process, teachers need to be sensitive to the understandings of individual students. Teachers need to continuously assess the level of students' understanding so that each student's participation is a genuine contribution to the construction of a shared understanding. Teachers' mediation in the learning process thus becomes a fundamental element in optimizing children's potential to learn. Furthermore, in co-constructing knowledge with their students, teachers need to become inquirers themselves. As Wells (2002) noted, teachers need to become 'the leader of a community of inquiry' (p. 145).

For children who learn and use more than one language, the use of tools and signs is necessarily complex and sometimes requires learning more than one orthography for reading and writing. The onslaught of change in technologies also means that children have to become adept in a range of multiliteracies. Recent research on how children learn to navigate literacy via technology and different symbol systems will also be a feature of this text.

Myths and legends of literacy teaching

One of the interesting things about working in a field of research for a long time is that we become very aware of the myths and legends surrounding a particular topic. In the early childhood sector, for many years, the myth that 'literacy belongs in the primary school' has often been encountered, as has the myth that early childhood teachers might do some harm if they get too involved with children's emergent literacy (or numeracy for that matter, but that's another story for another time!). Students have returned from their early childhood practicum/teaching placements reporting that when they have attempted to actively support children's literacy development through reading stories with strong repetitive rhyme, helping children to write or playing language games, they have been told 'we don't do that primary school stuff here'. Other more alarming advice has been overheard by student teachers, who have said that teachers have advised parents who speak another language that they should only speak English to the child, as speaking languages other than English will hamper their ability to learn to read and write in English. Although both positions were arguably well intentioned, they are both horribly wrong in light of recent research (Cunningham et al. 2004; Teale et al. 2009). We hope to explore and dispel the myths around when and how to support literacy in early childhood and primary education and how to best support literacy acquisition in second-language learners. These principles form the foundation for principles of teaching and learning in the primary school setting.

There are, equally, myths around teaching literacy in the primary school. In New Zealand, over many years, like other countries, the 'reading wars' have prevailed, staged between the advocates of 'whole language' approaches and the advocates of 'phonics' (see Nicholson 2000). Although the major reviews of literacy (e.g. NELP 2009) indicate that both approaches have their usefulness in supporting the ability to read and write, the belief system around this myth appears to be ideologically driven and the debates are often histrionic rather than rational. We will revisit the arguments behind these somewhat entrenched positions and find out what recent research has to say about when and how to teach literacy.

Added to approaches to teaching and learning are the myths about certain groups of children and literacy, in particular boys. We will explore the myths around giving children, and in particular boys, 'the gift of time'. We will also explore some of the myths around struggling readers and how they can best be supported in the primary school.

Vaughn listens to a bedtime story with his grandfather

What this text covers

This introductory chapter has so far provided an overview of the theoretical position adopted in this text, and it has introduced the myths surrounding reading acquisition and the effectiveness of common pedagogies in early childhood and primary settings. It later suggests ways the text can be approached by early childhood and primary pre-service teacher education students and their lecturers. We now summarise what the chapters that make up the bulk of this book cover.

Chapter 2 outlines recent theory and research on literacy acquisition. It involves a review of both the psycholinguistic research into how children gain the essential literacy skills that predict reading achievement (in particular, phonological awareness, alphabet knowledge and vocabulary), as well as a review of the **social practice** research, which shows that children have different pathways to literacy as a result of their immersion in diverse social and cultural settings. Using a **sociocultural** framework, Chapter 2 explores how children acquire literacy as a result of both access to resources and mediation of literacy in homes, communities, early childhood settings and schools.

Social practice: an explanation of the influences of social and cultural literacy practices on literacy acquisition.

The myths of when to begin formal reading and writing instruction are explored in Chapter 3. Enduring social and cultural beliefs about maturational readiness and delaying reading instruction are critically examined. The outcomes of international studies on literacy achievement, demonstrated in PIRLS (Progress in International Reading Literacy Study) and other data are explored. The differences in ages of starting school and the pedagogy of beginning and ongoing reading instruction are critically examined.

Chapter 4 examines in detail what research has shown us over the years and what is presently known and understood from literacy research internationally. This chapter explores the growing body of research on the different patterns and expectations of literacy in homes and schools. The research is international, drawing on both recent longitudinal studies in the United States, the United Kingdom and New Zealand, as well as in-depth studies of family literacy programs that have attempted to bridge the gaps between homes and schools to support literacy acquisition. This chapter also gives practical advice on how to engage parents in the reading process.

Sociocultural theory: a constructivist theory, originally developed by the Russian psychologist Lev Vygotsky, which explains the interaction of genetics; interaction with more competent members of the society; and the influence of cultural tools, signs and artefacts on children's learning.

Research on multiliteracies are explored in Chapter 5, as part of examining how children come to centres and schools with diverse literacy experiences, which may or may not match the literacy environment of the centre or school. This chapter is designed for teachers to reconsider how the nature of readers and the contexts in which reading occurs is changing with the advent of technology. Ideas to support an ever-increasing array of text types and multimodal applications for various ages in the classroom are investigated.

Catering for diversity in classrooms is the focus of Chapter 6. It leads into the notion of what it means to have a negotiated curriculum where learners make choices about what they value when it comes to reading. It looks at incorporating a variety of perspectives that acknowledge the variety of interests and experiences learners have to contribute to curriculum. This chapter also examines some of the recent research on children's literacy acquisition in bilingual, multicultural and multilingual settings. Research on the literacy outcomes of mainstream, bilingual and total immersion settings are explored, along with the barriers to literacy acquisition that bilingualism and multilingualism has been found to create in many countries. Research with Indigenous Australians in early year and primary school settings internationally is examined in this chapter and the implications for educational practice identified.

Chapter 7 examines the growing body of research on how to provide both access to high-quality literacy environments and effective mediation of literacy. Drawing on a range of research on the features of effective literacy environments, principles for curriculum and centre design are discussed. In addition this chapter examines the recent research on the role of teachers in supporting literacy acquisition. In particular, recent research which has explored the range, type and amount of teacher involvement in children's literacy acquisition is examined. This chapter considers in particular what Cunningham et al. (2004) call 'knowledge calibration' in effective early childhood teachers.

Chapter 8 explores the 'sound' foundation for learning literacy and looks in depth at how teachers and families can support alphabet knowledge, phonological awareness, vocabulary and comprehension prior to school entry, as well as ways in which teachers can support continuity between home and centre literacy learning. Recent research on how to integrate phonological awareness into holistic educational programs during the early years is examined. Drawing on Nicholson's (2005) work, guidelines for the scope and sequence of teaching phonemic awareness in early childhood are provided. Research on approaches to storybook reading, supporting socio-dramatic play and emergent writing is examined, as crucial vehicles for supporting foundational knowledge and skill development.

Chapter 9 reviews literature on effective assessment, particularly of literacy, and examines this in relation to methods of assessment that are commonly used in early childhood education. Principles for effectively assessing children's literacy progress before, during and after the initial transition to school are developed. A range of potential methods for assessing and documenting children's literacy acquisition prior to school entry are explored and critiqued. The importance of documenting literacy progression that can be effectively used by the early childhood setting, the primary school and parents is a particular focus of this chapter.

Chapter 10 examines how continuity from the early childhood setting to the junior primary school setting can be supported. It reviews the research on the discontinuities that children can experience and the research evidence on the most effective ways to avoid major mismatches in pedagogy and expectations. The issues of transition from early childhood to primary are be further explored, along with recommendations for the construction of the initial reading and writing program.

What does it mean to have a classroom of eager readers who love to talk books? Chapter 11 explores how teachers can create collaborative processes where all readers know that their opinions are heard and respected and examines how a teacher can get momentum happening so that learners want to read beyond the classroom walls. Catering for diversity in classrooms is also the focus of this chapter. It leads into the notion of what it means to have a negotiated curriculum where learners make choices about what they value when it comes to reading. It looks at incorporating a variety of perspectives that acknowledge the variety of interests and experiences learners have to contribute to curriculum. This is a practical chapter about planning and organising a classroom for learning. It contains the 'nitty-gritty' of how to be equipped for effective instruction for K–6 learners.

Chapter 12 takes a closer look at assessment in the junior primary school. Assessment is always hot on the agenda of teachers, and with the move to 'high stakes' assessment teachers feel increasing pressure to teach to the test. This chapter looks at accountability and considers: accountability for what? It provides a fresh look at self-assessment and how the learner needs to be an integral partner in the assessment process. Building on the earlier chapter on effective assessment in early childhood settings, this chapter examines recent research on the most effective ways to assess children's ongoing acquisition of literacy in the K–6 grades. Research evidence on the effectiveness of common literacy assessments is reviewed and recommendations for practice with diverse learners are examined.

Chapter 13 considers the research evidence on the powerful reciprocal relationship that exists between reading and writing development and how curriculum decisions can impact on children's achievement in the K–6 grades. The teacher's role in supporting children's emerging reading and writing abilities is critiqued and implications for practice are discussed. This chapter looks at tried and tested ways to inspire reluctant readers to read and write. It examines what makes a book worth reading and examines the secrets of success discovered in a range of studies.

Chapter 14 builds on the earlier chapters on establishing communities of readers and encouraging writing in the junior school. It explores how to build on children's interests in literacy, negotiating the curriculum to maintain children's interests and motivation, and making innovative use of multiliteracies approaches.

What happens when reading goes wrong? Chapter 15 investigates the origins of reading failure from the perspective of those who have lived the experience. The research literature including the fads and fancies associated with reading failure is examined. This chapter also examines research evidence around 'Matthew effects' (Stanovich 1986) for children who get off to a slow start in reading. Issues of diagnosis of dyslexia and other reading-related disorders are examined and the implications for educational practice are discussed. This chapter examines some of the recent moral panic around boys' literacy achievement and reviews the research evidence related to boys' achievement. The challenges for parents of children with reading difficulties are examined, along with the long-term implications for children with reading difficulties. The roles of families, communities and agencies in supporting children with reading difficulties are reviewed.

The final chapter draws together the key findings of each chapter and provides an overall summary of the principles for supporting children to make the transition from emergent literacy to fluent reading and writing. This chapter stresses the notion of literacy for life and reiterates the need to have readers be lifelong readers and what a difference that makes to what and how we learn, and how we learn with and from each other.

A few words on how to use this book

This book is designed to be used by early childhood and primary teachers as well as researchers and students in pre-service early childhood, early year and primary teacher education. Use of terms is something we need to clarify, as these terms are used slightly differently in Australia and New Zealand. For the purposes of clarity, we refer to 'early childhood education' as any education that occurs *prior* to entering a state or private primary/elementary school. If we ever refer to 'kindergarten', we clarify which country we are talking about. So, for example, in New Zealand children attend kindergarten from three to five years of age, but in other countries kindergarten age is often later.

We know that children usually start school on the day that they turn five years of age in New Zealand, but in Australia and other countries this may occur when children are in their sixth year. Thus the generic term 'school' refers to compulsory education for children, in which they are expected to engage in formal instruction in literacy.

Although we consider that most chapters will be useful to both early childhood and primary teachers and student teachers, there is also a logic to the structure of the text, which may make navigation a bit easier. Note that we consider that early childhood teachers need to understand how literacy is taught in primary schools and primary teachers need to understand how literacy is taught in early childhood, so use of part of the whole text is highly recommended, but it can be more selectively sampled. Our view of the structure is represented in Table 1.1.

Table 1.1: *Structure and audience for chapters in this text*

CHAPTER	TOPICS	AUDIENCE
Chapters 1–6	Part 1: Literacy acquisition: the child, the family and diversity in the modern world	Early childhood and primary
Chapters 7–9	Part 2: Learning about literacy in early childhood settings	Early childhood
Chapters 10–13	Part 3: Literacy learning in the primary school	Junior to middle primary
Chapters 14–15	Part 4: Literacy learning in the senior primary school	Senior primary
Chapter 16	Conclusion	Early childhood and primary

We hope that you will enjoy reading this text as much as we have enjoyed writing it. Each chapter is similar in format, with scenarios and examples for you to consider provided in boxes, and questions raised within and at the end of chapters for you to think about or discuss in your study groups or in class. Here's our first set of questions to get you thinking!

Reflective questions

1. Can you think of any myths or legends about literacy? What are they and where did you hear about them?

2. Can you identify your own theoretical position or philosophy on literacy acquisition? Has it ever changed?

3. What role do parents play in children's literacy acquisition before, during and after primary school? Does their role change over time?

4. What do you think is the single most important thing you can do to support a child who is learning how to read and write?

Part 1

Literacy acquisition: the child, the family and diversity in the modern world

Chapter 2

Literacy acquisition in the early years: past, present and future

Chapter objectives

1. To review the history of how literacy has been promoted in the early years, with particular attention to approaches in Australia and New Zealand.
2. To critically examine the contribution of psycholinguistic and social practice perspectives on literacy acquisition.
3. To consider the contribution of cultural historical theory to current thinking about literacy acquisition.

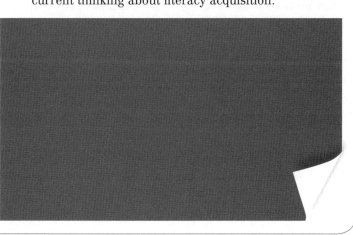

This chapter outlines recent theory and research on literacy acquisition. It involves a brief review of the psycholinguistic research into how children gain the essential literacy skills that predict reading achievement (in particular phonological awareness and alphabet knowledge). It also reviews the social practice research showing that children have different pathways to literacy as a result of their immersion in diverse social and cultural settings. Using a sociocultural framework, this chapter explores how children acquire literacy as a result of both access to and mediation of literacy in homes, communities, early childhood settings and schools.

Looking back: a brief history of literacy in the early years

Nicholson (2000) provides a compelling history of the teaching of reading in his text '*Reading the Writing on the Wall*', which outlines that humans have been using symbol systems to communicate for thousands of years. He cites evidence that alphabet (ABC) methods of teaching reading have been used for around 3000 years. Certainly this method of teaching reading prevailed in Australia and New Zealand through their respective periods of settlement into the late 19th century. It has only been in more recent history, however, that the notion of everyone being able to read and write has gained social and cultural acceptance. From feudal times, the main people who were likely to be literate were wealthy and male or belonged to a religious order. We will discuss New Zealand's history of reading instruction as an example of the changes over time, as the differences between states in Australia make presenting a simple history quite difficult.

As a migrant nation, New Zealand has only had compulsory schooling since the Education Act of 1877 and secondary schooling did not become compulsory until 1914, although some children attended private and church schools before this time. Similarly, in Australia schooling became compulsory between 1872 and 1893 in various states and territories, which is surprising considering Australia's much longer period of settlement than New Zealand.

Helen May (2005), in her history of schools for young children in New Zealand, cites that the first schools in New Zealand were run by the missionaries. There is evidence of a Maori 'primer' (an old word for a children's reading book) being written in 1815 for a school that opened in 1816 for 33 children, the youngest aged seven at the time. The school shut down in 1818 due to difficulties in getting supplies to feed the children, despite reports sent to London about the progress that Maori children were making in reading and writing. May explains that missionary education developed rapidly after this small beginning, with a printing press established in 1834 by

William Colenso which produced half a million pages of religious material for educational purposes before 1840. May cites a report sent to the British House of Lords in 1838 which claimed the success of missionary education: 'the great majority [of Maori] children can read' and the 'power of acquisition [of literacy by Maori children] is greater than our own, almost' (in May 2005, p. 33). It should be noted that in the early part of this period, Maori children were not educated with European children, although this began to change as time went on. There were notable differences between the loving and caring approaches to childrearing that were observed in Maori society and the 'spare the rod and spoil the child' approaches advocated by the early missionaries; the infant schools were regarded as places in which the promise of a civilised Christian Maori could be produced (May 2005).

The early infant schools were also influenced by the writing of Robert Owen, who founded the first British infant school at his cotton mill in New Lanark, Scotland, in 1816 (May 2005). Owen, like the missionaries, believed in putting children into school before their families could influence their characters. However, he was also heavily influenced by the writings of Jean Jacques Rousseau and Johann Pestalozzi, who argued for the potential goodness of children and the importance of pleasurable learning, and was opposed to the missionaries' rigid approaches to early education. Owen's ideas were adapted by Samuel Wilderspin, who designed the approaches to infant schools used in England from 1823, which later underpinned New Zealand's approach to primary education. In Wilderspin's approach, the three R's (reading, writing and arithmetic) and moral and religious training were advocated, along with opportunity for outdoor activity and play; a primary purpose was to make the children happy as well as instruct them. The focus was on producing an 'educable and orderly child' (May 2005, p. 44). It wasn't until after the signing of the Treaty of Waitangi in 1840, when the colony began to rapidly grow, that schools began to be organised in earnest. The majority were founded by churches in most regions, with a focus on the three R's and religion and practical crafts, although there were also a number of private schools of variable quality.

Achieving high standards of literacy for all children is an even more recent phenomenon. Following World War II, most children in New Zealand were 'streamed' at high school into academic, trades or domestic streams, with high levels of literacy achievement only being required for the mythical 5 per cent of all children who would attend university. Changes in educational policy, societal expectations and economic climate have meant that children are expected in New Zealand and Australia to stay at school until they are at least 16 years of age, and by that time they should have acquired highly developed literacy skills. Most governments have these aspirations for children as part of their economic strategy and have policies around what children will be able to read and how well (Olson 2009).

In both countries, children were first taught letters, then two-letter words, then three-letter words and so forth, with lots of practice and repetition. Nicholson (2000) explains that ABC methods of teaching reading have dominated reading instruction since Greek and Roman times. Our education systems have been heavily influenced by our British colonial roots and hence children used reading books called 'horn-books' and later 'primers', which typically had letters of the alphabet, followed by two-letter words, words of one and then two syllables, then a religious passage or prayer for children to learn (Nicholson 2000).

This pattern was also common in the United States, where Puritans had taken the British primers in the 17th century. By 1850 schools began to move away from ABC methods towards a 'word' method, advocated by Horace Mann, the secretary of the Massachusetts Board of Education (Coulson 2002). Coulson (2002) suggests that the time-honoured fashion of teaching reading through ABC and phonics lessons fell completely out of favour in the United States by the 1930s, not because the method was ineffective, but because academics such as G. Stanley Hall and John Dewey agreed with the spirit of the 'word' method advocated by Horace Mann, where children were expected to memorise whole words as an incidental part of the reading process. Coulson proposes that progressive educators believed that children should be released from what they perceived as the straitjacket of traditional schooling and set free to explore learning in their own way. Coulson further posits that although this 'word' approach to reading was not based on empirical research, it was soon adopted by policy makers and school boards across the United States and was bedded down into practice.

New Zealand was slower than the United States to change its approach to reading and continued to use ABC methods, using primers imported from the United Kingdom until around 1900 and then 'Imperial Readers' locally published by Whitcombe and Tombs. These followed the ABC method of alphabet and two letter-words, and were sometimes contextualised for Maori children in native schools (May 2005). Nicholson (2000) states that these readers were widely used in New Zealand schools until the end of World War I. Reading instruction in this model was based on lots of drill and repetition. Figure 2.1 shows an example of a school journal donated to Massey University Library used by Dorothy Harrow at Timaru School around 1914.

Following World War I, Whitcombe and Tombs published a new series of readers, called 'Live Readers', which were based on 'look and say' and **phonics** approaches to reading, designed by a Miss Dorothy Baxter and designed to be more fun than the skill and drill approaches of the ABC method. Teachers would begin by teaching children 'look and say' methods (which involved repeating a small number of common words) until they knew a few words and sentences and then would move on to teaching phonics, as part of children being able to read independently

Phonics:
a method of teaching
the relationship
between letters and
sounds.

and without teacher help. Teaching phonics involves teaching children the alphabet letter – phoneme (sound) relationship. A phonics program involves systematically teaching children all of the letter–phoneme correspondences over a course of time.

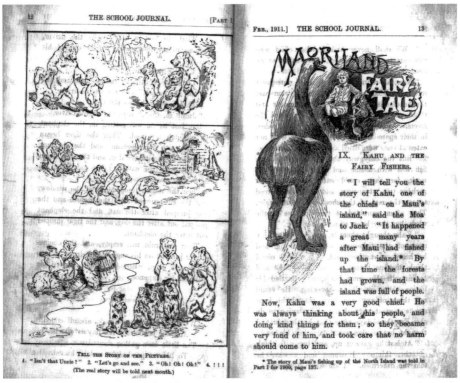

Figure 2.1 *Dorothy Harrow's* School Journal, *Part 1, nos. 1–3, nos. 5–9, 1911, pp. 12–13*

12]

$u = \breve{oo}$

LET'S PRETEND

1. Put some wood on the fire.
2. Put the cup on the hook.
3. Pull the cork out of the bottle.
4. Drive the bull into the paddock.
5. Push open the gate.
6. Fill the kettle, please. When it is full, put it on the fire.
7. Chase me round this big bush.
8. Mix the plum pudding.

could, would, should

Dick could not lift the sack.
Bob would not help him.
"You should help Dick to lift the sack, Bob," said Jane.

[13

or

MAKING HAY

One morning Joe put on his old clothes and his big sun hat. Off he went to the hay-paddock.

Father and Norman were there. Father was up on the stack. Norman tossed the hay on to the cart with his fork. Duke, the big brown horse, pulled the load to the stack.

Figure 2.2 *Progressive Primer, Book 3, pp. 12–13*

By 1928, Whitcombe and Tombs had published a new series, the Progressive Primers, which was a phonics-based reading series. Teachers could either use this series, the Live Readers or the Beacon Readers series from the United Kingdom, which used 'look and say' flashcards and phonics (Nicholson 2000).

After World War II, New Zealand adopted a new reading series from the United Kingdom, the 'Janet and John' series, which were stories based on two children, their parents and their dog. New words were introduced at a rate of six new words for every hundred. Children were taught using 'look and say' methods until they could recognise 400 words and then they were taught phonics. New words were taught before children progressed on to the next reader in the series, so that children recognised words before they encountered them.

I see something.

I see an aeroplane.

I want to go up.

I want to go up high.

I want to be in an aeroplane.

One day I shall go up high.

I shall go up high in an aeroplane.

Janet sat with her toys.

The doll was on her lap.

Mother came out.

" Come here," she said.

" Come and see what I have."

Figure 2.3 *Janet and John reader,* I Went Walking *(1949), pp. 12–13*

In 1960 the New Zealand government commissioned a new series, Ready to Read, to replace Janet and John, which had been criticised as too stereotyped. The new series was based on typical New Zealand family lives and 12 colour-graded books were initially produced. The approach to reading was based around reading for meaning and teachers were urged to use phonetic analysis of words as they were needed, rather than as part of a structured sequence or as part of sounding out words. New words were introduced at a faster rate of one in every 10, meaning the differences between levels of books were greater.

The cars are going to the fire.
The children are going
to the fire.
Frank and Harry and Father
are going to the fire.

Figure 2.4 *Ready to Read reader,* The Fire Engine *(1963)*

By the 1970s the notion of 'learning to read by reading' became pervasive, for example, in the United States under the influence of Ken Goodman and in Canada thanks to Frank Smith. In this approach, teachers taught strategies such as prediction of words based on clues from pictures or by drawing attention to the initial letters of words (Pressley 2006). This period was also powerfully influenced by the writing of Sylvia Ashton-Warner (1986), who advocated a language-experience approach in which teachers encouraged children to write and use words that were meaningful to them – what Ashton Warner called 'organic vocabulary'. By the 1980s and 1990s the notion of authentic reading experiences held sway, reflecting **whole language** or literature approaches to reading. The Ready to Read series was revised in 1985 to reflect this approach and was developed into further colour-graded levels for use with shared reading, guided reading or independent reading.

> **Whole language:** an approach to teaching reading that focuses on assisting children to understand the meaning of text, rather than on specific decoding strategies.

The reading wars

In the last 10 years, however, although the Ready to Read series is still in active use, there has been increasing debate over the effectiveness of the 'whole language' or literature approaches to reading instruction used in New Zealand schools, as research shows that New Zealand's standards of literacy have been declining and approximately 25 per cent of all children have dropped to below international benchmarks for reading achievement at the age of nine (Mullis et al. 2007). Other research has showed that the literacy skills with which children enter school predict their reading achievement seven years later, suggesting that greater attention needs to be paid both to what children do in school, but also in prior-to-school settings (Tunmer, Chapman & Prochnow 2006).

Stanovich (2000) argues that whole-language approaches are based on the notion that learning to read is like learning to speak – a natural process. However, as Stanovich points out, the use of the 'reading is like speech' analogy ignores the fact that although all communities of human beings have developed spoken languages, only a minority exist in written form and written language is an invention of the last three or four thousand years. Furthermore, 'virtually all children in normal environments develop speech easily by themselves, whereas most children require explicit tuition to learn to read and substantial numbers of children have difficulty even after intensive efforts on the part of teachers and parents' (Stanovich 2000, p. 364). As Stanovich argues, there is now robust research evidence about how children learn to read and it is crucial that teachers understand the research and its implications for classroom practice.

Pressley (2006) states that the whole-language approach to literacy acquisition can be summed up as follows: 'do not teach decoding directly. Rather, immerse children in print experiences and opportunities to write with invented spelling, and they will learn to read' (p. 25). Pressley says that although the whole-language approach can be effective, especially with children from middle-class homes where children have had rich and diverse literacy experiences, it is based on an incomplete model of literacy development. Pressley argues for a model of literacy instruction which includes what is good in whole-language approaches, combined with a more explicit approach to teaching decoding and comprehension.

These debates about which method is best culminated in the 1990s in the 'reading wars', which took hold in New Zealand, Australia, England and the United States. Soler and Openshaw (2009) state that both England and New Zealand openly argued and debated these issues at the personal, political and policy levels, through the media and through parliament. In England, the issue was brought to a head following the 1991 report of the Education and Science Committee, which suggested a decline in the reading levels of seven-year-olds. The report argued that the decline had followed the introduction of whole-language/real-books approaches advocated by Frank Smith and Kenneth Goodman (Education, Science and Arts Committee 1991). This resulted in an inquiry into teaching methods in primary schools and a resulting report which advocated against too much diversity in teaching methods (Alexander, Rose & Woodhead 1992, in Soler & Openshaw 2009). A Literacy Task Force and National Literacy Strategy was subsequently developed, which was an uneasy compromise between teaching phonics and giving children good books to supplement phonic decoding. Further debate led to the Rose Report of 2005, which stated that 'synthetic phonics' was the key method to teaching the relationship between letters and sounds and that a program of instruction in synthetic phonics should be followed faithfully by teachers. Synthetic phonics involves teaching the phonemes of letters and how to blend those phonemes to sound out words (Nicholson 2005). This method can be contrasted with the more traditional 'analytic phonics' method in which children are taught one letter–phoneme rule each week.

In New Zealand the debates similarly waged through parliament and the national media, leading also to the establishment of a Literacy Task Force, which was charged with ensuring that all nine-year-olds could 'read and write for success' (Ministry of

Education 1999). It should be noted that in New Zealand, despite the millions of dollars spent on literacy leadership programs, resource teachers and the development of further resources, the long tail of reading achievement failure, as evidenced in the PIRLS (Progress in International Reading Literacy Study) (Mullis et al. 2007) and other data, remains firmly in place. For a variety of political reasons, including the dominance of the whole-language reading intervention, Reading Recovery (RR), the whole-language approaches to literacy retain prominent positions in policy in New Zealand, with phonics methods on the margins (Soler & Openshaw 2009).

Pearson and Hiebert (2010) state that literacy has been the subject of considerable review over the last half century in many countries for the purposes of establishing consensus and synthesis within the field. This is often at governments' behest as the previous brief history demonstrates. Pearson and Hiebert argue that the most recent American review, the National Early Literacy Panel Report (NELP 2009), strengthens the recommendations from previous reviews, but still doesn't go far enough in extrapolating the implications for teaching in early childhood and primary classrooms; this is an issue we will address in later chapters of this text. A list of 11 **predictors of literacy** achievement is identified in the NELP Report, along with five interventions that have consistently shown to increase literacy competence and achievement, which should underpin any early literacy strategy. We will use the 11 predictors of reading achievement as a starting place for our discussions of early literacy and expand on these in the following chapters of this text.

> **Predictors of literacy acquisition:**
> factors that predict children's ability to learn to read and write.

How do children gain essential literacy skills? A psycholinguistic perspective

Early literacy, or 'emergent literacy' as it is more commonly called, is the period between early childhood and formal schooling when children gain their foundational understandings of what literacy is and what it means for them as learners. The term emergent literacy is used to:

> denote the idea that the acquisition of literacy is conceptualised as a developmental continuum, with its origins early in the life of a child, rather than an all or none phenomenon that begins when children start school. This conceptualisation departs from other perspectives in reading acquisition in suggesting there is no clear demarcation between reading and pre-reading (Whitehurst & Lonigan 1998, p. 848).

Emergent literacy means that children develop reading, writing and oral language concurrently and interdependently as a result of their exposure to social contexts in which literacy is a component and in the absence of formal instruction (Whitehurst & Lonigan 1998). Whitehurst and Lonigan, in their seminal 1998 paper on emergent literacy, further argued that children develop literacy as a result of what they call 'inside' and 'outside' processes, explaining the complex interplay between a child's maturing brain and the social context in which they learn about the purposes and functions of literacy.

Most young children develop an intuitive knowledge of sounds and can recognise rhyme and alliteration. Although most New Zealand children develop these literacy skills as part of their experiences at home and in early childhood settings, approximately 25 per cent of children do not (Nicholson 2005). These children benefit from receiving specific alphabetic and phonological awareness instruction (Phillips, Clancy-Menchetti & Lonigan 2008). Intervention studies that have taught phonological awareness skills to children prior to school entry have found that it provides an advantage for children (Schneider et al., 1997; Phillips, Clancy-Menchetti & Lonigan 2008). Some recent studies of how literacy knowledge and skills can be promoted within more naturalistic settings show that literacy acquisition concerns both access to interesting literacy resources and highly effective teachers who know how and when to step in and out of children's literacy learning and play (Phillips, Clancy-Menchetti & Lonigan 2008; Piasta & Wagner 2010; Justice et al. 2009).

A child's language development and family literacy patterns are also strong predictors of literacy achievement. Children who are language delayed or come from families where there is a known history of reading difficulties may likely have difficulties with literacy. Children who may be especially 'at risk' (Justice & Pullen 2003) of literacy failure include children with impaired vision or hearing, cerebral palsy, intellectual disability, specific early language disorder, attention deficit/hyperactivity disorder, emotional disturbance, and speakers of other languages.

According to the NELP Report (2009), there are six primary variables which predict reading achievement. These six variables include:

- *alphabet knowledge* (AK) – knowledge of the names and sounds associated with printed letters
- *phonological awareness* (PA) – the ability to detect, manipulate, or analyse the auditory aspects of spoken language (including the ability to distinguish or segment words, syllables or phonemes), independent of meaning
- *rapid automatic naming* (RAN) of letters or digits – the ability to rapidly name a sequence of random letters or digits
- *RAN of objects or colours* – the ability to rapidly name a sequence of repeating random sets of pictures of objects (e.g. 'car,' 'tree,' 'house,' 'man') or colours
- *writing or writing name* – the ability to write letters in isolation on request or to write one's own name
- *phonological memory* – the ability to remember spoken information for a short period of time.

An additional five early literacy skills were also moderately correlated with at least one measure of later literacy achievement. These additional potentially important variables include:

- *concepts about print* – knowledge of print conventions (e.g. left–right, front–back) and concepts (book cover, author, text)
- *print knowledge* – a combination of elements of alphabet knowledge, concepts about print, and early decoding
- *reading readiness* – usually a combination of alphabet knowledge, concepts of print, vocabulary, memory, and phonological awareness
- *oral language* – the ability to produce or comprehend spoken language, including vocabulary and grammar
- *visual processing* – the ability to match or discriminate visually presented symbols.

These ideas are discussed further in the next few chapters and in particular in Chapter 8, where the foundations of literacy learning in early childhood are explicitly explored.

Social practice perspectives on literacy acquisition

An alternative but complementary view of literacy can be found in research on literacy as a **social practice**, which focuses on how people participate in their social lives. In this world view, literacy cannot be separated from the social, cultural and historical context in which it is acquired. Jalongo, Fennimore and Stamp (2004, p. 62) cite the writings of Bakhtin (1981) about literacy, and argue that literacy is influenced by context, is part of the construction of self and affects participation in communities. They cite the following aspects of literacy as a social practice:

> **Social practice:** an explanation of the influences of social and cultural literacy practices on literacy acquisition.

- *Literacy is deeply influenced by context.* Each person and each use of literacy is situated in a world that is interactional and has certain ideologies. When the context changes, communication changes.

- *Literacy is part of the construction of self.* Bakhtin argues that we become who we are through dialogic relationships with people and texts. Literacy affects what attracts headlines, is merely mentioned or is marginalised. Bakhtin argues that our beliefs about ourself are constructed through interaction with people and texts. As he states, 'The word in language is half someone else's. It becomes "one's own" only when the speaker populates it with his own intention, his own accent, when he appropriates the word, adapting it to his own semantic and expressive intention' (1981, pp. 293–4).

  Susan Engels (1995) similarly argues that children develop a sense of self through the construction of narratives about the self, first by family, then friends and then finally through internalising. This identity includes a sense of self in terms of literacy, leading to children's definitions of self as 'good at reading' or 'dumb at reading' at remarkably early ages. Stanovich (2000) calls this phenomenon 'Matthew effects', linked to the gospel according to St. Matthew, which states that the rich get richer and the poor get poorer. In terms of literacy, children know from early in their school careers whether they belong to the rich or poor.

- *Literacy affects participation in communities.* As literacy learners engage with a multitude of texts (broadly defined to include images, symbols and signs) and build dialogic relationships with others either face to face or 'virtually' via social media, they learn how to participate in various communities. In this way, learners identify who has power, who speaks and who listens, who writes and reads, who leads and follows and whose story gets told.

Gee (2004) states that people adopt different 'ways with printed words' within different purposes, functions and contexts. In these practices, humans are always meaning producers, not just meaning consumers. As Gee proposes, literacy is always a social and cultural practice, which is integrally linked into ways of talking, thinking, believing, knowing, acting, interacting, valuing and feeling. He considers that it is impossible to just look at the 'print bits' and ignore the rest; in this way a child's first scribbles, a youth's graffiti on the wall, an athlete's comment on Twitter, a teacher's journal and a grandmother's handwritten letter to her daughter are all meaningful literacy acts, which are rooted in literacy identities adopted in relation to cultural and social context.

Knobel and Lankshear (2003), in their discussion of 'out of school' literacies, argue that there are four main research positions to be considered in terms of literacy as a social practice. 'Practice' in this context refers to the ways in which people think about and make practical use of literacy. As Knobel and Lankshear explain:

> A concern with literacy *practice* always takes into account knowing *and* doing, and calls into play the notion of *literacies* as a way of describing how people negotiate and construct patterned and socially recognizable ways of knowing, doing and using languages to achieve different social and cultural contexts (Knobel & Lankshear 2003, p. 55) (italics in original).

In this view, there is more than one form of literacy, hence the term 'literacies' that is used here and the understanding that different people use literacy in different ways in different social settings.

Knobel and Lankshear (2003, p. 55) propose that the research into literacy as a social practice has had the below focuses and can be categorised in these four ways:

1. any literacy practice engaged in by a preschool age individual outside a school

2. any literacy practice engaged in by persons of any age within non-school (i.e. non-formal education) settings

3. any literacy practice engaged in by preschool age individuals in settings outside the school that is not a formally recognised literacy within school pedagogy and curriculum

4. any literacy practice engaged in by persons of any age within non-school (formal education) settings that is not a literacy belonging to a formal education curriculum or pedagogy.

Knobel and Lankshear propose that Category 1 concerns literacy research which draws on developmental psychology, psycholinguistics and cultural psychology, informed by Vygotsky's theories, which aims to look at the influence of children's lives outside school in terms of emerging literacy. This type of research has three purposes:

• to document parent–child interactions with print

• to compare children's at-home literacy performance with school experience in order to better understand transitions

• to respond to what are seen as the limitations of emergent literacy studies that don't take full account of what happens to children outside of formal settings.

The last purpose encompasses studies of play culture, popular culture activities, telephone discourse, intergenerational socialisation and their relevance to early childhood education. Good examples of this type of research include Shirley Brice Heath's (1983) seminal study of language and literacy in middle-class and working-class communities in the Piedmont Carolinas in the southern United States and Tizard and Hughes' (1984) study of language and literacy patterns in working-class homes in England.

The Category 2 research involves the range of family intervention studies which aim to increase family literacy. We discuss these further in Chapter 4, where we look at family literacies and intervention studies. Typically this type of research looks at how parents/caregivers can provide more effective storybook reading and other literacy opportunities in the home.

The Category 3 research, which is of particular interest for early childhood and primary, is that which concerns comparing the in- and out-of-school literacy competencies and experiences of diverse school children. According to Knobel and Lankshear, this research shows that children who fail in one context (e.g. school) may be effective in other out-of-school contexts. Research has examined negotiated gender identities and literacy practices; multilingual identities and cultural, religious and school discourse; literacy in marginalised youth groups; and literacy outcomes for overlooked, marginalised or excluded-from-school children. The aim of this research has been to alert teachers to children's literacy proficiencies outside school and examine what literacies children want to use outside school.

The Category 4 research involves community and workplace literacy programs for adults, which are not centrally a focus of this text.

Studies in this field of literacy social practices reveal that children who are officially regarded as being 'literacy failures' or not 'having literacy at home' actually experience lives in which literacy is deeply embedded in familial, community and school relationships. The point of including such studies of literacy practice is to ensure teachers understand that children have different purposes for literacy inside and outside of school. As McNaughton (2002) argues, children are more likely to succeed in literacy if there is a close pedagogical match between home and school. Teachers need to understand the types of literacy experiences or 'funds of knowledge' (Moll 1990) that children experience out of school and make use of this knowledge to increase children's chances of achieving literacy within the school system.

Children participate in out-of-school literacy activities in great frequency and these events may have quite formal structures. The family is a major site of literacy development and it is clear that children experience multiple literacies in the home and that literacy is defined, used and supported in accordance with social and cultural differences (Cairney 2003). In addition, as Gregory and Kenner (2003) argue, families and communities have always ensured that children have access to important cultural practices through formal and informal classes during out-of-school time. Such classes include religious or first-language classes, often covering a range of subjects in the curriculum. They argue that these 'cultural and linguistic spaces' help children to develop cognitive, cultural and linguistic flexibility with which to tackle the world. For instance, a former colleague who grew up on Niue, a Pacific Island, taught Niuean language and culture classes in Auckland on the weekend to children from her community, whose parents were concerned that the children were not learning about Niue and its language and culture in the state school system. Second-language learners are a particular group for attention in New Zealand and Australia because of the growing cultural diversity of the two countries. The children of migrants and refugees are in danger of losing their emergent literacy skills in mainstream education settings (Tabors & Snow 2001). In Chapters 5 and 6 we further discuss multiliteracies and bilingualism and multilingualism in children's literacy learning.

A sociocultural perspective on literacy acquisition

So far this chapter has proposed that how literacy is promoted in early childhood centres and schools is a social, cultural and political act. How literacy is understood and taught at any time in an educational system is the result of people's belief structures about what is important at any particular historical juncture and what beliefs people hold about how children learn and learn literacy in particular.

In Chapter 1 we used Vygotsky's (1978) theory to explain that literacy develops as a result of the maturing brain and its functions, the input of families, teachers and communities in social interaction, and as a result of the use of the tools and signs of the culture. In this chapter we have further explained that research has told us about some of the predictors of literacy achievement, which develop as a result of maturation and delineation of neural pathways in the brain and as a result of social experiences – what Whitehurst and Lonigan (1998) have called the 'inside' and 'outside' process of literacy acquisition. The research around literacy as a social practice supports this view, by further elaborating the 'funds of knowledge' (Moll 1990) that children bring to their literacy learning, as a result of different social, cultural, religious and technological backgrounds, creating an extension of the notion of inside and outside in literacy learning. These 'funds of knowledge' may also include exposure to a range of signs and symbol systems that children learn to negotiate as part of their inside and outside school practices.

Vygotsky (1978) argued that children learn as a result of access and mediation. We will argue that the teachers of today need to understand what types of access children have had to literacy and to not fall into the easy habit of ranking the types of access that children have had; it's too easy to say that children have not had access to a literacy environment simply because it doesn't correspond to your own home and community experiences. In addition, teachers need to fully understand what it means to mediate children's learning when they have diverse social, cultural and linguistic backgrounds. We will explain how mediation means understanding how to work with a child within the context of his or her family, supporting both child and family. The examples used in subsequent chapters will explore the complexity of literacy acquisition, as well as highlighting strategies and solutions to issues and challenges in children's learning.

Conclusion

This chapter has examined how learning to read involves political decision making about what children will read, empirical evidence from reading research about how children learn the concepts and skills associated with literacy, and research on the social and cultural contexts that shape the experiences of literacy and the identities that children develop as learners in those communities. As previously proposed, learning to read is complex and multilayered and there are a range of developmental pathways to literacy that children take. We further explore these pathways in subsequent chapters.

Reflective questions

1. How were your parents and grandparents taught to read and write in primary school? Was it different or similar to today?

2. What 'outside' experiences of literacy did you have as a child? How did these experiences shape your literacy skills, abilities and understandings?

3. When did you last hear something in the media about literacy achievement in your country or approaches to literacy instruction? What was the focus of the media item?

4. Often governments use literacy as an election platform. What was your government's last 'big thing' concerning literacy and what do you predict will be the next?

Further reading

Hoffman, J.V. and Goodman, Y.M. (eds) (2009). *Changing Literacies for Changing Times: An Historical Perspective on the Future of Reading Research, Public Policy, and Classroom Practices*. New York: Routledge.

May, H. (2011). *I Am Five and I Go to School. Early Years Schooling in New Zealand, 1900–2010*. Dunedin, NZ: Otago University Press.

Openshaw, R. and Soler, J. (eds) (2009). *Reading across International Boundaries: History, Policy and Politics*. Charlotte, NC: Information Age Publishing.

Chapter 3

When should children start literacy learning?

Chapter objectives

1. To explain some of the misunderstandings and myths about when children should start literacy learning.
2. To explore the outcomes of international studies on literacy achievement and how this relates to when children start literacy learning.
3. To examine differences among countries and pedagogies in the ages of starting school.

This chapter explores our beliefs about when to begin formal reading and writing instruction. It examines enduring social and cultural beliefs about maturational readiness and delaying reading instruction. It also considers the outcomes of international studies on literacy achievement. Further, the chapter examines differences in ages of starting school and the pedagogy of beginning and ongoing reading instruction.

Overview

When did you first start learning to read? Many of us will not remember, especially if we had no difficulties, but we might remember one of our siblings having difficulty, even in the first stages of schooling. Our sister may have squirmed and been unhappy when an adult read a book to her, and she may not have liked books. At school, she might have said she was 'dumb' and may have had to sit alone at a desk to do her work while her classmates worked in groups, completing their worksheets with ease while their 'dumb' classmate had trouble even knowing what to do, and usually not completing the task the teacher set her.

Some children can read well before they start formal schooling. They are precocious readers. Studies on these children show they are interested in books from a very early age, even when they are babies, and often learn the letters of the alphabet by about two years of age. By the time they are four years old they are happily reading books and 'writing' letters, and making up their own invented spellings (Nicholson 2005).

How did this happen? Was it a good thing? Should they have waited until they got to school instead of deciding to teach themselves to read? This chapter will discuss this question of when to begin formal reading and writing instruction. It will also explain enduring social and cultural beliefs about maturational readiness and delaying reading instruction, the outcomes of international studies on literacy achievement, and differing views of what is the right age to start school and to teach beginners.

Scenario 3.1

Imagine you are at a restaurant. The family next to you have a three-year-old daughter. They call for the menu and ask for one for their daughter. She reads the menu aloud. What would you think about this?

Precocious readers

Most of us would be envious of the above three-year-old in the restaurant because most of us did not learn to read until we got to primary school. It is amazing to see a **precocious reader** like that because it is so rare. Very few children are able to read before starting school, probably no more than 3 per cent (Jackson 1992). Is it a good thing to be able to read early? Some people think it is a positive thing but others will worry that the child is reading too early and that it might lead to negative effects, such as boredom at school because they already know how to read.

> **Precocious readers:** children who can read before they start formal schooling.

Stories of precocious readers have been in the literature for a long time – for example, the book *Gnys at Wrk* (Bissex 1980). Stainthorp and Hughes (2004a) describe precocious readers as 'children who are able to read fluently and with understanding before attending school and without having received any direct instruction in reading' (p. 107). What are precocious readers like? They are a diverse group (Jackson 1988). They show a wide range of intelligence, some are good at using contextual clues for reading, others at using decoding skills, and nearly all have huge parent support. They differ in reading interests; for example, Susan was reading at three years of age and liked reading chapter books such as *Charlotte's Web* whereas Bruce began reading at three but liked factual books (Jackson 1988).

Are they also early talkers? A study of 21 children who were early talkers showed that they were above-average readers by the time they were six years of age (Crain-Thoreson & Dale 1992). These children were not precocious readers so their language skills did not help them at that time but their language skills probably helped them to develop, especially in reading comprehension, once they started school.

> **Phonemic awareness:** this is one aspect of phonological awareness. Phonemes are the smallest constituent units of spoken language. An operational definition that shows how to deconstruct words to phonemes is that by deleting a phoneme from a spoken word or adding a phoneme to a word, you can generate a new word – for example, replace the /s/ in /sun/ with an /f/ and you will generate a new word, /fun/.

Are precocious readers good at **phonemic awareness** (i.e. breaking spoken words into minimal sounds, as in /k-a-t/) and **phonics** (i.e. being able to use rules that show how to 'sound out' words correctly)? As adults, we are quite good at phonemic awareness; for example, we can tell if two words rhyme or start with the same sound, and we can break words into segments such as 'k-at' and /k-a-t/. We can delete sounds from spoken words; for example, we can say that 'steal' without the /t/ sound says 'seal'. Children in early childhood struggle to do even the simplest of these tasks, and still have difficulties even at five years of age. However, many precocious readers are quite good at this. They are also good at phonics. For example, the child who writes 'if I woz a dog I would brk and chas stiks oll da' has an excellent ability to write words with phonics skills. Applied to reading it is the ability to sound out words using explicitly taught or implicitly learned phonics rules. For example, we all know that the word 'hat' is different to 'hate' and phonics teaches that this is because the final 'e' signals to pronounce 'hate' in a different way where the vowel takes its name, rather than its sound. This is phonics.

> **Phonics:** an instructional method of teaching decoding skills, involving the teaching of 'rules' that specify the grapheme–phoneme relationships of alphabetic writing systems.

Stainthorp and Hughes (2004b) reported a case study of an English child who could read fluently at five years and four months. In reading development, she was five years ahead of her age (at the 10-year-old level) and four years ahead in spelling (at the nine-year-old level). At five years of age, she had excellent vocabulary knowledge, high levels of phonemic awareness and high levels of phonics skills. At seven years of age, she said 'I think I've read every book I've seen'. She had read books by Roald Dahl, J.K. Rowling, Paula Danziger and Terry Pratchett. She was still well ahead of her peers in reading and spelling when reassessed at 11 years of age. The researchers concluded that early readers like her have a phonological advantage. We will talk more about this advantage in Chapter 11.

> **Phonological awareness:**
> the ability to segment the speech stream into phonological units – that is, the ability to segment speech into words, words into syllables, syllables into their onset (initial consonant(s)) and rime (what comes after the onset), and syllables into phonemes.

In contrast, a case study of a boy called Max found that he memorised words at first and did not do very well on a test of **phonological awareness** that required the ability to break spoken words into their component sounds, but he was sounding words out at three years of age. Max's mother wrote stories about Max and they read these together – for example, 'Max is a funny fella. He checked my ears for cheerios yesterday' (Henderson, Jackson & Mukimal 1993).

Another contrasting study is by Fletcher-Flinn and Thompson (2000) who reported a detailed case study of a girl named Maxine. At three years of age she was identifying words at an eight-year-old level but did not score well at all on tests of phonological awareness. From three to seven years, her word reading developed from an eight- to a 16-year-old level. She was still not 'sounding out' words but could read non-words quickly and accurately.

How do we explain this case study? Maxine had developed implicit skills of decoding words phonologically and worked out the rules for herself through reading and exposure to print. She was not taught phonics but had implicitly built up letter–sound associations in her mind, as well as using other sources of information in reading such as context, visual representations of words (i.e. orthographic representation) and analogy with other words. The researchers called this 'implicit phonological recoding' which means she had high levels of phonics skills but she had internalised them herself. No one had taught them to her. The researchers made the point that she had learned to read without showing evidence of phonological awareness and without anyone teaching her phonics. The conclusion we gather from the studies of Max and Maxine is that they did have phonological coding ability just as in the case of the Stainthorp and Hughes study, but that Maxine's skills were implicit – she had taught herself the skills just through reading.

You might be wondering whether Maxine became a 'normal' person as a grown-up? One of the authors of this book remembers seeing her as a young girl in the library with her mother, looking at Harry Potter books. This author also met her again at her university just recently. She was a lovely person, bubbly and very smart (according to her mother), and seemed to have a very positive attitude to life. Learning to read early seemed to have done no harm at all.

What are the long-term effects if some children learn to read early? Are they positive or negative?

Positive effects

Evidence for positive effects comes from a longitudinal study by Cunningham and Stanovich (1997). They followed 27 United States children from Grade 1 to Grade 11. Children who started well at school had become 'lifetime readers' by Grade 11. In another longitudinal study, Nicholson, McIntosh and Ell (2000) found that New Zealand children with high reading scores at Year 1 also had high scores at Year 5. These indicate long-term positive effects on the academic side of school. Are there also positive emotional effects? Most children who learn to read well have positive attitudes to reading. For example, one of our students surveyed a group of 11-year-old good and poor readers and found that there was a highly significant difference in attitudes. The good readers were much more positive about reading (Liu 2000).

Negative effects

In contrast to this result, a recent longitudinal study of more than 1000 gifted and early readers over their lifetime found three negative effects. Their early academic success was followed by (a) less educational attainment (e.g. not going to University); (b) worse midlife adjustment (e.g. increased use of alcohol); and (c) a greater likelihood of early death compared with children who learned to read at an average age. They were less conscientious at school, less likely to take further education after high school, and less socially prepared for an early start to school (Kern & Friedman 2009).

The results are disturbing but we need to keep in mind that this was a sample of gifted children and not 'normally developing' children. Another cautionary note is that researchers assessed these gifted children starting in the 1920s and then tracked them through their whole lives, to the turn of the 21st century. They grew up in different times to present generations, and these cultural and historical factors may have accounted for the negative results found in the study.

What is the 'right' age at which to learn to read?

Most children in the world start school at age 6 or 7. They start at age four in Northern Ireland; age five in Australia, England, Malta, Netherlands, New Zealand, Scotland and Wales; age six in India and most of North and South America and Western Europe; and age seven in some large countries such as Brazil, China and Russia, and in some European countries such as Finland and Poland. They start at age 8 in Mongolia. The NationMaster website (2012) lists starting ages for all countries.

There seems to be no educational reason for this variation in starting ages, though one plausible explanation for the early start time of age five goes back to Victorian times in England when child labour was common and it was intended to protect children from having to work in mines and factories (Couglan 2008).

There has never been a shortage of opinions about the 'right' age to learn to read or the 'right' time to teach reading. More than 2000 years ago, Quintillian thought seven years of age was a good time to start learning to read; Plato thought 10 years of age. In 1612 the opinion was that five years of age was a good time and in 1660, between three and four years of age (see Coltheart 1979).

There are a number of myths about when to begin formal reading instruction, the main one being the myth of 'reading readiness'. These are myths in the sense that they are based more on anecdote and opinion than on research. In this section of the chapter we explain the myths of visual and mental readiness.

There was a view in the late 1800s that schoolwork caused eye problems, because many children seemed to need glasses once they went to school. The opinion was that reading small print in primers was bad for the eyes and children should only engage in music and gymnastics. They were not mentally ready, not able to sit still, and desks were not good for a child's posture (Huey 1908).

Another opinion was that children's eyes were not ready to read, and would not be ready to focus on small print until they were 10 years of age – though later research proved this idea to be totally wrong (Coltheart 1979).

Another opinion was that children were not mentally ready to learn to read until they were 10 years of age (see Coltheart 1979). The opinion that the minds of young children were not ready to read until 'the time is ripe' has been with us since the 1920s. It is the **maturational** view that if a child struggles to read, then the child is not 'ready' to read. Parents may say, 'He is not ready to read and write – he cannot even hold a pen'. The argument against the 'ripening' theory is that if it is true, then teaching children to read before the time is ripe should be totally ineffective and yet much research shows that reading instruction at an early age is effective.

> **Maturational readiness:** the idea that children are best ready to learn to read when they have reached a certain level of physical, social and emotional development.

There is also the complication that different countries start to teach reading at different ages. If the age of six, for example, is the right time to learn to read, then five-year-olds in countries such as England, Israel and New Zealand should be failing in droves but this is not the case.

In the 1930s there was evidence in support of the opinion that a mental age of six and a half years was needed to learn to read. (The formula for calculating mental age is intelligence quotient x chronological age ÷ 100. For example, if you have an intelligence quotient of 100 and a chronological age of six years and six months, then you have a mental age of six years and a half.) The evidence came from an influential study by Morphett and Washburne (1931) in the United States. The results were widely cited: for example, 'We have a mountain of evidence that a perfectly 'normal' child – IQ 100 – cannot learn to read until he is about six years and six months old' (see Coltheart 1979 for more quotations like this one).

The 'time is ripe' theory persevered from the 1930s through to the 1960s and beyond. Many researchers accepted the findings of Morphett and Washburne because it explained why a large number of children failed to read in their first year of school. The simple answer was because they were mentally 'not ready'. The argument was plausible but did not make sense because it goes round in circles, saying that if you are not ready to read you will not be able to read, and if you are not able to read it is because you are not ready to read – without taking account of the fact that you might not have the necessary pre-reading skills to learn to read, you might have a poor classroom reading program, you might come from a poor home, and so on.

Some researchers in the 1930s supported the mental readiness theory. They explained that children found it hard to learn phonics, for example, until they were seven years of age, though later studies found that six-year-old children who had been at school for only a few months were often able to break words into component sounds and to read simple non-words (for example, Firth 1972, in relation to Australian six-year-olds). The groundbreaking research of Read (1971) at Harvard University showed that kindergarten child could break spoken words into sounds and spell them before they had even learned to read, showing that they could use simple phonics, a feat that came to be known as 'invented spelling'. Coltheart (1979) summarised several research studies in the 1960s and 1970s which showed that in simple reading and pre-reading tasks requiring phonics skills such as decoding simple non-words and segmenting syllables into phonemes, even three-year-olds could do these tasks to some extent and five-year-olds to quite a large extent. These results indicated that the concept of 'reading readiness' was seriously flawed in terms of research, and was too simplistic a reason to explain reading failure.

The flaw (called the base rates fallacy) in the Morphett and Washburne study was that it was done in the United States. If their conclusion about a mental readiness age of six and a half years was correct, then it should have been found in other countries as well, where children started school at a younger age, but this was not the case.

A more fundamental problem with the 'reading readiness' theory of maturation was that it compared reading development with physical development (Coltheart 1979). The opinion was that it took a certain amount of time to learn to walk and talk, and so it would also take a similar amount of time to learn to read. The problem with this argument is that reading and writing were technological discoveries (for more on this, see Nicholson 2000); they were not part of physical and mental maturation. It was the wrong comparison to make because reading is an invention. It is not something we naturally acquire, like walking and talking. In many countries around the world there are many millions of children and adults who can walk and talk very well but who cannot read and write. We are wired through evolution to walk and talk but someone has to teach us to read and write.

Teaching babies to read

Programs for teaching babies to read have been in the literature for a long time, and especially since the 1960s (*Teaching Baby to Read* 1966). The latest versions of these programs are DVD series and computer apps such as *Baby Einstein*, *Brainy Superstar*, *Brainy Baby*, *Baby Wordsworth*, *Your Baby Can Read*, 'Jumpstart' and 'TV Teach Me'. Publishers of these programs claim that they are educational but there is not much research to verify these claims.

A recent study has tried to find out what children learn from a DVD. The DVD *Baby Wordsworth* (part of the 'Baby Einstein' series) is designed for 12-month and older babies. It runs for 39 minutes and it highlights 30 words of objects and rooms in a house. There is a picture of the item, a printed word and a sign language gesture for the word. Researchers randomly assigned 45 infants either to a group that watched the DVD or to a control group of babies who did not watch the DVD. The researchers found that although the DVD publishers implied it would increase vocabulary, the babies in the study did not learn any more words than the control group of babies (Robb, Richert & Wartella 2009). They concluded that children learn better from a live model than a DVD in that research on adults reading books to children seems to be effective whereas research involving watching television or DVDs does not show the same positive effects.

The conclusion is that babies do seem able to learn something about reading but it is better if an adult interacts with them and the interaction involves sharing books.

When is the best time to teach children to read?

Even if it is possible for children to learn to read at an early age, is it worth it, given that the effects wear off at a later age, and that children who start school when they are older catch up with those who start school when they are younger? We will now look at the evidence for starting formal instruction in school at an early age.

There may be initial advantages in teaching children to read at an early age but does this advantage wash out over time? International studies suggest that there is a washout effect in that the gains from early reading instruction disappear over time. Yet the existence of a washout effect does not prove that learning to read at an older age is just as good as starting earlier. It could be that children who start reading at an early age get off to a flying start and could make even better progress but teachers do not capitalise on their early gains.

There are some data in New Zealand schools to support this idea (e.g. Thomas & Ward 2010). They show that children who start school at five years of age make major gains in reading in Years 1 to 4, but they plateau after that, and fall below expectations by Year 8. It may be that once children learn the basics of reading – that is, once they have good decoding skills – teachers do not build on these foundations to extend these gains. There is some evidence that teachers pay less attention to good readers and think that good readers are 'masters of their own destiny' (Nicholson 2000) and prefer to spend time teaching those who are behind grade level.

An example of the washout effect is a comparison study by Ritter (2006) using a cross-sectional design. She assessed the reading levels of a sample of 300 children ranging in ages from six to 10, in two New Zealand and two United States schools. The sample of children in New Zealand started school at five and the sample in the United States started school at six. Ritter predicted that the New Zealand children would be ahead of the United States children in reading at age six because they had already been in school for a year. The results showed a significant advantage in reading for six-year-olds in New Zealand compared with six-year-olds in the United States, which suggests there are advantages in beginning formal reading instruction at five years of age, though by the time children were eight years of age, this advantage had disappeared (see Figure 3.1 which compares the two countries at five different age levels in oral reading accuracy and reading comprehension). The United States children scored ahead of the New Zealand children at 10 years of age, though this was probably because the children in the United States 10-year-old sample were slightly older. The practical implication is that the early start had positive effects for the New Zealand children in the short term, though not in the long term.

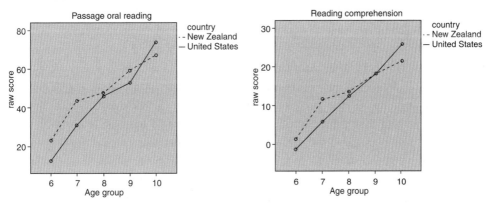

Figure 3.1 *A comparison of reading levels of children in New Zealand and the United States (Ritter 2006)*

Another interesting finding was that early gains for New Zealand children in oral reading accuracy occurred mainly for the below-average readers (see Figure 3.2, based on a sample of 137 below-average readers). The below-average New Zealand readers started ahead of the below average United States six-year-olds in oral reading accuracy but the gains washed out by eight years of age. In reading comprehension, above-average New Zealand readers stayed ahead of their United States counterparts until about nine years of age when the gains washed out (N=94).

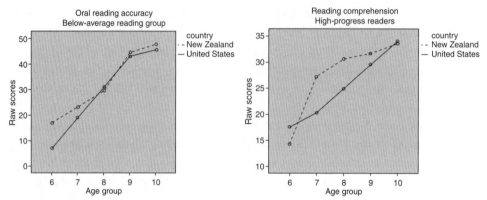

Figure 3.2 *A comparison of reading levels for below-average and above-average reading groups in New Zealand and the United States (Ritter 2006)*

The implication of the findings is that the early start for New Zealand children was beneficial in the short term but not in the long term. Further evidence of a washout effect comes from international studies that compare the reading achievement of large samples of pupils in different countries. Children learn to read at different ages in different countries, and their relative performance on reading tests can give insights about the best time to learn to read. A study of reading results for 10 countries at nine years of age showed that the best performing countries started school six months earlier (Elley 1992). In contrast, the results of the 2006 international survey (i.e. PIRLS) of the reading levels of 10-year-olds in 40 countries showed that high-performing countries that were ahead of countries such as England and New Zealand were those where children started school at six or seven years of age (Mullis et al. 2007).

In England one of the recommendations of the Cambridge Primary Review is to delay formal instruction until six or seven years of age, as is done in most other European countries, the United States and Australia (Alexander 2009; see NationMaster 2012 for details). In some ways, this seems sensible because, in learning to read English, many children struggle and if they start to learn to read at an older age it means that they will not have spent their early years labelled as a struggler, or 'backward'.

A problem with international studies is that there are other variables that may account for reading progress. Possible confounding factors include the quality of reading programs; quality of teaching; cultural differences in the extent to which parents 'push' their children to make strong efforts in school; immigration of peoples from different cultures with different languages; and socio-economics, such as the difference in living standards between rich and poor in many countries.

Time spent in school doing academic work seems much more effective in terms of formal learning than not going to school at all. Fitzpatrick, Grissmer and Harstedt (2009) found that a year of school results in gains of about one standard deviation (about a school year) above normal developmental gains in both reading and math. The implication is that starting school earlier, or extending the school year, will make a significant difference to academic learning. It may or may not be due to the quality of the teaching children receive at school but simply that they are required to learn. Some evidence that teacher quality is not the main reason for pupil achievement comes from Byrne et al. (2010); they found that identical twins taught in different classrooms by different teachers still made the same progress, suggesting that the quality of the teacher does not make a difference. The implication of both these studies is that government money should be spent to ensure that children attend school (every day makes a difference) and spend more time in school, rather than to improve the quality of teachers.

These findings about the effects of simply attending school suggest that school-entry age is important. They also suggest that if we want to improve the prospects of struggling readers we need to use effective teaching methods and give them more learning time.

Another way to study age effects is to compare children in the same year level who are the same age but either at the high or low end of that age group. A comparison study of older children with their younger peers of the same age found that the older children did better in reading up until nine years of age (Menet et al. 2000). A review of 12 studies found that older pupils in the same age group performed better in reading than their younger peers between the ages of five and 14 (Sharp et al. 2009).

A final way to assess possible age effects is to compare children in Steiner schools with children in regular schools in countries where children start at an early age. Researchers compared, in England, children in regular schools who started learning to read at five years of age with children in a Steiner school who started learning to read at seven years of age. They found that the Steiner children, after their first and second years of school, read as well as mainstream children even though they started school at an older age. The researchers found the Steiner children did not do as well in spelling (Cunningham & Carroll 2011).

In summary, research shows that it is possible to learn to read at an early age. It seems that getting off to an early start does no harm, and that for many children it does have very positive long-term effects. Although there is a 'wash out' effect of getting off to an early start in reading, this may be due to other factors such as differences in emphasis on academics from one country to another.

Conclusion

Only 2–3 per cent of children can read even a few words before they start formal schooling, which is why school is so important. We normally have to teach children how to read. It does not just happen like walking and talking, listening and viewing. The best predictors of learning to read are letter–name and letter–sound knowledge and phonemic awareness. Reading books to children at home sets them up for school because that is what will happen in the classroom. The teacher will read them a book every day. Research shows that going to school is important. Incredibly, even missing a day at school makes a difference. In spite of this, many children go missing from school for long periods. In some countries, schools do not start teaching reading until children are seven, but this does not mean you should keep your child at home when other children in your street are starting school at age five or six. The best thing a parent can do is to help his or her child at home and to send the child to school as soon as the system allows this to happen. There is research to show that accelerating a child to higher classes with older children may have negative social effects but a parent can take steps to make sure his or her child is doing well academically and socially. Research shows that reading makes you smarter. Getting off to an early start in reading is a good thing, because the child will be likely to succeed at school and not struggle. It is better to be a winner than a loser, or at least be at the same level as the rest of the class. The best insurance a child has for reading success is the support and help of their parents. Schools and parents have to work together.

Reflective questions

1. When you think back to learning to read and write as a child, do you think you started too early?

2. Did your parents help you to learn to read and write? How did they do this?

3. Do you think we should wait until children are seven or eight years of age before we teach them literacy?

4. Can teacher and parents work together if a child in the class is struggling to learn literacy?

Further reading

Nicholson, T. (2005). *The Importance of Phonemic Awareness in Learning to Read and Spell.* Wellington: NZCER Press.

Appendix

Possible answers to parent questions

QUESTION	ANSWER	REASON
1. Should I teach my baby to read?	Some television ads and internet ads say that babies can learn to 'read' but the evidence is that babies look for distinctive cues to remember words, such as the 'golden arches' at McDonalds, or a thumbprint on a flashcard to remember. They do not have the necessary skills to learn how to sound out words until a later age. We think youngsters can start to crack the code from about three years of age if they have the right pre-reading skills.	Research indicates that youngsters before about five years of age have trouble knowing that spoken words are made of phonemes and this makes it difficult to appreciate that letters stand for phonemes. They are likely to tell you that the sounds in 'cat' are 'meow'. When they can tell you that the sounds in 'cat' are k-a-t, then they are ready to learn to read.
2. My friend's child is in a Steiner school which does not start teaching reading until pupils are seven years of age. Should I discourage my child from learning to read until then?	In state and many private schools children start earlier than that, usually at five years of age. If your child attended a state school and you discouraged her from learning to read until she was seven, she would be two years behind her peers and that is not good.	Research shows that when we compare children who start school at five years of age with Steiner children when both groups are seven years of age, the ones who started school earlier are ahead of the Steiner children.
3. In Finland, children learn to read at seven years of age, and they have very high levels of literacy in that country. Why do we start school so young?	Finland has a writing system that is transparent. Each letter has just one sound but in English many of the letters of the alphabet have more than one sound. English is a lot harder to decode and children typically take at least two years to gain a reasonable level of skill.	It is not a good idea to compare countries because they are so different.
4. Should I teach my child things such as the letters of the alphabet? My friends say that they teach their four-year-old children the letters of the alphabet, and how to break words such as 'cat' into phonemes, but I am afraid that if I do that, my child might be learning the wrong things and get growled at when she gets to school.	Your child will be at a definite advantage if you help her to learn the letters of the alphabet and how to break words into phonemes before starting school. It will make school so much easier for your child and it will help her teacher as well to know that she already has these essential skills.	Research shows that these pre-reading skills are our best predictors of whether or not a child will learn to read.

Chapter 4

Family literacies and relationships with centres and schools

Chapter objectives

1. To consider the importance of family literacy and associated research.
2. To consider how schools and families can work together to help children to learn.
3. To critically examine the research on engaging families in the reading process.

This chapter explores the growing body of research, conducted with families internationally, on the different patterns and expectations of literacy in homes and schools. It examines recent longitudinal studies in New Zealand, the United Kingdom and the United States, as well as in-depth studies on family literacy programs that have attempted to bridge the gaps between homes and schools to support literacy acquisition. This chapter also gives practical advice on how to engage parents in the reading process, drawing on recent research to provide examples of effective involvement with families.

What is family literacy?

Research demonstrates that the family is a powerful force for literacy learning and that this finding is the case across social and cultural groups (Anderson & Morrison 2011; Taylor & Dorsey-Gaines 1988). According to Cairney (2003), research shows that the family's influence on children's learning does not stop at five years of age when the child starts school. Instead, differences in family backgrounds have been found to be a significant predictor of school achievement, and there are strong relationships between parents' knowledge, beliefs and interaction styles and children's school achievement. Because of this evidence, family involvement in children's education is widely recognised as a key component of effective education. Involvement includes parents, caregivers, siblings and extended family such as grandparents (Taylor & Dorsey-Gaines 1988).

As we argued in Chapters 1 and 2, literacy is a social practice which has many forms and is practised in culturally specific ways. For the purposes of this chapter, we define 'family literacy' as the social and cultural practices associated with written text. We need to be clear that **family literacy** refers to the research which focuses on literacy practices within family settings. Family literacy should be seen as distinct from family literacy programs, which focus on how to educate parents about school literacy, build partnerships between home and school, and raise literacy levels within family members.

> **Family literacy:** a range of issues associated with how children learn about literacy in homes, extended families and communities.

Morrow (2009) states that family literacy is a complex concept, but has some or all of the following features:

- It encompasses the ways families, children and extended family use literacy at home and in the community.
- It occurs naturally during the routines of daily living and helps children and adults to 'get things done' – for example, making lists, writing letters, sharing stories, and through engaging in reading, writing and talking.

- It may be initiated purposefully by a family member or may happen spontaneously as families go about their lives.

- It reflects the ethnic, racial or cultural heritage of the family.

- It may be initiated by the school to support the acquisition of school literacy – for example, storybook reading, writing or helping with homework.

- It can involve families going to school for concerts, parent–teacher conferences and programs in which children participate.

- It can include parents becoming involved in the school classroom, helping with reading, observing classes, sharing hobbies or speaking at mat times.

- It can also include parents' involvement in workshops designed to help them learn about and understand what they can do at home to help their children.

The last point usually concerns family literacy programs, which may include parent education, but also literacy education. We talk briefly about some examples of these programs in Australia, New Zealand and England later in this chapter.

Literacy in the home setting

As argued in Chapter 1, the study of children's literacy prior to school entry is relatively young. Prior to the emergence of research on emergent literacy in the 1980s, there was relatively little research on family literacy. There was a lot of research on children's early language acquisition, but considerably less on how children develop literacy within homes and families.

Cairney (2003, p. 86) states that research in the 1980s identified some key understandings about the role of families in children's literacy learning:

- Family support of literacy experiences was foundational to later learning.

- Guided interaction between parents/caregivers and children in relation to story reading or early print experiences was important.

- The development of the alphabetic code had its foundations in children's early experiences of environmental print.

Cairney further argues that research has shown that differences between the literacies of the home environment and the school environment and children's different knowledge bases mean that some children are disadvantaged in school settings, where their literacy experiences are not valued or recognised. In Chapter 5, we more fully explore the range of multiliteracies that children encounter in homes and communities and the role of schools, which are clearly also part of this topic.

In Chapter 1, we introduced Vygotsky's (1978) notion of *access* and *mediation* in children's learning; this is addressed further in Chapter 7, where we look at promoting literacy in early childhood settings in more depth. In terms of family literacy research, we know that some families provide a great deal of access for their children to literacy resources, such as books, writing materials, computers and televisions. Families can also provide mediation of these resources by reading to children, talking about print concepts (e.g. front/back cover, pictures) and defining new vocabulary, showing them how to use writing materials and environmental print (e.g. TV guides, newspapers, bibles) and explaining their purpose. They have an important role in supporting children's interactions with digital technologies such as computers, television, Playstation and Xbox. The research evidence is strong that families vary enormously in both the access and mediation that they provide and that this isn't necessarily because of socio-economic status, although poverty can be a major issue (Nicholson 1999; Wasik & Hindman 2010). For instance, you could have a home that is rich in material literacy resources, such as books, writing materials and digital technologies, but parents who are too busy or disinterested to support children to use these resources. In contrast, you can have homes that are materially poor, but language- and interaction-rich, in which parents actively engage in supporting children's growing understandings of literacy.

As an example, Claire McLachlan is one of six children and her father was a motor mechanic and the sole income earner. Claire says her family was always short of money, but her home had lots of books and writing materials and her father in particular, who loved to read, read to the children in her family every night. He exposed the children to stories with rich language and varied plots. His favourites were *The Wind in the Willows*, Rudyard Kipling's *Just So Stories* (in particular 'The Elephant's Child'), and *Alice in Wonderland* and *Through the Looking Glass*. In Claire's family, all six children hold a tertiary qualification of some type and have all been gainfully employed their entire lives. Claire's family is not the only example of low socio-economic status families being rich in literacy. As Nicholson (1999, p. 5) argues:

> Although many children from low-income backgrounds have low levels of reading achievement, some do not. There are well-known figures in history who were excellent readers and writers, yet came from humble backgrounds. Abraham Lincoln, President of the United States during the American Civil War, came from a background of rural poverty. D.H. Lawrence became a famous novelist, though his father was a coal miner.

No doubt you can think of many other examples of adults who have achieved high status in their chosen career in spite of the difficulties involved in their childhood, but unfortunately these individuals are often the exception rather than the rule.

The catchphrase 'parents as first teachers', used in many contexts, sums up what research and common sense tells us. Children learn about language and literacy and its purposes from their parents, caregivers, siblings and extended family. The role of a parent in relation to a child's development is obviously complex and includes adopting the role of listener, prompter, information giver, asker of questions and fellow meaning maker interested in the communication process (Cairney 2003). It is important to remember that language begins very early in the life of a child, and by only a few weeks old babies are intentionally vocalising in response to the human face and voice. Learning about language and literacy in the home environment is a not a neutral activity: parents actively socialise their children into the social and cultural life of the family, as the following photo shows.

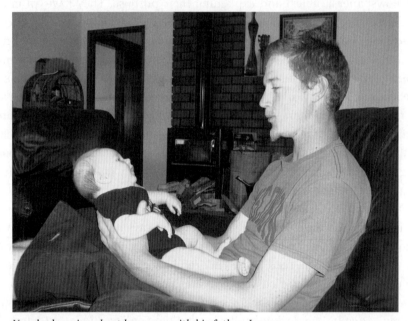

Vaughn learning about language with his father, Jeremy

There is now a considerable body of research which has demonstrated the differences in uses and purposes of language and literacy in different homes. Cairney (2003) states that many researchers have tried to explain difference in literacy achievement in terms of the different ways that language is used in homes, based on evidence that parents in middle-class homes use a more elaborated linguistic code, in which parents explain their meanings and intentions. However, more recent research has showed that it is not the volume of language and literacy experiences that make the difference to children's achievement, as most children have experiences with oral and written language in highly developed countries. The differences emerge because children are not familiar with the form of literacy practices used in schools and schools do not build on the literacy practices that children bring with them from home. Moll and Greenberg (1990, p. 320) call the knowledge of literacy that children have 'funds of knowledge' and strenuously argue that schools need to adapt western curricula to include these different forms so that children's learning is legitimated. One of the early examples of this type of research is the study of language and literacy in three different communities by Shirley Brice Heath (1983), in which she found variation in the acquisition of oral language and the ways that literacy was introduced to children and used.

Sénéchal (2011) proposes a **home literacy** model which explains the different outcomes in children's literacy. Sénéchal argues that there are two types of literacy experiences that children are exposed to: formal and informal. 'According to the home literacy model, informal literacy activities promote the development of language skills, whereas formal literacy activities promote the acquisition of early literacy skills' (p. 176). Sénéchal also argues that there is not a straightforward relationship between home literacy activities and the development of phonological awareness. Figure 4.1 provides a summary of the relationships that Sénéchal proposes exist with the home literacy model.

> **Home literacy:** literacy that occurs within family homes.

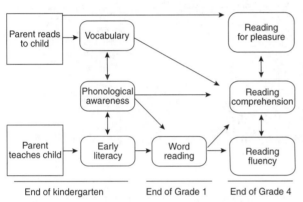

Figure 4.1 *Sénéchal's home literacy model (2011, p. 177)*

The caption reads 'Reliable relations among home literacy and child outcomes in the home literacy model. Arrows represent statistically significant predictors after controlling for potential confounds' (Sénéchal 2011, p. 177). Sénéchal argues that some parental factors influence this model. These factors include responding to the child's interest and encouraging the child to read a wide range of books for pleasure. Sénéchal also found a strong relationship between parents who had high expectations of children becoming literate, and belief in the importance of literacy and children's literary achievement in school. Clearly, involvement and offering both formal and informal opportunities for literacy in the home environment are important.

Most approaches to family literacy have focused on the role of mothers, with the role of fathers less commonly reported in research literature. However, the long-term benefits of fathers' involvement have been investigated; fathers' involvement in their children's education at age seven predicts educational attainment by age 20 (Saracho & Spokek 2010). Saracho and Spodek argue that modern fathers are more involved in family life than fathers of earlier generations; they assume multiple roles, including not only 'breadwinner', but also carer and educator, possibly because more mothers are also in the workforce.

In New Zealand McNaughton (1995) found significant differences between the literacy practices engaged in by Maori, Samoan and Pakeha (European) families with their preschool children. McNaughton identified that families used three main ways to socialise their children into literacy:

Jeremy reading a bedtime story to Vaughn

1. *Joint activities* – where another person provides guidance in a specific literacy event, such as story reading. This could be a parent, sibling, grandparent or other caregiver.

2. *Personal activities* – involving the child practising a specific form of literacy on his or her own, such as writing his or her own name or scribbling, or reading a book on his or her own.

3. *Ambient activities* – involving literacy practices where the child is immersed in daily life, which occur around him or her. This might be activities such as preparing a shopping list, reading a recipe or the newspaper, or being around other children doing their homework.

Similarly, in a study of 27 families in Australia by Cairney and Ruge (1998) found that literacy was used for four distinct purposes in homes and classrooms:

- establishing and maintaining relationships
- accessing or displaying information
- pleasure and self-expression
- skills development.

Cairney and Ruge found considerable variation in the extent to which literacy was visible in family life and the extent to which 'school' literacies dominated the homes, particularly in those families that already had school children, where homework was a common feature. They also suggest that parents' desire to prepare children for schools is a factor. Current family literacy programs are built upon Vygotsky's (1978) theory, theorising that learning occurs in social contexts as competent adults and others engage in meaningful activities in their daily lives (Anderson & Morrison 2011).

The research by Taylor (Taylor 1983; Taylor & Dorsey-Gaines 1988) in middle-class white and poor, urban, black American communities demonstrated that there is a richness of literacy experiences that occur in homes and that institutional factors, rather than lack of parental support, have a greater impact on school success for these children. Findings by Taylor and Dorsey Gaines (1988) in particular were significant, because they identified that race, socio-economic status and social settings are not necessarily correlates of literacy. Rather, there is a rich diversity of literacy practice occuring in homes that needs to be acknowledged and tapped into by centres and schools to support continuity in children's literacy learning.

Wasik and Hindman (2010) investigated the nature of 'Head Start' children's home literacy environments in the United States and the correlates between these environments and children's early language skills and literacy skills. At the beginning of the preschool year, families of 302 children completed a family literacy survey. In general, Head Start families reported providing a variety of activities for young children; however, variability was observed across families in several aspects of the home literacy environment. The findings also revealed that the average family reported employing academically focused activities approximately once or twice per week, whereas play-related activities took place significantly more often, close to every day. Wasik and Hindman (2010) propose that teachers can help families understand how literacy can be supported through play activities and they also make useful suggestions about how teachers can identify the literacy practices in home settings using observations and interviews, rather than relying on self-reports or surveys.

Dickie and MacDonald's (2011) study of the literacy practices of 14 Year 7 and 8 Samoan children in New Zealand showed that older siblings introduced school ways of learning to younger family members and that church literacy also involved techniques for understanding and assessment that were similar to those of the school. They also found that parents who worked in literate occupations or were involved in further study had greater amounts of literacy materials and behaviours, indicating a possible factor in differences in literacy outcomes. However, they also found that the amount of time spent on church activities sometimes reduced the time that could be used for school literacy and that Samoan families differed in the amount and type of literacy that children experienced. Dickie and MacDonald (2011, p. 30) further argue that New Zealand's assessment of literacy needs re-examination, concluding:

> standard reading tests measure the literacy taught in schools. How well would Samoan pupils compare with others if their literacy was assessed by measures such as committing verses written in formal language to memory to be recited and publicly tested for accuracy?

It is important not to underestimate the other difficulties that children can face in the home environment. As Nicholson (1999, p. 17) states:

> Data from a number of studies indicate that children from low-income backgrounds do less well in school than children from middle-class backgrounds. There are many factors which militate against success for children from low-income homes, including the need to do lots of chores at home, lack of study facilities, books, money for school materials, ostracism at school, attendance at schools with a preponderance of other pupils from low-income backgrounds, stress and feelings of inadequacy on the part of the parents of these children, and possible miscommunication between parents and schools about the academic progress of their children. In addition to these social disadvantages, there are linguistic disadvantages as well for children from low-income backgrounds. Compared with children from middle-class homes, they have less knowledge of the names and sounds of the letters of the alphabet, less knowledge of books, less knowledge of the phonemic structure of spoken words.

For all these reasons, it is imperative that teachers find ways to provide extra support for children who face considerable contextual difficulties in their journey to literacy and also to do their best to support families in helping children to become literate. Working with children's different literacy experiences requires an open-mindedness to different forms of literacy that teachers may find challenging. However, as Cunningham, Zibulsky and Callahan (2009, p. 488) state:

> Whether children come from impoverished or enriched language environments, their preschool teachers are in a unique position to provide opportunities to build the fundamental skills and knowledge they will need for the transition into the first years of formal schooling – the years when reading and writing will be among their most significant core achievements.

Helping families to support children's literacy achievements

McNaughton (2002) considers that children enter early childhood centres and primary schools with very different literacy backgrounds and experiences, some of which map well to the context of the centre or school and some which do not. He argues there is often a mismatch between the literacy practices of homes, communities and cultures and those of the school, which studies discussed in this chapter support. Tunmer, Chapman and Prochnow's (2006) longitudinal New Zealand study found that these differences at school entry in what they term 'literate cultural capital' (which loosely translates to something like 'literacy knowledge/money in the bank') predicted reading achievement seven years later. Differences in the levels of knowledge and awareness that children have during early childhood can impact on the efficiency in which they can transition into conventional literacy in primary school (Tunmer, Chapman & Prochnow 2006).

Second-language learners are a particular group for attention in Australia and New Zealand, because of the cultural and linguistic diversity of the populations created by waves of immigration from a wide variety of nations. We will discuss this in more depth in Chapter 6, but it's worth mentioning here too. Second-language learners are in danger of losing their emergent literacy skills in their first language and gaining unstable language and literacy understandings in the second language (Tagoilelagi-Leota et al. 2005). A lower literacy achievement is not inevitable, of course, but these children may need dedicated help in order to develop literacy skills in both languages, as Tagoilelagi-Leota et al. (2005) demonstrated with Samoan and Tongan children in South Auckland. In this study, children who experienced an enriched emergent literacy environment with skilful, knowledgeable teachers gained language and literacy skills in both their first and second languages over an 18-month intervention period. The study followed children from six months before school entry until a year after school entry and found that teachers who focused on quality of teaching in reading to children, guided reading and retelling of stories made significant gains in emergent literacy in both Samoans and Tongans. Earlier research by Phillips, McNaughton and McDonald (2001) found that many early childhood teachers had limited knowledge of how literacy develops and that professional development improved literacy outcomes for children. The 'Picking up the Pace' project suggested that greater collaboration and negotiation between early childhood centres and primary schools could support continuity in language and literacy development.

Family literacy studies have shown that the role of parental storybook reading has an impact on children's success in school-based literacy instruction (Saracho & Spodek 2010). Storybook reading is when adults read an appropriate text to their children and has been found to promote children's language growth, emergent literacy and reading achievement. As Saracho and Spodek (2010, p. 1385) explain:

> Family storybook reading consists of a parent or another adult family member reading books to young children. In addition to reading the book, it includes the adult engaging the children in dialogue about the book before, during, and/or after the actual story reading. This literacy experience has significant effects. It promotes the children's language and literacy development; increases their vocabulary; improves the chances of children's success in school-based literacy instruction; and increases the children's reading achievement, vocabulary and comprehension skills. The children develop a positive awareness of the structure of stories, the language of stories and the nature of reading behaviour. The influence of the experience may be felt through the third grade.

Carter, Chard and Pool (2009) propose a model for improving early literacy skills that:

- recognises children within the context of their unique family system and natural home environment
- focuses on family strengths, and
- identifies a system for embedding learning opportunities within meaningful and contextually relevant everyday experiences.

As they argue, 'If families and practitioners begin by recognizing the common routines in their life and their own unique strengths, they are able to identify activities and learning opportunities that fit within the context of their life' (p. 524).

The **family strengths model** starts with identifying the unique routines, strengths and resources of an individual family as a way to better pinpoint natural and meaningful opportunities for embedding early language and literacy experiences. Carter, Chard and Pool propose four family strategies:

- creating opportunities
- modelling reading and language
- interacting with their child
- providing recognition that families can create multiple meaningful opportunities for their child to engage with language and print.

To facilitate implementation of this model, they suggest organising activities into three steps:

- Step 1 – Identify family routines.
- Step 2 – Identify family strengths.
- Step 3 – Identify language and literacy opportunities.

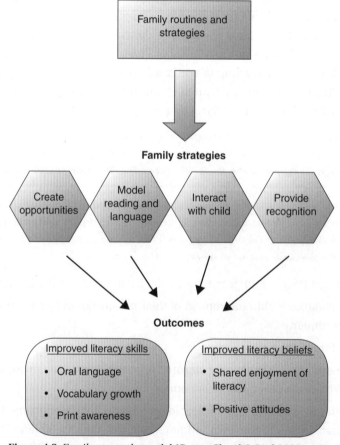

Figure 4.2 *Family strengths model (Carter, Chard & Pool 2009, p. 8)*

Zeece and Wallace (2009) argue that creating and sharing take-home literacy bags is a literacy-promoting activity that may be shared with children and families to provide support for emergent literacy. The BAGS (Books and Good Stuff) take-home literacy kits are advocated as a simple method of promoting literacy. Zeece and Wallace provide suggestions for content, construction, implementation and evaluation. They suggest the following contents for BAGS (2009, p. 37):

- Books with varying formats, including old favourites and new finds with the same theme or skill level. Books do not need to be new. Having gently used books encourages children to become more familiar with classroom resources and to consider the positive results of recycling.
- Developmentally appropriate activities including pictures to colour, dot-to-dot, phonics and math games, letter trace-and-write sheets, interactive mini-books, and puppet patterns.
- Small games related to the theme or specific skill development.
- A surprise (e.g. manipulatives, stamping materials, miniature plush book character or other prop tied to the themes of the BAGS).
- A journal to pass from student to student with themed writing paper, allowing developmentally appropriate writing or drawing at all stages.
- A parent letter suggesting ideas for use and care of the books and materials.
- Additional materials suggested or donated by children or families that enhance the themes and learning.

In a review of the literature on learning literacy in families and communities, Spedding et al. (2007) identified the following principles for supporting family literacy in Australia:

- A proactive approach is crucial, ensuring that families are supported in their role as their children's first literacy educator.
- Family literacy programs must take account of family differences and avoid 'one size fits all' approaches.
- Family literacy models must be sensitive to specific cultural, community and family needs and be empowering for families.
- Children need a literacy-rich learning environment and opportunities for meaningful, enjoyable experiences.
- Teachers need to use literacy practices in the home as the basis for curriculum, rather than force school practices into the home.
- In order to be effective, interventions must be developed in partnership with those they serve. Each must provide a multipurpose and flexible program with families, concentrating on enhancing the quality of parent–child interactions and the home literacy environment.

There is some evidence that programs that are designed to support family literacy don't always recognise the literacies of the home environment, as Spedding et al. suggest. An example can be found in the recent study by Billings (2009) of the American 'Reach Out and Read' (ROR) early literacy promotion program. Billings' study investigated literacy values and practices among Latino families with pre-school-age children. This was part of a larger study that looked at the efficacy of the ROR program. Participating families were given advice by paediatricians in training at the child's routine medical exams. The advice was based on a sociocultural framework, advocating story reading and scaffolding approaches to learning. The results demonstrated that families were engaged in a range of culturally relevant literacy activities not always recognised or supported by early literacy programs such as ROR, suggesting that 'one size fits all' approaches to family literacy are not most effective.

Engaging families in children's literacy learning

Family literacy programs: typically these are parent education programs aimed at increasing literacy activity in the home environment, to support children's developing literacy knowledge and skills.

This section provides some examples of recent **family literacy programs** which aim to ameliorate some of the family literacy issues identified in this chapter. There are obviously more examples and you can look at some of these on this book's companion website, if you are interested. What follows are some contemporary examples. What you should take note of is who is involved in funding and promoting these programs.

The Manukau Family Literacy Program (MFLP), run by the City of Manukau Education Trust (COMET) in South Auckland, New Zealand, is a good example of a program aiming to increase literacy, as well as improve the quality of time that parents spent with their children. The MFLP had the following components (COMET 2012):

(1) Adult Education – Delivered by an accredited tertiary institution on the school site. The adult education programme runs for approximately 20 hours per week (plus additional self-directed learning) and focuses on developing literacy skills. Adult students work towards gaining a Certificate in Introduction to Early Childhood Education.

(2) Parent Education – Woven throughout the Adult Education Programme, this component of MFLP works to strengthen the parents' role as 'first-teachers' and build family literacy.

(3) Child's Education – As delivered by the school or early childhood education centre.

(4) Parent and Child Time Together (PACTT) – A pivotal part of MFLP. PACTT gives the adult student an opportunity to actively engage in their child's school or early childhood activities. There are three types of PACTT:

  – Tahi PACTT – Each day the adult student spends approximately 10–15 minutes in their child's classroom working one-on-one with their child.

- Roopu (Class) PACTT – Once a month, adult students and PACTT children engage in a planned literacy experience such as a library visit.
- Whanau PACTT – Once a term, whanau and extended family are invited to join the group for a shared event such as a quiz night or a barbeque.

A summative evaluation of the MFLP (Benseman & Sutton 2005) identified the following key outcomes of the program:

- foundation skill gains for both adults and children
- an increase in parents' levels of self-confidence and self-efficacy
- an increase in the long-term aims and aspirations of both parents and children
- greater parent involvement in their children's education
- improvement in parenting skills
- strong learning communities among parents, their children and participating institutions.

COMET's website suggests that this program has temporarily ceased, despite its success for children and their parents. Anecdotal reports suggest this is due to changes in government policy on the use of community education funds.

The aim of the 'Bridging the Gap' project (Freeman & Bochner 2008) was to enhance the early literacy skills of Indigenous Australian kindergarten children through a home shared-book reading program designed to:

- foster child–family interactions with books at home, and
- bridge the gap between children's literacy experiences at home and the school's reading curriculum.

The program also provided an opportunity for relationships to be developed between Indigenous parents and school staff. The following description of the program is sourced from Freeman and Bochner (2008).

The project was funded by a grant from the Australian Government Department of Education, Science and Training Innovative Projects to Support Improved Literacy and Numeracy Outcomes of Educationally Disadvantaged Students. It was implemented in conjunction with Jarara, the Indigenous Catholic Education Unit within the Catholic Schools Office (CSO), Parramatta Diocese, New South Wales. The home book-reading program was designed by Louella Freeman, a literacy specialist from Macquarie University, and implemented by four Aboriginal Education Assistants (AEAs) from Jarara.

The experimental group comprised 19 Indigenous children and their families. Most of the children attended CSO schools in the Parramatta area and the others were at government schools but attended a homework centre operated by Jarara. The proposed design of the study included a matched non-participating control group to be located in kindergarten classes within the Parramatta area. However, there were not enough Indigenous children identified in the local schools to form this group. As an alternative, a non-equivalent contrast group was formed comprising 15 children in their second year at school. Several of these children had siblings in the experimental group, so there was some overlap between participating families.

The main aim of the Bridging the Gap project was to encourage Indigenous families to use a home book-reading program, using shared-book reading, to help the children become actively involved in the reading process. At post-test, the children's mean reading age was higher than their mean chronological age, and there were increases in listening comprehension, phonemic awareness and receptive language. The project had a positive impact on the children's self-esteem, interest in books, experiences with books at home, and home-school links. The project also had a positive impact on the role of the AEAs within the Indigenous Education Unit and their support of the literacy needs of Indigenous children in the first year at school.

The REAL (Raising Early Achievement in Literacy) project (Morgana, Nutbrown & Hannon 2009) aimed to promote pre-school children's literacy through the implementation and evaluation of a parental involvement program. Ten teachers located in the north of England worked with 80 families for the duration of the 18-month program. The project was based on the ORIM conceptual framework which views parents supporting their child's developing literacy through four key roles:

- *opportunities* – giving children pens and paper, joining the library, making a space in the home where literacy can take place, placing books and writing equipment in an accessible place
- *recognition* of the child's achievements – displaying writing, discussing with the child what they have achieved (e.g. 'You found all those letters yourself, didn't you?')
- *interaction* – sharing times of interaction with the child in literacy activities, for example, by reading a book together, playing an alphabet puzzle or writing a birthday card
- *model* – modelling being a user of literacy in everyday life, for example, by reading a recipe, doing a crossword, completing a form or writing a note.

According to Morgana, Nutbrown and Hannon (2009), four strands of literacy formed the main focus of the REAL project program: environmental print, books, early writing and aspects of oral language. The program included a combination of home visiting by teachers and group meetings. Teachers kept records of contacts with parents. There was also an optional adult learning component leading to accreditation of parents' learning. Of particular interest was investigation of the role of fathers in children's literacy, as the majority of research looks at the role of mothers. In this study, the majority of fathers are reported to be involved in their young children's literacy development. It should be noted however, that mention of fathers as involved in literacy activities with pre-school children is associated with higher socio-economic status. Morgana, Nutbrown and Hannon make two major recommendations in terms of building successful family literacy programs:

- Family literacy programs need to acknowledge that they are building on families' existing knowledge, skills and cultures and this must include recognition of fathers' contributions.

- Family literacy programs may need to review their modes of delivery in order to increase fathers' involvement. In this study, an emphasis on flexible home visiting was more successful than centre-based meetings for encouraging father involvement; indeed, centre-based meetings were poorly attended by fathers and mothers in comparison to home visits.

Conclusion

This chapter has explored the meaning of family literacy and some of the now vast body of research about how children are socialised into literacy in their homes and communities. We have also touched on some examples of family literacy programs, which are typically organised by local communities to support families in their community in their role of raising the next generation of readers. These programs are often of mixed success, unless they are essentially home-grown, involve the families in the conceptualisation of how they should work best and build on family literacy practices. As argued, 'one size fits all' models of how teachers and communities can support family literacy are often unsuccessful. What this chapter has also argued is that teachers can play a powerful role in supporting children who come from challenging home backgrounds and that learning to read is a powerful force for overcoming the inequities of socio-economic status and opportunity. It is important that teachers look for opportunities to support and encourage and build on the knowledge and skills that children bring to their learning from homes and communities.

Reflective questions

1. Think about your own home background. What form did family literacy take in your home?

2. Did you experience both formal and informal teaching of literacy in your home environment?

3. Thinking about your role as a teacher, what are some key things you might do to support families in their role as literacy educators of their children?

4. Do you know of any family literacy programs in your local community? Are they successful? Try to find out what has worked and what hasn't worked in your local community.

Further reading

Harvard Family Research Project. 'Family Literacy: A Review of Programs and Critical Perspectives'. http://www.hfrp.org/publications-resources/browse-our-publications/family-literacy-a-review-of-programs-and-critical-perspectives.

State Library of Western Australia. Better Beginnings. http://www.better-beginnings.com.au.

Chapter 5

Multiliteracies: growing the next generation of readers

Chapter objectives

1. To define and examine the concept of multiliteracies.
2. To consider the notion of literacy in a changing world.
3. To reconceptualise literacy in the classroom.

This chapter explores multiliteracies as part of examining how children come to centres and schools with diverse literacy experiences, which may or may not match the literacy environment of the centre or school. The chapter encourages students and teachers to reconsider how the nature of readers and the contexts in which reading occurs are changing with the advent of technology. Ideas to support an ever-increasing array of text types and multimodal applications for various ages in the classroom are investigated.

What are multiliteracies?

Multiliteracies: the understanding and skills associated with different forms of literacy available in both hard-copy and electronic formats.

The term **multiliteracies** is used to capture the complexities of the range of types of texts in which gestural, spatial, verbal and visual elements are included and which use a wide range of communication channels that influence people's literate practices (New London Group 1996; Makin, Jones Diaz & McLachlan 2007). People today live in an increasingly globalised world, in which finance, global capital, trade, information, communication and media technologies merge across economic, political, cultural and social fields, all requiring understandings of specific forms of literacy. People of all ages, including children, are drawn into globalisation, consumerism and interaction with technology, media and communication systems. Globalisation has led to shifting conceptions of what constitutes literacy and this shift in thinking has important implications for teaching the next generation of children. New technologies emerge daily, bringing with them new everyday functional community literacies, such as changes in the internet, email, MP3s, mobile phones, electronic maps, signs and advertising. The internet, according to an advertisement on New Zealand television at the moment, has been in New Zealand for more than 20 years; in this period it has brought about enormous changes in the ways people connect, interact and communicate.

Reflection 5.1

Think back to when you first used a computer. When was it and what did you use it for?

Think back to when you first used a mobile phone. What features did it have compared to the one you may use now?

Thinking about the changes in uses of technology you have personally experienced, what do you predict children in the schools of the future will use for learning literacy in five, 10 or 20 years?

The term multiliteracies was coined by the New London Group (1996) to highlight two related aspects of the increasing complexity of texts:

- the proliferation of **multimodal** ways of making meaning where the written word is increasingly part and parcel of **aural, gestural, spatial and visual** patterns
- the increasing salience of cultural and linguistic diversity characterised by local diversity and global connectedness.

> **Multimodal:** learning through aural, visual, gestural or spatial learning, or a combination of all four with different forms of literacy.

Children born into this new world have been termed 'digital natives' (New Media Consortium 2005), as they are often more familiar with new literacies than traditional forms. The term can differentiate adults from children, suggesting the differences that digital technologies play in each generation's lives. Zammit (2010) suggests this differentiation is overly simplistic; not all children are natives and not all adults are immigrants. Furthermore, the generalisation hides the realities that not all children have access to digital technologies, have the requisite skills or are critical users of electronic media. Teachers need to recognise that not all families can afford to provide children with electronic resources.

> **Aural, visual, gestural and spatial learning:** learning that is based on hearing, seeing, comprehending space issues and engaging in non-verbal communication.

The term multiliteracies includes the ways subcultures use literacy in specific ways – for instance, technical groups, sports groups, religious groups and adolescent peer cultures. There are multiple literacies that children experience in their homes, communities and cultures which shape the ways in which they experience literacy (Makin, Jones Diaz & McLachlan 2007). Literacies are experienced both inside and outside formal settings (Knobel & Lankshear 2003), within culturally specific ways.

Knobel and Lankshear (2003) argue that reading and writing are not the same things within a youth culture, an online chat space, a school classroom, a feminist reading group or within different kinds of religious ceremonies. A quick look at how teenagers interact on Facebook or in mobile phone text messages, compared to how their parents do, can indicate how literacy is enacted differently by different groups.

Children's experiences with these literacies bring them into contact with shifting social practices and understanding of social relations. Luke (1997, p. 29) states that 'children are immersed in the texts of popular culture, and their understanding of narrative, good versus evil, of heroes and heroines, gender, race and power, is learned from those texts'. Conceptualisations about literacy must take account of the social practices of which literacy is part, including practices around listening, speaking, writing, viewing and critiquing. For example, Game Boys and Xbox bring children into contact with narratives of popular media and digital culture, often presenting gendered and racialised identities which may not be necessarily identified or understood.

Luke (1997) argues that children often come to school well versed in a different set of literacy skills and have in reality learned another language of interaction; they have learned the codes and conventions through which moving images tell stories.

Thus teachers need to understand the role that images and visual communication play in children's out-of-school lives.

A new generation of readers: skills and abilities of children in the new millennium

Hill and Mulhearn (2007) argue that the term multiliteracies is a useful way to combine understandings of the ways in which print-based literacy and digital technologies combine. Commenting on their study of Australian children's engagement with multiliteracies, Hill and Mulhearn (2007, p. 61) state:

> Digital literacies and print based literacy are not oppositional concepts, both are required. In fact, traditional print based reading and writing was found to be vitally important. For example, writing was significantly important as a memory tool, for planning, designing and recording ideas and information. Reading was critically important for predicting, scanning, interpreting, analysing and selecting from the abundance of information. Interestingly the children switched effortlessly between genres, scanning material for information, following procedures, searching by scrolling through menus, and interpreting icons and written instructions on tool bars. In other words, although reading, writing, listening and speaking are paramount, today's students must be able to do more, as they decipher, code break, achieve meaning and express ideas through a range of media, incorporating design, layout, colour, graphics and information.

Martello (2007) suggests that children today experience:

- Multiple sign systems.
- Multiple modalities of literacy.
- Recursive communication and cognitive processes. (Recursion is the process of repeating items in a self-similar way; it involves, for instance, trying out all possible routes through electronic games.)
- Literacies which encompass electronic, techno, digital, visual and print-based media.

Martello also argues that children experience most of these multiliteracies in their homes and community backgrounds and often their knowledge and experiences outstrip those of their teachers. Martello suggests that children use their experiences and knowledge for multimodal communication which encompasses either spoken or written language, visual images or all three together (multimodal). The New London Group (1996; Cope & Kalantzis 2000) explain that these understandings involve what they call 'design elements', which include audio, visual, gestural, linguistic and spatial meaning, or all five elements together, which they term 'multimodal'. As an example, Hill (2005) found the three- to four-year-old children could represent meaning with digital photos and text and could also import slide shows, change layout and so on.

Information technologies impact on children's experiences of literacy, from the food and clothing they consume to the toys, media and electronic games by which they are entertained. Children's access to and experience with these literacies in early childhood and the junior school will situate them in a variety of new social practices. As Luke and Grieshaber (2003, p. 8) argue, new information technologies influence the 'everyday practices of child-rearing and play, socialization and cognitive development, and of course, text practices and pathways to literacy'.

Vaughn explores the computer at his early childhood centre

Marsh (2005b) proposes that children construct their identities in relation to the media and popular culture that they encounter in homes and communities. She argues that the texts and artefacts rooted in popular discourse are pivotal to the range of skills, knowledge and understanding which facilitate decoding and encoding of a variety of multimodal texts and are essential ingredients of play, rituals and developing identity. McNaughton (2002) similarly argues that the centre or school curriculum must be wide enough to incorporate the familiar while unlocking the unfamiliar, thus building on the knowledge and understandings that children bring from engagement with literacy practices at home. For this reason, teachers need knowledge of the literacies that children encounter out of the school or centre so that they can build on children's literacy understandings, as well as introducing them to approaches to literacy that they have not encountered at home.

Marsh (2005a) states that children are immersed in digital technologies in their homes and wider community settings, which are part of cultural, media and digital literacy practices. Marsh cites a survey of 1852 parents and caregivers of children aged birth to six years in England which found the following:

- Children spent an average of just over two hours engaged with a screen each day (TV, DVD, computers, games etc.)
- 22 per cent of children can turn the TV on by age one, 49 per cent by age two.
- 53 per cent of children used a computer at home on a typical day.
- 27 per cent below four years of age used a computer independently at home.
- 47 per cent could use a mouse and click by age four.
- 27 per cent had used a digital camera to take photos.
- 15 per cent had used a video camera.

Although the survey revealed significant use of information and communication technologies (ICT) by children at home, a parallel survey of these children's teachers revealed that many teachers were uncomfortable with the use of digital technologies in the classroom. In particular, 25 per cent of teachers did not plan for the use of computers in the early childhood setting, 74 per cent never planned for the use of digital cameras and 81 per cent never planned for the use of video cameras. In addition, 83 per cent said that they would never plan for children to visit websites during their time in early childhood. Marsh states that this mismatch of home and centre or school experiences is of obvious concern for children's developing knowledge and skills.

In a similar study in Australia, Zevenbergen and Logan (2008) found that 95 per cent of four- to five-year-old children had access to computers somewhere outside of the educational setting, with 87.31 per cent of children having access to a computer in the home context. The majority of use was for educational games (59.9 per cent), non-educational games (79.54 per cent) and drawing (48.92 per cent), with some use of software packages, writing activities, modelling or copying of others, internet searching and free play. According to the parents, these children

Vaughn investigates how a mouse works

were developing a range of computer-related skills, such as using a mouse, finding letters and numbers on a keyboard, using drawing tools, loading CDs and DVDs and using a printer. Of interest is that boys were more frequent users of computer technologies and are more likely to play games, both educational and non-educational, which has implications for curriculum planning for boys in educational settings. Roberts, Djonov and Torr (2008) also identified gender differences in their study of children's use of e-games.

In a small study of 11 four-year-olds in Tokyo, Yamada-Rice (2010) found that visual-based media were well utilised in all homes, with most children using DVDs, drawing, picture books, television, websites, cameras, mobile phone cameras, drawing-based software, visual email and webcams for use with Skype in their weekly or monthly activities at home. Yamada-Rice suggests that the study, while small and with a relatively privileged group of children, suggests the importance of working with the visual mode with young children.

The implications of these studies are obvious. Children are entering early childhood and primary with a range of skills, abilities and experiences that children of the past did not have, and therefore teachers of the future need to both understand ICT, and plan for their use in the classroom if they are going to provide a curriculum that is culturally and socially meaningful to children. As Turbill (2002, n.p.) argues:

> Reading and the learning-to-read process is certainly a far more complex process in the '00s than it was in the '60s. It is imperative, I believe, that teachers of reading – and particularly teachers of early reading – broaden their view of what reading is in today's world. The digital world is here to stay, and it is a highly literacy-dependent world in which readers and writers need to have highly refined skills and access to multiple strategies that go beyond paper-based print texts.

Yelland (2006) argues that there has been a 'moral panic' around the use of technology and computers, in particular in the early childhood setting. She says this is often framed around the notion that children will spend so much time on a computer that they will not experience traditional play materials, although this myth has not been reinforced by research. In fact, Yelland cites a study by Shields and Behrman (2000) that demonstrated that children between two and seven years of age spend on average 34 minutes per day using computers at home, with use increasing with age, and that computer use at home is associated with slightly better school achievement. Furthermore, children score better on literacy, maths, computer knowledge and following instructions than children who have not experienced computers (Blanton et al. 2000). Yelland argues that the computer and other **digital technology** should just be considered like any other resource in early year settings, like blocks or puzzles. She considers that the 'moral panic' position has raised questions about what children will get out of using technology. These questions are not usually

Digital technology: technical devices, such as computers, that are used for learning.

asked in relation to traditional play materials such as books, puzzles, blocks and play dough.

So, should popular culture feature in early childhood education? In prior-to-school settings, few would regard children's knowledge of the characterisation, storylines and narrative plots in popular culture as valid or even remotely related to literacy, even though children enjoy reading this material and it motivates interest in literacy (Marsh 2007). In contrast, children's knowledge of characters in traditional children's literature, book-handling skills, concepts about print, print directionality and conventions are often used as the sole indicators of children's orientation to literacy (Makin et al. 1999).

This focus on 'school literacy' alienates some children, who feel that their knowledge and skills are not valued. Centres and schools need to have a range of images and texts that reflect diverse cultures, languages and family structures (Marsh 2007) and to encourage text reconstruction through retelling, replaying, rewriting and redrawing from different perspectives, with different characters and values. Gee (2004) proposes that children cannot feel that they belong when their homes and community practices are ignored, dismissed and unused. Many children who are exposed to popular media and digital literacies, such as the internet, video and computer games, use forms of language that are complex and technical, which is very different from that valued in schools and centres. While the children may find these literacies more compelling, they may not be utilised in the educational setting (Marsh 2007). These children often disengage with 'schooled' literacies and pedagogies that fail to draw on knowledge and experiences gained outside schools and centres.

Thinking about technology and teaching for the next generation of learners: multimodal approaches

So, if traditional approaches to literacy are unlikely to engage the new generation of learners, who are more likely to have experienced multimodal approaches to gathering information, then what do teachers need to do in the classroom? Luke and Freebody (1999b) argued some time ago that for children to be able to engage with multiliteracies, they need to be able to do the following:

- break the code of text
- participate in the meaning of text
- use text functionally
- critically analyse and transform texts.

Encouraging understanding of multiliteracies requires teachers to be able to promote critical literacy, so that children can engage with different literacies and understand their strengths and weaknesses. Teachers need to encourage children to question taken-for-granted values, beliefs and assumptions underpinning texts and social relationships. They need to open them up to alternative perspective taking. For example, teachers could encourage children to search for resources on the internet for their project topic on 'recycling' and consider the various arguments put up for either use of natural resources and the disposal of waste. For children who have never experienced composting, worm farming or recycling plastics and papers, all the ideas will need critical discussion and evaluation of what perspective is being presented.

The main elements of a multiliteracies pedagogy (New London Group 1996), or the approach to teaching and learning, include:

- situated practice, in which learning is based in children's experiences
- overt instruction of the metalanguages needed to talk about designed artefacts
- critical framing, which takes into account the cultural context of the designs
- transformed practice – application of ideas in new contexts.

These elements require teachers to think about children's progress in literacy in different ways – an idea that is further developed by Bearne (2009).

Bearne (2009) argues for the development of a framework for describing children's multimodal texts, based on the semiotic theory of Michael Halliday (1978). **Semiotics** is the study of signs and sign processes and includes the meaning of language. Bearne suggests the following analytic categories for analysing children's texts:

Semiotics: the study of language and in particular different meanings of language.

- *image* – content, size, colour, tone, line, placing/use of space
- *language* – syntax and lexis
- *sound/vocalisation* – content, emphasis, volume, vocal intonation, pause, pace
- *gaze* – direction of gaze of communicator or character in representation
- *movement* – gesture and posture.

Bearne states that analysing children's texts using this framework provides more information about the child's thinking and understanding than an analysis within a traditional literacy lens (spoken or written language), as much would be missed. She suggests teachers provide models, examples and deliberate teaching about different features of texts and modes and how they communicate to an audience. In addition to a multimodal pedagogy, Bearne suggests there is a need for some way of describing and assessing children's progress, as current national testing in most countries is based on written evidence. Assessment of children's multimodal text production is not readily catered for.

In Australia, the Department of Education, Science and Training's (DEST) *Raising the Standards* proposal (2002) notes that teacher competency in the use of ICT is related to dimensions of ICT. Teachers with higher levels of ICT competence are argued to be best placed to support children's learning within a multiliteracies framework.

Table 5.1 *Dimensions of ICT use in teaching and learning*

DIMENSIONS OF ICT USE	STAGES OF ICT COMPETENCE	KEY GROUPS
ICT as a tool for use across the curriculum or in separate subjects where the emphasis is on the development of skills, knowledge, processes and attitudes related to ICT	Minimum	Underpins all teaching practice
ICT as a tool for learning to enhance students' abilities to deal with the existing curriculum and existing learning processes	Developmental	For pre-service/beginning teachers
ICT as an integral component of broader curriculum reforms that change not only how students learn but also what they learn	Innovator	For practising teachers who are beginning users of ICT and for accomplished users of ICT
ICT as an integral component of the reforms that alter the organisation and structure of schooling itself	Leader	For highly accomplished users of ICT and for school leaders and teacher educators

(DEST 2002, p. 33)

There are a few frameworks for multiliteracy teaching and learning that are worth thinking about for use in classrooms. The first framework is by Unsworth (2001), which employs a dual model framework. Both models have a circular design. The first, the 'Literacy Development cycle' (LDC), focuses on pedagogy and includes stages of modelled, guided and independent practice. In this model, students move from teacher-guided lessons to independent construction of multimodal texts. Zammit (2010) states that the LDC draws on an approach to literacy developed in the late eighties in Australia, utilising the theories of Jerome Bruner (1978, 1985) and Lev Vygotsky (1978), emphasising scaffolding and working with students towards independence.

Unsworth teams the LDC model with the CAMAL (Curriculum Area Multiliteracies and Learning) framework, which provides a structure for designing learning experiences that integrate explicit teaching about what texts and images mean. Although both models draw on the notion of scaffolding learners towards independence, Zammit (2010) argues that the dual model is cumbersome, is only focused on written and visual modes, and doesn't make explicit that teachers need to teach the 'critical framing', which is the final stage of independent practice in the LDC.

The New London Group (1996) pedagogical approach and the revised version entitled 'Learning by Design' (Healy 2008; Kalantzis & Cope 2005) can be seen to be similar to Unsworth's dual framework, in that both recognise the active, developmental nature of learning and describe an 'active pedagogy' (Cope & Kalantzis 2000) which moves students from understanding to challenging existing ideas and creating their own products in different formats. The Learning by Design framework has four processes of learning: experiencing, conceptualising, analysing and applying within a curriculum area. These are roughly equivalent to the New London Group's four processes of situated practice, overt instruction, critical framing and transformed practice, mentioned earlier in this chapter. Zammit (2010) argues that although these models offer insights into curriculum and teaching, they do not assist teachers with critiquing existing practices and identifying future changes.

As an alternative, Zammit (2010) suggests a 'New Learning Environments' curriculum and pedagogical framework which suggests how teachers can select new learning components beyond what is currently part of the classroom curriculum. Zammit states that the model is a dynamic one, focused on moving students towards developing and demonstrating their understandings of a topic or concept. The relationship between each layer is dynamic and was 'developed to assist teachers in designing units of work that provide opportunities and support for students to engage in a range of learning processes and texts that use different forms of communication or mediums' (Zammit (2010, p. 328).

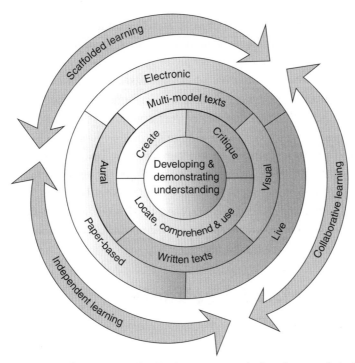

Figure 5.1 *The New Learning Environments curriculum framework, including pedagogical cycle (Zammit 2010, p. 328)*

The outer circle is the medium of communication – paper-based, live (such as speeches, plays) or electronic, but boundaries between media may be merged or blurred. The next layer is the range of modes or texts that students work with as they are learning and gaining competence with a range of media – this circle draws on the New London Group's modes of aural, gestural, linguistic, spatial, visual and multimodal. The next circle includes the processes of teaching and learning involved as students develop understandings and engage with texts. The inner circle recognises that literacy occurs in authentic contexts and that students develop understandings within other subjects, drawing on literacy-related activities.

Zammit cautions that teachers need to exercise professional judgements, as medium (paper-based, electronic or live) cannot always be matched directly to mode (written, visual, aural, multimodal). For example, an aural mode cannot be presented in a paper-based medium. Zammit also says teachers need to consider which aspects need explicit instruction and which need less teacher support. The pedagogical cycle is represented outside decisions about curriculum, thus differentiating the 'how' from the 'what'. The model is based on moving students to independent practice, through explicit scaffolding.

Zammit describes the implementation of the New Learning Environments model in two classrooms (a Year 5 and a Year 6) in a Catholic primary school in the southern suburbs of Sydney, Australia, over four school terms. The two teachers had differing levels of knowledge and skills about the uses of technology in the classroom: one was confident with ICT and used it in her classroom, but with a skills-oriented focus; the other was apprehensive about her lack of knowledge and had only recently returned to teaching from maternity leave.

The first teacher initially didn't use electronic texts with her ability-based reading groups, but moved to including reading and critiquing internet sites as part of her reading group activities. The second teacher gradually ceded control to students about what medium they would use for demonstrating understandings and adopted the role of student as the children taught her about webpage construction, while she provided content direction, selection of learning processes and mode focus. The second teacher and her students often referred to the New Learning Environments framework as they worked. Both teachers used the framework to reflect on which medium children were being encouraged to work in and made deliberate decisions to include all media in curriculum planning.

Multiliteracies in schools: some examples

The Multiliteracy Project (2012) is an example of how teachers in Canada are meeting the challenges of multiliteracies in the classroom. It comprises a national study exploring pedagogies or teaching practices that prepare children for the literacy challenges of a globalised, networked and culturally diverse world. Under the project, teachers engaged Grade 4 and 5 children with three core themes: mindfulness, exploring friendship, and social responsibility. A visit to the project website shows how children have used a range of media and critical reflection to engage with these three themes.

Hill (2010) reports an Australian study that explored how children aged 4–8 years understood and worked with new forms of literacy at home and at school. The study involved 25 teacher researchers from urban and rural settings, who visited the homes and communities of two focus children to gather 'funds of knowledge', using 'learning stories' (Carr 2001) to document what children could do with new literacy both at home and at school. The teachers then analysed the learning stories in order to develop a responsive literacy framework, to identify and build on what children could already do with new forms of literacy. The teachers explored ways to encourage children to understand and use new forms of literacy in early childhood and junior school settings. They collected further learning stories of how to work with literacy in ways that built on what children knew and could do with new literacy technologies.

The teachers in Hill's study reported the results of what they termed the 'technotour' of 48 homes, which revealed far greater use of new technologies than they had expected – in many cases it was far in advance of what centres and schools had access to. Computers, next to television, were the most popular form of entertainment and access to knowledge available in homes. In this study, children as young as four went online to websites linked to television shows, used search engines to find information and played interactive games online. Regardless of socio-economic status or geographical region, children had regular access to computers. The teachers concluded that children needed to be involved in in-depth inquiry-based or project-based activities to encourage them to question information, pose problems and make decisions as creative and critical thinkers, rather than experience curriculum based on fragmented or isolated skills.

The teachers developed a literacy framework, based on the four resources model of Luke and Freebody (1999), where a learner is seen as a code breaker, meaning maker, text user and text critic, which involves cracking the code of text, focusing on comprehension, understanding text type or genre, and unpacking the intention of text and cultural meanings. They also used the Durrant and Green (2000) framework, which has three integrated dimensions: operational, cultural and critical. These three dimensions concern technical competence, understanding the cultural uses of texts and technologies, and understanding that there is no one universal truth in any story or curriculum.

They developed a multiliteracies map, which showed how children interacted with literacies as functional users, meaning makers, critical analysers and transformers. Use of the map enabled teachers to analyse learning across all four quadrants and to identify that although children needed to learn skills to be functional users, this needed to be balanced against opportunities to create new texts using a range of technologies. Children were found to fit the definition of being 'digital natives', while most teachers were 'digital immigrants' (Prensky 2001).

The teachers in Hill's study also explored ways to use new forms of literacy in the classroom and found that the pedagogy that incorporated new technologies was most often inquiry-based, with questions and problems arising from the interests of a group of children or from individuals. They found that explicit or overt instruction was needed to assist children on how to use computers and software, but also in the teaching of frameworks or questions to support children's exploration and critique of media. The teachers said they needed a 'metalanguage' (Hill 2010, p. 325) to be explicit about how learning skills, strategies and problem solving could be used in one medium and transferred into another type of text. Some children were found to act as coaches and mentors as they capitalised on their learning from home with their peers.

Although the teachers developed a metalanguage to describe multimodal texts, they also found that children's knowledge of traditional print-based reading and writing were crucial for success in digital texts. Writing was used for planning, designing and recording ideas and information, and reading for predicting, scanning, interpreting and analysing and selecting from information. Children were thus found to decipher, code break, make meaning and express ideas through a range of media incorporating design, layout, colour, graphics and animation. Interestingly, Hill does not comment on how differences in children's reading and writing ability affected their ability to engage in multimodal learning.

Another Australian study (Harrison et al. 2009) examining pedagogy for multiliteracies involved following 48 children from 12 early childhood centres (and 24 teachers) in disadvantaged communities in three different states as they made the transition from early childhood to primary. Teachers in each centre collected case study data for two children, which included samples of the children's work, conversations, narrative observations of play, photographs, video footage and teachers' reflections. Teachers all wrote a 'learning story' (Carr 2001) about each focus child and the data collection was continued as the child moved from early childhood to primary school.

The multiliteracies pedagogy was found to facilitate relationships between participants in the transition process – children, families and teachers in early childhood and primary settings. Harrison et al. (2009) argue that the collaborations that were formed were based on the conversations that needed to be had with children and families about the ICT 'funds of knowledge' that children brought into the classroom and that teachers often knew less about how to use various technologies than children and had to become learners. The study also found that enriching access to digital technologies in early childhood centres led to an increased range of literacy practices. In the classrooms which utilised the multiliteracies pedagogy, teachers made effective use of drama, dance, construction, visual arts and access to ICT to support children's learning. Harrison et al. argue that this research supports the direction of the Australian National Early Years Framework (Commonwealth of Australia 2009) in that it highlights the importance of continuity and similarity between educational settings.

Harrison et al. advocate the use of a 'digital suitcase' that children take with them when they start school, which includes information about children's existing ICT and multiliteracies skills, knowledge and experiences that teachers can build on in the primary classroom. In an earlier phase of this study, based in Western Australia, Lee and O'Rourke (2006) found that through professional development and support, early childhood teachers were able to move from minimum or developmental levels of competence with ICT to being innovators and in some cases leaders in their educational settings.

Moody, Justice and Cabell (2010) examined the effectiveness of storybook reading under three conditions: adult led e-storybook condition; child led e-storybook condition; and adult-led traditional condition. E-story books are books for children that are online and children read them on a computer or iPhone application.

Two measures were used in this study: measures of children's reading engagement and measures of children's communicative initiations. An adapted form of the Minnesota Teaching Task (Egeland, et al. 1995) was used to quantify reading engagement on three scales: persistence, enthusiasm and compliance. These scales were used to codify children's ability to maintain participation in the book, to display motivation and excitement, and their willingness to listen to the reader's suggestions and to comply with requests. A coding measure, derived from several studies examining e-storybooks, was used to quantify children's type and quantity of communicative initiations and was checked by two researchers. Five categories were examined:

- labelling (e.g. 'What is that?')
- story/comprehension (e.g. 'Why is he sleeping?')
- external referencing (e.g. 'My classroom looks like that one')
- medium specific referencing (e.g. 'Help me click here')
- miscellaneous referencing (e.g. 'Cool' and 'Yes').

The results are extremely interesting in terms of our focus on teaching multiliteracies, as they showed that children demonstrated significantly higher levels of persistence in the e-story book condition, confirming studies which have shown the benefits of e-storybooks for reading engagement. Reading engagement is important, because children who persist with reading tasks increase exposure to literacy, which has known benefits to emergent literacy (Whitehurst & Lonigan 1998), including increased language and literacy skills. Notably, there were no differences between conditions on enthusiasm or compliance. Children were significantly engaged in both the child-led and adult-led conditions, but there were more communicative initiations when the storybook was adult-led.

Another significant finding was that children's labelling references were significantly higher during the traditional storybook condition, which suggests that children had more active participation in a traditional storybook reading session. This is consistent with research findings that traditional storybook reading supports oral language development, emergent literacy, communicative initiations and engagement in sustained dialogue. Moody, Justice and Cabell (2010) conclude that both computerised and traditional storybook reading can influence children's language and literacy development, especially when they are paired with an adult who uses scaffolding and questioning techniques to extend the children's thinking and understanding. Moody, Justice and Cabell suggest that there are caveats to these conclusions, however, as this was a relatively small study of a homogenous sample of Head Start children, using only one episode for each condition. They argue that 'descriptive studies examining the effects of e-storybooks on comprehension, vocabulary, print awareness and oral language for this population should be pursued with rigor' (p. 308). Although these findings are indicative of the need for further research, they do suggest that **e-books** and **e-games** can offer valid literacy learning experiences for children, especially when offered with adult support and guidance.

> **E-books and e-games:** books and games that are available in an electronic format on DVD or on the computer.

In a study of preschoolers' use of the I-Spy CD-ROM produced by Scholastic Australia, Roberts, Djonov and Torr (2008) found that the manner in which children engage with e-games varies according to social context, textual features of the game and children's proficiency in using computer hardware and software. The I-Spy software involves word matching, puzzles and riddles for children to play on a computer. Roberts, Djonov and Torr argue that their findings, although based on a small sample, challenge the myth that young children engage easily and naturally with computers compared with adults. Their findings suggest, like Moody, Justice and Cabell (2010) that children need certain skills in order to learn how to play e-games, they need to use language to reflect on strategy and ask the right questions and they have to be able to elicit constructive help from others. Roberts, Djonov and Torr also found that children need sensitive, focused guidance and that such guidance was more likely to come from an adult, rather than a peer or more experienced sibling.

Conclusion

Being literate in today's culture can mean many things and involves a range of skills, abilities and knowledge that may or may not be learned in the classroom. Helping children to learn may mean involving literacies that have not typically been used in classrooms and may require teachers to increase their own knowledge and skill with digital technologies. It is also highly likely that children use multimodal methods of learning and will make more successful transitions between home and school if the literacy resources used in the classroom are also used at home. As this chapter has suggested, there is growing evidence of the teaching strategies that teachers can use to make the most of children's multimodal learning. Given the pace of electronic change, this is an area of literacy learning that needs to remain high in teachers' consciousness!

Reflective questions

1. Think about a centre or classroom you have been in recently. What access did children have to multiliteracies?

2. Did children use e-books or e-games?

3. What was the role of the teacher in relation to the learning experiences?

4. How could the experiences offered to children be improved?

Further reading

ED Talks. http://edtalks.org.

Ministry of Education (NZ). 'A Pedagogical Approach to ICT'. http://www.educate.ece.govt.nz/learning/exploringPractice/ICT/PedagogyAndICT.aspx.

Turbill, J. (2002). 'The Four Ages of Reading Philosophy and Pedagogy: A Framework for Examining Theory and Practice'. Reading Online, February. http://www.readingonline.org/international/inter_index.asp?HREF=/international/turbill4/index.html.

Upwardly Mobile – Mobilizing Education. http://tonitwiss.com/mobile.

Diverse classrooms and learning in bilingual and multicultural/multilingual settings

Chapter objectives

1. To understand how and why children learn differently.
2. To examine how literacy can be promoted in multicultural contexts.
3. To examine the issues that bilingual or multilingual children face in becoming literate.
4. To explore how to provide differentiated instruction for diverse learners.

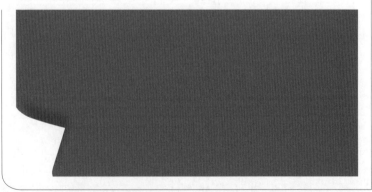

Catering for diversity in classrooms is the focus of this chapter. It leads into the notion of what it means to have a negotiated curriculum where learners make choices about what they value when it comes to reading. This chapter looks at incorporating a variety of perspectives that acknowledge the variety of interests and experiences learners have to contribute to a curriculum. It also examines some of the recent research on children's literacy acquisition in bilingual, multicultural and multilingual settings. Research on the literacy outcomes of mainstream, bilingual and total immersion settings is explored, along with the barriers to literacy acquisition that bilingualism and multilingualism have been found to create in many countries. Further, research on Indigenous Australians in early years and primary settings is examined and the implications for educational practice identified.

Diversity: what does it mean?

We can begin with a quotation from an excellent synopsis of educational research.

> Individual differences in the ability to benefit from instruction (the zone of proximal development) and individual differences between children are large in the primary years; *hence any class of children must be treated as individuals* (Goswami & Bryant 2007, p. 21) (emphasis added).

Levine (2002) suggests that the biggest mistake we can make as teachers is to treat everyone equally when it comes to learning.

Do these two ideas mean that we should provide individual learning plans for all of the children in our classrooms or are there other ways in which we can accommodate **diverse learners** in our classrooms?

Diversity is a natural phenomenon. If you are lucky enough to have siblings just think of how different you are from each other. If siblings who have the same upbringing/environment and similar genes can be so different from each other, imagine how different other children might be from each other.

> **Diverse learners:**
> children who face a range of issues or challenges to learning.

> **Diversity:**
> a term used to explain the social, cultural and linguistic differences between learners.

Reflection 6.1

What are some of the things that make us different from each other? Try to list at least five things that distinguish you from one of your friends. You may like to include things that make you different in the area of literacy specifically. For example: do you prefer to read using a tablet device or traditional paper-based texts?

Ecological differences

Ecological differences include the home environment, the school and the cultural background of our students. All of these factors must be taken into consideration when planning for diversity in classrooms.

The home environment

The home is where the child experiences his or her first five years of literacy instruction. The parents are the child's first teachers and lay the foundations for future literacy learning. Research has confirmed that home literacy activities profoundly influence children's academic success (Bus, van Ijzendoorn & Pellegrini 1995).

This is Joel reading to his two-year-old son and his three-month-old daughter. You can see that both children are engrossed in the book.

Unfortunately what you might remember as your first experiences with books and storytelling may not reflect the majority of children's experiences in your classrooms. Some children will come to school with little or no experience of sharing books in the home but others will come already knowing how to recite the alphabet and may even know how to read a few words. This is what diversity in the classroom is all about: the need to get to know each individual child and identify the child's needs and strengths in relation to literacy. Early assessment and targeted teaching is essential.

Some parents will be happy to be involved in their child's literacy learning but others may not and this point should be respected by teachers. Some parents, particularly those with low socio-economic status, believe that teachers are better qualified to teach their children and there are parents who generally feel powerless to help their children (Lareau 2000).

Ways to support parents include:

- Value different of forms of home literacy, such as parents writing notes and shopping lists, reading magazines, playing word games and searching for information on the internet.

- Keep parents informed about current literacy learning in the classroom. Provide clear directions about how parents can extend this learning in the home. For example, they could cut out pictures from magazines that start with the particular sound that you might be studying for that week.

- Form partnerships with families. Demonstrate that you are willing to discuss ideas with parents. Communication is the key to success.

Reflection 6.2

Try to think of some literacy activities that you might be able to share with parents and other members of the children's families in your classroom.

Shared-book reading is a valuable activity to encourage in the home (Fielding-Barnsley & Purdie 2003). See Chapter 15 for more information about this form of 'dialogic reading'.

The school environment

The school should be a place where every child is valued. The child's acceptance at school will have considerable ramifications for his or her learning. Many children, particularly those with learning difficulties, will experience problems developing positive relationships with both teachers and peers; they will receive less praise and are more likely to be criticised, shown disapproval or even ignored (Brooks 2000).

Can you imagine how difficult it would be for some children to make progress in your literacy classes if they have had such negative experiences, sometimes on a daily basis?

The cultural and linguistic environment

It is imperative that teachers understand and appreciate the children's cultural and language backgrounds. Our schools are made up of a diverse body of students from many different ethnic, language and cultural backgrounds. We refer to these children as having English as an Additional Language (EAL). There is a small school in the suburbs of Brisbane with children representing 16 nationalities.

Many of these children are refugees from the Sudan and had suffered terribly before arriving in Australia. This particular school embraced the opportunities of having these children in its community by inviting the parents to share in their learning. One way they fostered this was by inviting the parents into the school garden. The parents were asked to grow plants native to their country of origin and then to cook the produce in the school kitchen. You might ask, 'How did this improve the children's literacy skills?' The answer is, 'in many ways'. For example, the children learned the names of exotic plants such as okra and taro and they kept diaries of what they were growing in the garden. Many of the children made visual entries in their diaries and took them home to share with their families. Recipes were written to share with all the families in the classroom and beautiful posters of good and bad foods adorned the classroom walls (Tangen & Fielding-Barnsley 2007).

Teachers should make every effort to create a welcoming atmosphere that builds on cultural and linguistic diversity (Montgomery 2001). Here are some suggestions:

- Include content that is relevant. For example, when teaching on the topic of animals include some animals from the children's ethnic background.
- Allow children to share their cultures with the other children in their class; this may be involve oral or written communication.
- Provide materials from different cultures such as books representing different religious festivals. There are also many good books that you can share which look at issues facing immigrant children in their own lands. See the 'Further reading' section at the end of this chapter for some suitable titles.
- Provide a truly inclusive classroom by organising cooperative learning groups so that the children can share and discuss their differing ideas.

Every opportunity should be taken to allow this special group of children to learn English. This does not mean that you devalue their own language; opportunities should also be given for them to share their own language with the rest of the class. For example, you might include a language component in a theme on animals and learn the names of a few animals in another language. The study of words, etymology, could be used to teach the many words that are derived from the root word for dog, *caninus* – for example, 'canine' teeth. Imagine how much fun you could have looking for the origins of other words and discovering how people and their languages are interconnected.

One of the most difficult aspects of literacy for these children is the complex language of information and content area texts. The complex vocabulary should be pre-taught and visuals should be utilised wherever possible. If the content is particularly difficult, you might try using another text or reading the text with the class.

Be sure to build up background knowledge as these children may never have encountered the topic previously. For example the concept of going on a picnic may be quite incomprehensible for children from Africa.

Reflection 6.3

Try to think of a way of introducing the concept of a picnic. A teddy bears' picnic perhaps?

Here is a summary of useful strategies to use when you are considering the needs of the EAL children in your literacy class:

- Have children work in small collaborative groups.
- Introduce main ideas and vocabulary prior to new topics.
- Use visuals to support all literacy learning.
- Include graphic organisers to link main ideas.
- Allow children to express their ideas in spoken and written forms.

Regarding assessment, you need to be aware that some children from other cultures will not be confident in answering oral questions posed by the teacher. The teacher should be patient and allow sufficient time for the child to process the language and to construct an answer.

Also, some children from other cultures may have been taught not to be competitive; this is particularly pertinent to Indigenous Australian children. On the other hand some children from an Asian background may be quite competitive and not want to share information such as in group work situations.

Indigenous Australian students

We must recognise that Indigenous Australian students should be treated the same way as all students – that is, as individual learners. If we fail to do this we are guilty of stereotyping and stigmatising this group of learners. This is not to say that we should not appreciate the cultural heritage of this group. It is important to acknowledge that by Year 3 Aboriginal students are disproportionately represented in the lower bands of the national literacy tests (Hanlen 2010). Indigenous students do not generally speak standard Australian English and their families may have little experience with schooling in literacy. It would be wise to include books that value Indigenous Australians in your classrooms. One such book that combines traditional art with culture and language is *Tjarany Roughtail* by Gracie Green. You could also include the alphabet book *Possum and Wattle* for younger children; it also features traditional Aboriginal art. See the 'Further reading' section at the end of this chapter for more recommended books.

Chris Sarra (2007) sums up what our philosophy of teaching Aboriginal students should be when he says that we should have the same high expectations of Aboriginal students as we have for all students.

Ruth Fielding-Barnsley provides the following reflection. Her own personal experience of teaching Aboriginal students caused her to reflect on why they performed so badly on a test of vocabulary. She decided to test some of her students using The Hundred Pictures Naming Test (HPNT) (Fisher & Glenister 1992). She noticed the students were failing because the answers that they were giving, although perfectly correct in a non-testing situation, were scored as incorrect. Ruth gives two examples. The test is one of expressive language and requires children to name an individual picture on a page. The first example was a picture of a fishing net with a handle (something like a butterfly net) and one child's response was 'thing to go fishing'. The response could only be marked as correct if the child responded with the word 'net' or 'fishing net'. The second example was a picture of a ladder; the response was 'thing you go up'. So while this child had a perfectly acceptable knowledge of what these items were used for, he couldn't actually name them. This is just one example of cultural differences in how we classify objects. It is also an example of a culturally biased test!

Alternative assessment is covered in Chapters 9 and 12.

Differentiated instruction

It is important to take individual differences into account when you plan your instruction. **Differentiated instruction** is particularly key for struggling readers and writers and also for the other end of the spectrum: the gifted learners.

> **Differentiated instruction:** a method of adjusting teaching and learning to suit individual learners.

There are three main elements of differentiated instruction: content, process and product (Tomlinson 2001). Content refers to the goals and objectives of learning which will vary according to the student. Process relates to the way that the learning is done; children must be active learners in order to make sense of the content. Product refers to how the children will demonstrate their learning. There are many ways that we can differentiate each of the three elements.

Example 6.1

Mrs Pennington has 26 children in her Year 2 class. The class is made up of 12 children of Anglo-Saxon origin who have been at this school since Year 1, four children from Vietnam, five from China, three from the Sudan and two from New Zealand. One of the children from New Zealand has recently been diagnosed with dyslexia and one of the children from China appears to be autistic but has not been diagnosed. Some of the overseas children have been at the school for a few years but the Sudanese children have only just arrived and they are all refugees.

Mrs Pennington has travelled widely but she has never been to China or to the Sudan. This term she is planning a unit on 'healthy eating', and being a truly inclusive teacher she wants all the children in her class to achieve her planned objectives.

This is Mrs Pennington's first lesson.

Content and process

Objective

For all children to understand the difference between good foods and bad foods.

Building background knowledge

Read the original *The Very Hungry Caterpillar* to the whole class.

Questions to ask:

Who has read this book before?

Did you ever think about that poor caterpillar's weekend diet?

Let's make a list on the board of the good food and the bad food.

Questions to ask about why they have chosen the particular foods:

Who has eaten watermelon before? Do you have watermelon in China? Who does not have watermelon in their country? What is it called in your country?

I want everyone to think of a healthy food and we will write it on our list of good foods.

Product

Please go to your groups. (small groups of five, mixed ability)

I want you to write your own Very Hungry Caterpillar *book but this time the caterpillar will only eat healthy foods.*

Instructions for the class

Select one member of your group to find some other foods that are healthy but not on our list. Include some foods from other countries (use the internet perhaps).

Select one member to write a sentence for each page including one healthy food from another country. For example: 'On Tuesday the very hungry caterpillar went to Vietnam and ate a mangosteen.'

Select one member to choose the foods that you will include from the list on the whiteboard and researched foods and the order in which the foods will appear for each day of the week.

Select two members to illustrate your book.

All members will proofread your book and think of a new title for it.

Mrs Pennington provides each table with a written copy of the instructions and moves around the tables to answer any questions or assist children who may not be on task. The above breakdown of tasks is not meant to be prescriptive. For example, if group member number one has finished his task of finding the information on the internet, he could quite easily help group member number two with the task of writing the sentences. Or they could both search the internet and both write; be flexible with your groupings.

The following day Mrs Pennington asks the confident children to read their books to the rest of the class.

The surprise: Mrs Pennington reads the school's politically correct version of the very hungry caterpillar!

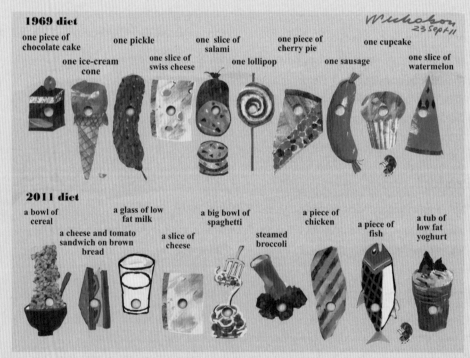

Figure 6.1 The Very Hungry Caterpillar – *old and new diets*

Example 6.2

Mrs Fellows takes a Year 2 class in the same school as Mrs Pennington with similar children. The objectives of the lesson are the same as Mrs Pennington's but Mrs Fellows plans her lesson this way.

She reads *The Very Hungry Caterpillar* to the class. She tells the class that the caterpillar ate some good foods and some bad foods and distinguishes between them.

The class is then asked to go to their individual desks and write their own book titled *The Healthy Hungry Caterpillar.*

The children read their finished products to a peer.

Mrs Fellows returns to her desk to complete marking of the children's work from the previous day.

Reflection 6.4

Which of these teachers would you see yourself as? Which would be the easier way to teach?

The preferred model is of course Mrs Pennington's, but why? Let us consider a list of characteristics developed by Heacox (2002). Differentiated instruction should be:

- *Rigorous*. Teachers should provide challenging instruction that encourages students' active engagement in learning.

- *Relevant*. Teachers need to address literacy standards to ensure that students learn essential knowledge, strategies and skills.

- *Flexible*. Teachers should use a variety of instructional procedures and grouping techniques to support students.

- *Complex*. Teachers need to engage students in thinking deeply about books they read, compositions they write and concepts they learn.

Mrs Pennington would be able to tick off all of those requirements for her diverse class, right?

Another important component of a good differentiated lesson is that it should accommodate a range of learning abilities in the one group. This is often termed layering or tiering instruction (Tompkins 2010). You may notice that in Mrs Pennington's lesson the tasks were arranged in order of complexity and also in a range of skills.

Some tasks involved skills in design while some required skills in ICT. There are possible pitfalls in this approach, however.

Reflection 6.5

Consider possible problems with and also possible solutions to this method of grouping your students.

You may have thought of some or all of these reasons:

Problem. Some children may always choose their preferred area of interest/strength. Imagine if you always allowed some children to fulfil the visual component of literacy but ignored their ability to write a sentence.

Solution. Never delegate tasks to the group as children need to take ownership of their learning but sometimes it might be necessary to encourage them to try something new. This may work well if you partner children with different abilities; have one child instruct another on how to search the internet, for example.

Problem. Some children may not work well in groups – for example, those with High-Functioning Autism (HFA). This special group is discussed later in this chapter.

Solution. Let the child choose their preferred learning buddies; this may be a very small group or even a pair to start with. Let the child choose his or her area of strength to develop confidence in working in a group situation.

Problem. Some children may prefer always to work with the same group of friends.

Solution. Sometimes teachers should choose the groups. It may be advisable in some situations to have heterogeneous groups and at other times to have groups of similar ability levels. This will allow you to give more input and support to those children who may need it.

Problem. Some children may not contribute as much as other children; those with learning difficulties may use the group situation to escape their weaknesses.

Solution. Regular monitoring of the group should avoid this situation. You may need to provide some scaffolding for children who are at risk. If you have a teacher's aide in your class you might consider having him or her work with the more able groups while you assist those more in need of specialist teaching. Be aware that many teachers will use their teacher's aide to support the at-risk group but this is not a wise decision. These children need professional teachers if they are to overcome their difficulties.

Of course group work would only be part of your literacy program in a diverse classroom. You would also consider whole class work and individual work. The important thing to remember is that every child should be given the opportunity to learn and to be successful.

Another face to diversity: students who are different in terms of how you might teach them

While all students exhibit attention and behavioural challenges to the teacher to some extent, some students have medical conditions that make these challenges more extreme.

AD/HD

To be truly inclusive we need to take into account those children who for one reason or another may find it more difficult to learn in an inclusive classroom. One such group is the children diagnosed with **Attention Deficit/ Hyperactivity Disorder (AD/HD) or Attention Deficit Disorder (ADD)**. This is a medical diagnosis that describes people who are experiencing significant behavioural and cognitive difficulties. The difficulties are related to problems of impulse control, hyperactivity and inattention. ADD describes the disorder that does not include hyperactivity. The AD/HD diagnosis was devised by the American Psychiatric Association. Twenty per cent of children with AD/HD have reading difficulties and 60 per cent have serious handwriting difficulties (Cooper & Ideus 2000, p. 9).

> **Attention Deficit/ Hyperactivity Disorder (AD/HD)/ Attention Deficit Disorder (ADD):** involves children demonstrating difficulties with both concentration and impulse control.

Children who are diagnosed with AD/HD are often of average or high ability but because of the associated behaviours they may find it extremely difficult to perform in the classroom. There are many ways we can assist this group of children to be productive in an inclusive classroom.

As with any group of children who may appear to be 'different' in some way, it is important to understand and celebrate their differences. We should be careful not to stigmatise these children.

It is mostly a matter of common sense when you prepare to accommodate these children in your inclusive classroom. If you think about the diagnosis and what it entails, you should be able to think of ways to improve your teaching and your teaching environment. There are three components of the diagnosis and each of these should be seen separately. First, there is attention; second, hyperactivity; and third, inattention. You may consider that attention and inattention are the same thing but they do differ. You may notice that a child is more interested in the wind blowing through the trees outside the classroom but another child might just be daydreaming and not concentrating on anything at all; the first is an attention problem and the second is an inattention problem. We sometimes refer to the first group as 'highly distractible'.

So how can we best cater for these children specifically in relation to literacy instruction? Of course these suggestions are also useful for all the children in your class but they are particularly relevant for this group.

Example 6.3

Because Marcus upsets the rest of the class, Miss Sergeant has placed him on his own at the back of the class. Miss Sergeant has asked her Year 2 class to write a story about their farm visit last week.

Marcus: 'What are we supposed to be writing about, Miss?'

Miss Sergeant: 'The farm visit, I've already told you Marcus.'

Marcus: 'I need a rubber, Miss. My writing is really messy.'

Miss Sergeant: 'Go and fetch one from the front desk.'

Marcus: 'I've forgotten how to write a capital Q, Miss. What was the name of the farm. Miss?'

And so on, with the result that Marcus ends up writing very little at all.

The reasons for Marcus's behaviour are directly related to his diagnosis of AD/HD. His inattention has caused him to miss the instructions and the name of the farm. As mentioned previously, these children tend to have difficulties with handwriting; they also may be disorganised and impulsive and may have missed vital instruction related to literacy, such as how to write a capital Q. They do not readily raise their hands and tend to shout out for assistance in the classroom. You can imagine that this becomes very difficult for a busy teacher with up to 30 children to teach in her classroom.

Miss Pleasant has placed Marcus at the front of her class, away from the window, with one other boy who seems to get along with Marcus. Marcus is able to concentrate on Miss Pleasant's instructions without the distractions of the other children being in front of him. If Marcus has forgotten some of the instructions or details about the farm he is able to ask his friend or the teacher without distracting the rest of the class. Miss Pleasant has also written the instructions and prior knowledge including relevant vocabulary on the board. Marcus only needs to check the board for information. Marcus is allowed to write the final draft of his story on the computer.

You can see that with a little thought and consideration for Marcus's difficulties, life will be easier for everyone in your inclusive classroom.

Autism:
involves children displaying a range of difficulties with social interaction, social communication and social imagination, flexible thinking and imaginative play.

High-Functioning Autism (HFA):
involves children displaying a less severe range of autistic behaviours, previously called Asperger's Syndrome.

For further information on teaching literacy to this special group of learners, refer to Cooper and Ideus (2000) and Zentall (2006), both listed in this chapter's 'Further reading' section.

Autism

Children with **High-Functioning Autism** (HFA, previously referred to as Asperger's Syndrome) are another special group that will need special consideration in your inclusive literacy classes. HFA involves three areas of impairment:

- impairment of social interaction

- impairment of social communication
- impairment of social imagination, flexible thinking and imaginative play.

This is known as the 'triad of impairments' (Wing & Gould 1979).

A lack of social imagination presents significant difficulties in relation to creative writing and comprehension. If you ask a child with HFA to write a story about 'My best friend', for example, the child will stare blankly at his or her paper and refuse to write anything. It is best to give the child a concrete personalised example to write about and then to help him or her expand and imagine 'what if' situations. For example, the child could write about a real experience of having visited the zoo. You can help to develop the child's imagination by asking, 'What if a lion had escaped and was running free around the zoo?' Or, 'What if it was the baby panda's first birthday?'

Children who have HFA are often very good at learning to read and are good decoders with good vocabulary but they still seem to have trouble comprehending what they read. One thing you can do here is to help the child use the illustrations to aid his or her comprehension of the written text. Children with HFA are often very good at interpreting visual information. Another weakness for these children is sequencing and this will sometimes interfere with comprehension. You can assist them by asking them questions referring to sequencing, such as 'What happened first?' 'What happened next?' Again you might use their visual strengths to draw the sequence of events.

Because children with HFA prefer realism they will tend to choose non-fiction over fiction. While this can be encouraged to give them practice and confidence in reading it must not constitute their sole genre of reading.

Children with HFA can be obsessive about certain things and may choose to read and write about their current obsession. Again this can be encouraged to a point but you may need to use their obsessions as a form of reward. Allow them to research their preferred topics on the internet after they have completed some set class work, for example.

Reflection 6.6

How can you use a diagnosis of AD/HD or HFA to assist you in your literacy planning? Is it better for a beginning teacher to know if a child in their class has a diagnosed learning disability or should you treat all the children the same despite their disabilities?

For further information on teaching literacy to this special group of learners, refer to Attwood (1998) and Cumine, Leach and Stevenson (1998), both listed in the 'Further reading' section.

Gifted and talented

We have discussed two special groups of children and you will have noticed that both of these groups are potentially very capable of high achievement, as long as teachers know how to include them in our inclusive classrooms. There will

Gifted or talented: children identified to have exceptional knowledge and skills for their age.

also be other children in your class who may be **gifted or talented** in areas of literacy and they can be as challenging as some of your other students. These children need to be extended in the classroom to avoid boredom and all the negative behaviours that go along with this boredom. You may refer to the tiered activities that we mentioned earlier in this chapter, for example. There are many things about these children to take into account. One thing is that they tend to hide their talents; this is particularly relevant for older children. You should refer to Chapters 9 and 12 on assessment and always be aware that there will be children in your classrooms who will require extension work. This should not be more of the same work that the rest of the class is doing but it should be something tailored to their interests or strengths.

Clark (1983) recommended six cognitive domains that should be considered when planning for gifted children in your literacy classroom:

- to be exposed to new and challenging information about the environment and the culture
- to be exposed to varied subjects and concerns
- to be allowed to pursue ideas as far as their interests take them
- to encounter and use increasingly difficult vocabulary and concepts
- to be exposed to ideas at rates appropriate to the individual's pace of learning
- to pursue inquiries beyond allotted time spans.

It is important to know that some children may have a complex set of behaviours and may be diagnosed with more than one disability. For example, it is quite common to have a dual diagnosis of dyslexia and AD/HD and even more common for a diagnosis of HFA and gifted and talented. This is referred to as 'co-morbidity' or 'co-occurring' learning disabilities.

Conclusion

This chapter has discussed diversity in the classroom and how to handle it in an effective way to create productive learning experiences. We have argued that it is better to be a teacher like Miss Pleasant than Miss Sergeant, or to be a teacher like Miss Pennington who values diversity in her classroom and makes use of this to enhance learning.

Diversity in modern classrooms is the norm rather than the exception. Teachers can take advantage of their range of experiences and the many ways of thinking outside the square that this diversity brings to learning. All children, no matter what their characteristics or backgrounds, can be provided with challenging yet achievable goals. The important thing is to acknowledge their differences and plan your inclusive classroom accordingly.

Reflective questions

1. Thinking about the range of possible challenges discussed in this chapter, consider whether you have seen any teachers with children with these challenges in classrooms or centres you have visited or taught in. How did the teacher cater to the child's (or children's) challenges?

2. Do you think the strategies the teacher used could have been improved? Why or why not?

3. Multicultural classrooms are a reality in many Australian and New Zealand schools. What are three key things that you need to think about when working with potentially bilingual or multilingual children?

Further reading

Books about children from other parts of the world and how we interconnect

Hume, L. (2006). *Clancy the Courageous Cow*. Malver, SA: Omnibus/Scholastic.
Macaulay, D. (1990). *Black and White*. Boston: Houghton Mifflin.
Nivola, C.A. (2008). *Planting the Trees of Kenya. The Story of Wangari Maathai*. New York, NY: Frances Foster.
Winter, J. (2009). *Nasreen's Secret School. A True Story from Afghanistan*. New York, NY: Beach Lane Books.

Books about HFA and AD/HD

Attwood, T. (1998). *Asperger's Syndrome: A Guide for Parents and Professionals*. London: Jessica Kingsley Publishers.
Cooper, P. and Ideus. K. (2000). *Attention Deficit/Hyperactivity Disorder: A Practical Guide for Teachers*. London: David Fulton Publishers.
Cumine, V., Leach, J. and Stevenson, G. (1998). *Asperger Syndrome: A Practical Guide for Teachers*. London: David Fulton Publishers.
Zentall, S.S. (2006). *ADHD and Education*. New Jersey: Pearson Education.

Books about Indigenous Australian children

Bancroft, B. (2010). *Possum and Wattle: My Big Book of Australian Words*. Surry Hills, NSW: Little Hare Books.

Greene, G., Tramacchi, J. and Gill, L. (1992). *Tjarany Roughtail: The Dreaming of the Roughtail Lizard and Other Stories*. Sydney: Magabala Books.

Longer books
Davis, A. *Sit-in. How Four Friends Stood up by Sitting Down*. New York: Little, Brown.
Partridge, E. (2009). *Marching for Freedom*. New York: Viking.

Part 2

Learning about
literacy in early
childhood settings

Chapter 7

Effective practice and the role of teachers in supporting literacy

Chapter objectives

1. To critically examine the notion of a high-quality literacy environment for early childhood.
2. To identify the features of an enriched literacy environment that supports literacy acquisition.
3. To critique the role of teachers in promoting young children's literacy.

This chapter explores the growing body of research on how to provide both access to high-quality literacy environments and the effective mediation of literacy in early childhood settings. Drawing on a range of research on the features of effective literacy environments, this chapter discusses principles for curriculum and centre design. In addition it examines the role of teachers in supporting literacy acquisition and, in particular, recent research which has explored the range, type and amount of teacher involvement in children's literacy acquisition. This chapter critiques what Cunningham et al. (2004) call 'knowledge calibration' in effective early childhood teachers.

High-quality literacy environments: what are they and how can you create one?

A quality literacy environment is one that is well resourced with literacy materials and in which children experience effective teaching and learning practices that make a difference to their literacy learning outcomes. This section explores what 'quality' means and how definitions have changed over time.

Both New Zealand and Australia have looked to reconceptualise what quality in early childhood means. In New Zealand in 1985 the Education Department (now the Ministry of Education) began to regulate all the diverse sectors of early childhood for the first time. Prior to this, the Department of Social Welfare regulated childcare services, while the Education Department regulated play centres, kindergartens and Kohanga Reo (Maori language immersion) centres. This sort of fragmentation of management of early childhood was also common in Australia, where each state had its own regulatory arrangements for early childhood centres. In New Zealand the fragmentation of governance was considered a barrier to achieving quality, as services could not achieve what was called a 'uniform standard'. The Meade Report of 1988, *Education to Be More* (Department of Education 1988) recommended that early childhood education should include equitable access, greater involvement of families and more equitable funding. As a result, the charter system was implemented and the Education Review Office was established to provide ongoing review of schools and centres. With these changes, quality came to mean 'inclusion', plus a uniform standard. The Education (Early Childhood Centre) Regulations of 1998 came to be known as the 'minimum standards', which were based on research that suggested for quality to exist certain structural indicators needed to be present. In the 1991 regulations, these *structural* features were defined as:

- appropriate staff–child ratios
- appropriate group size
- appropriate caregiver qualifications
- developmentally appropriate curriculum planning
- acknowledgement of Te Tiriti o Waitangi (the Treaty of Waitangi)
- partnership with parents
- a safe and healthy environment
- a close relationship with the community.

In both New Zealand and overseas the structure of adult–child ratio, group size and trained staff became known as 'the iron triangle of quality', equating quality with structural indicators (Smith et al. 2000). In New Zealand a higher rate of funding was given to centres that met the iron triangle of quality.

The dominant discourse of early childhood education at this time was developmental psychology, based primarily on Piagetian theory and a modernist approach. Piaget proposed a cognitive stage theory, which proposed that all children go through an irreversible pattern of development (Piaget 1962). Modernism can be defined as a socially progressive trend of thought that affirms the power of human beings to create, improve and reshape their environment with the aid of practical experimentation, scientific knowledge, or technology (Gutek 2011, p. 122). For example, structural features could be defined on the basis that quality could be researched, defined and objectively stated by an expert more knowledgeable than others (Dahlberg, Moss & Pence 2007). It promoted a 'one size fits all' solution, implying the iron triangle of quality would always guarantee learning and development of all children – the 'universal child'. However, the concept of the universal child was increasingly questioned by researchers as being limited because of significant differences in children's cultures and social contexts. More recent sociocultural and postmodern theorising (e.g. Rogoff 1990; Anning, Cullen & Fleer 2008; Dahlberg, Moss & Pence 2007) has demonstrated that children's learning is significantly shaped by experiences within home and community settings. This focus on the outcomes of structural quality is most clearly seen in the guidelines for developmentally appropriate practice drawn up by the National Association for the Education of Young Children (NAEYC) in the United States (Bredekamp & Copple 1997), since revised to recognise the influence of social and cultural contexts (Copple & Bredekamp 2009).

From the late 1980s onwards, quality in early childhood education was viewed as something complex and having many dimensions (Smith et al. 2000). These were:

- the *structural* aspects that form the foundations of quality
- the dynamic or *process* aspects that are part of the child's daily experiences (such as interactions)
- the *contextual* aspects, such as type of setting and staff stability.

In New Zealand the Regulations and Statement of Desirable Objectives and Practices (DOPS) of 1997 were revised to reflect this more dynamic aspect of quality, which included both **structural and process quality**, and to allow more flexibility for context. *Quality in Action* (Ministry of Education 1997) was published to give guidelines on how to incorporate the new DOPs into practice, although it was recognised that external review, such as the cyclic Education Review Office reviews, were more effective at assessing structural quality than process quality. Accordingly the Ministry of Education released two major resources to support early childhood centres in their ongoing self-review of quality: *Quality Journey* (Ministry of Education 1998) and *Self Review Guidelines for Early Childhood Education* (2007c), as well as revisions to the Education (Early Childhood Centre) Regulations of 2008 and the licensing criteria for centres. A recent literature review by Dalli et al. (2011) suggests that these issues apply to quality for infant care and education too. As Dalli et al. (2011, p. 9) argue:

> **Structural and process quality:** aspects of quality that are associated with specific measurable issues associated with the provision of education, such as class size, resources and teachers' qualifications; and aspects of learning associated with types and frequency of interactions between teachers and learners.

> The overwhelming consensus across studies, and contexts, is that quality ECS for under-two-year-olds are characterised by attuned relationships between children and adults. These relationships are underpinned by a number of interrelated elements that can be addressed in policy. These include high ratios, on-going professional development and low stress environments.

In Australia moves towards national quality standards are also underway. A National Quality Framework will be phased in from 2012 (see Department of Education, Employment and Workplace Relations 2012).

Since the early 1990s it has been considered that quality in early childhood education is constructed in part by the beliefs and values of the stakeholders (Dahlberg, Moss & Pence 2007). For example, a definition of quality for a Kohanga Reo might be how much Te Reo Māori (Maori language) was spoken; for a play centre how many families are involved and are doing play centre training; for an early childhood centre, what percentage of staff are fully qualified teachers.

Quality is thus the interrelationship between the structural, process and contextual aspects of any early childhood environment and all are important for literacy acquisition. Children need access to high-quality resources and the structural features of good teacher–child ratios and mediation of the environment and resources through interaction with more knowledgeable peers and teachers. We revisit this issue later in the chapter when we examine what an enriched literacy environment includes.

Much of our current understanding of 'what counts' for quality in early childhood curriculum is based on the outcomes of longitudinal studies of children in early childhood settings – mainly British and American studies. Most of these studies (e.g. Siraj-Blatchford et al. 2006; Howes et al. 2008) demonstrate clear links between the quality of an early childhood program and children's later educational achievement.

They also demonstrate long-term social outcomes, as well as short-term cognitive gains (Golbeck 2001).

Many people simply blame outcomes of education on teaching quality and teacher education programs, and there is some justification for this position. The Kane Report (Kane 2005) on initial teacher education in New Zealand argues that teachers have significant impact on the quality of teaching and learning. The notion of what a teacher *knows* (knowledge), *shows* (attitudes) and *does* (skills) has an impact on the learners they work with (and on what they learn). Teachers are seen to gain 'theoretical knowledge' during initial teacher education and 'craft knowledge' during practicum placements and when they commence teaching. However, in early childhood the situation is more complex because teachers are not working in isolation in their classroom with a group of children. Quality in early childhood is affected by the nature of the relationships between the teachers in the centre (Smith et al. 2000; Dalli et al. 2011).

Given these conditions, self-review can be really useful for establishing and maintaining a high-quality learning environment because teachers can then identify what sort of practice they collectively want to promote and can work as a team to achieve this. Hamer and Adams (2003) advocate that centres should prepare a policy for literacy which is regularly reviewed and revised to meet the needs of children and families attending the early childhood service.

One large study of quality in early childhood education is the Effective Provision of Preschool Education (EPPE) project (Siraj-Blatchford et al. 2006). This research contested the postmodernist notion from Dahlberg and Moss (2005) that quality is a 'constructed concept' and attempted to identify features of process quality that could be found across different types of services. The project involved over 3000 children and 141 centres and 300 plus children in homes who had no early childhood education experience from 4–7 years of age. The Early Childhood Environmental Rating Scale (ECERS-R) (Harms, Clifford & Cryer 1998), together with a United Kingdom adaptation (ECERS-E), was used to evaluate centre quality in 141 centres. Measures of centre quality helped to predict child outcomes and statistically account for variation in centre effectiveness. Both quality and duration of time spent in early childhood education were found to be significant predictors of better cognitive and social outcomes at the start of primary school; and the combination of high quality and a long duration was found to have the strongest positive impact on child outcomes. The largest effects identified were for language development and peer sociability. In particular, children who had longer duration (three or more years) between start at the target centre and primary school showed most positive outcomes (an effect size of over 0.6, meaning there was a strong relationship between length of experience and positive outcomes) compared with children who had no early childhood education experience. Individual preschools varied in their 'effectiveness' for influencing a child's development and children were found to make better all-round progress in settings where:

- adults formed warm interactive relationships with children
- a trained teacher acted as manager and a good proportion of the staff were (graduate, teacher) qualified
- settings viewed educational and social development as complementary
- the pedagogy included interactions traditionally associated with the term 'teaching' – that is, the provision of instructive play and learning environments and 'sustained shared thinking' to extend children's learning (adults guiding rather than dominating).

Siraj-Blatchford et al. conclude that while quality may in part be 'subjective', it is certainly not arbitrary and can be planned for.

Research has shown that there are strong relationships between quality in early childhood and children's outcomes. Children gain academic skills through quality learning environments – research shows effect sizes ranging from .26 to .79 (1.0 being the strongest) across numerous American studies (Howes et al. 2008). Howes et al. found that structural and process classroom quality contributed to relative growth in both academic and social skills. Children who experienced positive

Table 7.1 *Structural and process features of quality*

Structural quality

Teachers have a bachelor's degree.
Teachers' preservice training includes specialised training in early childhood education.
Assistant teachers have a Child Development Associate (CDA) degree or equivalent.
Teachers attend at least 15 hours of professional development per year.
The state has comprehensive standards for curricula that are specific to pre-kindergarten.
Classes have no more than 20 children.
At least one teacher/staff member is present for every 10 minutes.
Screening and support services are provided, including parent conferences or home visits,
    parenting support or training, referral to social services, or information relating to nutrition.
At least one meal per day is served.

Process quality

Emotional support
Positive climate
Lack of negativity
Regard for student perspectives
Sensitivity to children's academic and emotional needs

Classroom organisation
Effective behaviour management
Productive use of class time
Instructional formats that promote learning

Instructional support
Feedback that extends learning and encourages participation
Interactions that promote higher-order thinking and problem solving
Activities that facilitate and encourage language use

(Mashburn 2008, Table 1.2, p. 15)

teacher–child relationships and effective teaching showed the most gains, parallel-ing the results of the EPPE study in the United Kingdom. Children showed the most gains in classrooms where teachers provided instructional activities and learning opportunities for literacy. The same results were not found for maths or numeracy, but lack of creativity in maths teaching was one of the findings. Howes et al. note that standards for structural quality did not guarantee findings of process quality and enhanced outcomes for children, confirming the importance of process quality in early childhood classrooms. Mashburn (2008, p. 15) provides a useful summary of the structural and process quality features associated with effective early child-hood programs.

In the next section, we will look at the guidance that **curriculum** documents can provide in promoting both structural and process quality in literacy environments.

> **Curriculum:** a system for organising learning that includes aims or objectives, contents or subject matter, methods or procedures, and evaluation and assessment.

Literacy in the curriculum: Te Whāriki and the Early Years Learning Framework

It can be argued that children's successes in school and in life are dependent to a large extent on their ability to learn to read. Reading and writing skills serve as the major avenue for achieving the essential learning areas of the New Zealand Curriculum (Ministry of Education 2007b) and in the Australian Curriculum too (Australian Curriculum Assessment and Reporting Authority 2012), in which competence in literacy is stressed. Reading is necessary for learning about other people, about history and the social studies, the language arts, science, maths, technology and other content subjects that are taken at school. If children do not learn to read, their general knowledge, spelling, writing and vocabulary devel-opment suffer. Reading skills are the foundation for all school-based learning (Stanovich 2000). It's not surprising, then, that many countries have been look-ing at the precursors of reading achievement and asking about what experiences children should have with literacy before compulsory schooling and exploring the implications for early childhood curriculum (Allington 2010; McLachlan & Arrow 2011; Olson 2009).

Internationally there are a number of early childhood curricula available, but few nationally agreed curriculum documents. New Zealand and, more recently, Australia are exceptions to this rule as there are nationally accepted curricula for early child-hood for both countries. New Zealand's curriculum, Te Whāriki (Ministry of Education 1996), is the oldest and is discussed first. Australia's curriculum, the Early Years Learning Framework (DEEWR 2009a), is much more recent and not surprisingly includes more current thinking and research about literacy. We will briefly explore

Figure 7.1 *Cover of the Te Whāriki curriculum document*

both documents, but urge you to do your own comparisons of the relative strengths of the two curriculum documents.

An analysis of Te Whāriki (Ministry of Education 1996) reveals that it is holistic and deliberately open to diverse interpretation by different early childhood services (May 2011). The principles of empowerment, holistic development, family and community and relationships are all relevant as a framework for literacy, but can be interpreted in many ways. Within the principles of holistic development, for instance, it argues that 'the early childhood curriculum takes up a mode of learning that weaves together intricate patterns of linked experience and meaning rather than emphasising the acquisition of discrete skills (Ministry of Education 1996, p. 41). Although literacy is a pattern of linked experience and meaning, it also involves discrete knowledge and skills. The lack of specific guidance on how to promote literacy knowledge and skills is problematic, as argued elsewhere (see McLachlan & Arrow 2011). Te Whāriki is loosely based on a sociocultural perspective of learning, but it does not specifically advise teachers on how to promote literacy or any of the other essential learning areas.

Research supports the principle of relationships for literacy, as children need people who persist in supporting and understanding their attempts at literacy (Bus & van Ijzeendoorn 1995). Similarly, the strand of belonging, in which links with families and communities and establishment of routines, customs and regular events are advocated, provide a context for meaningful literacy opportunities to occur (Neuman 2007). Strand 4, Communication-Mana Reo (Ministry of Education 1996, p. 16) contains the strongest statements about literacy. It states that the languages and symbols of children's own and other cultures are promoted and protected in an environment where children:

- develop non-verbal communication skills for a range of purposes
- develop verbal communication skills for a range of purposes
- experience the stories and symbols of their own and other cultures
- discover and develop different ways to be creative and expressive.

The strongest statements are in Goal 2: 'children experience an environment where they develop verbal communication skills for a range of purposes' (p. 76), where language skills, appreciation of rhythm, rhyme, alliteration, understanding of syntax and meaning, and the ability to listen to and enjoy verbal communication is encouraged. Unfortunately, key predictors of literacy achievement – alphabetic awareness and phonemic awareness – are not named explicitly (Adams 1990; Nicholson 2005), although it does discuss children having experiences with rhyme, rhythm and alliteration. Although awareness of numbers is listed in Goal 3, awareness of the alphabet and phonological awareness are not specifically mentioned; unless 'a playful interest in repetitive sounds and words' (p. 76) is meant to indicate this. In addition, it does suggest that children will make the transition to school having developed some of the following skills and abilities (p. 73):

- language skills for a range of purposes
- experience with books
- development of vocabulary, syntax and grammar
- awareness of concepts of print
- enjoyment of writing
- playing with and using words
- opportunities to hear and use Te Reo Māori and other community languages.

Apart from affirming the role of home languages and community involvement, the document does not discuss multiliteracies or bilingualism and biliteracy in any depth, both important issues resulting from immigration and global change, but this is not too surprising given the age of the document. It was first released in draft form in 1993, revised in 1996 and has not been revised or evaluated since, although there is some indication via national media that the Minister of Education is considering this.

The Early Years Learning Framework (EYLF) (DEEWR 2009a), by comparison, addresses many of these issues by much more specifically identifying what learning children will display, along with providing specific guidance to teachers about how they can support learning. In the EYLF, the learning outcome for communication has the strongest statements about literacy and there is also a definition of literacy (p. 38):

> Literacy is the capacity, confidence and disposition to use language in all its forms. Literacy
> incorporates a range of modes of communication including music, movement, dance, storytelling,

Figure 7.2 *Cover of the Early Years Learning Framework curriculum document*

visual arts, media and drama, as well as talking, listening, viewing, reading and writing. Contemporary texts include electronic and print-based media. In an increasingly technological world, the ability to critically analyse texts is a key component of literacy. Children benefit from opportunities to explore their world using technologies and to develop confidence in using digital media.

This learning outcome includes the following (p. 39):

OUTCOME 5: CHILDREN ARE EFFECTIVE COMMUNICATORS
- Children interact verbally and non-verbally with others for a range of purposes.
- Children engage with a range of texts and gain meaning from these texts.
- Children express ideas and make meaning using a range of media.
- Children begin to understand how symbols and pattern systems work.
- Children use information and communication technologies to access information, investigate ideas and represent their thinking.

Each of the sub-learning outcomes for Outcome 5 is accompanied by specific guidance to teachers on what they need to do to help children achieve each outcome. For instance, for the sub-outcome 'children engage with a range of texts and gain meaning form these texts', the predictors of reading achievement are made explicit in the following guidance (p. 41):

- Read and share a range of books and other texts with children.
- Provide a literacy-enriched environment including display print in home languages and Standard Australian English.
- Sing and chant rhymes, jingles and songs.
- Engage children in play with words and sounds.
- Talk explicitly about concepts such as rhyme and letters and sounds when sharing texts with children.
- Incorporate familiar family and community texts and tell stories.
- Join in children's play and engage children in conversations about the meanings of images and print.
- Engage children in discussions about books and other texts that promote consideration of diverse perspectives.
- Support children to analyse ways in which texts are constructed to present particular views and to sell products.
- Teach art as language and how artists can use the elements and principles to construct visual/musical/dance/media texts.
- Provide opportunities for children to engage with familiar and unfamiliar culturally constructed text.

In addition, in other learning outcomes there are further links to literacy, in a similar way to Te Whāriki. Outcome 1 refers to building on family and community context, children's knowledge, language and understandings and providing resources that reflect children's social worlds. Outcome 2 suggests that children should be exposed to different languages and dialects and should be encouraged to appreciate linguistic diversity. Outcome 4 suggests that teachers introduce the tools, technologies and media and provide the skills, knowledge and techniques required to enhance learning.

Reflection 7.1

Both curriculum documents are available online.

Te Whāriki

Ministry of Education, 'Te Whāriki', http://www.educate.ece.govt.nz/learning/curriculumAndLearning/TeWhariki.aspx.

Early Years Learning Framework

Department of Education, Employment and Workplace Relations, 'National Quality Framework – National Quality Framework for Early Childhood Education and Care', http://www.deewr.gov.au/earlychildhood/policy_agenda/quality/pages/earlyyearslearningframework.aspx.

Take a look at each website and identify in each curriculum document the major links to literacy. For each point that you identify, check to see if any links to theory and research are provided. Consider what has been highlighted and what has been omitted from the literacy focus.

The role of teachers: knowledge calibration and effective teaching of the very young

Cunningham, Zibulsky and Callahan (2009) argue that although the importance of children's early literacy experiences and the links to later academic achievement have been clearly demonstrated, limited attention has been paid to teacher knowledge and its effects on children's learning, primarily because of the complexity of the task. As they explain: 'It is daunting to determine what teachers need to know, under what circumstances, and how they need to know it to be masterful, adaptive and responsive in the preschool classroom' (p. 488). Research also indicates that many teachers have an inadequate understanding of how literacy develops (e.g. Moats & Foorman 2003) and consequently miss many opportunities to encourage children's development within naturalistic settings. Cunningham et al. (2009, p. 491) argue that teachers:

> need to understand that early oral language development is the main precursor of reading development, and that it unfolds with steady growth of vocabulary, a deepening syntactical awareness, ever maturing grasp of pragmatics, and an evolving ability to hear, blend, segment and manipulate phonemes in words and sentences.

In earlier research, Cunningham et al. (2004) examined the relationship between their knowledge and their teaching practice, and outcomes for children's learning. In their study of 722 teachers, Cunningham et al. focused on three domains of literacy knowledge recognised as important for kindergarten to Grade 3 teachers to have: children's literature, phonological awareness and phonics. Cunningham et al. state that teachers need to know what constitutes good children's literature and how to use it, as well as understanding phonological awareness and phonics, particularly for children who need extra assistance with beginning reading and writing. In addition, Cunningham et al. explored a metacognitive skill: knowledge calibration. Simply, this means whether a teacher is aware of what they do and do not know.

Cunningham and colleagues' results revealed that teachers did poorly in all three areas: they showed poor knowledge of children's literature; relatively little knowledge about phonemic awareness (e.g. knowing how many sounds are in the word 'stretch'); or phonics (e.g. knowing that 'what' is an irregular word). In addition, their results showed that teachers tended to overestimate their actual literacy knowledge. As Cunningham et al. (2004, p. 161) point out, 'It is important to note that these findings in no way imply that the teachers in this sample were not literate individuals; rather it points out that they lack a degree of technical knowledge that is relevant and that many consider fundamental to the teaching of reading'.

These findings parallel the findings reported by the Education Review Office (2011) into literacy in the early childhood setting in New Zealand. In the review of 353 early childhood services in the fourth quarter of 2009, it was identified that although most services provided an appropriate range of literacy resources and opportunities for children, a number of centres used commercial phonics packages inappropriately with very young children, held large formal mat times that did not cater to the diverse abilities of children, and used formal and teacher-led literacy teaching which limited children's opportunities to engage with literacy activities that were meaningful to them. The Education Review Office recommended to the Ministry of Education that written guidelines and expectations for literacy teaching and learning in early childhood be developed.

Allington (2010) also argues that many teachers are unaware of what effective teaching of literacy to young children looks like and estimates that as few as 25 per cent of teachers are effective teachers of literacy and have sufficient knowledge of how to promote it in young children. The following example illustrates the point.

Scenario 7.1

One of the authors of this text witnessed a teacher who 'didn't know what she didn't know' during a visit to a student on a practicum. During the visit, a teacher in the early childhood centre ran a morning mat session. She began to read the Dr Seuss book *Fox in Socks* – a good choice for supporting phonological awareness, as it features rhythm, rhyme, alliteration, lots of repetition, and is usually fun for all participating. The teacher had clearly never read the book before and she stumbled along, getting increasingly tongue-tied, before slamming the book shut and proclaiming to the children on the mat, 'This is a really stupid book, let's do something else'. There were multiple messages sent to children that day: that Dr Seuss's books are not fun; that being playful with language is not fun; that rhyming books are hard; and if it gets too hard to read a book, you should just give up. Did this teacher know when she selected *Fox in Socks* about the layers of literacy opportunity it provided and how valuable her reading of that book might be to children's phonological awareness?

In addition to evidence on the importance of supporting the predictors of literacy achievement (Nicholson 2005), there is now significant evidence on the most effective pedagogies for supporting literacy acquisition in early childhood. We discuss these further in Chapter 8, after we look at how to prepare for literacy in the early childhood setting.

Access *and* mediation: making the most of a literacy-rich environment

Remember, quality has two major components in the early childhood setting: structure *and* process. Structure includes a well-structured and well-resourced **literacy-rich environment** (Morrow 2009). Although this takes time, thought and sometimes financial investment in resources, providing a literacy-rich environment is the *access* part of the equation.

> **Literacy-rich environment:** a classroom or home environment that has a lot of literacy resources and lots of opportunities for language development.

There is now robust evidence that enriching classrooms with literacy resources and literacy teaching strategies leads to significant gains in children's understandings of the purposes and functions of literacy. The National Early Literacy Panel (2009) report found evidence that centres that have a richly stocked library area, interactive story reading, lots of common literacy resources and environmental print (e.g. posters, collage materials, signs and labels) lead to an increase in socio-dramatic play and literacy knowledge and skills. Furthermore, teachers who are responsive to literacy play can positively enhance literacy learning (Morrow & Shickendanz 2006). Hannon (2007) proposes that early childhood settings offer quite constrained opportunities for play and that it is more likely that most literacy play occurs in homes and community settings. Hannon argues for a home-like environment to encourage literacy play.

Morrow (2009) has written about the purposes, organisation and outcomes of literacy environments for young children, and has very specific guidance about what needs to be included. She argues that children who have access to a literacy centre in an early childhood setting read and look at books 50 per cent more often than children who do not have a specific space for literacy. Furthermore, literacy centres which have specific design characteristics are highly correlated with children's use of centres during free play and conversely poorly designed centres are the least popular. Morrow (2009, p. 288) argues that good design of physical space plays an important role in motivating children's interest and stresses these requirements:

> [There] should be a focal area, immediately visible and inviting to anyone who enters the classroom. To provide privacy and physical definition, it should be partitioned on two or three sides with bookshelves, a piano, file cabinets or freestanding bulletin boards. The dimensions will vary with the size of the classroom. Generally, it should be large enough to accommodate five or six children comfortably.

Morrow further explains that the following resources should be considered:

- a rug
- pillows and/or bean bag chairs
- small table and chairs
- headsets and taped stories
- a rocking chair – Morrow calls this the 'literacy chair of honour' for teachers, children or guests
- elements of softness, such as stuffed animals
- books related to the stuffed animals (e.g. a stuffed rabbit next to *The Tale of Peter Rabbit*)
- a felt board with figures of story characters
- puppets
- posters
- the author's spot – this needs the table and chairs, crayons, pens and pencils, a range of paper, one or more computers, book-making materials, coloured construction paper, a stapler and scissors.

Note that in this increasingly digital age, you could add e-books and e-games to this list, which children can use on the computer. Refer back to Chapter 5 on the outcomes of children using interactive e-books.

Morrow argues that children have little opportunity for privacy or quiet in early childhood settings, so the literacy corner offers an opportunity for individual activity such as writing or listening to recorded stories with headphones. Morrow also suggests that children should be part of planning the literacy corner, be responsible for keeping it neat and should be invited to select a name for it.

Within the literacy corner, Morrow states that a well-stocked library is essential. Bookshelves should be of two types: one houses the bulk of books, which are shelved with spines facing out; the other is open-faced and features a revolving selection of books, which draws attention to special books. Morrow suggests a revolving circular rack would also work. Regardless of type, the selection should be changed regularly according to different themes or interests in children's learning to maintain interest. Morrow considers that books should include the following categories: picture books, picture storybooks, traditional literature, poetry, realistic literature, informational books, biographies, novels, easy-to-read books, riddle and joke books, participation books, series books, textless books, TV-related books, brochures, newspapers and magazines (the latter need not be current).

There are a few other factors about books that need to be considered:

- About 5–8 books per child are needed (i.e. 240 books total for 30 children).
- Books should be narrative and expository, rather than exclusively narrative.
- Non-fiction books should comprise one third of the collection.

- Books should cover at least four levels/ages, so there is opportunity for extension for early readers.
- Approximately 25 new books should be introduced every two weeks. These can be rotated out of the existing collection and/or borrowed from the public library.
- A check-out system is ideal, so children can take books home for a week.

Anecdotally, some kindergartens in New Zealand find a check-out system problematic in terms of having books returned, especially from families who move around a lot, so teachers in these communities typically either take children to the library or arrange for the mobile library service to visit the kindergarten on a regular basis.

Although Morrow advocates for a literacy centre in the early childhood setting, opportunities for literacy should not be constrained to one place in the early childhood centre. High-quality literacy environments also offer relevant opportunities for literacy in other areas. For instance, there may be sign-up sheets for using some resources, name tags by the painting tables so children can write their name and clipboards that will travel into the sandpit for drawing designs for constructions or making lists of resources.

Access and mediation: student access to learning resources and assistance provided to students using the resources by more competent adults or peers.

Co-construction: a process of learning that involves a teacher/adult or more competent peer identifying possible solutions to learning problems with a child or more inexperienced learner.

Scaffolding: a process of learning that involves a more experienced teacher, adult or peer providing a learner with specific guidance or support on how to manage a task that is just beyond their own independent problem-solving ability.

Guided participation: a method of learning in which children learn social and cultural knowledge and skills through involvement in everyday activities, being given instruction by more experienced members of the society.

In terms of knowledge calibration (Cunningham et al. 2004; Cunningham, Zibulsky & Callahan 2009), we know that teachers need to understand how literacy develops, what resources to use and how to promote literacy knowledge and skills. They also need to know what understandings of literacy children bring to early childhood and plan how to integrate this knowledge into practice, within the context of their curriculum and regulatory requirements. Neuman (2007, p. 157) provides a clear explanation of **access and mediation** and how adults can support **co-construction** of knowledge using **scaffolding** (Wood, Bruner & Ross 1976) and **guided participation** (Rogoff 1990).

Although Table 7.2 was designed for a family literacy program, the ideas are very applicable to early childhood teachers too. These four stages of involvement in the child's learning move from enticing the child into literacy play, to extending thinking and gradually handing over responsibility so that the child achieves independent mastery, aiding construction of literacy identity (Neuman 2007).

Casbergue, McGee and Bedford (2007, p. 171) identify three aspects of interactions among children and their teachers within language- and print-rich environments that determined differences in children's literacy achievement:

Table 7.2 *Mediation of literacy*

Definitions of the four processes in guided participation
Get set • Recruits the child's interest in an activity. • Gives the child a reason to become involved in an activity. • Focuses children's attention on something observable: 'Look at this …' • Attempts to keep their attention throughout an activity.
Gives meaning • Helps the child understand what is important to notice and the values associated with it. • Labels objects that are seen in the environment. • Adds descriptive comments or elaborations about an object. • Adds animation or affect to objects to make the activity come alive and provoke interest. • Demonstrates or models a behavior.
Builds bridges • Makes connections to the child's past or future: 'Do you ever …' • Elicits connections from a child: 'Tell me if …' • Encourages imagination: 'Can you imagine if …' • Induces hypothetical, cause–effect type thinking: 'What if …'
Step back • Gives the child a strategy for completing a task: 'This is a way you can make it work …' • Encourages turn taking on the part of the child. • Provides elaborative feedback: 'No … it works this way …' 'How about trying …' • Responds to the child's initiatives: 'So you are building a train?'

(Neuman 2007, p. 157)

- extensions of teacher-directed activities from whole and small group lesson to children's free play time
- the quantity and quality of teachers' interactions with children during free play
- the amount of children's spontaneous interactions with print during their free play.

Casbergue, McGee and Bedford (2007, p. 170) summarise the features of high-quality literacy-rich classrooms in Table 7.3.

Justice and Pullen (2003) also reviewed the literature on literacy-rich environments and argue that although enriching the literacy within an environment leads to an increase in literacy play, further gains in literacy understandings are achieved if adult mediation is part of the planned environment. Building on Vygotsky's (1978) notions of access and mediation, research shows that those children who have experienced literacy-rich environments with adult mediation display greater gains in print awareness, particularly alphabet knowledge and environmental print recognition.

There is a range of ways that teachers can assess if they have an enriched literacy environment. One way is to use the Early Childhood Environmental Rating Scale (ECERS-R), as the EPPE project in the United Kingdom did, along with the

Table 7.3 *Features of high-quality literacy-rich classrooms*

TEACHER PRACTICES AND LANGUAGE	READING AND WRITING ROUTINES	LITERACY MATERIALS AND CLASSROOM SPACE	CLASSROOM DISPLAYS
Teacher provides opportunities for extended talk.	Teacher provides daily modelling of several reading and writing routines (read aloud, shared and interactive reading and writing).	Materials are age-appropriate, authentic, and functional.	Print displays represent a variety of purposes for writing, including furthering pretense, experimenting with print and recording ideas.
Teacher frequently uses 'rare words'.	Teacher provides access to abundant reading and writing materials, including those that the teacher has read or written.	Materials are varied, clustered thematically, located in proximity to props, and easily accessible.	Print displays include materials that are produced by the teacher with input from the children.
Teacher regularly employs language extension strategies.	Teacher encourages children's daily participation in reading and writing activities.	Room is divided into clearly defined and labelled play spaces that include reading and writing materials.	Print displays include pieces produced by children.
Teacher provides opportunities for children to use analytic and predictive talk.	Teacher acknowledges children's attempts to read and write.	Ample space is provided for more than one dramatic play centre.	Print displays include connected text and themed words.
Teacher plans for conversations with children throughout the day.	Teacher scaffolds children's reading and writing efforts.	Dramatic play centres include themes and 'scripts' that are familiar to children.	Print displays are usable and accessible to children.
Teacher plays with and talks to children in centres.		Purpose of centres is evident.	Print displays change frequently in content, format and sophistication.
Teacher extends children's dramatic play by modelling new 'scripts'.		Centres are organised for children's independent use.	

(Casbergue, McGee & Bedford 2007, p. 170)

United Kingdom extension (ECERS-E, Siraj-Blatchford et al. 2006), which are both used for evaluating the quality of early childhood environments against items on a seven-point scale. Alternatively, a more recent literacy-specific scale, such as the Early Language and Literacy Classroom Observation Scale (ELLCO) published by Brookes Publishing, could be used. This scale has three sections: a literacy environment checklist of resources available; a global classroom environment observation which looks at organisation of the environment, opportunities for child initiation, oral language facilitation, curriculum integration and approaches to writing; and a description of the literacy activities observed in the classroom.

Conclusion

This chapter has examined four important factors in creating an effective literacy environment for young children:

- how to recognise both structural and process quality for literacy
- the importance of understanding the implications of a curriculum framework
- how to design a literacy-rich learning environment
- the role of teachers in mediating children's learning in that environment.

We know that providing a high-quality literacy environment is a predictor of enhanced outcomes for children and that effective teachers make a substantial difference in children's literacy learning. There is clear evidence that teachers who have strong 'theoretical knowledge' of literacy and can integrate this well with appropriate 'craft knowledge' achieve the greatest overall gains for children.

Reflective questions

1. Thinking about your knowledge about literacy, what things are you confident about and what do you know you still need to learn?

2. Think about an early childhood centre you have worked in or are working in. How well does it relate to Morrow's (2009) definitions of a literacy-rich environment?

3. If you were going to write a literacy policy for a centre, what would you include and how would you ensure both structural and process quality in the literacy environment?

Further reading

Brookes Publishing Co. 'The Preview: Education' (September 2009). http://www.
brookespublishing.com/newsletters/ed-article-0909.htm.
Ministry of Education (NZ). 'Te Whāriki'. http://www.educate.ece.govt.nz/learning/
curriculumAndLearning/TeWhariki.aspx.
UK ECERS. http://www.ecersuk.org/10.html.
UNC FPG Child Development Institute. 'Environment Rating Scales'. http://ers.fpg.unc.edu.

Chapter 8

'Sound' foundations for learning literacy

Chapter objectives

1. To examine if the predictors of literacy acquisition can be promoted in early childhood settings.
2. To explore specific teaching strategies which have proven effective in promoting literacy knowledge, skills and dispositions.
3. To critically examine the roles that teachers and parents play in ensuring continuity of literacy learning between the home and early childhood setting.

This chapter examines in depth how teachers and families can support alphabet knowledge, phonological awareness, vocabulary, comprehension and emergent writing prior to school entry, as well as ways in which teachers can support continuity between home and centre literacy learning. Recent research on how to integrate phonological awareness into holistic educational programs during the early years is also considered. Drawing on Nicholson's (2005) work, guidelines for the scope and sequence of teaching phonemic awareness in early childhood are provided. Finally, the chapter explores approaches to storybook reading, supporting socio-dramatic play and emergent writing as crucial vehicles for supporting foundational knowledge and skill development.

A starting point

If we return to the National Early Literacy Panel Report (NELP) (2009) and revisit the six evidentially based predictors of literacy achievement, we have a starting point for examining what teachers need to promote in early childhood.

Reflection 8.1

What were the evidentially based predictors of reading acquisition identified in the NELP Report? Hint – there were six major variables. Write your list and then check back to Chapter 2 for the right answers!

This chapter focuses on the teaching of five key concepts in early childhood, stemming from this list:

1. *phonological awareness* – including the alphabetic principle
2. *alphabet knowledge* – including rapid naming of letters
3. *vocabulary* – including oral language, grammar and rapid naming of objects or colours
4. *comprehension* – taking meaning from print, concepts about print and print knowledge
5. *writing* – includes writing and phonological memory.

> **Phonological awareness:**
> an umbrella term for the understanding children develop that words are made up of separate sounds – syllables, beginning sound (onset), ending sounds or word families (rime) and phonemes (the smallest unit of sound in a word).

Phonological awareness

Phonological awareness is the ability to hear sounds in words, such as syllables, rimes and phonemes, and is an important skill linked to the acquisition of literacy. Children who have been taught phonological awareness prior to beginning formal instruction have been found to be better equipped for learning to read and spell than children who have not and children with greater phonological awareness at kindergarten or at school entry tend to be better readers (Stanovich 2000).

Phonological awareness is most commonly understood to be a single ability that manifests itself in different ways at different points throughout child development (Anthony & Francis 2005). The conceptualisation is similar to that of a continuum; as indicated in the simple diagram below, during early childhood word, syllable, and rime awareness are most likely to develop.

word ➡ syllable ➡ onset and rime ➡ phoneme

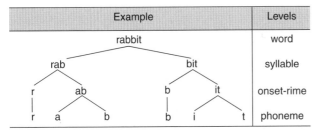

Example	Levels
rabbit	word
rab / bit	syllable
r ab / b it	onset-rime
r a b / b i t	phoneme

Figure 8.1 *Phonological awareness continuum – early part (Nicholson, 2005, p. 27)*

Phoneme awareness typically develops in older children. In this chapter, we focus on the early part of the continuum – namely, word, syllable and rime awareness. Later chapters examine the more complex aspects of phonological awareness in greater depth.

Rime awareness is the ability to distinguish between words that rhyme and words that do not rhyme and typically develops during early childhood (Anthony & Francis 2005). It also includes the ability to produce rhyming words, a more complex manipulation task. Based on the assumption that phonological awareness is a single unified ability, it is expected that rime awareness contributes to the future development of phoneme awareness (Lonigan, Burgess & Anthony 2000). By teaching children rime awareness, it may directly, or indirectly through phoneme awareness, contribute to the development of reading.

Further along the continuum of phonological awareness development is phoneme awareness. At the far end of the continuum is phoneme manipulation, which includes the ability to delete and substitute phonemes. Closer to the centre of the continuum is a sensitivity to phonemes which is the ability to identify whether two phonemes are the same or different. A sensitivity to phonemes may be the first step to developing the alphabetic principle (Byrne 1998), providing the initial understanding that words consist of sounds. Noel Foulin (2005) suggests that phoneme sensitivity is required for children to be able to make use of letter names in early word learning, even prior to the acquisition of the alphabetic principle.

Alphabet knowledge and phonological awareness together form the basis for the acquisition of the *alphabetic principle*, which is the understanding that speech sounds in spoken words are represented by graphemes in print (Moats 2000). The combined knowledge means that children can use letters and their sounds to make phonemically correct representations of words when both reading and spelling (Nicholson 2005). Together phonological awareness and alphabet knowledge form part of the inside-out processes that comprise emergent literacy (Whitehurst & Lonigan 1998).

According to Ehri's (2006) phase theory of reading development, even very young children are able to learn to read words. Once they acquire letter knowledge and some phonemic awareness, they move from a *pre-alphabetic phase* to a *partial alphabetic phase* and they can read some words from memory by accessing partial connections between letters and sounds at a previous reading. Boyer and Ehri (2011) argue that these children also use the partial knowledge for spelling, but are unable to read unfamiliar words. Boyer and Ehri (2011, p. 441) state that although spoken language is acquired easily, children usually require explicit instruction to learn how to segment and blend phonemes in words, because speech is perceived as an unbroken flow of sound with no pauses between phonemes in words.

> Letters are thought to facilitate learning because they provide visible, concrete representation of phonemes that are transient and disappear as soon as they are spoken or heard. Letter markers allow children to hold phonemic segments in memory and to inspect and manipulate them during training. Letters facilitate the transfer of phoneme segmentation skill to reading and spelling tasks that require letter knowledge.

Boyer and Ehri's (2011) study of 60 children aged 4.1 to 5.8 years showed that children gained phonemic segmentation and phonemic spelling abilities when they were explicitly taught letters and sounds or letters combined with articulation pictures. Stahl and Yaden (2004) state that children who have even rudimentary phonological awareness are more likely to make sense of letter–sound correspondence and, as they explain, 'Children who do not have this phonological insight do not make sense of decoding instruction or of the relation between written and spoken words and thus fail to learn to read' (Stahl & Yaden 2004, p. 153).

In terms of promoting phonological awareness, it's important to differentiate between phonological awareness and phonics; they are commonly misunderstood. Phonological awareness is a capability that children develop, whereas phonics is a specific method of teaching that focuses on the links between letter sounds with printed letters or groups of letters (Philllips, Clancy-Menchetti & Lonigan 2008). As Phillips, Clancy-Menchetti and Lonigan (2008, p. 4) state:

> Children's understanding that words are made up of smaller sounds such as syllables and phonemes helps them to 'break the code' of written language and acquire the alphabet principle. The alphabetic principle

refers to the fact that written words represent spoken words in a sound by sound correspondence. Sounds are signified by a single letter, or in some cases, several letters indicating a single sound in a word (e.g. *sh* or *ch*). When teachers and parents tell a child to 'sound it out', this suggestion only makes sense if the child grasps the concept that the word can be broken down into smaller components. Phonological awareness, letter name knowledge and letter sound knowledge come together in young children to forge this conceptual understanding and to facilitate reading and writing development.

Phillips, Clancy-Menchetti and Lonigan (2008) explain that as children will present a range of skills along the phonological awareness continuum, it is quite important be able to identify children's level of awareness. They also explain that phonological awareness will not develop 'naturally', so it is important to identify children who are displaying difficulties with awareness in relation to their peers.

Phillips, Clancy-Menchetti and Lonigan (2008) advocate teaching phonological awareness using scaffolding and guided participation. They argue that targeting activities at subgroups may be useful to support children's range of abilities. They cite evidence that holistic curriculum can support phonological awareness through independent exploration, socio-dramatic play and free play, as long as it is supported with brief and interactive small group or individual sessions supporting phonological awareness lasting no more than 10–15 minutes per day. The authors stipulate that early childhood teachers should begin with helping children to enjoy nursery rhymes, Dr Seuss books and other rhyming texts, but should not push children into rhyming manipulation tasks (e.g. 'say words that rhyme with boat'), as this is a conceptually difficult task related to skills later on the continuum. They suggest that rather than starting with rhyming activities, teachers are better to focus on tasks that encourage these levels of awareness: word, syllable, onset (beginning sound in words), rime (vowel plus letters that follow or word family) and phoneme.

Similarly, Nicholson (2005, p. 37) states that teachers need to understand the scope and the sequence in which children learn about phonemes. In early childhood, teachers can experiment with this sequence depending on where they perceive a child to be on the continuum of phonological awareness.

To promote phonological awareness, there is a range of actions that teachers can readily adopt within a holistic curriculum.

- Encourage knowledge of nursery rhymes.
  - singing nursery rhymes
  - emphasising rhyming parts in the rhyme
  - pointing out humour in the nursery rhymes
  - using rhymes at appropriate moments – 'we know a rhyme about that'
  - making up 'our very own rhymes' or changing the words in rhymes.

- Encourage knowledge of beginning sounds:
  - during story reading – group and one to one

Table 8.1 *Scope and sequence of phonological instruction*

STEP	PHONOLOGICAL TASK	EXAMPLE
1	Syllable awareness	Let's clap the syllables in RABBIT.
2	Rhyme awareness	Which word does not rhyme with the others? HOT CAT POT
3	Phoneme identity	Which picture starts with /s/? Which picture starts with /g/?
4	Blending	Turtle talk: Find the B-A-G.
5	Deletion: initial final	Say CAT without the /k/. Say CAT without the /t/.
6	Segmentation	What are the three sounds in DOG?
7	Substitution	Point to the MOP. Instead of the /m/, start a new word with /p/.

(Nicholson 2005, p. 38)

- during songs, rhymes, language games (e.g. I spy something that begins with a /b/ sound)
  - using the first sound of a name to send children off the mat (e.g. names beginning with /k/ sound)
- When engaging in storybook reading:
  - play with rhymes and rimes (word families) in storybooks
  - identify beginning sounds – e.g. f is for frog, football, friend – so that children learn they begin with the same sound
  - talk about links between pictures and words
  - define unfamiliar words.

Alphabet knowledge

Alphabet knowledge: recognition of the letters of the alphabet.

As mentioned in the previous section, knowledge of the alphabet is a fundamental skill that children need to learn. **Alphabet knowledge** provides beginning readers with the knowledge necessary to make connections between the spoken word and its print representation (Piasta, Purpura & Wagner 2010) and is used for making phonemically correct attempts at reading, writing and spelling (Ehri & Roberts 2006). Ehri and Roberts (2006) point out that in English, children have to learn 26 upper- and lower-case letters; with duplication of shape (e.g. S and s) removed, there are 40 distinct shapes for children to learn. The relationships between letter shapes and letter sounds then need to be learned, which is foundational to children being able to decode words. Sénéchal (2006) found that this knowledge of letters can continue to influence reading ability up to Grade 4, as he found when French parents provided their preschool children with tuition in the alphabet.

Vaughn explores the alphabet

There are at least two ways in which alphabet knowledge can be used in the acquisition of reading and spelling ability: through either *letter name* knowledge or through *letter sound* knowledge. *Letter-name* knowledge has been found to influence children's early spelling attempts and can make learning to read easier, if the words contain letter name cues, such as JRF for giraffe (Ehri & Roberts 2006).

Additional studies have also shown evidence of the role that letter names may play in the development of word knowledge before children have acquired the alphabetic principle (e.g. Treiman & Rodriguez 1999). This could be due to the use of the orthographic cues that letter names generate. Orthography is a method of representing a language or the sounds of language by written symbols or spelling. For example, a two-year-old boy might identify his letter name for his own name every time he saw it. One of my friend's children would always say 'that says Paige' when she was about three and saw the letter P or any word that started with a P, demonstrating that she understood the link between the letter and the her name in print,

Piasta, Purpura and Wagner (2010) argue that although the importance of alphabet knowledge has been established (e.g. NELP 2009), little is known about how alphabet knowledge should be taught. Early studies have been criticised for their research design or for combining teaching of alphabet with teaching of phonological awareness. Piasta, Purpura and Wagner state that curricula designed to facilitate early literacy skills vary considerably in how alphabet knowledge is taught, especially with respect to whether teaching targets letter names and sounds, or just letter sounds.

Letter-sound knowledge is one of the more important skills that children need to develop for attempting new and unfamiliar words (Ehri & Roberts 2006). For example, a child who knows the letter sound for /f/ will know the beginning sound in any word beginning with f and can recognise that 'foot', 'furry' and 'funny' all begin with the same sound and that the sound is represented in print by the letter 'f'.

Piasta, Purpura and Wagner (2010) found that children who had letter name and sound instruction learned an average of two more letter sounds than children who had just learned letter names, a finding consistent with the effect sizes identified in the NELP Report (2009). Piasta, Purpura and Wagner (2010) explain that support for the idea that letter name knowledge is used to acquire letter sound knowledge is provided by the *letter name structure effect*. Some letters, such as B and F, include cues to letter sounds (i.e. /b/ and /f/) in their names. Other letters have names that do not provide cues to their sounds, such as W and H. When children's patterns of alphabet acquisition are examined, a letter name structure effect is apparent: letter names and sounds are most likely to be known for letters that include cues to their sounds as opposed to letters with unrelated names and sounds.

A meta-analysis of 60 studies on alphabet knowledge by Piasta and Wagner (2010) revealed that letter name knowledge, letter sound knowledge and letter writing outcomes all showed small to moderate effects to teaching in the early childhood context, suggesting that specific domains of alphabet knowledge can be enhanced through appropriate teaching. They also note that children receive a lot of incidental teaching of alphabet knowledge through involvement with family and community, which aids understanding.

Alphabet knowledge can be taught in a variety of ways within a holistic curriculum, including storybook reading, games, writing names and routines within mat sessions. Some simple ways to encourage alphabet knowledge include the following:

- name boards
- dictating names onto artwork
- signup lists for activities (e.g. computer time)
- using a letter card to send children off the mat
- talking to children about alphabet charts – sing the alphabet song while pointing to the letters
- using cards and magnetic letters to make words.

Vocabulary

Vocabulary:
the number of words that children can understand (receptive vocabulary) or can say (productive or expressive vocabulary).

A large and rich **vocabulary** is one of the strongest predictors of reading comprehension and the size of a child's individual word knowledge is not only predictive of comprehension in primary school, it is also related to fluency and comprehension in high school (Neuman, Newman & Dwyer 2011). Arguably, as children transition into and through primary school, the richness of vocabulary assists them with understanding the specific meanings of academic terms, such as the words 'sign' and 'operation' in mathematics (Stahl & Nagy 2006). Typically children learn vocabulary at home, over meals, during daily activities and household chores, but often gain the wider and more sophisticated vocabulary in early childhood through story reading. It is this reason that most of the intervention research in homes and early childhood settings is framed around story reading (Neuman, Newman & Dwyer 2011). As Stahl and Yaden (2004, p. 147) propose:

> As children learn more about reading, they develop more language knowledge from exposure to books … and, subsequently, more phonological awareness from their growth in language.

Vocabulary development is a socially mediated process and much literacy research has focused on storybook reading as a context for learning new vocabulary (Silverman & Crandell 2010). As Silverman & Crandell (2010, p. 319) argue, 'children learn words when adults label objects, actions and characteristics. As children encounter words in more and more situations, they learn to generalize words across contexts. The more words children learn through this labelling process, the more likely they are to encounter words that are related or similar'. Beauchat, Blamey and Walpole (2009) state that shared storybook reading has a range of potential language and literacy 'targets' that teachers need to actively promote, including oral language, vocabulary, comprehension, phonological awareness and concepts about print.

Amber being read a story by her uncle

Justice et al. (2009) argue that storybook reading has traditionally been used for supporting a range of literacy knowledge and skills. However, they also argue that the way in which teachers read to children determines quite different outcomes. In their randomised control trial of 106 preschool children in 23 centres over a 30-week period, they found that children who experienced a 'print referencing' style of storybook reading made significant gains in concepts about print, alphabet knowledge and name-writing ability compared to children who received 'business as usual' storybook-reading styles from teachers. In a print-referencing style, teachers use verbal and non-verbal techniques to heighten children's attention to and interest in print within a storybook. Justice et al. (2009, p. 68) suggest a number of simple techniques including the following:

- asking questions about print (e.g. Can you see the letter S on this page?)
- commenting about print (e.g. that word says 'splash')
- tracking a finger along the text while reading.

Justice et al. suggest that the print-referencing style of storybook reading can be readily adapted by parents at home too.

Justice and Pullen (2003), in their analysis of evidence-based interventions for promoting literacy, also identify a 'dialogic reading' style as useful for supporting oral language and emergent literacy. When reading to children, dialogic reading involves the following behaviours:

- asking open-ended questions and limiting use of yes/no questions
- following children's answers with additional questions
- repeating and expanding on what children say
- offering praise, encouragement and feedback for participation
- following children's interests.

This method of reading encourages children's engagement, creates a dialogue and provides adult models of language. It has been found to be particularly useful for encouraging phonological awareness.

Neuman and Dwyer (2009) reviewed a number of commercial vocabulary 'packages', which are designed to teach children new words in a sequenced pattern. Typically these are purchased and downloaded from the internet or are available on a CD-ROM and they are typically graded from kindergarten to Grade 6. Children work through a set of pre-scripted exercises. Neuman and Dwyer caution against teachers using such packages without critical scrutiny and thoughtful use within early childhood environments. They summarise the evidence of effective teaching strategies for vocabulary as the following:

- Be systematic and explicit, providing children with plenty of opportunities to use words in interactions.
- Involve a great deal of practice that is active, guided and extensive.
- Incorporate periodic review of new words over time, to check that understanding of new words has been retained.
- Include observation and progress monitoring assessment to inform further teaching.

Morrow (2009, p. 126) considers that children learn new vocabulary through language interactions with other children and often without the involvement of a teacher. She suggests that children use the following types of talk:

- *Aesthetic talk* – this type of talk occurs when children discuss literature, tell stories and participate in drama.
- *Efferent talk* – this is used to inform and persuade. This type of talk occurs when children discuss themes or projects, present at mat sessions (i.e. in show and tell) or give oral reports or interviews. It often requires preparation and is more formal than other talk.
- *Talk in dramatic activities* – during socio-dramatic play, children adopt roles, share experiences, use props and puppets to act out stories and engage in dialogue with peers.

Morrow suggests that teachers can promote language and vocabulary development by encouraging children to engage in these different types of talk.

Wasik, Bond and Hindman's (2006) vocabulary intervention in early childhood classrooms involved the following teaching strategies to promote vocabulary growth in preschoolers:

- Provide feedback.
- Ask descriptive questions.
- Use active listening strategies.
- Demonstrate word meanings (visually or kinaesthetically).
- Ask predictive, reactive and recall questions outside of book reading.
- Make connections between storybook context and classroom experiences.

The results showed that children outperformed control classrooms in receptive and expressive vocabulary over the course of the school year. Children who had 'rich instruction' doubled word gains over children who didn't, and those who had 'more rich instruction' (a greater amount) made doubled word gains over those who had 'rich instruction'.

Coyne et al. (2009) also trialled different methods of vocabulary instruction during story reading. They used three different strategies:

1. Children were exposed to new words incidentally during story reading.
2. Children were directly taught new words through embedded instruction in story reading. Teachers would teach new words before story reading and ask children to raise their hands when they recognised the word. Teachers reread words, defined them and showed pictures which supported the words.
3. Children received embedded and extended instruction in which they were introduced to new words in new contexts, shown pictures of target words in various contexts, and asked to respond to discrimination and generalisation questions about target words.

Coyne et al. found that children learned new words more readily in conditions two and three, but only fully learned and understood the new words using the third strategy.

Neuman, Newman and Dwyer (2011) trialled the World of Words (WOW) curriculum with 12 schools, 28 early childhood classrooms, and 604 children. The WOW curriculum is an intervention to support vocabulary and conceptual development in pre-kindergarten-aged children. The curriculum is organised across three units of learning: healthy habits, living things and mathematics. There were four topics in each unit and each topic was taught over an eight-day period. Each topic typically started with a song, rhyme or wordplay on a DVD; this was followed by a definition of the category on DVD, then discussion of the words associated with the topic (e.g. 'what is an insect?') and finally the teacher read something meaningful related to the topic. Over subsequent days, words related to the topic were introduced and other words reviewed. Children were then presented with 'time for a challenge' items and review learning through journal activities, such as writing or drawing. The sequence of teaching was based on the notion of scaffolding children's vocabulary and drew on research highlighting the importance of singing, interacting and playing with words, shared-book reading of informational text, and writing (Neuman & Roskos 2007). Results showed that children in the intervention learned not only curriculum-related vocabulary, but they were also better able to identify concepts and their conceptual properties and categories (e.g. properties of insects). These findings support Stahl and Nagy's (2006) proposition that children need not only the words, but the rich network of knowledge that underpins comprehension and reasoning.

In their observations of 16 teachers and 244 children, Silverman and Crandell (2010) identified teaching practices that were associated with greater vocabulary growth. These included the following:

- acting out and illustrating words
- analysing words semantically
- applying words in new contexts
- defining words explicitly in rich contexts
- word study
- read-aloud and non-read aloud times.

Harris et al. (2011) reviewed the research on vocabulary acquisition in early childhood and suggest six principles for vocabulary learning emerging from the research evidence:

1. *Frequency matters*. Children learn the words that they hear most.
2. *Make it interesting*. Children learn words for things and events that interest them.

3. *Make it responsive.* Interactive and responsive contexts rather than passive favour vocabulary learning.

4. *Focus on meaning.* Children learn best in meaningful contexts.

5. *Be clear.* Children need information about word meaning.

6. *Beyond the word.* Vocabulary learning and grammatical development are reciprocal processes.

Harris et al. recommend that teachers avoid passive approaches to vocabulary instruction and instead attempt to embed these principles in the pedagogies of the early childhood setting and through promoting children's play, which heightens interest, enjoyment and motivation to learn.

Comprehension

In order to make the most of story-reading sessions to aid **comprehension**, it's important to also make use of the visual cues that most storybooks provide. Teachers and parents can aid children's comprehension of stories by drawing attention to the illustrations. There is a lot of learning involved in the 'reading' of illustrations – children will come to understand that the pictures depict meaning and represent movement or actions on the part of the character. At a more advanced level, children can 'read' mood depicted by colour and tone suggested by style of illustration (Morrow 2009, p. 189). Adults who share books with

> **Comprehension:** understanding what is being said or being read out.

Amber reading visual print

children and draw attention to visual elements that draw attention to characters, plot or theme enable children to become readers of visual material, which will aid both comprehension and their experiences of multimodal learning (refer back to Chapter 5 on multiliteracies). Because pictures provide a context for the words, the beginning reader who can 'read' visual material is able to use this as a source of additional information and being able to read pictures is a useful short-term reading-related skill for beginning readers.

Dymock and Nicholson (2010b) outline strategies for enhancing comprehension in primary school children, which is also of relevance to early childhood teachers. Their 'High 5!' approach is built on research evidence of up to nine comprehension strategies that good users use (Pressley 2006), but focuses on five key strategies:

1. *Activating background knowledge.* Simple questioning helps the teacher find out what children already know about a topic, so that children can make links.

2. *Questioning.* This involves questioning the text in older children, but for younger children might involve asking questions about what might happen next or more specific questions about the content of each page.

3. *Analysing text structure.* Teachers can help children to understand text structure by drawing attention to the type of structure the story has – cause and effect, problem and solution, webs, sequential strings. Discussions about things such as the effects of earthquakes or the sequential development of a butterfly help children to understand these sorts of text structures.

4. *Creating mental images.* In primary, this might involve developing a diagram of a topic, but for early childhood, it is more likely that children would draw pictures of their mental images of topics. Neuman, Newman and Dwyer (2011) also advocate this strategy for assisting vocabulary and comprehension.

5. *Summarising.* This strategy involves identifying and summarising key ideas. This might come before or after drawing pictures in early childhood, to check that children have clear understandings of what has been discussed in the story.

Although Dymock and Nicholson give a clear plan of how this might be used as named strategies in a primary setting, in early childhood it is arguably more important that the teacher draws on the strategies as part of planning for story reading, including choices of texts and possible ways of reading and critiquing the text.

Blum et al. (2010) propose something simpler, but similar for promoting comprehension in early childhood. They suggest that teachers use a set of prompts for promoting discussion:

• 'Tell me in your own words what happened in the book.'

• 'Talk about your favourite parts.'

- 'This book reminds me of …'.
- 'Add something new to the book.'

Mem Fox, the acclaimed Australian author, said in a keynote speech at a Reading Association Conference in New Zealand in 2002 that there were three successive readings associated with the reading of a new book:

- *reading to* (where the teacher reads the story to the children pointing out interesting features)
- *reading with* (where children engage and discuss the story as it is read)
- *children reading it back to the teacher* (where children present their 'reading' of the story as they understand it) (Fox 2002).

In terms of checking children's comprehension, there is value in such simple advice!

Writing

You may be wondering why we have included this heading in a chapter on promoting literacy in early childhood, when teaching writing is not a common practice. The simple answer is that **writing** begins very early in the life of a child and children's attempts at writing also involve phonemic attempts at spelling by the time they have developed what Ehri and Roberts (2006) call the 'partial alphabetic phase' of reading. There are parallels between reading and writing – children teach themselves to write in much the same way as they learn to read – through trial and error and gradually recognising patterns and similarities. They mix drawing with writing, they invent messages in various forms and shapes, and they invent and decorate symbols, letters and words. They continue to use invented forms of writing after they have mastered conventional forms (Teale et al. 2009). As the NELP Report (2009) suggests, writing your own name is a significant act, primarily because it begins the process of naming objects in writing.

> **Writing:**
> a cognitive and motor skill that involves the ability to produce written language using the writing system of specific societies and cultures.

Writing is a key part of most families' lives. Rowe (2008) proposes that writing should be viewed as a social practice and that as soon as children begin to participate in the writing practices of homes, schools and communities, they begin to learn which textual intentions, procedures and reading and writing processes are valued in specific literacy events. Children move from playfully making marks on paper through to communicating messages on paper and then on to making texts as products or artefacts, such as making their own books or cards, with some practice happening on the wallpaper along the way!

Children's writing develops through constant invention and reinvention of the forms of written language and obviously includes the development of motor skills as well as cognitive development. Children's involvement in written language, though embedded in social situations and interactions, is typically self-initiated and self-directed. Children learn about writing by observing more skilled others and participating with them in literacy events, but they need to work independently on mastery. From this framework, learning is defined in terms of children's increasing expertise of use of social and cultural literacy practices. Rowe's (2008) study of two- and three-year-olds' writing showed that teachers negotiate what she terms 'social contracts' with children about the uses of materials and purposes of writing that shaped children's participation in writing, which arguably also happens in homes. The implications of this study are that children develop local, social and cultural understandings of what constitutes writing and what is acceptable in terms of writing and this will shape the skills and abilities they have as they transition between early childhood settings and primary school.

Rowe and Neitzel's (2010) observation study of two- and three-years-olds' participation in emergent writing revealed that children of this age showed conceptual, procedural, creative or socially oriented interests which were reflected in the ways they used writing. Rowe and Neitzel define the categories as follows:

- *conceptual interests* – used writing to explore and record ideas on topics of personal interest

- *procedural interests* – explored how writing worked and practised conventional literacy (e.g. writing alphabet letters)

- *creative interest* – explored writing materials to generate new literacy processes and new uses for materials

- *socially oriented interests* – used writing to mediate joint social interaction and align activity choices with those of other participants.

Rowe and Neitzel conclude that children have different experiences of early writing, based on their orientation and interests, which become part of agency and identity as a literacy learner. Rowe and Neitzel propose further research which investigates if these interests remain stable over time and if they lead to different literacy outcomes for children, but suggest that teachers need to be aware that children use writing for different purposes and that teachers need to offer a wide range of materials and opportunities to meet children's interests.

Love, Burns and Buell (2007) suggest that one of the best ways to align with the child's needs for writing, balancing guidance with autonomy, is through 'scaffolded writing'. In this approach, teachers provide children with support and guidance (scaffolding) to develop their understanding of the function and conventions of writing in several ways, which they argue is particularly effective with preschoolers. Children get direct experience with making and executing a plan, an everyday function of writing. The teacher's directed instructions and guidance on how to represent the children's thoughts on paper in writing decrease as the children learn the task. As new complexities are added, such as asking a child to write a longer line for words with many sounds and a shorter line for words with fewer sounds, the teacher again offers assistance. Generally, young children are most successful when teachers provide structure and instruction about a new aspect of writing. Once the concept is introduced, the teacher then steps back to allow children the freedom to incorporate and master the new skills (Love, Burns & Buell 2007, p. 17).

Some strategies for promoting writing include the following:

- Children's attempts should be responded to as meaningful communication. Express pleasure in children's writing.
- Children need exposure to a rich literacy environment, which has good resources for writing. Alphabet charts, plastic, magnetic, wooden and felt letters are all useful resources, in addition to conventional writing materials.
- Children need opportunities to experiment with writing. They need encouragement but to be left alone to make decisions about writing. Model writing by writing in their presence.
- Writing should be integrated through the curriculum and used for a range of purposes. Many centres use clipboards and pens near lots of activities, so that children can use writing as a meaningful part of their play. Provide writing materials and sign-up lists throughout the centre.
- Assist children to hold pencils, crayons and so on by guiding the child's hand to the paper. Show children the simplest and most comfortable way to hold a pencil or pen.
- Use clay, play dough, finger paint, and chalkboards for writing – anything that requires finger dexterity is useful for promoting coordination.
- Provide a writing centre – an inviting and well stocked space for writing and making books and other written works (see Chapter 6 for further ideas).
- Provide a writing folder with 'very own words' for older children.
- Provide mailboxes, bulletin boards, and displays of children's work.

Reflection 8.2

Think about a centre that you have visited or worked in recently. What opportunities for writing did that centre provide? How could the opportunities for writing be improved?

Continuity between home and centre literacy learning

Chapter 4 outlined a number of ways in which families can support children's literacy acquisition and, as previously argued, teachers need to understand and build on children's literacy practices if they hope to ensure continuity in children's learning.

Justice and Pullen (2003, p. 110) argue that early childhood programs need to follow three principles for literacy curriculum:

1. Intervention activities should address both written language and phonological awareness.

2. Intervention activities should include naturalistic, embedded opportunities for knowledge attainment as well as explicit exposure to key concepts (an 'explicit embedded balance').

3. Practices should be evidence-based.

This notion of a balanced curriculum is a useful one. As McNaughton (2002) argues, the curriculum must be wide enough to incorporate the familiar while unlocking the unfamiliar. For this reason, teachers need knowledge of the literacies that children encounter out of the school or centre and tailor their teaching to build on children's strengths, but they also need to identify what is unfamiliar and support children's developing repertoire of literacy knowledge.

There are a number of ways in which teachers can establish continuity. In New Zealand the learning stories framework for assessment (Ministry of Education 2004) is premised on the notion of including parents' and children's voices, which can aid continuity and involvement. Portfolios of children's learning are regularly shared with parents and children. Teachers can also arrange regular opportunities for families to be involved in centre activities and events. Teachers can also send home journals documenting children's play and developmental milestones or sharing anecdotes from the day's activities. Parents (and children) in turn can write in the journal, sharing their observations with the teacher and other children (Love, Burns & Buell 2007).

Conclusion

This chapter has included some key actions teachers can take to support children's emergent literacy within an early childhood setting, building on the ideas introduced in previous chapters. Using the framework of the predictors of literacy acquisition (NELP 2009), this chapter has reviewed some recent research on how alphabet knowledge, phonological awareness, vocabulary, comprehension and writing can be promoted in the early childhood setting. Clearly, these ideas are also important in the junior school and this chapter hasn't addressed the issues of supporting children's spelling development, which develops in conjunction with knowledge of the alphabetic principle and children's emergent writing abilities, but this issue is addressed more fully in later chapters. What this chapter does suggest, however, is that teachers need to be fully aware of the potential of the literacy resources in the early childhood context and have a range of teaching strategies in place for making best use of them to support children's literacy.

Reflective question

Think about an early childhood setting that you are familiar with. For each of the below topics, identify how the teachers in the centre supported children's learning:

- phonological awareness
- alphabet knowledge
- vocabulary
- comprehension
- writing.

Further reading

Early Childhood Australia. 'About Early Literacy'. http://www.earlychildhoodaustralia.org.au/everyday_learning_and_play/language_and_learning/about_early_literacy.html.

Education Review Office (NZ). http://www.ero.govt.nz/National-Reports/Literacy-in-Early-Childhood-Services-Teaching-and-Learning-February-2011/Introduction.

Ministry of Education (NZ) – Education Counts. 'Literacy Learning Progressions: Report on Feedback on the Draft Document'. http://www.educationcounts.govt.nz/publications/literacy/43632.

——'Foundation Years'. http://www.minedu.govt.nz/theMinistry/PolicyAndStrategy/KaHikitia/StrategyOverview/StrategyFocusAreas/FoundationYearsGoalsandActions.aspx.

——'Report of the Literacy Taskforce'. http://www.minedu.govt.nz/NZEducation/EducationPolicies/Schools/ResearchAndStatistics/LiteracyResearch/ReportoftheLiteracyTaskforce/Background.aspx.

University of South Australia – The Researcher. 'Babies Bounce Ahead in Early Literacy Program'. http://www.unisa.edu.au/researcher/issue/2006July/story3.asp.

Chapter 9

Uses of assessment before, during and after transition to school

Chapter objectives

1. To develop an understanding of the principles of effective literacy assessment.
2. To review the purposes and types of assessment that occur before, during and after a child's transition to school.
3. To critically examine a range of methods for assessing and documenting children's developing literacy skills and strategies.

This chapter reviews literature on effective assessment, particularly of literacy, and examines this in relation to methods of assessment that are commonly used in early childhood settings. Principles for effectively assessing children's literacy progress before, during and after the initial transition to school are developed. A range of potential methods for assessing and documenting children's literacy acquisition prior to school entry are explored and critiqued. The importance of documenting literacy progression that can be effectively used by the early childhood setting, the primary school and parents is a particular focus of this chapter.

Setting the scene for assessment

In Chapter 1 we introduced you to four students to help you begin thinking about literacy as well as the theoretical frameworks and pedagogies that underpin literacy development in early childhood and primary settings. In this chapter, we'd like you to think about two of these students (Scenarios 1.1 and 1.2) again: the active four-year-old boy with little interest in learning indoors, and the five-year-old girl who is already reading (and comprehending) chapter books. You will undoubtedly meet children like this boy and girl in your teaching practice.

Take a moment to think about these children as well as others that you have met during your practicums.

- What do you know about these children?
- What do you need to know in order to be an effective teacher of both children?

The information that you need will be much broader than you might at first think. In addition to gathering specific information about each child's emerging literacy skills, you will want to find out about his or her particular interests and family background, and any factors that may be hindering or supporting his or her development. Later in this chapter, we will consider these factors in greater detail. For now, however, be thinking about the importance of knowing about a child's developmental history, language and cultural background, and interest in books and learning.

As an educator working with these two children and others, your focus would be primarily on **assessment for learning** (DEECD 2009a); that is, you would be looking for specific information that would inform your teaching and the learning of each of the children in your class both in school and beyond. As children make the transition into school, 'assessment as learning' and 'assessment of learning' (DEECD 2009a) will become more frequent. We will discuss these two additional types of assessment in Chapter 12, when we are considering literacy assessment in the junior school years.

Assessment for learning: occurs when teachers use information gained from an assessment of students' learning to inform their instruction (DEECD 2009a).

Before we move on to consider principles of effective literacy assessment, however, it is important to be clear about the differences between *testing* and *assessment*. Testing is typically a singular activity in which an educator is looking for specific information about a child's achievement in relation to particular objectives or standards. Testing can be thought of as the major component of 'assessment of learning' (DEECD 2009a) and it is unlikely to figure largely in your work in an early childhood educational setting. In contrast to testing, which is typically a discrete event, assessment is an *ongoing multidimensional process* that involves gathering and evaluating information about a child's learning that will assist an educator to plan for instruction. Although assessment may involve the use of some tests, the process more typically utilises focused observations, anecdotal records, checklists, narratives, and portfolios of work samples as the basis for evaluating children's knowledge and skills and communicating their progress with the children themselves as well as their families.

Learning to use assessment wisely

Much has been written about principles of effective assessment. In order to consider what is really important for you to incorporate into your practice as a thoughtful early childhood educator, in this section we consider the assessment guidelines within relevant policy and curriculum documents from New Zealand and Australia and close with a consideration of the developmentally appropriate practices recommended by the International Reading Association and the National Association for the Education of Young Children in 1998–2000.

Early childhood educators in New Zealand and Australia have in common increasingly diverse populations of children and governments that are concerned about the provision of quality early childhood education and services. In both countries national early childhood strategies that include national early learning frameworks have been developed. We hope that you will explore the documents and resources of both of our countries because the materials have much in common as well as important elements that are unique to each country (e.g. the specific and well-articulated focus on bicultural as well as multicultural learning in New Zealand). New Zealand's curriculum, Te Whāriki (Ministry of Education 1996), is the oldest and is discussed first.

New Zealand's early childhood curriculum, Te Whāriki (Ministry of Education 1996), provides a framework for supporting children's early learning within a sociocultural context. It emphasises the learning partnership between teachers (kaiako), parents (mātua), children (tamariki) and family (whānau). The principles of Te Whāriki have provided the framework for *Kei Tua o te Pae/Assessment for Learning* (Ministry of Education 2010a), a best-practice resource that has been designed to assist educators in understanding and strengthening children's learning. Importantly, the resource also considers how children and their parents and family can contribute to the assessment and ongoing learning of a child.

Kei Tua o te Pae/Assessment for Learning (Ministry of Education 2010a) is readily available on the web. We recommend that you explore this learning resource because the text encourages educators to be deeply reflective about their everyday practices and move beyond thinking about the assessment of children in terms of identifying deficits. As noted in the introductory section:

> Effective assessment is an everyday practice that involves noticing, recognising and responding to children's learning. It is formative in that it affects learning and teaching. It requires knowledgeable practitioners that understand children's learning. It includes and actively involves children and their families/whānau.

Kei Tua o te Pae/Assessment for Learning is presented in the form of 20 download-able booklets and you will undoubtedly be interested in *Book 17: Oral, Visual and Written Literacy* (Ministry of Education 2009a). In this book exemplars of assessments of specific children are presented in relation to their developing repertoire of literacy practices: namely, observing and listening in to literacy practices, playing with language and literacy practices, using literacy for a purpose and critically questioning or transforming (Ministry of Education 2009a, pp. 5–6).

The exemplars include a range of considerations including a brief description of the child and the assessment tasks; a reflection by the educator on 'what is new' and 'what is needed next'; a brief text conveying the perspective of the parent and an extended reflection by the authors of the resource in relation to a number of thought-provoking questions, such as: 'What's happening here? What aspects of noticing, recognising and responding to literacy learning does this assessment exemplify? What does this assessment tell us about literacy learning? How does this assessment exemplify developing competence in literacy?' (Ministry of Education 2009a). The exemplars will assist you to think deeply and critically about your work with children, their parents and the community in relation to instruction and assessment for learning.

In Australia The Early Years Learning Framework (DEEWR 2009a) was developed in response to the Council of Australian Government's (COAG) reform agenda and is a key component of the Australian Government's National Quality Framework for early childhood education and care. The framework is part of a drive to ensure the delivery of nationally consistent and quality early childhood education across the nation (DEEWR 2009b).

The Early Years Learning Framework curriculum document, *Belonging, Being and Becoming* (DEEWR 2009a), includes two sections that we are sure you will find extremely valuable in relation to supporting the literacy development of young children. The first section, 'Assessment for Learning' (pp. 18–19), describes assessment in much the same way that assessment for learning was described in the New Zealand document, in that assessment is viewed as an ongoing collaborative practice. *Belonging, Being and Becoming* (DEEWR 2009a) notes that:

Assessment for children's learning refers to the process of gathering and analysing information as evidence about what children know, can do and understand. It is part of an ongoing cycle that includes planning, documenting and evaluating children's learning. It is important because it enables educators in partnership with families, children and other professionals to:

- plan effectively for children's current and future learning,
- communicate about children's learning and progress,
- determine the extent to which all children are progressing toward realising learning outcomes and if not, what might be impeding their progress,
- identify children who may need additional support in order to achieve particular learning outcomes, providing that support or assisting families to access specialist help,
- evaluate the effectiveness of learning opportunities, environments and experiences offered and the approaches taken to enable children's learning, and
- reflect on pedagogy that will suit this context and these children.

The second section of the document that you will undoubtedly find of interest covers the fifth of the five learning outcomes described for children from birth to five years of age. 'Outcome Five: Children are Effective Communicators' is highly relevant to a consideration of young children's emerging literacy skills. Of special note is the statement that: '[children] have the right to be continuing users of their home language as well as to develop competency in Standard Australian English' (DEEWR 2009a, p. 38).

Within Outcome Five, there are (yes, you guessed it) five descriptors that are considered in relation to 'what can be observed' (evidence) and how educators can promote learning (instruction). The five descriptors along with some examples of evidence are as listed below.

1. Children interact verbally and non-verbally with others for a range of purposes. An example of evidence: the child can 'convey and construct messages with purpose and confidence, building on home/family and community literacies' (DEEWR 2009a, p. 42).

2. Children engage with a range of texts and gain meaning from these texts. An example of evidence: the child can 'sing and chant rhymes, jingles and songs' (DEEWR 2009a, p. 43).

3. Children express ideas and make meaning using a range of media. An example of evidence: the child can 'begin to use images and approximations of letters and words to convey meaning' (DEEWR 2009a, p. 44).

4. Children begin to understand how symbols and pattern systems work. An example of evidence: the child can 'on memory of a sequence complete a task' (DEEWR 2009a, p. 45).

5. Children use information and communication technologies to access information, investigate ideas and represent their thinking. An example of evidence: the child can ' use information and communication technologies as tools for designing, drawing, editing, reflecting and composing' (DEEWR 2009a, p. 46).

The learning frameworks in both New Zealand and Australia emphasise the importance of collaboration among educators, young children, their families and community members in the assessment of children's learning skills and strategies and in the planning of activities, experiences and opportunities that will support each child's development. By providing a common language, the learning frameworks facilitate communication and collaboration among these partners.

Now that we have examined relevant sections on assessment for learning from the frameworks being utilised at present in New Zealand and Australia, we'd like you to consider the principles for the assessment of young children's reading and writing skills that was developed jointly by the International Reading Association (IRA) and the National Association for the Education of Young Children (NAEYC) in 1998. Their seminal text, *Learning to Read and Write: Developmentally Appropriate Practices for Young Children*, was republished in 2000 in an expanded form and includes a chapter, 'Informing Instruction in Reading and Writing', which specifically focuses on assessment for learning in reading and writing (Neuman, Copple & Bredekamp 2000).

The five principles of assessment in reading and writing (Neuman, Copple & Bredekamp 2000) are consistent with the broader principles of *Kei Tua o te Pae/ Assessment for Learning* (Ministry of Education 2010a) and *Belonging, Being and Becoming* (DEEWR 2009a). Nonetheless, we want to draw your attention to IRA/ NAEYC's position statement for several important reasons. First, the principles apply directly to literacy learning. Second, the principles are expressed in clear unambiguous language. Third, the principles are followed by a number of specific examples of assessment procedures appropriate to foundation literacy skills. Finally, the statement makes it very clear that professionals from both domains – early childhood and early literacy – view teaching and assessment as complementary processes; that is, teaching informs assessment and assessment informs teaching. We will discuss this reciprocal relationship in detail in the next section on assessment before and during children's transition to school.

The five principles of assessment in reading and writing (Neuman, Copple & Bredekamp 2000, p. 104) include:

1. *Assessment should support children's development and literacy learning.* That is, assessment information should inform program planning and decision making so that learning activities are appropriate to each child's current level. For example, if, as described in Scenario 1.2 in Chapter 1, you have a five-year-old girl in your new entrant class who is independently reading chapter books with good comprehension, then you know that you need to acquire books at a more advanced level for your library and design relevant reading and writing extension activities.

2. *Assessment should take many different forms.* That is, valid and reliable assessments are multidimensional and involve a range of methods and records;

nonetheless, the core of high-quality assessment is focused daily observation of children's performance in authentic learning activities including play. For example, if a child is able to print all of the upper-case letters when they are presented in alphabetical order but can't print many of them when asked to do so in random order, then you would know that the child's knowledge of the letter forms is still consolidating. As a consequence, it would be valuable to discuss your perceptions with the child and his or her parents in order to ensure that practice in naming and printing the letters at home is being approached playfully with random ordering of the letters.

3. *Assessment must avoid cultural bias*. That is, although the goal is for all children to attain high standards of learning and performance, it is recognised that children with diverse language, cultural and experiential backgrounds may differ in the type and timing of activities they need to develop their reading and writing skills. For example, a child who is learning English as an additional language may need explicit instruction, extra practice activities and rich opportunities to play with sounds (chants, jingles, nursery rhymes and songs) in order to develop awareness of the 44 phonemes in the English language.

4. *Assessment should encourage children to observe and reflect on their own learning progress*. That is, asking children to contribute their thoughts about their learning is a powerful way to involve them as collaborators in assessment and learning. For example, very young children can set their own goals, keep evidence of their growth in their literacy portfolios, and share their progress with their 'teacher' and parents in student-led conferences.

5. *Assessment should shed light on what children are able to do as well as the areas where they need further work*. That is, assessment can help educators and children to look at literacy learning as a constructive process in which skills are extended and mistakes regarded as learning opportunities, thereby building children's motivation and self-confidence. For example, children can see the growth in their ability to illustrate and write about their experiences when they keep a cumulative literacy portfolio that includes samples of their language-experience stories.

Now that we have developed a good understanding of the principles of effective assessment, it is time to examine the *focus* and *methods* for assessment before and during a child's transition to school.

Assessment before and during a child's transition to school

Most of the children with whom you will be working will have experienced assessment long before they even enrol in an early childhood program. Indeed, many children will have been assessed before they are born. Such assessment is conducted to monitor the health and development of the unborn child as well as that of the mother. During the early childhood years, children continue to be assessed by community professionals (e.g. general practitioners and public health nurses) to ensure that each child's growth and development reach optimum levels.

When a child enters an early childhood program, further assessment is appropriate to ensure that each child is making expected progress. Many learning centres will utilise a developmental history questionnaire to gather relevant information about individual children as they enter the program. Questions typically focus on the child's early development (e.g. birth, illnesses/accidents and age at which the child achieved milestones for cognitive, motor, social and language development) as well as current development (e.g. health, appetite, sleep, day-care experiences, and relationships with peers), family context (e.g. number of siblings) and possible risk factors (e.g. chronic ear infections). In the case of children who are experiencing significant difficulties with learning as the result of hearing, vision, physical and/or social-emotional and behavioural functioning, professionals within the community (e.g. family doctors, paediatricians, optometrists, audiologists, speech and language therapists, and physiotherapists) will be involved in supporting the child and family. You may be asked to collaborate with these community professionals in supporting individual children, but as an educator your primary focus will be on assessment for learning.

Let us now turn to the *focus* of your assessment for learning. You will want to know how each child's literacy skills and strategies are developing as a result of their learning within the centre, at home and within the community (Anderson & Morrison 2011; Taylor & Dorsey-Gaines 1988). Would focusing on what you want children to learn be a good place to start for thinking about assessment for learning? You bet. In the previous section where we discussed the IRA/NAEYC joint position statement, *Learning to Read and Write: Developmental Appropriate Practices for Young Children* (Neuman, Copple & Bredekamp 2000), we learned that teaching and assessment could be viewed as complementary processes; that is, teaching informs assessment and assessment informs teaching. This means that any method utilised to teach a specific skill (e.g. teaching children how to 'stretch' out words to hear the individual sounds – phonemic awareness) could be reversed to assess a child's skill (e.g. you could ask a child to 'stretch' out the word 'elephant' and tell you how many sounds he or she could hear). As a consequence, it makes very good sense to think about all you learned in the previous chapter, '"Sound" Foundations for Learning', as an excellent place to begin when thinking about assessment for learning.

In Chapter 8 you learned that the five key concepts of literacy learning in early childhood were derived from the evidentially based predictors of literacy achievement identified by the National Early Literacy Panel (NELP 2009). In 2002 the National Early Literacy Panel (NELP) was set the task of identifying instructional practices and parenting activities that would promote the development of children's early literacy skills. After reviewing more than 500 high-quality research papers, the panel established that 11 skills or abilities can be regarded as precursors or predictors of later literacy achievement. (NELP 2009, p. vii).

The first six skills, which were found to be strongly predictive of later literacy development regardless of the influence of children's cognitive abilities and the relative economic advantage of their home environment, included: alphabet knowledge (AK), phonological awareness (PA), rapid automatic naming for letters and digits (RAN-LD) as well as colours and objects (RAN-CO), the ability to write letters in isolation or name (WRT), and phonological memory (PM). A further five skills, which were also found to be potentially important, included: concepts about print (COP), print knowledge (PK), reading readiness (RR), oral language (OL), and visual processing (VP).

These 11 precursor skills were found to be strongest in predicting the literacy achievement of children at the end of kindergarten or the beginning of Year 1. As a consequence, we have chosen to discuss a combination of these skills in this chapter. In Chapter 12, when we consider the assessment of literacy during the junior school years, we examine a somewhat different set of skills and a new framework upon which to plan assessment.

In the following section, we consider the strongest independent predictor skills in the 'big five' concept format of Chapter 8 in relation to *methods of assessment* – that is, the ways in which an early childhood educator could assess and monitor a child's development in a busy learning centre. We also discuss ways in which family members could contribute to the assessment given the important role that parents and other family members have to play in ensuring the validity of an assessment and in contributing to plans for skill development and practice.

Methods for assessing and documenting children's developing literacy skills and strategies

Early childhood educators typically utilise a wide range of approaches and methods to collect, document, organise, synthesise and interpret information concerning a young child's literacy development. Information collected during instructional and play activities relating to each child's literacy skills, engagement, use of strategies, interests and attitudes, as well as perspectives on learning, will be of interest to the educator who seeks to 'assess for learning' as well as to the child and family. Many educators develop a portfolio for each child, which contains information such as that listed above along with photographs, drawings and reflections and narratives periodically dictated by the child. The portfolio will of course contain the educator's anecdotal records, reflections and narratives and may also contain similar written contributions from the child's parents. Such a portfolio provides a rich, inclusive and graphic account of the child's learning across time (DEEWR 2009a). As noted in Book 17 of *Kei Tua o te Pae/Assessment for Learning* (*Oral, Visual and Written Literacy*), when early childhood educators make portfolios, especially those containing narrative assessments, available to the children themselves, it is:

> a particularly powerful way of building children's identities as literate beings. In many cases, the children's portfolios have become books that they can 'read', contribute to, revisit and retell. These portfolios are meaningful literacy artefacts for children, who find it compelling and engaging to be able to contribute to and revisit stories of personal achievement. They provide natural opportunities for children to assess their own literacy knowledge and skills. When teachers also draw children's attention to some of the literacy conventions that exist within such documented assessments, their value for literacy learning is noticeably strengthened (Ministry of Education 2009a, p. 3).

Within each child's portfolio it will be important to collect information and evidence of literacy learning that focuses on the 'big five' skill domains that you explored in relation to instruction in Chapter 8. In this chapter we will explore the five concepts – *phonological awareness* (including the alphabetic principle), ***alphabet knowledge*** (including rapid naming of letters), *vocabulary* (including oral language, grammar and rapid naming of objects or colours), ***comprehension*** (taking meaning from print, concepts about print and print knowledge) and *writing* (includes writing and phonological memory) – in relation to assessment.

Phonological awareness (including the alphabetic principle)

As noted in Chapter 8, young children's **phonological awareness** develops over time (Anthony & Francis 2005) across a continuum of skills – awareness of *words*, *syllables*, *onset* and *rime*, and *phonemes* (Nicholson 2005). In an early childhood setting, children's awareness of words can be assessed in a number of ways, primarily through planned and focused observation of each child's performance during instruction, practice and play activities.

Words

When reading a familiar story, can the child match voice to print? For example: 'Point to the words as I read.'

Syllables

Can the child clap each syllable in a familiar word while saying the word? For example: 'Clap the syllables in your name. Now clap the syllables in 'hopping'.'

Alphabet knowledge: a student's knowledge of the upper- and lower-case letters (graphemes), which are used to represent the sounds (phonemes) in an alphabetic language such as English.

Comprehension: a student's ability to develop an accurate understanding of the intended meaning of oral (listening comprehension) or written language (reading comprehension).

Phonological awareness: a student's developing awareness of the sounds of language (e.g. syllables, onset and rimes, and phonemes) as they learn to read and spell words.

Onset and rime

Can the child break a syllable into its constituent onset and rime? For example: 'Say "hop"; now say /h-op/. Now tell me all the words you know that rhyme with "hop"' (e.g. 'top', 'mop' and 'drop'). You would begin with single consonant onsets and then move to consonant blends.

Phonemes

Can the child play with the separate sounds in language? A child's abilities in this critically important domain generally develop across a developmental continuum from *phoneme isolation* through to *phoneme blending*, *phoneme segmentation* and *phoneme manipulation* (Konza 2011b).

Phoneme isolation

Can the child isolate the first sound in a word? For example, 'What is the first sound in "hop"?' /h/. Can the child isolate the last sound in a word? For example, 'What is the last sound in "duck"?' /k/. Finally, can the child isolate the middle sound in a word? For example, 'What is the middle sound in "map"?' /a/. You would assess the child's ability with single consonant words with short vowels (cvc words) first and then move to words with consonant blends (ccvc and cvcc words) and words with long vowels sounds (e.g. 'meat').

Phoneme blending

Can the child listen to a sequence of phonemes (sounds) and combine them into a word? For example, 'Listen to the sounds I make and then tell me the word'. We have /rrraaannn/'ran', /piiig/'pig' and /mmmuuussst/'must'. Again, you would assess the child's ability with cvc words first and then move to ccvc and cvcc words, before assessing words with long vowels sounds.

Phoneme segmentation

Can the child break a word into its separate phonemes by sounding out and tapping each phoneme? For example, 'Listen to the sounds in "hat". Say and tap out each sound.' /h/ /a/ /t/. As before, you would assess the child's ability with cvc, ccvc, and cvcc words as well as those with long vowels sounds. Many early childhood educators and primary teachers use the 22-item Yopp-Singer Test of Phoneme Segmentation that Hallie Yopp has made available to the educational community (Yopp 1995).

Phoneme manipulation

Can the child *delete* phonemes from a spoken word? For example, 'What word do you make if you say "stop" without the /s/?' 'Top.' Can the child *add* phonemes to a spoken word? For example, 'What word do you make if you add an /s/ to "hot"?' 'Shot.' And finally, can the child *shift* and *combine* phonemes within a spoken word?

For example, 'What word do you have if you take away the /s/ at the beginning of "shoot" and move it to the end of the word?' 'Hoots.'

Alphabet knowledge (including rapid naming of letters)

As you read in Chapter 8, a child's knowledge of the phonemes and the alphabet together form the basis for the acquisition of the *alphabetic principle*, which is the fundamental understanding that speech sounds in spoken words can be represented by graphemes (the letters that represent those sounds) (Konza 2006; Moats 2000). In terms of assessment, it will be important for you, the child, and the child's family to monitor how the child is progressing in terms of: *letter name knowledge, letter sound knowledge* and, to a lesser extent, the ability to *rapidly name letters* (and digits).

Letter name knowledge

Each child needs to learn to name (and later to print) the 26 upper- and lower-case letters or, with S and s removed, 40 distinct letter shapes (Ehri & Roberts 2006). A child's knowledge can be assessed quickly at regular intervals by asking him or her to name each of the 40 letter shapes presented in random order.

Letter sound knowledge

To attain mastery of letter sound knowledge, the child faces a monumental and ongoing challenge during the early childhood years as well as across subsequent years because the English language has approximately 44 phonemes and 1200 orthographic representations or spelling variations (Konza 2006, p. 40). During the early childhood years, the best way for you to assess and monitor a child's development of letter sound knowledge is to utilise a checklist that includes the letters of the alphabet (upper and lower case) as well as the common letter combinations (e.g. initial consonant blends, consonant digraphs, double consonant endings and the silent letters) that you could expect the children to be acquiring at this stage of his or her literacy development. Konza (2006) has developed useful checklists with the initial consonants presented in the *Carnine Order* (Konza 2006, p. 41). The instructional sequence was developed by Carnine (1976) in response to the finding that young children were more successful in learning letters and sounds when lessons focused on letters with similar shapes and/or sounds were separated by time and the teaching of dissimilar letters.

Rapid naming of letters (and digits)

The ability to rapidly name letters (and also digits) has been identified as a strong predictor of reading abilities primarily because the task requirements of speeded naming of serially presented visual stimuli are not dissimilar to those involved in reading. Indeed, functional magnetic resonance imaging studies conducted by Misra

Rapid automatic naming (RAN): a student's ability to rapidly name a series of letters, digits, colours, or pictures of objects (RAN tests are most typically used by cognitive psychologists as part of a multidimensional assessment of an individual's reading and cognitive abilities).

et al. (2004) have indicated that **rapid automatic naming** (RAN) tasks (especially of letters) utilise a network of neural structures in a reader's brain that is also activated during complex reading tasks. Additional studies indicate that rapid automatised naming of letters is more strongly related to reading fluency than reading accuracy (Georgiou, Parrila & Liao 2008; Savage & Frederickson 2005). Accordingly, assessment of a child's ability to name the upper- and lower-case letters (40 letter shapes) presented in random order under timed conditions (e.g. 'Read along this line and tell me the name of as many letters you can until I say stop') can provide important information about a child's emerging mastery of letters (and digits) as well as an indicator of possible future challenges in relation to reading fluency. At this time, however, there is insufficient evidence to indicate that instruction to improve naming speed is warranted (Kirby et al. 2010).

Vocabulary (including oral language, grammar and rapid naming of objects or colours)

Vocabulary: those words known by a student – may include knowledge of the meaning of particular words (semantic knowledge) as well as the ability to read the word by sight (sight vocabulary).

As we learned in the previous chapter, the breadth and depth of a child's **vocabulary** during the early years is a strong predictor of reading comprehension during the primary and secondary school years (Neuman, Newman & Dwyer 2011). As a consequence, it is critically important to immerse children in a word-rich environment in which they have frequent informal and formal encounters with words and to monitor their acquisition of vocabulary (Blachowicz & Fisher 2011; Silverman & Crandall 2010).

Ways in which you could monitor the development of children's *receptive* (listening) and *expressive* (speaking) vocabulary, their ability to name colours and objects rapidly, and the quality of their oral language including grammar during instructional and play activities include:

- *Focused observation.* For example, you could keep individual anecdotal records in relation to a child's use of specific target words, ability to act out or illustrate a word, and to express ideas in complete sentences.

- *Oral language samples.* For example, you could tape a child when responding during shared-book reading, when retelling a story just heard or telling a story based on a wordless picture book.

- *Teacher-developed curriculum-based checklists.* You could monitor children's development for both *receptive* (e.g. Can the child point to the correct picture from an array of pictures?) and *expressive* vocabulary development (e.g. Can the child correctly label pictures representing specific words and basic concepts?) in relation to vocabulary words related to classroom themes as well as to the basic concepts of

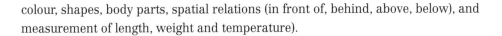

colour, shapes, body parts, spatial relations (in front of, behind, above, below), and measurement of length, weight and temperature).

Comprehension (taking meaning from print, concepts about print and print knowledge)

A young child's ability to comprehend oral language (listening comprehension) is strongly predictive of their later ability to comprehend written language, largely because language comprehension and reading comprehension share a common core. In comprehending both oral and written language, the child is seeking to understand – to take in new information, make links with prior knowledge and develop a coherent mental representation (Kendeou et al. 2005). As a consequence, it is important for early childhood educators to continue developing and monitoring children's comprehension of oral language (e.g. abilities to retell stories, recount information, make predictions and draw inferences during shared-book readings as well as during non-text-based experiences such as viewing a DVD or television program) while increasingly focusing on the development of children's skills in making meaning from texts.

In relation to comprehension of text, three essential skills that you need to develop and assess for learning during the emergent reading phase include: a child's ability to take meaning from print and illustrations (Morrow 2012, p. 203), a child's **concepts about print** (Clay 1989) and his or her developing knowledge of print (Justice & Ezell 2004).

Taking meaning from print and illustrations

Lesley Mandel Morrow, an American educator and academic, has written passionately over and over again about the need for excellent preschool programs that robustly support the development of children's language and literacy skills. Morrow (2005a, p. 8) noted that 'Children who have high quality preschool experiences with an emphasis on language and literacy are more likely to acquire strong language and literacy skills that translate into achievement in the early grades and throughout their schooling'. In particular, Morrow has been interested in the need for preschool children to learn about the many different types of text (e.g. stories, information materials, menus, signs, newspapers and environmental print – to which we could add digital texts) as well as the relationship that exists between texts and their accompanying illustrations (photos, logos, drawings, etc.).

> **Concepts about print:**
> a student's understanding of how print, texts and books work; for example, that printed words have meaning and that in English, we start reading at the top of the page, we read from left to right and from the top to bottom of a page, and that spaces and punctuation marks have meaning (Clay 2000a).

Researchers have known for many years that the ability of young children to 'read' texts (storybooks and their own dictated stories) diminishes considerably when illustrations and drawings are removed (Vukelich & Edwards 1988). More recently, psychologists in Canada have found additional evidence indicating that when young children (aged 2–5 years) are being read to, they focus on the illustrations rather than on the text. These findings remind us that early childhood educators and adults engaging in shared-book reading with young children need to make deliberate and sustained efforts to help young children see that meaning can be derived both from text and from illustrations (Evans & Saint-Aubin 2005).

Understanding concepts about print

Dame Marie Clay (1926–2007), a distinguished New Zealand educational psychologist, began developing the *Concepts about Print* (CAP) observation schedule in 1963 while conducting pre-tests for a research project examining the literacy development of preschool children (Clay 1989). In particular, Clay was interested in discovering exactly what elements young children attended to when engaging with a book and also in what developmental order children's attention for these elements developed (Clay 2000a).

Clay's observation schedule has been published as a testing program, revised and republished over the years (Clay 2005) and it continues to be widely utilised in its entirety or in teacher-made adapted short formats across numerous countries where English is the language of instruction.

In Australia the newly developed national curriculum for English has included elements of concepts about print across the early years. For example, the Foundation Year Content Descriptions of Language – Text Structure and Organisation published by the Australian Curriculum, Assessment and Reporting Authority (ACARA) indicates that children should 'Understand concepts about print and screen, including how books, film and simple digital texts work, and know some features of print, for example directionality' (ACARA 2012). The ACARA description includes a link to 'elaborations', which include learning about print (direction and spaces between words), about the construction of books and digital texts (title, author, layout and navigation) and about the simple functions of keyboard and mouse, including typing letters, scrolling, selecting icons and using a drop-down menu.

Developing print knowledge

Although the development of print knowledge appears to be a fairly discrete skill and one that children have typically mastered in a relatively short time period, we know that print knowledge is really a marker of a child's understanding of two 'big ideas' – that is, that print is a meaningful, symbolic communication system and that the symbols within the system include the alphabet as well as other conventions of print (e.g. punctuation marks and spacing) that contribute to meaning (Piasta et al. 2012). Accordingly, print knowledge is an important skill for you to assess and monitor in relation to the development of each child in your program.

Children's print knowledge has typically been developed during shared-book reading sessions in which the adult (teacher or another adult) periodically interrupts the reading to point out and discuss specific features of the print (e.g. use of capital letters and use of question marks). In order to ensure that educators were providing adequate attention to important features of print, Justice and Ezell (2004, p. 186) developed a framework of five print-referencing actions to assist adults in using appropriate 'non-verbal and verbal cues to direct a child's attention to the forms, features, and functions of written language'.

You may wish to incorporate these cues into your own shared-book reading practices and monitor the development of your children's print knowledge by means of your own simple checklist. The cues include two non-verbal references (pointing to print and tracking print) and three verbal references: questions about print (e.g. 'Do you know this letter?'), comments about print ('This says, "Go away!"'), and requests about print ('Show where the A is').

Writing (including phonological memory)

The writing skills that you could expect typically developing children to acquire during the early childhood years include emerging abilities to write their own name and perhaps those of important others (e.g. immediate family members and pets); to print letters in isolation on request (e.g. 'Write a capital or big F for me'); and to begin sounding out words and trying to spell them (e.g., 'What word would you like to write for me? Good ... sound it out again, /c – a – t/, and write it for me here').

As might be expected, a child's ability to print isolated letters upon request at the end of the preschool year is a better predictor of their subsequent spelling development than is their ability to print their name. This is because a broader knowledge of letters (and phonemic awareness) is involved in printing isolated letters upon request than in printing one's own name (Puranik, Lonigan & Kim 2011). Nonetheless, being able to print one's own name is often seen as a significant milestone by a child, the child's family and the child's teachers, and there is cause to celebrate a child's achievement in establishing written evidence of their identity. Welsch, Sullivan and Justice (2003) developed a useful scoring continuum (based on a doctoral study conducted by Evelyn Jackson Leiberman in 1985) for monitoring and communicating a child's progress in representing self (illustration) and name (print form) on paper.

In beginning to sound out and spell whole words beyond their names, children are demonstrating numerous emerging skills in a highly complex domain. Spelling requires the mastery and integration of a number of critical skills, including letter knowledge, phonological awareness, specific phonemic awareness (especially phoneme isolation and blending), knowledge of letter–sound (phoneme–grapheme) relationships, as well as phonological memory and working memory (e.g. holding in memory the letters that need to be printed).

A powerful way in which to assess, monitor and communicate a child's development in writing abilities (including spelling and all the essential foundation skills mentioned above) is to file a child's illustrated and dictated (later self-scribed) stories, journal entries and functional writing (e.g. wish lists and letters) over the course of a year. A portfolio containing such samples vividly illustrates a child's developing literacy skills as well as their increasing ability to manipulate tools and illustrate their work.

Sulzby (1985) suggested that children's writing develops across six broad stages including:

- drawing
- scribbling
- making letter-like forms
- making learned units or letter strings
- invented spelling
- conventional spelling.

Comparing a child's writing samples with such a continuum or similar frameworks (e.g. the Writing Skills Checklist developed by Morrow in 2005b) will assist you to monitor a child's development and communicate your observations with the child and family members (Morrow 2007, p. 193).

Children take great pride in their portfolios and enjoy seeing the progress they have made in printing and writing across various genres, such as narrative writing, informational writing, functional writing, interactive writing, independent writing, journal writing, and response writing (Morrow 2007, pp. 184–9). They also enjoy 'reading' the notes and observations of their family members and teachers that can be incorporated into their portfolios. With support, children enjoy setting themselves goals and evaluating their progress with their parents and teachers.

Conclusion

This chapter has reviewed literature on effective assessment, particularly in relation to young children's development of literacy skills before, during and after the transition to school. The chapter has also considered principles of effective literacy assessment, which are to be found in New Zealand and Australian policy and curriculum documents as well as the seminal work of the National Association for the Education of Young Children (NAEYC) and the International Reading Association (IRA), *Learning to Read and Write: Developmentally Appropriate Practices for Young Children* (Neuman, Copple & Bredekamp 2000). Following a consideration of the principles of effective literacy assessment, this chapter has reviewed purposes, types and general methods of assessment, including the value of portfolios for monitoring and providing evidence of individual progress to children and their families. The chapter concluded with a review of ways in which to assess the skills known to be precursors and/or predictors of later success in literacy (McLachlan 2010). In doing so, the chapter has linked back to the previous chapter, '"Sound" Foundations for Learning Literacy'. This approach was taken in order to re-emphasise the critical links between instruction and assessment for learning. In the next chapter on literacy assessment in this text (Chapter 12), we will consider assessment of the essential foundation skills for literacy development during the junior school years.

Reflective questions

1. In your experience of early childhood settings, how do teachers usually assess children's literacy development?

2. Do you think the ways of assessing (and recording assessment information) that you have observed focus adequately on the essential foundation skills of reading and writing?

3. Do you think the ways that teachers usually assess children's literacy learning could be strengthened in any way?

4. Why is it important to focus your assessment for learning on the evidentially based precursor skills when monitoring young children's literacy acquisition?

5. Finally, why is it important to include the child and the family in the assessment for learning process?

Part 3

Literacy learning in the primary school

Chapter 10

The first year of primary school: building on foundations

Chapter objectives

1. To examine major issues and problems experienced by young children and their parents during the transition to school.
2. To identify specific strategies that you, the teacher (preschool or primary), can adopt to prepare and support children and parents as they face the many changes involved in the transition process.
3. To provide a framework for the construction of the literacy program in the first year of schooling.

This chapter examines how continuity from the early childhood setting to the primary school setting can be supported. It reviews research on the discontinuities that children can experience during transition to school and the research evidence on the most effective ways to avoid major mismatches in pedagogy and expectations. The issues of transition from early childhood education to primary school are explored and recommendations for the construction of the initial reading and writing program provided.

The importance of the transition to primary school

The **transition** from early childhood education, childcare and home settings to the primary school is a significant period in a child's life and the experience can be very exciting and, at times, daunting for the child and his or her parents. This period of transition marks an important milestone and a new phase in a child's life. Beginning school marks an era of growing independence for the child as he or she embarks upon the journey from preschool to primary.

Transition:
a period during which change takes place, involving moving from one stage to another.

Exploring issues during the transition from early childhood to primary

A growing body of educational research highlights the importance of the transition to school as having a lasting impact on a child's confidence and attitude towards school/learning and on their social success (Fabian & Dunlop, 2007). This is a critical period of adjustment for children and change is often discussed in terms of **continuity** and **discontinuity** between the two settings (Hill et al. 2002). Di Santo and Berman (2011) argue that discontinuity during this phase of life is unavoidable and that adults should support children by seeking their views throughout the process of transition. Peters (2010) reassures us that allowing children to gain familiarity with school expectations will assist in providing continuity in their transition experience. Fabian (2002) identified three main areas of discontinuity: physical, social and philosophical variables that include teaching practices. The transition period presents a number of changes and challenges for children and their families that relate to the physical, social and cultural environment. Let's briefly discuss some of these aspects of the transition before we focus on supporting children's literacy development during this time.

Continuity:
continuous, connected, smooth movement or sequence.

Discontinuity:
lack of connection, disjointed, interrupted.

The child

In the process of beginning school, the young child is led to identify him- or herself colloquially as 'a school girl or school boy'. During this period, the child's self-concept evolves from being an individual with particular interests, skills and knowledge, to becoming a member of a new social group: the primary school (Fabian & Dunlop 2007; Dockett & Perry 2006). Surprisingly, it doesn't take long for new school children to learn to state, upon request, which primary school they attend and who their teacher is.

Be aware that some children will be transitioning to school from public or private preschool environments, and some from childcare settings that have an integrated preschool program (known in Australia as 'long day care'), while others may be transitioning from their home environment, with school as their first institutionalised educational experience. In light of these differences and the fact that each child is an individual, coming from their own unique family environment and community, it becomes clear that the schoolteacher's role in supporting transition into school is no easy task.

New-entrant child writing

The new learning environment

'Transition to school is not just about the classroom, but about the whole school environment' (Bartram 2010, pp. 10–11). Although some parents get anxious about their child beginning school, most have the advantage of some familiarity with school environments and processes by drawing upon their own past schooling experiences. It is very important that teachers provide parents with ample information prior to beginning school, as schools and their cultures are likely to have changed since the child's parents attended school. As adults we often become blinded to the peculiarities of the school environment, forgetting that our own familiarity with aspects of school environments such as fences, buildings, timetables and routines may be something strange and unfamiliar to young children.

In their study of 100 children beginning school, Hill et al. (2002) identified a group of boys who had difficulty adjusting from preschool routines into primary school routines. They struggled to organise their work and manage their belongings and they missed the freedom that they had at preschool to select their own tasks and move around the room.

As well as adapting to changes in the physical environment, children soon become aware that primary school is pervaded by many routines and protocols compared to the early childhood centre or their home. Examples include:

- sitting on the mat for extended periods of time (listening to a story, explanation or instructions)
- raising your hand and waiting for your turn to speak
- reading quietly
- sitting still at tables to draw and write independently
- doing a daily array of teacher-directed activities.

Let's briefly consider what a timetable from a school day might look like. View Figure 10.1 (over the page).

Note the reference to 'school care' in Figure 10.1. An increase in the number of working parents has resulted in some parents paying for before- and after-school childcare services. When you calculate how many hours children spend in school and school care you begin to realise that they could be spending most of their waking hours in the school environment. You are likely to become a significant adult in the life of a child and this highlights the importance of your role and responsibility as his or her teacher.

Listed below are some aspects of schooling that children may find confusing:

- Bell ringing – What makes that noise? What does it mean?
- Why are there fences and gates everywhere?
- Why is it so busy and crowded?
- Where can I cross the road safely? Who is that person at the crossing with a whistle?
- Assembly – What is it? Why is it important?
- Who are the other teachers?
- What takes place in the other classrooms?

You will note from Figure 10.1 that the school bell rings many times throughout the day. Pupils and adults who can read the time on clocks soon become familiar with the purpose of each bell, but what of the child who is a new entrant to

TIME	EVENT	DURATION
7–8.50am	Before hours school care	1–2 hours
8.50am	Outside time	10 minutes
	BELL RINGS	
9.00am	Line-up	2 hours
	Class organisation	
	Literacy	
	BELL RINGS	
11.00–11.30am	Morning recess (playtime)	30 minutes
	BELL RINGS	
11.30am	Numeracy	1 hour
12.30pm		
	BELL RINGS	
1pm	Lunchtime	2 hours
	BELL RINGS	
2pm	Class	
	Specialist	
3.30pm	School is finished	
	BELL RINGS	
3.30–6.30pm	After hours school care OR Go home	1–3 hours

Figure 10.1 *A typical school-day timetable*
Note: Some schools have an additional 10-minute afternoon recess.

school? Remember, the same bell tone is rung at different times of the day, to signify different things. How can young children differentiate one bell ringing from another?

Peters (2010) highlighted the importance of explicitly explaining school routines to children beginning school, describing an incident where young children were confused by the multiple bell ringing and consequently went without food for much of that day. Teachers and schools need to inform children and apply strategies that ensure these sorts of misunderstandings are avoided. Some schools play three minutes of music during outdoor breaks to indicate that it is time to stop playing, go to the toilet or get a drink, as needed, and to line up in the designated place for their class ready for the teacher to escort them indoors.

In their research on transition, Briggs and Potter (1995) reported that toileting and washing hands were two major sources of anxiety for children beginning school. Consider this list of differences between the toilets in the two settings.

EARLY CHILDHOOD SETTING	PRIMARY SCHOOL SETTING
Unisex	Gender-segregated
Few toilets	Many toilets
Child-sized toilets	Full-sized toilets
Close proximity	Some distance away
Open plan design	Enclosed walls and doors, urinary wall
Adult view and support available	No adult assistance available
Available at any time	Available at specified times and requests

It is no wonder the decision to use the toilet can be a stressful one for young school entrants. Children beginning school should be inducted to become familiar with the toilets, the protocols and procedures for requesting a toilet visit and for getting changed into spare clothing when toileting mishaps occur to avoid accidents, upset and embarrassment.

Social challenges

Children face a number of social challenges during transition as they are expected to become more independent, to interact with unfamiliar children and adults, and to understand and abide by social and school rules (Margetts 2002; Fabian & Dunlop 2007). Fabian and Dunlop (2007) identified a number of areas that can be sources of difficulty and worry for new school children and these included:

- leaving old friends behind
- making new friends
- becoming a member of a new group
- coping among crowds of children and increased noise levels
- relating to older children
- receiving less adult attention due to increased staff-to-student ratios.

A growing body of research suggests that:

- children's views on learning and the nature of their social relationships during transition may be related to their future academic achievement (Gordon, O'Toole & Whitman 2008; Li-Grining et al. 2010)

- forming positive relationships relates to children's sense of wellbeing and happiness (Lippman, Moore & McIntosh 2011)
- children's sense of wellbeing increases when they
  - have a playground area designated for their age group
  - are encouraged to choose and direct their own play
  - are provided with support and encouragement from a trusted adult (Department of Education and Children's Services 2008).

As children are inducted into the primary school community it is important to be aware that it may be the first time that they have been expected to become familiar with and relate to a large number of adults without the presence of their parents or guardians. Consider the following list of adults that children may be expected to interact with throughout the school week:

- their classroom teacher
- other classroom teachers
- specialist teachers (e.g. art, physical education, music/drama, computer, language other than English, religious instruction)
- integration aides
- the principal and vice-principal
- parent volunteers (e.g. classroom, canteen)
- office staff
- the school crossing attendant
- guests and visitors.

As you can imagine, there will be a lot of names to remember!

The majority of research studies about children's transition into school have been conducted from the perspectives of early childhood and primary teachers and/or parents, with little regard for children's voices. A recent study of Canadian preschoolers by Di Santo and Berman (2011) considered children's (three- and four-year-olds') perceptions about starting school, focusing on aspects of continuity and discontinuity. Their study revealed three main themes that underpinned children's perceptions and expectations:

1. *Play versus academic activities and homework*. The children expected to be able to 'play 'at school just as they had at preschool, with only a few indicating that they were aware that 'play' might be somewhat different in the school context. Most children assumed the school curriculum would be similar to the play-based curriculum that they had experienced and they wanted to be able to paint, do puzzles, have circle time and play outside. Only a few children spoke

of expecting to do academic work in the form of homework and they hoped to receive assistance from parents and teachers.

2. *Getting bigger but still needing help.* Many children spoke about themselves 'getting bigger' in terms of their age and physical size, but despite this they still had expectations that their parents and teachers would help them with many of their personal care skills, putting on jackets, tying shoes etc.

3. *Rules.* Most of the children believed that it would be very important for them to learn the school rules.

Di Santo and Berman's (2011) study revealed that children do begin to develop their own ideas about beginning school and they recommend that children be viewed as co-constructors of knowledge and be given the opportunity to contribute to the planning of transition practices.

It is idealistic to think that we can follow 'a magical recipe' that has all the ingredients to guarantee a successful transition into school; it is just not that simple. We cannot define the perfect pathway to a 'successful transition in school' as the notion of what success looks like or is; it is complex and varies from individual to individual and from context to context. Peters (2010) identified aspects of successful and unsuccessful transitions and argued it is more useful to identify a range of key areas that parents and educators need to address:

* belonging, wellbeing and feeling 'suitable' at school
* recognition and acknowledgement of culture
* respectful, reciprocal relationships
* engagement in learning
* learning dispositions and identity as a learner
* positive teacher expectations
* building on funds of knowledge from early childhood education and home.

Each of these areas is important; however, the final point explicitly states the need for school teachers to work together with early childhood teachers and with the child's family. Developed extensively in previous chapters of this text, this point is argued further below.

Reflection 10.1

List each of Peters' (2010) key areas to address and then brainstorm how you would tackle each of these areas if designing a transition program.

So what can early childhood and primary school teachers do to support children during the process of transition? Let us now consider what educators can do individually and collectively to assist the child in the transition to primary school.

Educators from different settings such as long day care centres, kindergartens and schools, have a lot to contribute to children's positive start to school. They develop strong relationships with children and their families and bring professional knowledge and experience about children's learning and development (DEEWR 2009b, p. 5).

The important role of the early childhood educator in the transition process

Having spent at least a year with the transitioning child, the early childhood teacher develops important knowledge about the child as an individual, a family member and a member of the preschool group. The teacher is familiar with many of the child's likes, dislikes, fears, strengths and challenges and his or her social, emotional and physical development and learning capabilities. It is important that the teacher ensures there is a means by which to share this knowledge with the child's future primary school teacher. Providing insight into the child's learning and capabilities prior to school attendance will assist the school teacher in planning to further engage the child in his or her learning in the school environment. As Margetts (2000, p. 10) states:

Preschool child reading

How well a child adjusts to school can affect their future school progress. The identification of the skills and behaviours that indicate adjustment can assist early childhood staff in identifying children at risk of maladjustment, and in the implementation of appropriate strategies.

Sharing information about the child and his or her learning

Although logical, sharing information between the early childhood and primary school spheres about the transitioning child is a relatively new process in many parts of the world. In some places the onus for organising this process is upon individual teachers, while in others it is organised at a departmental level. In 2009 in

Victoria, Australia, for instance, the state government introduced an initiative called 'Transition: A Positive Start to School'. This involved the issuing of policy guidelines, a kit for every early learning centre, professional learning for early childhood teachers about transition to school, and the mandatory introduction of the use of 'Transition Learning and Development Statement'. The Transition Statement is a document about the child's learning and development which is completed by the early childhood teacher towards the end of the child's final year of preschool and then shared with the child's parents and future school teacher. It identifies the child's achievements and also any learning difficulties, disabilities and developmental delays that may need to be addressed early. The Transition Statement enables teachers to support children's continuity of learning and development as they transition into school (DEECD 2009c).

Although completing Transition Statements can be time consuming, an evaluative study (DEECD 2011a) confirmed that 96 per cent of schoolteachers read them and that 91 per cent considered all sections of the statements as valuable for preparing children for the transition. The Victorian Early Years Learning and Development Framework (DEECD 2009c) proposes that the statements support effective transitions as they are a tool for parents, children, and early childhood and primary teachers to begin the process of development of communicating and sharing valuable information and knowledge about the child.

Strategies and ideas for preparing for transition to school

Early childhood teachers play a key role in preparing children socially and emotionally for the transition to school and there are a range of strategies and activities that they can implement in order to prepare a child for the pending transition to school. They can:

- provide parents with information and resources about transition (e.g. weekly newsletter entries, an information session, conversations)
- talk to children about school and the similarities and differences
- ask the children how they feel about transition
- determine what the children know or want to know about school, and whether there is anything they are concerned about
- read and discuss stories about transition to school and school experiences
- include 'school' props within the room (e.g. dress-ups, school bags, lunch boxes and writing materials)
- provide a range of interesting reading and writing materials as part of the daily play-based program

- invite guest speakers (e.g. students, teachers and principals)
- support children's general wellbeing, self-help and social skills
- ask children to bring their own lunchboxes and water bottles to establish the habit of independent management of food
- encourage habits of regular, consistent attendance (Margetts 2002)
- introduce show and tell/share time in a manner similar to school
- allow children to borrow books
- introduce behaviours and protocols common to schools, such as lining up quietly, raising one's hand to indicate a turn to speak, packing one's own bag, and group time.

The 'group time' strategy

Throughout the primary school day, teachers address the class as a whole group and expect children to be able to sit still, listen and remain focused for extended periods. Group time may involve explaining an activity or discussing an issue or event, and it often leads to opportunities for class discussions where children are expected to share their ideas and experiences with their teacher and peers. The rules for contribution are clarified – for example, one speaker at a time, raise your hand if you want a turn or sit in a circle with legs crossed and pass the 'talking stick', 'teddy bear' or item that indicates it is your turn to speak (the latter is a way of ensuring that all children contribute to a class discussion).

By engaging in group time sessions you are preparing the children with many of the language and literacy skills that they will need in school, including speaking, listening, turn-taking, concentrating, understanding, seeking clarification, asking questions and cooperating.

The important role of the primary school teacher in the transition process

The introduction of transition programs

Many schools specifically plan and implement a transition program by which to induct preschool-aged children into the first year of schooling. These programs vary according to the school's interests, goals and community and should be tailored to suit the incoming students. In order to promote continuity, it is important for schools to work in partnership with local early childhood education providers and to share knowledge about the children and about each other's practices. The transition program will commonly include brief activity sessions conducted at the school for the potential school entrants to attend towards the end of their final preschool year. The focus of these events varies but may include story time, art, sing-along or picnics as activities. The organised visits provide children and parents with opportunities to visit and familiarise themselves with the school and to ask questions of staff. The value of these transition programs is becoming evident in research, with Margetts (2002, p. 13) finding that 'Children's participation in greater numbers of transition activities reliably predicted higher levels of confidence, self-confidence, self-control, overall social skills, and academic competence'. Similarly, Westcott et al. (2003) found that children entered school with greater levels of confidence when they had met their teachers, had some familiarity with the playground and experienced similar classroom activities prior to their first day of school.

Strategies and ideas for preparing for transition to school

Primary school teachers can adopt a number of strategies to support children and their families in the transition process to school. They can:

- plan the transition program with local preschool teachers (e.g. organise visits, fun sessions for children to attend)
- negotiate a way in which the preschool teacher will be able to provide you with some information about the child and his or her learning (e.g. Learning Statements or portfolios)
- visit children at their kindergarten
- plan non-threatening initial visits for the children (e.g. during story time and thematic literacy activities, and at learning centres)
- provide parents and children with as many opportunities for orientation at the school as possible
- invite families from local early childhood centres to attend information sessions, open days, transition activities and so on
- establish effective communication with parents and children to discuss differences in expectations and perspectives of children transitioning to school
- provide parents and children with information about the school (e.g. goals, vision, expectations, school grounds, facilities, routines)
- once school begins, be sure to allow children sufficient time to pack up and also to eat before going outside
- use a 'communication book' for each child by which to communicate with parents daily through writing (school notices can be pasted into this book)

- ease the children into the school program over the first few weeks (e.g. shorter days/week, smaller class size; also introduce supportive programs such as a buddy program in which new entrants can develop a positive rapport with older children).

Dockett and Perry (2006) provide specific guidelines for developing effective transition programs using documented goals and evaluations and recommend that teachers and parents communicate and work together.

In summary, experiencing some discontinuity during transition is inevitable; however, if we support children in becoming familiar with school expectations and practices they are more likely to have a positive transition experience (Di Santo & Berman 2011; Peters 2010) and become happy and confident, ready to learn and grow (Hill et al. 2002).

Now that we have discussed aspects of the transition process in general, it is time to consider how to support children's development in the area of language and literacy during this transition period.

Preschool child drawing

Children's ongoing language and literacy development – a crucial period

Dispelling the myth that learning to read and write starts in primary school and not before is no easy task. For many, the primary school is viewed as the place where formal instruction in reading and writing begins for children. A broader view of literacy and its development, as *emergent*, means that literacy skills and

Concurrently: occurring at the 'same' time.

Interdependently: reliant or dependent upon one another.

Emergent literacy: the early period of literacy development that begins from birth and continues into the preschool years. Viewing literacy development as emergent recognises that literacy develops over a long period of time.

knowledge emerge and develop over time, **concurrently** and **interdependently** (Whitehurst & Lonigan 1998; De Temple, Dickenson & Tabors 2001). Johns (2010, pp. 30–1) advocates that literacy develops 'from the result of our teaching (in the vast majority of cases), but builds from the critical brain capacities we nurture and shape in the critical years before formal education begins'. In this light, literacy learning can be viewed as a developmental continuum, with its origins beginning from birth, or arguably, even in utero.

Just as children arrive at preschool with a diverse range of abilities, skills, knowledge and life experiences, so too do they arrive at the primary school with as much diversity in their literacy development (Makin, Jones Diaz & McLachlan 2007). It would not be uncommon in the first year of schooling to have one child who can read a book, some children who can write their name and others who can barely recognise letters of the alphabet, let alone, write them. Elliott (2005) cautions that learning gaps evident upon school entry tend to broaden for most children as they continue through primary school. Similarly, Hales (2006, p. 45) warns that 'the first three years of formal schooling are a critical period for literacy development, with research showing that children who experience significant difficulties in literacy learning in early childhood will most likely establish a continuing problem'.

Ideally, the primary school teacher will support the child's literacy learning by *building on* the literacy foundations that have been partially developed through prior experience. Areas important to **emergent literacy** include: oral language; speaking, listening and understanding; and, more particularly, alphabet knowledge, phonological awareness, vocabulary and comprehension prior to school entry. Furthermore, the primary school teacher should seek to support continuity between the child's home and early childhood centre literacy learning and the school. But how are we to go about finding out this information? As discussed in previous chapters, early childhood teachers, primary school teachers and parents are perfectly positioned to provide opportunities and environments that promote literacy development and that is why we need to work together.

Recommendations for the construction of the initial reading and writing program

Although educational settings often prescribe curriculum, policies and assessment practices, it is still up to the primary school teacher to construct a literacy program that supports children's development in this area. There are a number of important areas that need to be considered when developing a literacy program for young children; these include building on the child's existing funds of knowledge; building partnerships between the teacher, the child and his or her family; developing records of the child's literacy development; considering key understandings about children's literacy learning in the early years of school; and providing engaging strategies and activities to support children's learning. Each of these areas will be discussed in turn.

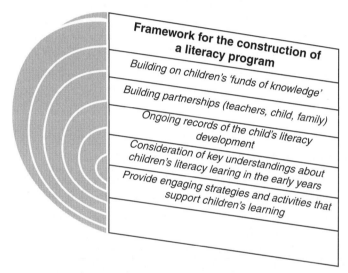

Figure 10.2 *Framework for the construction of a literacy program*

Building on the child's funds of knowledge

As mentioned earlier, it is important that early childhood and primary teachers share information prior to the child's transition. During transition, it is equally important for the primary school teacher to begin building a positive rapport with the child and his or her family. As Peters (2010) suggests, learning should be built upon children's **funds of knowledge** from early childhood education and home. What are funds of knowledge and why are they important?

> **Funds of knowledge:** unique knowledge that a person gains from his or her family, community, cultural background and experiences.

The phrase 'funds of knowledge' was coined by Moll et al. (1992) to describe the body of knowledge that an individual accumulates and develops, including that which is learned from social and cultural contexts. Their argument was that 'teachers rarely draw on the resources of the "funds of knowledge" of the child's world outside the context of the classroom' (1992, p. 134) and that teachers therefore work with a distorted, shallow view of the child as a learner. By excluding or discounting knowledge that the children have acquired from home (or other sources outside of school), we are failing to value the child as an individual and the knowledge that is meaningful to him or her. Tapping into a child's funds of knowledge can not only motivate and engage the child with the classroom activity, but also allows him or her to make meaningful connections between the prior knowledge and the subject matter.

Scenario 10.1

You decide that your class will engage in diary writing every Monday morning so that the children will all have something to write about: the weekend. Some children have a range of exciting outings and events to report and others are content to report about fun had during daily events such as shopping, cooking and playing. But Nathan has never written anything and you are beginning to grow concerned. When asked what he did on the weekend he routinely replies, 'Nothing'. You ask him to draw what happened on the weekend, but he doesn't respond. He tells you that his parents work on the weekends while he stays home with his grandmother. He is not motivated to write about this.

How can you tap into his funds of knowledge?

You telephone Nathan's parents and soon find out that although Nathan spends a lot of time with his grandmother doing household chores, he has a keen interest in dogs and skateboards. You are told that Nathan and his grandmother recently selected a puppy for him to adopt from the local dog pound.

Next week, during diary writing, you ask Nathan if he has any pets and his eyes light up as he begins to talk and laugh about his pet puppy, Sparky. Nathan explains that he is teaching Sparky a range of tricks, the first of which is not to chew people's shoes. Nathan also plans to teach Sparky how to ride a skateboard. Before you know it, Nathan is keen to write about Sparky and is busy drawing pictures to match. In the coming weeks Nathan writes about the time he spends with his grandmother and Sparky and other information such as how to take care of pets and train them.

Thomson's (2002) adaptation of the notion of funds of knowledge asks us to consider that each child is carrying a 'virtual school bag'. Although invisible to the human eye, these bags contain different knowledge, narratives, interests and understandings; however, only some children get the opportunity to open their school bags and draw upon their home- and community-based knowledge during school. In this manner, teachers can unknowingly be favouring some children and their funds of knowledge and disadvantaging children whose social, cultural and economic backgrounds do not match the mores and practices of the school. What is important is that teachers understand 'where the child is at' in terms of his or her learning and then build upon the different cultural and social knowledge that the child has in his or her virtual schoolbag. To ignore children's backgrounds and knowledge would be to implement what Freire termed a 'pedagogy of oppression' (Freire 1972).

Freire (1972) was well aware of the potential disadvantage that a mismatch of home and school literacy understandings creates and he has advocated for many years that literacy is not neutral, that it is socially and politically construed, used to empower and disempower; it is a tool for taking action in the world. His work pleaded for teachers to ensure that children could be empowered by valuing and drawing upon their existent developing literacy knowledge and skills. This view is well supported by research in the field of literacy where children of varied sociocultural and socio-economic status have been found to be disenfranchised by the teachers' pedagogical teaching style and the types of knowledge that they privilege (Heath 1983; McNaughton 2002).

Freire's main argument that teachers should be mindful that literacy is:

- not neutral
- socially and politically construed
- used to empower and disempower
- a tool for taking action in the world (Freire & Macedo 2000).

Hill et al. (2002) conducted a study of 100 children beginning school and followed their literacy development up to the age of 10. They found that:

> in many cases the language, social and textual practices of the home and the school were similar, creating an easy connection between home and school values and attitudes. For some children these connections did not exist, making it difficult for them to fit in easily into established ways of behaving, speaking and interacting with the sorts of texts valued in school (2002, p. 7).

They also noticed that some parents mistrusted the school's diagnosis of learning difficulties or disability in their child and were concerned that teachers judged them as having poor parenting skills, while others felt unwelcomed in schools because of the unspoken valuing of certain forms of cultural and social capital over than others.

Building partnerships between the teacher, child and the family

Valuing children's funds of knowledge as an important factor in supporting literacy learning stems from a sociocultural view of literacy development and the understanding that children will build their learning upon their prior learning experiences. In this light, the need to respect and value the views of the child's parents as the child's first educators is a given and an important part of building partnerships with parents.

Teachers who respect their students' home languages and cultures, and who understand the crucial role they play in the lives of the children and families, can help children make the necessary transition in ways that do not undercut the role that parent and families must continue to play in their education and development (Wong Fillmore & Snow 2000, p. 12.)

The importance of parental practices and children's exposure to literacy-oriented activities to children's emergent literacy is well supported (Raban & Nolan 2005; Zajicek-Farber 2010). Raban and Nolan's study of preschool literacy practices identified that:

Parents need relevant information about ways to enhance literacy experiences at home and this information needs to be culturally sensitive and easily accessible, as literacy still stands as one of the best chances for individual upward mobility (Raban & Nolan 2005, p. 296).

It is thus very important that early childhood and primary teachers identify and acknowledge a family's prior and current literacy practices and then work in partnership with the parents to support the child's literacy development by discussing and adopting a range of effective strategies. Together they should create social contexts in which children can have opportunities to participate in developing reading, writing, and oral language. Please refer to Chapters 4, 7 and 8 for further information about this. The teacher's task, therefore, is to find out what children know, to build upon this to develop meaningful and purposeful literacy experiences, and to monitor progress over time using a robust range of measures.

Literacy assessment: developing records of the child's literacy development

The challenge for any teacher of a new group of students is to 'get to know' the students as individuals – their likes/dislikes and strengths/weaknesses – and to identify how they learn best and what they need to learn next. As stated previously, teachers should take the time to receive information from parents and the early childhood educator about the child and his or her language and literacy development. This may take the form of a parent–teacher interview early in the year or the use of tools such as the ORIM framework (outlined in Chapter 4) that identify parents' and children's home literacy practices. Following this, the teacher should begin to adopt other strategies including assessment, as a means of finding out where the child is at with specific aspects of literacy.

A common practice in the first year of primary school is to engage children in a range of pre-tests to identify their pre-existing knowledge in areas of literacy. The activities are usually quite simple and relate to the following:

- alphabetic knowledge
- letter recognition (capitals and lower case)
- knowledge of letter names
- phonemic awareness
- phonics
- name writing
- concepts about print (Marie Clay's notion)
- word recognition.

Once you are given the role of teaching children in the first year of primary school, it is important that you familiarise yourself with the policies and practices that apply to your school and context. Your school may have purchased existing resources or developed templates to use, which will save you time and money.

Many of the literacy assessments undertaken in the first year of schooling include or are based on the foundational work of renowned Professor Marie Clay of New Zealand, whose work in early literacy assessment has had a global impact upon literacy in the early years (Clay 1979, 2005). In New Zealand, teachers commonly use the School Entry Assessment (SEA) assessment kit to assess children's understanding in the areas of oral language, early literacy and numeracy of new entrants. The kit is available in English, and in Maori as 'Aro Matawai Urunga-a-Kura' (AKA) (Davies 2001). The children are given tasks that provide them with opportunities to demonstrate their skills and understanding while the teacher keenly engages in detailed observations of the class. These assessments are used to establish what children already know on arrival. Many teachers have found that it is also valuable to later implement the Six-Year Net test as a means of diagnosing literacy difficulties. This is an observation survey which largely involves teachers observing students after one year of schooling to identify if they are making expected progress in literacy. Importantly, these tools help teachers identify children who are in need of extra help and support, allowing intervention strategies to be employed before children fall further behind their peers.

A similar process takes place in Australia, involving initial assessment and reassessment after one year to identify those in need of intervention. In Victoria the use of the online 'Prep Entry Assessment' is mandated. This incorporates a parent–teacher interview and an online literacy interview/assessment administered to individual students, whereby the teacher observes and records the child's responses to a series of online activities. The parent–teacher interview (DEECD 2011b) focuses upon the following:

- the child's preschool/child-care experiences, what they have already learned
- level of independence

- ability to socialise with children of various ages
- languages spoken and understood
- particular health and medical requirements
- family events that may be affect the child (e.g. births, deaths, separation and divorce).

This assessment incorporates an online interview to assess children's skills in reading, writing, speaking and listening in the early years of schooling, from new entrants up to and including Year 2. Children are reassessed in Year 1 to identify those in need of intervention.

As a proactive approach towards minimising the number of reading difficulties, primary school teachers are advised to notice, recognise and respond to the predictors of reading achievement (McLachlan 2008; Wong Fillmore & Snow 2000). Snow, Burns and Griffin (1998) identified an array of early reading accomplishments that primary school teachers should focus upon in an attempt to prevent reading difficulties in young children which are well recognised by other researchers (Meiers & Khoo 2006). These key accomplishments include:

- the alphabetic principle
- reading sight words
- reading words by mapping speech sounds to parts of words
- achieving fluency
- comprehension.

Many school-entry assessment tasks used today to reveal children's understandings and literacy practices on arrival at school involve activities related to:

- environmental print
- phonemic awareness
- book orientation
- retell – the ability to describe what the story was about in one's own words
- concepts of print
- others (e.g. writing, making meaning from text).

A recently conducted review of research literature on literacy assessment for the first three years of schooling (Care et al. 2011) highlighted the following important points:

- All children benefit from explicit instruction in code breaking (Snow, Burns & Griffin 1998), but it must be noted that this ability to decode does not necessarily lead to understanding the meaning of text (Stahl & Yaden 2004).
- Phonological awareness and phonics are decoding skills that need to be taught early.

- Language skills need to be taught, including vocabulary building and comprehension strategies.
- Comprehension develops as children gain exposure to more words and gain knowledge and experience with texts.
- Developing 'fluency' is important. This can be explicitly taught and assessed or developed through the increasing development of decoding and comprehension skills (Westwood 2009).

If you are working in a rural school or a school that does not have policies for school-entry assessments in place, you may choose to purchase or even develop your own templates to be used. For more information about assessment of literacy, please refer to Chapters 9 and 12.

Figure 10.3 *Child's alphabet chart*

Key understandings about children's literacy learning in the early years of school

A major study by Hill et al. (2002) of the literacy development of 100 children from pre-school to primary transition until 10 years of age produced the following findings.

1. Most children make substantial growth in literacy

Although children's literacy developed over the 10-year period, it was also noted that children who were not achieving were 'overwhelmingly from schools serving families living in poverty' (Hill et al.2002, p. 4).

2. Children take different pathways and have different patterns of growth in literacy development

'Not all children follow predictable trajectories based on early literacy assessments' (Hill et al. 2002, pp. 5–6). Late starters and 'catching up' depended on economic and cultural capital and the joint efforts of the teacher, parent and child. Not all 'early starters' kept their accelerated progress as the assessments delved deeper to include not just reading aloud, but also critical thinking and so on.

3. Home and community experiences influence children's literacy development

'Within the school communities the many diverse families had a range of relationships with the school and its staff. Several parents experienced significant differences, misunderstandings and communication breakdowns about their children. Families and communities had differing views about schooling' (Hill et al. 2002, p. 7).

4. 'Teaching that made a difference'

Teaching practices that were based upon teachers' philosophical and ideological understandings about the purposes of literacy were more important and effective than relying upon particular teaching strategies or prepackaged curriculum. These included measures such as adapting practice to meet the needs of students; using data-driven, diagnostic and responsive teaching to make a difference; developing a positive teacher–student rapport; and responded to children's work and views.

Supportive literacy strategies and activities

As significant adults in the child's life, parents and teachers are role models who impact upon the child's literacy beliefs, values and practices. Teachers' literacy practices stem from their values and beliefs (Ohi 2007) and so it is important during your teacher preparation to develop and confirm the underpinning beliefs that you have about literacy development (see Chapters 2 and 3).

Reflection 10.2

Pause for a moment and reflect upon the following questions about what literacy learning and development mean to you. Write down your responses.
- What is literacy?
- How does it develop?
- What can you do to support children's literacy development?

Although not exhaustive, Table 10.1 provides a range of ideas, activities and strategies that teachers can implement in their classrooms. The categories include the five key concepts mentioned earlier in Chapter 8.

Children's literature can be a rich resource for educators as they support young children's learning to understand the world around them. With this in mind, remember

Table 10.1 *Engaging strategies and activities*

Alphabet knowledge & Phonological awareness	• Arrange sing-songs (Murdoch 2002). • Recite and read rhymes and poems. • Be selective in choosing educational software. • Hold games – e.g. Bingo, I Spy, memory game (match pictures and letters). • Read books.
Vocabulary	• Scaffold children's speech as needed. • Introduce new vocabulary. • Encourage extension. • Read, read, read! (Justice & Pullen 2003). • Arrange cloze activities. • Show and tell. • Provide many opportunities to talk.
Build comprehension of what was read	• Retell what has been read. • Discuss it. • Write about it. • Follow instructions that have been read. • Adopt a Dialogic reading style/ask questions (Justice & Pullen 2003). • Allow for reading, songs, rhymes and games. • Read for a range of purposes: information, interest, fun, relaxation. • Read a range of genres: narrative
Writing	• Introduce name cards for the children to copy their names from and to be written on each piece of work. • Use language-experience strategies. • Model writing techniques. • Provide scaffolding for writing. • Create class and individual wordbanks. • Make individual and class books. • Write and draw to retell what was read. • Write for a range of purposes. Express thoughts, feelings and ideas, report/retell of experiences. • Write in a range of genres – utilise diary writing, letters cards, recipes, invitations, lists, poems, songs, etc.
Handwriting	• Model correct pencil grip. • Use a range of implements and a range of surfaces. • Promote the appropriate script. • Practise tracing. • Encourage writing.

that it is important to also explicitly teach children to care for books and materials used. All classrooms would do well to have a reading corner or area where a range of reading materials (genres, types, formats) are kept and are available for use during classwork and during periods of free time. The area should make children feel physically comfortable and be kept clean. Book choice is incredibly important and teachers should be mindful of selecting appropriate reading materials considering children's engagement in terms of length, topic, illustrations, style, design and content. Ensure that you read and evaluate the content prior to placing it in the children's reading area as you may be surprised to find that many books contain stereotypes, issues and political views, which are better avoided or introduced with supportive discussion.

Murdoch (2002) reminds us how important it is to consciously make time to talk with children as 'opportunities for children to talk with others and receive feedback can be limited, due to the competing demands on teachers' time and attention in the classroom' (Bond & Wasik 2009, p. 467).

Reflection 10.3

Next time you are on professional experience in a school, consider the following:

- Who is doing the most talking: you or the children?
- Do you allow the children to speak and share their views?
- Purposefully engage in talk and activities with the children, individually and in varied group arrangements (large group, pairs, small groups, interest groups).

Just as the school day has a routine, *build literacy routines* into your class's daily schedule until they become habitual and almost natural. Schedule some timeslots throughout the day for children to engage in the range of activities and learning centres that you provide and ensure that these are available during periods of free time. When would you like the children to engage in silent or shared reading of free choice? At what time of the day will you read to the whole class?

Let the children see you using literacy in meaningful ways for authentic purposes and talk openly about the processes involved and tasks achieved. Genuinely value and respond to the children's efforts to engage in these practices. Building a literate culture can involve explicit and implicit literacy teaching and children can experience literacy as a positive, enjoyable and valuable area to develop.

Hill et al. (2002, p. 9) state the following in relation to developing an effective literacy program:

> First it requires an understanding that effective teaching of early years' literacy cannot be 'contained' in a single program, approach or philosophy. It is a dynamic process that is responsive to the particular rather than the general, to the differences that children bring with them rather than to the general conceptions of a normal child development.

Consider who the children are in your class, what they are interested in, and their literacy development and what they need, and then use your knowledge and creativity to develop an engaging program for them. Promote a healthy love for reading and writing, offer a mix of directed and undirected activities where children can have freedom of choice, and do your best to foster healthy literacy habits and a natural love for literacy.

Conclusion

Child starting school with her sibling

This chapter has reviewed research and identified common issues that affect continuity and discontinuity during the process of transition from early childhood to primary education. A number of strategies have been suggested to support children and adults as they strive towards achieving a positive transition experience for everyone involved. This chapter also discussed the development of emergent literacy during transition to school and how to ensure continuity in literacy achievement for young children during this period and provided recommendations for the construction of the initial reading and writing program.

The transition into school is viewed as a critical time of learning and development for the child, important for later school success. Although every child's transition experience will be unique and different and problems and unexpected challenges may arise, the children that we are responsible for will have more chance if we as educators, along with parents and children, maintain a shared goal to ensure the every child experiences a positive transition process.

As a teacher, you will play a valuable role in the child's transition into school and in nurturing the development of his or her skills in language and literacy. Remember, it is of utmost importance that children receive the support that they need during these early years to assist them in developing firm foundations for their ongoing literacy development. Not only are you empowering children to engage in school literacy practices but you are also supporting them in developing literacy skills, knowledge and practices to assist them throughout their life.

Reflective questions

1. Why is the transition to school important?

2. Why is it important to work in partnership with families to support children's language and literacy development?

3. What can we (as early childhood educators and teachers) do to support children in their language and literacy development during the transition period?

4. How can kindergarten or new-entrant teachers further involve children and families in children's language and literacy development?

Further reading

Dockett, S. and Perry, B. (2006). *Starting School; A Handbook for Early Childhood Educators*. Castle Hill, NSW: Pademelon Press.

McLachlan, C. (2010). 'What Do Teachers Need to Know and Do about Literacy in the Early Childhood Context: Exploring Evidence'. He Kupu/The Word (August). http://www.hekupu.ac.nz/index.php?type=journal&issue=13&journal=243.

Tunmer, W., Nicholson, T. and Freebody, P. (2010). 'The Development and Teaching of Word Recognition Skill'. In M.L. Kamil, P.D. Pearson, E. Birr Moje and P.P. Afflerbach (eds), *Handbook of Reading Research, Volume IV*. Washington, DC: International Reading Association.

Chapter 11

Establishing a community of readers

Chapter objectives

1. To identify the principles for catering for diverse learners in the primary classroom.
2. To explain in detail how to set up effective reading programs in the primary classroom.
3. To explore the concept of a community of readers and how to establish one within a classroom setting.

What does it mean to have a classroom of eager readers who love to talk books? How do teachers create collaborative processes where all readers know that the teacher hears and respects their opinions? How does a teacher get momentum happening so that learners want to read beyond the classroom walls? Catering for diversity in classrooms is also the focus of this chapter. It leads into the notion of what it means to have a negotiated curriculum where learners make choices about what they value when it comes to reading. It looks at incorporating a variety of perspectives that acknowledge the variety of interests and experiences learners have to contribute to curriculum. This is a practical chapter about planning and organising a classroom for learning. It contains the 'nitty-gritty' of how to be equipped for effective instruction for K–6 learners.

Strategies for cooperation

Watching an experienced teacher in action is like watching the conductor of an orchestra. We are awed by the ability to keep a class of 30 pupils productively working. Experience comes from many hours of practice and planning but you can gain a lot by watching a teacher in action. Sometimes a trainee teacher out on practicum in schools is too shy to get involved in the classroom. He or she sits in a corner of the classroom with his or her laptop looking busy but not really getting involved in the nitty-gritty of teaching. Other trainees get right into it. They sit with the children, soaking up the atmosphere, making mental notes of how they can teach this way themselves. To illustrate the idea of using time in the classroom to make notes for teaching, Example 11.1 presents the notes of one of the authors of this book from a morning in a first-grade classroom in an inner-city school in Chicago (Nicholson 2011). The teacher used a range of strategies to teach reading but what came through was a **community of readers**, where pupils worked together. Even when completing skills worksheets, there was a cooperative spirit in the classroom.

> **Community of readers:** in this model there is an emphasis on interactive teaching, small-group learning and working together and in cooperation; pupils help each other and there is freedom to learn.

Example 11.1

Class: Grade 1
School: Chavez Elementary, Chicago
Teacher: Sara Strasser

7:50–8:30 Teacher takes small groups for guided reading – independent reading by rest of class.

Children eat breakfast in the classroom from 8 am to 8.30 am – and work on their writing projects. The teacher makes use of this time to work with some struggler readers with guided reading. Each group reads aloud to the teacher their graded text. Teacher asks questions: 'What does "webbed" mean? That's right, a platypus has feet like a duck'; 'What do we expect to find in a non-fiction book? Yes, real things, real pictures, and diagrams'; 'Is "gumball" a compound word? Yes, because it is made up of two words'.

8:30–8:40 Bathroom break
The whole class goes for a bathroom break (it is too dangerous in inner-city schools for children to leave class on their own).

8:40–9:20 Centres and guided reading

The regular reading program begins. Students work in small groups at various centres. The skills they are practising include word family work, sight words, phonic reading, reading comprehension, and spelling. The centres change daily. During this time more small groups of students are with the teacher for guided reading. The goal of the centres is for students to independently practise and further develop skills of reading and spelling.

Focus of the day is on OO. The OO pattern has two sounds, like the cuckoo clock, OO as in 'look', and OO as in 'zoo'. There are different activities for each group – for example, one group is with the teacher, writing OO words. Each group puts its skills-based teaching work onto the teacher's table and then the children go to the mat. They get 10 seconds to do this: 10, 9, 8, 7, 6...

9:20–9:40 Skills-based teaching

Students have a poem of the week that focuses on a particular word family or vowel pattern. This week the key words are OO words. Students participate in a cloze activity to practise new words (a cloze activity is one where a word is left out of the sentence and the students have to guess the missing word). The teacher has written a list of OO words – spoon, cool, zoo, books, good, crooks – some fit the poem, some do not. The students make predictions about which words make sense in the missing spaces – for example, putting in an OO word that does not make sense, so that you have 'Woody is a spoon detective. He reads mystery crooks'. After completing the cloze activity they read the poem together to learn the new words. The goal of the activity is to learn words that have the OO vowel combination, as well as develop reading fluency.

For this activity, there is a large chart on the board. It is a cloze activity. Part of the story reads:

Woody is a _____ detective.
He reads mystery _____.
Woody watches out for clues and is always chasing _____.

When finished they sing the poem to the tune of 'I'm a Yankee Doodle Dandy'.

9:40–10:10 Shared reading

Students have been learning about non-fiction and informational texts. They have been focusing on identifying important information in the texts. The teacher reads the class a book about recycling. Before reading, students predict which words they think will be important words in the text. They discuss the ideas in the text and the teacher explains unfamiliar vocabulary.

The teacher then reads another book to the class, *Where Does the Garbage Go?* The teacher reads the text aloud.

Teacher: 'We are learning new words today. "Landfill" – what is that?'

Teacher: 'I like how my first row has their eyes up here, looking at the book.'

After the shared reading, there is a follow-up activity related to the book. Pupils work in pairs to think of interesting words from the book that are about the topic. Pupils share with the class the words they selected, such as 'plastic' and 'garbage'. The class gives them a clap.

Teacher: 'Esther, Andy, can you show the class your two words?'

10:10–10:20 Play reading – puppet show

Pupils practise their puppet show. There is a special puppet show stand for this, and costumes. They read their parts.

10:20–11:00 Lunch

11:00–12:00 Writing workshop

Students have been working on topics they are interested in. Topics include dolphins and hamsters. Pages are lined, and pupils illustrate their writing.

How do you set up your own reading program?

Two to three weeks before school starts. Set up the classroom. It is hard to describe this in words but when you see a picture of a classroom set up with lots of books in it you know that it will work, as in Figure 11.1. Work out which children will work at each class table. Usually this means dividing them into ability groups. You will have a class list from the school that has student reading levels from the end of the previous

Figure 11.1 *Setting up a reading classroom (Ministry of Education 1985)*

year. There are likely to be 3–4 groups of different levels. Select no more than eight pupils for each group and for the lowest readers make the group small, about five in the group. Students may have slipped back over the summer break, due to the summer slide phenomenon, so it is wise to reassess them at the start of the next year.

Weeks 1–3. Establish the routines you want. Show the class how your program will work and what they have to do. Keep a simple program – for example, in the first 10 minutes the class does sustained silent reading on its own with books the children can read. Then the teacher has shared book reading where he or she reads a big book interactively with the class. Then the class does reading activities for the rest of the time period. Reading activities can include independent reading, buddy reading, skills-based worksheets, rereading of 'big books', and comprehension quizzes. The lowest level of readers need a mix of reading mileage with books that are at their reading level, and lots of decoding instruction. In Week 3, start to work with small groups, one at first, and then build to four (see the next section on the 'four-group' approach).

When to teach reading? Each school is different but the typical pattern is a first block from 9:00 to 10:30 for oral language, handwriting, and writing of stories. The second block, after break, is 10:50–12:30, lunchtime, and is usually for reading. In the senior school, this pattern is often in reverse. Schools run a four-day program where you must teach literacy Monday to Thursday. Friday can be a mix of different activities.

Preparation. Most teachers set up the reading activities for the next day in the evening. A suggestion is to have a basket for each group's activities, with one basket per table in the classroom, so that pupils have something to work on straight away when you ask them to go to their workstations. One basket at the blue table, for example, will have the graded readers for the day that you will be using with the group for guided reading. It will also have a follow-up vocabulary quiz or similar. At the next table, the basket will have skills quizzes – for example, words with the OO pattern that pupils have to fit into sentences. At the next table the basket will have big books that the class has read before, so pupils can read the books to each other. At the next table, the basket will have a worksheet with a template to write about the story that the class has read that morning. The template will have ideas on how to structure their writing – for example:

The main character in the story was _____.
The action in the story was 1. –, 2. –, 3. – .
The outcome of the story was that _____.

In the senior primary school, teachers use tumble boards that set out the day's program. In the junior primary school, teachers often explain to each group what they will do, and then send them to the table with the advice of 'Do your work – keep quiet so that I can help others in the class while you are working'.

Assessment. At some schools the minimum requirement in the junior school is to record pupils' reading on a regular basis, usually four analysed running records per pupil per year (one each term at least) and sometimes more than this. For pupils reading below their chronological age, the teacher may need to do more than four per year. Teachers try to slot in some spare time each day to take an individual assessment. Sometimes this is in the reading period, sometimes before school, and so on.

Planning the program. Most schools have a planning template that summarises the lessons each week so you will need to ask for one. Every beginner teacher will have a mentor at the school to go to for help with planning.

Catering to diversity. When lesson planning, relate instructional material to the experiences of your students. Ask them if they know what you mean when you explain something. Ask questions to check. An interesting example of the difference between the formal vocabulary of school and the informal vocabulary of children is in the anecdote below where children's understanding of a 'large book' was different to that of the teacher.

Teacher: 'What large book do we consult if we do not know the meaning of a word?'

Pupils: 'The Bible?'

Teacher: 'Can you think of another book?'

Pupils: 'The dictionary!'

Teaching in small groups

In the reading period, after shared reading, most classrooms follow the 'four group' approach. The teacher works with four different groups through the school week. Each day the teacher takes guided reading with a different group. Each day pupils move to a new group (Ministry of Education 1985; Cunningham 2007).

Group 1 does self-selected reading. The aim is to build reading mileage. Some studies have found that pupils do not get much time each day to read on their own. This will give them time. Teachers orchestrate their choices of books to some extent, encouraging them to read books at their reading level, books that are not too hard and not too easy.

The teacher does guided reading with Group 2. This means having individual copies of the book or other text for each pupil to read. It is an opportunity for the teacher to focus on areas of need for that group, whether decoding skills or comprehension strategies, or both.

For Group 3 the teacher sets up activities for the students to build word knowledge. In the junior school much of this work might focus on the mechanics of decoding – for example, there are 100 high frequency words that account for more than half of all the words that pupils read. In this block, students can work in pairs and quiz each other on these words – for example, one pupil times the other pupil, reading the words as fast as they can. Other activities may focus on skills, such as working through activity sheets with another classmate to learn spelling patterns.

The teacher encourages the pupils in Group 4 to write about what they have been reading. This is an opportunity to encourage pupils to write with a template (e.g. problem–action–outcome), or to write out the text structure of the 'big book' the teacher used in shared reading. Students can check each other's writing and give feedback.

An example of a reading lesson for a beginning Year 1 class

In the following example, the teacher encourages a community of learning, where pupils help each other. The teacher has pupils working in groups together. When she teaches she involves all the class. She encourages children to help each other. There are no favourite pupils or groups.

Example 11.2

At 11:00 the class has reading, which includes a review of skills. The teacher writes 'at' – then 'cat', 'mat', 'bat', 'that', 'fat', 'sat'. Pupils read the words together chorally – then she has them read chorally a skills story: 'Sit on a mat, and knit a hat. No, no, no, I can't do that. Ring the bell, Ring the bell. I can't do that. I don't feel well.'

This finishes at 11:05. The teacher then explains the reading tumble board for the day.

DAHL	ROWLING	COWLEY
Worksheet	Teacher	Worksheet
Teacher	Worksheet	Book box
	Alphabet match	Teacher

At 11:10 the class has shared book reading. The teacher does a skills-based teaching warm-up activity before the shared reading. The class reads aloud a skills poem with regular words, including: 'Away went the cat, away went the dog, and away went the frog, to sit on his log.' The teacher shows the class the shared book for the week, called *Mrs Wishy Washy*. The class reads the text aloud as the teacher turns the big book pages. On the last page, the teacher reminds the pupils to make their voices sound exciting! Wishy washy!

The teacher reminds the pupils to bring their book bag to school each day (a zip-up bag to take a book home each night), their frog card (with a list of high-frequency sight words to learn), and their homework book (which the parent signs to verify the pupil has done his or her reading).

At 11:25 the class finishes shared reading by reading aloud the words on the frog card (e.g. 'went', 'come', 'this', 'house'). The teacher reminds the class that she will test their spelling of the frog card words this Friday.

At 11:30 the teacher assigns pupils to group work. The advice she gives is 'Don't rush', 'Read quietly' and 'No talking'. When the pupils are finished their group activity, the rule is that they go to the book corner and read a book. The teacher has grouped the pupils into three groups according to their reading levels. The names of the groups are the names of famous authors. Dahl group is the high group. Rowling group is the middle group. Cowley is the low group. The teacher gives everyone in the Rowling and Cowley groups a copy of the 'Sit on the Mat poem' – they have to 'colour in the bell' and 'draw a hat or mat' and 'colour in your drawing'. When the pupils are finished the rule is that they go to the book corner and read a book.

At 11:35 the teacher works with the Dahl group at the teacher's workstation at the front of the class, where there is a whiteboard. At the moment, there is just one pupil in the Dahl group – she reads *Brave Father Mouse* in a guided reading lesson with teacher. She is a good reader so most of the time they discuss vocabulary meanings and comprehension.

At 11:45 the teacher works with Cowley group. They read *Off Goes the Hose* in a guided reading. They discuss the title, put a finger on each word and read aloud together in choral fashion. There is a follow-up worksheet.

At 12:00 the teacher works with the Rowling group. They read *Best Big Bear*. The teacher asks them to find some high-frequency words on the page – words such as 'my' and 'is'. She writes these words on the whiteboard and encourages the pupils to point to each word with a finger (this is encouraged in Year 1 but discouraged by Year 3). They then do a choral reading of story. There is a follow-up worksheet – they colour in the bear on the worksheet.

At 12:30 the pupils put their group work books in their book bags to take home to read to mum that night.

At 12:32 the teacher closes the lesson with a karakia, a Maori blessing (they also start the day with a karakia).

Creating a community of readers

The key to creating a community of readers is to have a classroom well stocked with books at the right reading levels for the range of ability in the class. Research shows that books vary widely in reading difficulty and that pupils lose interest and motivation if they have to struggle to read books, so it is important to have books that the class can read with success. To do this, the teacher needs access to graded books. In New Zealand graded readers published by the Ministry of Education's commercial arm, Learning Media, are freely available to schools. This is the Ready to Read series and consists of a wide range of levelled readers for pupils in K–3. Learning Media also publishes the *School Journal* containing stories, factual writing, poems and plays, for different grades. In New South Wales there is *The School Magazine*, which is similar. There is an online site for the magazine that also provides teacher lesson plans and specifies the reading levels catered for.

Most schools also purchase sets of graded readers from commercial publishers. These books are available in the teacher resource rooms of schools and teachers can borrow and use them. In addition, school libraries have a wide range of books for teachers to borrow for their classes. In New Zealand there is also the National Library's Schools Collection, which has a huge store of children's books that teachers anywhere can borrow. The teacher can select from these resources to establish a classroom collection of books at different reading levels in labelled boxes in the classroom so that pupils know exactly what they can read according to the level they are at.

Graded readers in most reading series are divided into reading levels using the Reading Recovery 1–30 system, as well as a colour system. In New Zealand Learning Media's Ready to Read series, for example, has a colour wheel that indicates the reading level of each book. The colour wheel also indicates at what reading level the book is suitable for shared reading, guided reading or independent reading.

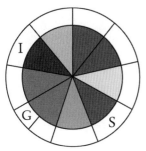

For example, a book might be at gold level, which is the average level expected at the end of Year 3 in school. The colour wheel will indicate that the book might be suitable for shared reading (S) with pupils below this level, or guided reading (G) for pupils at this level, or independent reading (I) for pupils above this level.

For more information on the resources described above, please see the 'Further reading' section at the end of this chapter.

Figure 11.2 *The colour wheel in the Ready to Read series*

Teaching beginning reading

The question of how to teach beginning reading is related to beliefs about how we read and how best to teach reading. The first approach is explicit, where pupils are taught to read words according to their sounds. This is skills-based teaching. The second approach is implicit where pupils are taught to read with books. It is called book experience.

In Europe, the traditional approach to teaching beginning reading is explicit – that is, it is skills-based teaching. The sounds of letters are taught, and pupils are encouraged to 'sound out' words. This approach suits a transparent orthography where most letters have only one sound. An example of this was manifested in a recent study comparing the rate of learning to read of pupils learning to read Welsh, which is a transparent orthography, with pupils learning to read English, which is a deep orthography in that many of the letters of the English alphabet have more than one sound (Spencer & Hanley 2003, 2004). This has led to criticism that the explicit approach is best suited to transparent writing systems such as Welsh, and not to English. Most researchers agree, however, that some skills-based teaching is necessary to learn to read English. Otherwise, the code will be a puzzle for many pupils, like looking at gobbledygook or Chinese writing. Skills-based teaching explains to the class the history of English writing patterns and the intriguing stories of how spellings changed, and this is useful information for any reader and writer of any age (Nicholson 2000; Nicholson 2006; Tunmer & Nicholson 2011).The difficulty of learning the code of English – that is, how to read words aloud accurately and automatically – means that we need to take advantage of both methods of teaching. In this chapter we argue that every classroom needs to have both kinds of programs combined with each other. There are negative aspects of each approach if you rely just on the one approach, but together they cancel out the negative aspects of each other's approach, so they are a formidable combination, as shown below.

	BOOK EXPERIENCE	SKILLS-BASED TEACHING
Pros	You read lots of books and learn to use context clues and illustrations to help work out words.	You learn the code and how to sound out words so you can read on your own without help.
Cons	You can rely too much on context and illustrations and never learn the code.	You can spend too much time on skills-based teaching of rules without actually reading books.

The book-experience approach: pluses and minuses

The book-experience approach has a strong interactive approach that sets the scene for cooperative learning in a community of readers. The teacher and the class 'share' a book together. The reading lesson is cooperative, with the teacher asking questions and the pupils expressing their opinions in a non-threatening atmosphere where all opinions are valuable. **Book experience** has a strong emphasis on teaching beginners to read words by using multiple cues from the text rather than sounding the word out. The main strategies it teaches are reading and rereading books many times; using book illustrations as cues to support decoding; studying words with similar patterns called word families; and guessing words using context and the initial letters of the word. It does not strongly encourage sounding out words, especially out of context.

Since the 1980s New Zealand has emphasised the book-experience or implicit teaching approach (Thompson 1993). It is implicit teaching of reading because it does not teach skills. Pupils learn skills through reading experience. The typical program has an emphasis on shared reading, with rereading of books by the teacher and the pupils. In shared reading, the teacher will read the book aloud to the class on Monday and reread it with the class joining in on Tuesday, Wednesday, and Thursday. On each day the teacher asks questions about some aspect of the book, such as questions about figurative language, inferences, letter patterns (e.g. 'at' and 'ing'), punctuation, illustrations and vocabulary.

The following illustrates a shared book lesson for six-year-olds (Tse 2011).

> **Book experience:** an instructional method that has a strong interactive approach which sets the scene for cooperative learning in a community of readers. The reading lesson is cooperative, with the teacher asking questions and the class expressing their opinions in a non-threatening atmosphere where all opinions are good.

Example 11.3

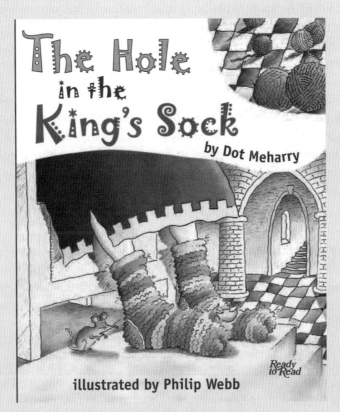

Introduction

Story: *The Hole in the King's Sock* (level – orange)

Teacher: 'I have a book for you to read that is about the king and his socks. How many of you are wearing socks today? Where do you get your socks from?'

Students: 'The supermarket, warehouse, the two-dollar shop.'

Lesson

Story: *The Hole in the King's Sock* (first reading)

1. Discuss the illustrations on the front and back covers of the book and read the title. Who is this person? Where does he live? What might you expect to see in a book about a king?
2. Read the title and the names of the writer and the illustrator. Talk about the use of possessive apostrophe in 'King's'.
3. Read the story to the students.
4. During the reading, encourage students to predict what might happen next.

Activity: Comprehension questions (oral)
1. What is the King's problem?
2. Did he find a solution? What is that? Did it work? If not, why didn't it work? Was the problem solved at the end?

Pupils have available to them a wide range of books that are graded from beginners to more advanced levels. The teacher encourages pupils to use multiple cues from the text to read the words. The teacher teaches the names and sounds of letters, but only emphasises these for spelling in the writing block of the school day. During this part of the day pupils learn to break words into their phonemes and match these to sounds of letters to spell words.

Example 11.4

Shared reading in Year 1

12:05 Reading
The text is *Greedy Cat's Door*. One of the pupils is allowed to hold the pointer – she points to each word as the class reads aloud with the teacher. The teacher makes some comments such as 'I can see exclamation marks here – what should we do?'
Class: 'Read louder!'
Teacher: 'Put expression in your voices, please.'

In the 1980s the theory behind book experience was that the combination of context clues plus a sampling of the initial letters was usually enough for pupils to learn to read most words, and certainly enough for them to grasp the meaning of the text. The argument was that context clues are used by the skilled reader as a major strategy for 'predicting' or 'guessing' words when reading. After much debate on this topic in the 1980s and 1990s (see Nicholson & Tunmer 2011; Tunmer & Nicholson 2011), researchers concluded that this assumption of the implicit approach had been overstated. On the other hand, the fact that many pupils do learn to read with the implicit approach, and only 20 per cent struggle, indicates that pupils do crack the code of English.

In the 1990s a new theory of implicit learning emerged. Researchers had a different explanation of why the book-experience approach worked (Thompson 1993; Tunmer & Nicholson 1993; McKay, Fletcher-Flinn & Thompson 2004). This new implicit theory said that pupils have four sources of information available to them to help them recognise words they read (context cues, letter–sound correspondences they have been taught explicitly, letter–sound correspondences they have learned implicitly themselves while reading, and sight words) so they have a range of sources of information for identifying seen and previously unseen words.

The book-experience approach does not teach letter–sound correspondences or how to blend letter sounds together to approximate a spoken word when reading. This is what skills-based teaching does. Instead, the book-experience approach encourages pupils to work out unfamiliar words by using a mix of context clues, illustrations and initial letters, and 'large grain size' skills-based teaching (Goswami & Ziegler 2006), as in working out words by comparing them with similar words that have the same rime patterns (e.g. 'sock' has the same 'ock' rime as 'clock'). The concept of 'grain size' in decoding words refers to the level at which you work when you decode, whether it be at the letter sound level or the rime level, or even at the whole-word level. The best explanation of how this approach fits with book experience is knowledge sources theory (Fletcher-Flinn & Thompson 2000, 2004).

On the other hand, book experience is not enough for an estimated 20 per cent of six-year-old pupils who somehow fall behind their peers and need 'Reading Recovery' tuition (Nicholson 2008a; Nicholson & Dymock 2011; Greaney 2011). It explains how good readers read but it does not have anything to say about struggling readers. This is where skills-based teaching can be of great value to the struggler reader. It explains the code in detail, teaching skills to help the child to say a word that was previously just a blur. For example, one of the authors of this book remembers one pupil who could say 'rain' and 'coat' when the teacher wrote them on the whiteboard, but when she wrote 'raincoat' he was lost and said, 'I've never seen that word before'. What happened is that he was trying to remember each new word separately and did not realise that sometimes we combine words. Most good readers figure this out while reading but some children need more direction than this. This is where skills-based teaching can give the struggler other strategies.

The skills-based teaching approach: pluses and minuses

The skills-based approach to teaching reading only works well in a community of readers. Otherwise, it can become a 'factory-type' model where pupils listen while the teacher teaches. On the other hand, skills-based teaching can be much more interactive and this is where it works best. The teacher is involved in explaining and discussing the skills with the pupils and checking to see if they understand. The pupils can show they understand by writing, circling and pointing to skills patterns, and engaging with the teacher and other pupils to explain and show understanding. This is the 'every pupil response' approach where every pupil joins with the teacher to use the skills effectively to read.

Phonological awareness: the ability to segment the speech stream into phonological units – that is, the ability to segment speech into words, words into syllables, syllables into their onset (initial consonant(s)) and rime (what comes after the onset), and syllables into phonemes.

Phonics: an instructional method of teaching decoding skills, involving the teaching of 'rules' that specify the grapheme–phoneme relationships of alphabetic writing systems.

Phonemic awareness: this is one aspect of phonological awareness. Phonemes are the smallest constituent units of spoken language. An operational definition that shows how to deconstruct words to phonemes is that by deleting a phoneme from a spoken word or adding a phoneme to a word, you can generate a new word – for example, replace the /s/ in /sun/ with an /f/ and you will generate a new word, /fun/.

The skills-based teaching approach is an explicit way of teaching the phonological rules of the writing system (**phonological awareness**). The plus is that it gives the pupil independent skills to read words. It is not an overnight solution because the code in English is complex, but skills-based teaching can quickly give the child a handle on how to work out words. After that, lots of reading practice will make the pupil skilful in sounding out words.

Meta-analyses comparing the skills-based approach with the book experience approach have found that skills-based teaching is more effective. The report of the National Reading Panel (see Ehri et al. 2001) indicated that skills-based teaching (or **phonics**) was moderately more effective than the book-experience approach. Another meta-analysis by Hattie (2009) found that the skills-based approach was 10 times more effective than the book-experience approach. Stuart (2005) has compared skills-based teaching and book experience and found that skills-based teaching was better. However, as we saw in the case of Maxine in Chapter 3, many pupils still learn to read with book experience so both approaches are helpful.

While **phonemic awareness** is necessary for skills-based teaching, it is not sufficient. The pupil has to work out the code. This means knowing how to turn letters into phonemes and then how to blend the phonemes together to reveal the word that is on the page. That is, under this method explicit skills-based teaching is a way to reveal to the pupil the nature of the cipher, the system we have for writing. Phonemic awareness is likely to make this task of learning the cipher much easier for the pupil because it shows pupils that spoken words are made of phonemes, and many struggling readers have not worked this out. Strugglers tend to think that the letters on the page do not correspond to phonemes, or they misunderstand what phonemes the letters represent.

In skills-based teaching, the teacher has a scope and sequence of teaching where the class learns the common sounds of the single letters of the consonants and vowels of the alphabet and then the sounds of other letter patterns, such as /ch/ and /th/ (Nicholson 2006). There are 21 consonants and five vowels (a-e-i-o-u) in the alphabet. Most skills-based teaching programs teach about 40 basic rules but sometimes they can teach a lot more than that. As Example 11.5 shows, skills-based teaching follows a scope and sequence (see also the appendix to this chapter).

Example of a skills-based teaching lesson

In the following lesson plan (Tse 2011), designed for six-year-olds who are average readers, the teacher plans to explain the ai/ay and oi/oy patterns. The basic rule is that the /ay/ sound is spelled 'ai' in the middle of a word and 'ay' at the end of a word because in the olden days printers did not like to end a word in the letter 'i'. The same rule operates for the 'oi' and 'au' patterns in English.

Example 11.5

Lesson: vowel digraphs AI/AY and OI/OY

Today we are going to learn about putting two vowels together to make a new sound. The first one is the /ay/ sound and the second one is /oy/ sound.

The AI-AY pattern represents the /ay/ sound. The AI spelling is usually in the middle of the word, and the AY spelling is usually at the end of the word.

Look at Lists 1 and 2 and read them aloud with me.

List 1	List 2
rain	ray
pail	pay
sail	say
train	tray
plain	play
mail	may

Question: What is the difference in the way we spell the /ay/ sound in each of the lists? (Answer: usually AI is in the middle of the word and AY at the end of the word).

The OI-OY pattern has one sound, as in /oi/. OI is always spelled in the beginning or middle of a word and OY at the end of a word. Let's read these OI and OY patterns together.

List 1	List 2
oil	boy
boil	joy
foil	toy
join	roy
noise	enjoy
toilet	annoy
poison	

I have underlined all the /oy/ sounds. The (oy) is spelled as OI in the beginning or middle of the word, and OY spelled at the end of the word.

Note: Meanings of the words are also explained to the students while learning the sounds.

Activity: phoneme awareness
Using turtle talk (see p. 205) to sound out words

rain	paint	boy
play	toy	toilet
day	point	joy

Wrap-up

1. Each student listens to the sounds of the word when the teacher uses turtle talk and circles the correct word on the whiteboard.
2. Remember the AI-AY pattern has the sound of /ay/, and OI-OY has the sound of /oy/.

To review learning of the skills-based teaching pattern, the teacher gives the pupils a follow-up quiz (Tse 2011). This will reveal if each pupil has learned the pattern. In the quizzes below, one pupil has learned the pattern but the other is still unsure:

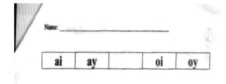

Phonemic awareness

Many researchers think that children will have an even better start in learning to read if they have good phonemic awareness when they start school. Phonemic awareness is not sufficient to learn to read but it sure is necessary. It helps pupils to see that letters stand for spoken sounds, that is, phonemes. Many classrooms have book experience and skills-based teaching but they forget to include phonemic awareness, perhaps thinking that pupils learned it in preschool – but this is not the case. Studies show that they have very little of it when they start school.

Phonemic awareness involves the ability to segment spoken words into their constituent phonemes. This is not the same as being able to recite nursery rhymes such as 'Humpty Dumpty'. It is more than that – it is knowing that 'cat' can be said as 'k-a-t'. Gough and Lee (2007) reviewed research showing that phonemic awareness is a strong predictor of successful reading achievement. Dozens of studies have shown this but the important thing is that the purpose of phonemic awareness skill is to enable the pupil to work out the code, the system of letter–sound correspondences, of alphabetic languages such as English and Spanish. Once the pupil has worked out the code, then it is possible to read words independently, without help from parents. Knowing the code also means you do not have to rely on context clues to read words. The code brings freedom to read on your own without help.

Researchers see a lack of skill in phonemic awareness as the major stumbling block in learning to read. Studies have found that pupils up to five years of age struggle to break words into sounds. They seem to learn phonemic awareness more easily when they are about five years of age and this has implications in terms of the timing of beginning reading instruction if you want to provide explicit skills-based teaching instruction. They have trouble distinguishing the form of words (phonemes) from their meaning – for example, a young pupil may say that the sounds in 'dog' are 'woof woof'. They have trouble tapping the phonemes in words and breaking off phonemes. Gough and Lee (2007) argue that the most important phonemic skill for cracking the cipher is phonemic segmentation, breaking the spoken word into its full set of phonemes, as in 'd-u-ck' and they use a technique called turtle talk that teaches pupils to say a word slowly like a turtle.

In a similar vein Byrne and Fielding-Barnsley (1991) produced a program called Sound Foundations that taught pupils the initial and final sounds of a number of words, using posters that contained illustrations of objects that began or ended with those sounds. The original program is now out of print but Fielding-Barnsley and Hay (2012) have produced a new program that is similar in concept to the original. It is designed to be downloaded from the Apple iTunes website to iPods or iPads. The positive point about this app is that it is based on much field-tested research. The app teaches phonemic awareness and letter sound knowledge to very young pupils, even those younger than five years of age, focusing on initial and end sounds.

Conclusion

In this chapter we discussed how to create a community of readers. The key is to make books accessible and easy enough to read so that pupils want to keep reading.

We explained some ideas for hooking the class into reading and how the teacher can inspire the class to read by reading books aloud to them in an interesting way.

Most pupils will learn to read whatever approach you use to teach reading but some will not. This is where you need flexibility. Rather than wait for some children to fail because they do not respond to one particular program, a better insurance policy is to use both approaches from the start, to ensure that there is a learning path for everybody.

Once pupils learn to decode and are reading well, it is tempting to leave them to their own devices. Some teachers say that good readers are 'masters of their own destiny' and let them follow their own reading interests. However, as we will discuss in Chapter 13, statistics show that good readers plateau between the ages of five to eight and we think this is because they are not challenged enough. The most important goal is to keep them reading books, to increase their reading mileage simply because this is the best way we know to increase vocabulary and general knowledge, which are essential for reading and writing success.

There is so much that good readers can still learn! There are new text genres to challenge them that are different to the typical diet of narrative texts, such as complex factual writing with different text structures. Anyone taking a close look at good readers in senior primary will see that these books often look good and the pupils seem busy reading but they are just cruising. There is a huge vocabulary to learn in English (none of us know all the words, of course, since there are more than 500 000 words in the language). In Chapter 13 we show how to stretch the stronger pupils to expand their vocabulary with a combination of extra text reading and activities such as quizzes to glue new vocabulary in memory.

Reflective questions

1. Do you remember your own time in primary school? Which years were the most interesting and helpful? Were they the ones when the class would work together to achieve reading outcomes, or learn together as a group when the teacher read the class a picture book showing how we can achieve more if we work together? (An example is *Clancy the Courageous Cow* – see Hume 2007). In contrast, was your time in school more like the 'factory model'?

2. Do you remember the instructional approach that helped you learn to read? Was it the skills-based approach or the book-experience approach, or both together? What was it that helped you learn to read?

3. In the practical examples provided above, what aspects suggest that the class and the teacher are working together as a community of readers?

4. What other things can a teacher do to create a community of readers? Are there ways, for example, to make links to parents to enlist their help to create a community that works together for the common good?

Further reading

Ministry of Education (NZ) – Literacy Online. http://literacyonline.tki.org.nz.

——Ready to Read. http://www.tki.org.nz/r/literacy_numeracy/professional/teachers_notes/ready_to_read/index_e.php.

——School Journal Teachers' Notes. http://www.tki.org.nz/e/r/literacy_numeracy/professional/teachers_notes/school_journal/index.php.

National Library of New Zealand. 'National Library Schools Collection'. http://www.natlib.govt.nz/collections/a-z-of-all-collections/national-library-schools-collection.

Sound Foundations. http://www.soundfoundationsbooks.co.uk.

Appendix

Figure 11.3 *Skills-based teaching – scope and sequence (Nicholson 2006)*

What to teach and when to teach it			
Age 5–6	**Age 5–6**	**Age 6–7**	**Age 6–7**
1. Knows all letter names and sounds. **Aa** 2. Aware of phonemes in spoken words	3. Knows all CVC 3-letter words, e.g. cat, log, sun, big. **c-a-t in cat** 4. Knows most frequent 50 sight words	5. Knows all consonant blends, e.g. crab, glad, stop, swim. **cr in crab**	6. Knows all consonant digraphs, e.g. ch, sh, th, wh, ph. **sh in fish**
Age 6–7	**Age 6–7**	**Age 6–7**	**Age 7–8**
7. Knows the 'silent e' rule for long vowel sounds, e.g. hat-hate, cut-cute. **o_e in bone**	8. Knows the doubling rule for short vowel sound, e.g. hoping-ho**pp**ing.	9. Knows the R- and L-affected vowel sounds – ar, er, ir, or, ur, all. **ar in car** 10. Knows the 300 most frequent sight words and the 'advanced' list	11. Knows all 1-sound vowel digraphs, e.g. ai, oa, oi, au, ew. **ee in bee**

Figure 11.3 *(cont'd)*

What to teach and when to teach it			
Age 7–8	**Age 8–9**	**Age 8–9**	**Age 9–10**
12. Knows all 2-sound vowel digraphs, e.g. ea, ei, oo, ow. **oo in book** **oo in roof**	13. Knows compounding patterns, e.g. hot/dog, rain/coat, night/fall, steam/roller. 14. Knows silent letters, e.g. gh, kn. **h in ghost**	15. Knows Greek letter patterns with special sounds **ch**=/k/, **ph**=/f/, **y**=/i/ sound. **phone** 16. Knows the 6 syllable rules: closed, open, r-affected, silent 'e', -LE, vowel team.	17. Knows simple Anglo-Saxon prefixes (e.g. by-, for-, over-) and suffixes (e.g. -ed, -ing, -ly) and simple Latin based prefixes (e.g. pre-, dis-) and suffixes (e.g. -age, -ance).
Age 10–12	**Age 12–14**	**The reader**	
18. Knows more complex Latin-based prefixes (e.g. anti-, trans-, inter-, intro-, sub-) and suffixes (e.g. -cian, -cial, -tious, -age, -ance, -ive). **station**	19. Knows advanced Greek root words (e.g. chron, graph, sphere, thermo), prefixes (e.g. semi-, photo-, tele-, hydro-, hyper-) and suffixes (e.g.; -phobia, -scope, -cracy, -phile).		

Chapter 12

Uses of assessment in the primary school years

Chapter objectives

1. To develop an understanding of the roles of assessment during the primary school years (assessment *for*, *as* and *of* learning).
2. To examine the important role of self-assessment within the assessment process (assessment *for* and *as* learning).
3. To develop an understanding of accountability (particularly the question of accountability for *what* in the assessment *of* learning).
4. To develop an understanding of the key domains of literacy assessment.
5. To critically examine a range of methods for assessing and documenting pupils' developing literacy skills and strategies across these key domains during the primary years.

Assessment is always hot on the agenda of teachers, and with the move to 'high-stakes' assessment teachers feel increasing pressure to teach to the test. One of the major themes of this chapter is accountability, particularly the question of accountability for *what*? It takes a fresh look at self-assessment and how the learner needs to be an integral partner in the assessment process. Building on Chapter 9, which covered effective assessment in early education settings, this chapter examines recent research on the most effective ways to assess pupils' ongoing acquisition of literacy in the K–6 grades. Research evidence on the effectiveness of common literacy assessments is reviewed and recommendations for practice with diverse learners are considered.

Assessment *for* learning: occurs when teachers use information gained from an assessment of students' learning to inform their instruction.

Formative assessment: when the information yielded by the assessment is used by the teacher and student to inform teaching and learning respectively.

Collaboration: occurs when individuals work together to achieve common goals – in the present context, best practice is when a pupil works with his or her parents and teacher to ensure that educational goals are being met.

Assessment *as* learning: occurs when students reflect on and monitor their progress in learning in order to develop goals for future learning.

The roles of assessment during the primary school years (assessment *for*, *as* and *of* learning)

In Chapter 9, on assessment during the early childhood years, we focused primarily on **assessment *for* learning**. As you will recall, this type of assessment is deliberate, ongoing and the specific information it yields about a student's strengths and needs (e.g. mastery of consonant blends) is used to plan for instruction as well for additional practice at home and at school. 'Assessment *for* learning' is often described as **formative assessment** in that the information is used to shape teaching and learning and not to grade a student's achievement. The fine-grained information yielded by 'assessment *for* learning' can be used as the basis and catalyst for **collaboration** among students and their parents and teachers as they work to develop a student's literacy capabilities.

During the primary school years, however, teachers' assessment necessarily expands beyond a primary focus on 'assessment *for* learning' to include 'assessment *as* learning' and 'assessment *of* learning' (DEECD 2009a). There are very good reasons for this expansion and all relate to the increased range of purposes for assessment as well as the number of individuals who have an interest in monitoring school-aged children's literacy development (see Table 12.1 below).

First, let's consider **assessment *as* learning**. Although this form of assessment is also ongoing (i.e. part of a teacher's everyday practice), it may well involve some of the same tools as those that are used in 'assessment *for* learning' (e.g. observations, anecdotal records, quizzes, logs, reflections and portfolios) and it may also be classified as formative. 'Assessment *as* learning' involves students and their peers more directly in the assessment process in dialogue with their teacher. It involves students in examining evidence of their learning and that of their peers, in establishing personal learning goals, in monitoring and reflecting on their individual progress, and in taking responsibility for their own learning, thus enabling them to become more autonomous learners (Earl 2003). It is during 'assessment *as* learning' that students' involvement in self-assessment is of critical importance. We'll discuss self-assessment in greater detail in the next section of this chapter.

Before discussing self-assessment, however, let's consider '**assessment *of* learning**'. This is likely the type of assessment that you remember mostly clearly from your own days as a student in school because of the tendency of many of us to feel threatened by an assessment of our abilities. 'Assessment *of* learning' generally occurs at the end of a period or unit of learning and involves an evaluation of performance or achievement. The assessment, which is **summative**, typically utilises **formal** curriculum-based or standardised tests that yield a mark or grade for each student. The results of an 'assessment *of* learning' are of great interest to a range of individuals – from the students themselves and their teachers and parents who want to know 'how they did' to school administrators, government officials and members of the public who want to know whether schools (and teachers) are producing literate individuals who will contribute to society – for example 'become successful learners, confident and creative individuals, and active and informed citizens' (MCEETYA 2008). In a later section on accountability, we will give further consideration to 'assessment *of* learning' in Australia and New Zealand.

> **Assessment *of* learning:** occurs when teachers use evidence of student learning to make judgements about students' achievement and learning progress with respect to specific goals and standards.

> **Summative assessment:** when the information is used to evaluate the student's learning against a specific set of standards or benchmarks upon completion of a unit of learning

> **Formal assessment:** when a teacher uses a published assessment instrument.

Table 12.1: *Assessment types, purposes and audience*

TYPES OF ASSESSMENT	PURPOSES FOR ASSESSMENT	AUDIENCE
Assessment *for* learning	• To determine a student's strengths/needs. • To plan for instruction/learning. • To support home–school collaboration.	Students Teachers* Parents
Assessment *as* learning	• To examine learning strengths/needs. • To establish personal goals and monitor progress. • To take responsibility for learning.	Students* Teachers Parents
Assessment *of* learning	• To determine the effectiveness of literacy instruction. • To provide information about students' progress. • To establish teacher/school/ministry accountability.	Students Teachers* Parents* School* Ministry* Community*

* Denotes primary recipient(s) of assessment information.

The roles of self-assessment within the assessment process (assessment *for* and *as* learning)

Students of all ages can reflect on their learning and when they are given explicit instruction and scaffolded opportunities to become involved in **self-assessment**, numerous positive outcomes have been noted for students from pre-school through to university (Bingham, Holbrook & Meyers 2010; Ibabe & Jauregizar 2010; Kostons, van Gog & Paas 2010).

Self-assessment: a form of assessment that provides students with opportunities for greater ownership and responsibility for their learning in that students must necessarily learn what assessment criteria are regarded as important and judge their learning or performance against those criteria.

An excellent example of self-assessment during the primary years can be found in the work of Munns and Woodward (2006) with students in schools located in poor communities surrounding Sydney, Australia. Munns and Woodward found that when students had opportunities to reflect on what and how they were learning, how it connected to their lives, what they had achieved, how to improve their performance, how their future learning experiences could be designed and evaluated (i.e. student voice) and how they saw themselves as learners, the students began to demonstrate greater engagement with learning, increased self-regulation (i.e. control of their social-emotional/behavioural functioning to support academic learning), improved learning outcomes, and a stronger sense of self as learners. If you find that you are particularly interested in the work of Munns and Woodward, especially in relation to their Fair Go Project and REAL Framework (for enhancing students' reflection) and their subsequent work with young Indigenous Australian students, we suggest you conduct an internet search to connect with their most recent work.

An approach to assessment that is particularly conducive to encouraging students to become involved in regular self-assessment is the 'portfolio performance assessment' (Farr 1999), which we will discuss further in relation to methods of assessment. This widely used approach requires regular deposits of work (reading responses, letters, notes, samples of best work, photographs, etc.) by the student, with frequent self-analysis of the work samples and artefacts supported and scaffolded by the teacher (Vizyak 1999). These regular focused conversations between the student and the teacher can be extremely valuable but it is very important that the portfolio is viewed as belonging to the student. The portfolio is the student's evolving collection of works in progress, emerging ideas, beginning thoughts and reflections as well as the place to store self- and teacher evaluations along with feedback from the teacher, peers and parents (or carers). In this type of approach to self-assessment, the teacher's role is viewed as that of a consultant working with the student to support their self-assessment of progress and development (Farr 1999; Vizyak 1999).

Accountability (and accountability for *what* in the assessment *of* learning)

In both Australia and New Zealand the work of teachers is governed by national curricula, which specify core content, achievement standards and a reporting framework, and the learning of students is evaluated periodically by national and international assessment programs. In Australia, for example, the National Assessment Program (NAP) utilises tests endorsed by the Ministerial Council for Education, Early Childhood Development and Youth Affairs (MCEECDYA), replaced in 2012 by the Standing Council on School Education and Early Childhood (SCSEEC). The tests include the National Assessment Program Literacy and Numeracy (NAPLAN) and three-yearly sample assessments in science literacy, civics and citizenship, and ICT literacy. The NAP also includes the Programme for International Student Assessment (PISA) (which oversees the participation of Australian children in international assessments) and the Trends in International Mathematics and Science Study (TIMSS) (ACARA 2011). As a beginning classroom teacher you may well feel overwhelmed by these measurement and accountability demands. The words 'testing' and 'assessment' tend to spark a range of emotions – pressure, stress, anxiety, failure and success – for everyone involved (Berry & Adamson 2011). Nevertheless, as a teacher you are obliged to participate in national and international assessment programs as directed by your school administrator. It is important to realise that these **high-stakes assessments** have purposes and implications far beyond your classroom – indeed, across the education sector and beyond in terms of accountability, resource allocation, and research (Klenowski 2011). Regardless of the current preference in Australia and New Zealand for standardised testing and accountability (in assessment *of* learning), however, you need to remember that assessment *for* learning is a critical component of your practice as an effective teacher.

> **High-stakes assessment:** where a student is required to complete a single assessment, the results of which have significant consequences for the student in terms of 'passing' or 'failing' (i.e. there is something 'at stake' for the student).

Accordingly, your primary focus will be on assisting your pupils, those young people for whom you are responsible, to approach an assessment *of* learning (group-administered standardised test) as a positive learning opportunity – an opportunity to demonstrate their best work and learn from the experience of being tested in such a manner. Glasson (2009) has suggested that by helping students to focus on results of an 'assessment *of* learning' as but a single indicator of their present learning and the experience of the assessment as one that can contribute to their knowledge of themselves as learners and testees, additional value can be extracted from 'assessment *of* learning.' We agree. We think it is critical for students to develop the attitude and resilience that will help them to complete tests successfully because they are likely to encounter standardised testing periodically throughout their schooling and beyond (e.g. testing to obtain a driver's licence, a professional position, employment certification, professional registration, and entry into graduate programs).

What other levels of accountability should you consider? We have noted that your first duty is to the pupils in your class. But you are also accountable to the parents of your pupils, your colleagues and your school administrators. And your school administrators are not only accountable to those in positions above them within the educational system; they are also accountable to you and your colleagues as well as the pupils and their parents. By now you should have a mental image of an entire web of accountability over which spreads another layer of accountability that includes bureaucrats in the Ministry of Education, the present government(s), and finally the taxpayers and businesses whose funds support the government. If you are feeling stressed by all these levels of accountability, you might want to reflect on the fact that there are records of formal assessments dating back to more than 3000 years ago in China, where candidates had to pass gruelling examinations in order to qualify for positions with the Imperial Civil Service (Berry & Adamson 2011).

Let's return now, however, to your first level of accountability – that is, your pupils and their parents. Your first priorities are to ensure that your pupils are receiving a high-quality education and that assessment of their learning is aligned with the curriculum and their learning experiences, is focused on improving your teaching and your pupils' learning, and provides authentic opportunities for your pupils to be involved in self-assessment and discussions of their progress and achievements with you and their parents. Klenowski (2011, p. 68) has noted that in the current accountability climate in which teachers are working, it is critically important for teachers to 'maintain a strong sense of responsibility by developing their professionalism through building their assessment literacy and practices'.

The key domains of literacy assessment

Foundation literacy skills: a student must develop a number of essential skills (such as phonological awareness, phonics, fluency, vocabulary and comprehension) in order to develop effective reading and writing skills.

Large-scale comprehensive reviews of research focused on the ways in which children learn to read have been conducted in a number of countries, including Australia (DEST 2005), the United Kingdom (Rose 2006) and the United States (NICHD 2000). There is compelling evidence across the findings of these inquiries that there are a number of essential **foundation literacy skills** that need to be addressed in an effective reading program during the early years of schooling. These five key components – *phonological awareness*, *phonics* (for *word reading* and *spelling*), *fluency*, *vocabulary* and *comprehension* – will be discussed in this chapter in relation to assessment during the primary school years. To these five, we will also add *writing* given that our focus in this chapter is upon literacy more broadly and not just reading.

In order to grasp the important relationships among these foundation skills, we'd like to introduce you to a model that clearly illustrates that we must never forget that the foundation of reading (a receptive language skill) and writing (an expressive language skill) lie within the fundamental core of one's oral language – both listening (receptive) and speaking (expressive) at the word level (vocabulary) and at the level of language (listening or language comprehension, world knowledge and ideas).

We stress the importance of this model as a heuristic (or cognitive) framework for thinking about each child's literacy development for several reasons. First, as already mentioned, the model visually demonstrates the position of oral language as the *central core* from which reading and writing develop. As noted by Snow, Burns and Griffin (1998), a child's development of oral language is a precondition for literacy development. It is extremely difficult for children to learn to read and write words that are not part of their listening or speaking vocabulary (Hill 2006).

Second, for the purposes of both instruction and assessment, the model supports an understanding of the reciprocal relationships among reading and writing at both the word level (reading and spelling words) and at the language level (reading comprehension and written expression); for example, the development of decoding skills (phonics) is necessary for and supports the development of encoding skills (spelling). Similarly, a child who enjoys expressing ideas in writing (written expression) is generally a child who also reads voraciously with good understanding (reading comprehension).

Third, a teacher can mentally plot a child's development across the seven key domains on the model and look for consistent and inconsistent relationships as a way of identifying and addressing the additional needs of particular pupils. An example of the need for concern is a pupil with well-developed oral language abilities (especially listening comprehension), a wealth of general world knowledge, and the ability to participate in discussions at a high level but with unexpected difficulties with phonics and spelling. For a pupil who has received consistent good instruction and home support, this inconsistent pattern is highly indicative of a specific reading difficulty likely in the domain of phoneme–grapheme (letter–sound) relationships.

Before we begin discussing specific methods to assess and document pupils' developing literacy skills, take some time to plot the eight skills – *oral language, phonological awareness, phonics, vocabulary, fluency, comprehension, spelling* and *written expression* – across the model. Note that components at the word level are necessary but insufficient for development at the 'text' level (e.g. oral vocabulary for listening comprehension and the development of world knowledge and ideas, word-reading skills for reading comprehension, and the ability to spell words for written expression).

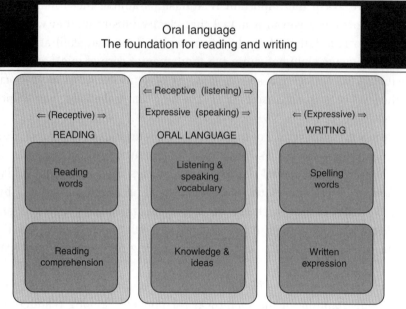

Figure 12.1. *Relationships between oral and written receptive and expressive languages*

Methods for assessing and documenting pupils' developing literacy skills and strategies

Informal assessment: when the teacher uses a teacher-constructed and/or curriculum-based measure.

Teachers of pupils in the primary school years use many of the same **informal** methods (tasks and activities) utilised by early childhood educators, such as planned observations, anecdotal records, narratives, checklists, skill inventories and work samples (Harp & Brewer 2000; Westwood 2001). Observations in particular can yield very important information about how a pupil is functioning (e.g. ability to focus and sustain attention, listen and follow directions, engage with literacy activities, persist with tasks despite frustration, and work collaboratively with peers) across various settings (e.g. individual, small group and whole class (Westwood 2008a, p. 30). You will likely find yourself using focused observation and other methods in combination – for example, conducting a planned observation and making anecdotal records during or on completing a session of work with an individual pupil or a small group of pupils who seem to be having difficulties acquiring a particular skill.

During the primary school years, teachers also use methods that are uniquely suited to gathering information about pupils' more developed (and developing) abilities in specific domains so that they have a deep understanding of how their pupils are learning and can identify the next steps for teaching and learning. Three excellent examples of such methods are surveys to record students' perceptions of their reading interests and levels of motivation (Harp & Brewer 2000), running records to assess beginning readers' skill development in oral reading as well as reading comprehension, and co-constructed rubrics, which move the responsibility for assessment of writing from the teacher to the student (Allington 2012).

> **Performance portfolio:**
> a student's ongoing purposeful collection (portfolio) of samples of work along with relevant assessment criteria and examples of critical self-assessment that provides evidence of his or her effort, progress and achievement (performance) in particular domains.

As was the case during the early childhood years, it is extremely useful to develop a literacy **performance portfolio** with each of your pupils. As we described in Chapter 9, the portfolio provides a clear basis for you to work collaboratively with each of your pupils to select representative samples of their work and evaluate their developing knowledge and skills. Portfolios also provide perfect opportunities for a teacher and a pupil to meet with the pupil's parents each term to review the pupil's goals and progress and perhaps engage in wider-ranging conversations about the pupil's engagement with literacy at home and in the community as well as the pupil's aspirations.

> **Student-led conferencing:**
> refers to a three-way conference among a student and his or her parents and teacher in which the student leads a discussion focused on his or her goals for learning as well as his or her performance and progress (often referring to specific examples from their performance portfolio).

Discussions among a student, his or her teacher and parents regarding the student's performance portfolio can be informal or more formal as in the case of '**student-led parent conferences**'. In the latter, the teacher develops a script with students that may include scaffolding such as how to greet and thank participants, how to describe goals, how to present evidence and how to elicit feedback. Scripts and practice enable even very young students to participate successfully in student-led conferences. Studies have shown that student-led conferences from the early years to the middle-school years have resulted in positive outcomes being reported by students, their parents, their teachers and their school administrators, which have included more-focused and higher-quality student work, higher results in statewide tests, a decrease in student discipline problems, and an increase in parent satisfaction and participation. Not surprisingly perhaps, negative outcomes were few and included finding adequate time for preparation and streamlining the paperwork (Borba & Olvera 2001; Tuinstra & Hiatt-Michael 2004).

As noted in Chapter 9, it will be important to collect information and evidence of your pupils' literacy learning across the important foundation skills for literacy (DEST 2005; NICHD 2000; Rose 2006). In the next section, we consider assessment methods across the six skill domains discussed earlier in relation to the model of the relationships between oral and written receptive and expressive languages – namely, *phonological awareness, phonics, fluency, vocabulary, comprehension* and *writing*. Before doing so, however, we have to confess that we are going to slide a few more skills into your approach to assessment. As you will know only too well by now, reading and writing are extremely complex processes that involve the integration of many skills. These additional skills (described in the following paragraph) are important to

Receptive and expressive language: a student's ability to understand the language of others, whether oral or written, is described as *receptive language* (i.e. language that is received either by listening or by reading) while a student's ability to communicate his or her ideas, whether by oral or written means, is described as *expressive language* (i.e. language that is expressed either by speaking or writing).

developing a deep understanding of how a pupil is developing **receptive and expressive language** abilities in both oral and written language.

We will begin with a consideration of assessment in relation to *vocabulary*, which lies within the central core of oral language. Before leaving this core, however, we will discuss *language comprehension* because this foundation ability underpins a student's success in developing both reading comprehension and expressive writing abilities. Next, we will move to the 'word level' of the model and consider *phonological awareness* and *phonics* in relation to *word reading* and *spelling*. The next component for us to consider is *fluency*. In relation to fluency, we will also consider briefly *sight words* and *sight vocabulary* because the recognition of a large number of words by sight has an enormous impact on a student's reading fluency. Finally, we will move down to the 'text' level and consider methods for assessing *reading comprehension* and *written expression*.

1 Vocabulary

It is important for students to continue developing their vocabulary or knowledge of word meanings throughout their years of schooling (and hopefully beyond). The size of a student's vocabulary in preschool and the early years of schooling is a significant predictor of reading comprehension and academic achievement in secondary school as well as later vocational success (NICHD 2000). Although the best way to assist students to develop their knowledge of words and word meanings remains under debate (Konza 2011c), there are ways that a classroom teacher and specialists can assess a student's vocabulary.

For the classroom teacher, vocabulary assessment needs to be do-able; that is, it needs to be an activity or task that is relatively brief yet capable of providing an insight into the progress of individual children. The best way to measure *receptive* vocabulary (i.e. children's understanding of the words they hear or read) is to observe closely children's functioning in the classroom. Do they understand and follow simple directions? Do they seem to understand your use of abstract words such as 'under', 'over', 'behind', 'before' and 'fewer than'? A method for assessing your pupils' *expressive* vocabulary (i.e. their ability to use appropriate words in context) is to listen carefully to their oral language when they are answering questions, describing pictures, speaking during sharing time or class discussions or when they are telling a story from a wordless picture book. You can make anecdotal notes about the length of the pupil's phrases and sentences. Are they shorter than the child's typically developing peers? Are the pupil's sentences grammatically correct? Are they using pronouns correctly? Are they confusing past and present tense?

If your pupils are in Year 2 or above, you might like to try a method of conducting an informal written expressive vocabulary assessment suggested by Peter Afflerbach and his colleagues (Afflerbach et al. 1995). Ask your pupils to write as many words as they can think within a 5–10-minute period. The children's lists of words are scored on the basis of the number of words that are spelled correctly and that they are able to read back accurately. The pupils can start with their names and then move on to any other words they can think of. The task described by Afflerbach and his colleagues is very similar to the Writing Vocabulary subtest of Marie Clay's *An Observation Survey of Early Literacy Achievement* (Clay 2005). If these writing tasks were repeated over time, you would have a very good indicator of each pupil's ability to generate words – that is, of their writing vocabulary.

If you continue to have concerns about a pupil's receptive and/or expressive vocabulary development, you should discuss your concerns with the pupil's parents and with your school-based specialist teacher. In the Australian state of Queensland, these teachers are most typically known as Support Teachers in Literacy and Numeracy (STLaN), while in New Zealand they are generally known as Supplementary Learning Support Teachers (SLST). In the case where a child is not reaching the widely held expectations despite additional instruction and practice at school and at home, the school-based team (teacher, pupil, parents, specialist teacher and school administrator) may wish to refer the pupil for an assessment by a visiting specialist (e.g. a speech and language pathologist). Pathologists can use formal standardised measures such as the Peabody Picture Vocabulary Test (PPVT-4) (Dunn & Dunn 2007) and the Expressive Vocabulary Test (EVT) (Williams 2007) to give you and the members of the school-based team an assessment of the child's development in relation to age-based norms. It must be remembered, however, that many of the standardised assessment instruments we use were developed and normed in the United States. As a consequence, we need to interpret the results with caution. Norms developed in relation to the language functioning and academic achievement of children in the United States may not be representative of the functioning and achievement of children in Australia and New Zealand who are of the same age or completing an equivalent year of schooling.

2 Language comprehension

A student's ability to comprehend oral language, especially oral literate language (or the language of books), is a significant indicator of his or her later success in reading comprehension as well as in oral and written expression (Berninger & Abbott 2010; Gunning 2006). You will be able to identify the students who are having difficulties in understanding literate oral language (or with listening comprehension) because they will struggle to follow the stories that you read aloud to your class (Konza 2006).

If you want more concrete information concerning the listening comprehension skills of particular students who seem to be making slower than expected progress and you are already using an informal reading inventory to assess the student's reading comprehension skills, you might consider using one of the set of the parallel texts for assessing listening comprehension skills. Most informal reading inventories consist of at least three parallel sets of texts, which facilitate assessment of oral reading, silent reading and listening comprehension. An example of a readily available and much-used informal reading inventory that assesses students' abilities with both narrative and expository (information) texts is the Qualitative Reading Inventory (Leslie & Caldwell 2011).

3 Phonological awareness

In Chapters 8 and 9 we noted that children's phonological awareness develops across a continuum, ranging from awareness of words, syllables, onset and rime, and finally to phonemes, over time (Nicholson 2005) and we reviewed informal methods for assessing a child's progress in these particular skills. Monitoring the development of students' phonological awareness skills continues to be important during the primary school years because phonological awareness and its subcomponent, phonemic awareness, are significant predictors of students' later success in reading and writing.

As a classroom teacher, the best way to monitor your pupils' development is to observe their functioning carefully during instruction and practice activities. You will want to know whether your pupils are aware of words and able to identify when words rhyme, how many syllables are present in a word, what onset and rime they can hear in a particular word, and whether they can blend, segment and manipulate sounds (Konza 2011b). Most teacher-resource materials for teaching phonological awareness contain checklists of skills that you could use to monitor each of your pupils' progress.

In the case of a pupil who isn't making satisfactory progress in developing phonological or phonemic awareness skills, despite additional support, you would consult with your school-based specialist teacher. Learning support teachers who have received graduate-level training in measurement and reading assessment, as well as speech and language pathologists, can assist you in identifying the specific skills a pupil needs to develop. Nicholson (2006) recommends the Gough-Kastler-Roper Test of Phonemic Awareness, an informal measure developed at the University of Texas at Austin, for assessing young pupils' phonemic skills. Nicholson provides a copy of this unpublished measure in his seminal book, *Phonics Handbook* (Nicholson 2006). Standardised measures that are often used by learning support teachers and speech pathologists to compare the abilities of a particular student with those of same-aged peers include the Comprehensive Test of Phonological Processing (C-TOPP) (Wagner, Torgesen & Rashotte 1999) and the Phonological Awareness Test (PAT) (Robertson & Salter, 2007) and the Test of Phonological Awareness (TOPA) (Torgesen & Bryant 1994).

4 Phonics (for word reading and spelling)

An understanding of the 'alphabetic principle', by which the individual sounds in language (phonemes) are associated with particular letters or groups of letters (graphemes), is fundamental to developing phonics skills – skills that are essential for both sounding out words (decoding) and spelling words (encoding) (Konza 2011a). As a classroom teacher you will need to approach the teaching of phonics skills systematically, especially for children who are experiencing difficulties in learning the relationships between phonemes and graphemes. As we discussed in Chapter 9, the English language is extremely challenging in that it has 44 phonemes and approximately 1200 orthographic representations or spelling variations (Konza 2006).

Many teachers and schools in Australia and New Zealand and have adopted specific phonics teaching programs in the early primary school years to ensure that explicit, systematic instruction is provided to all children. Two programs that are quite widely used include 'Jolly Phonics' (Jolly Learning 2012)) and 'Teaching Handwriting, Reading and Spelling Skills' (THRASS) (Davies & Ritchie n.d.). Both of these programs provide checklists that you can use for monitoring your students' development.

You will also find developmental phonics checklists in many recent teacher-resource materials and texts. Two very useful charts, which could be used as checklists, are Nicholson's (2006, pp. xv–xvi) Phonics Scope and Sequence chart, which gives a broad indicator of which phonics elements should be taught/mastered from ages 5–6 to 12–14 years; and his developmental Decoding Charts (Nicholson 2006, pp. 395–410), which you could use to track your pupils' decoding (word reading) and encoding (spelling) skill development. The charts begin with a phoneme-alphabet chart and move across the key phonic elements; these include words containing short vowels, silent 'e', initial consonants and consonant blends, initial and final consonant blends and digraphs, 'r' and 'l' affected vowels, vowel digraphs, and words containing common suffixes and prefixes. In the following sections, we will discuss how such phonics charts or checklists could be used to monitor a pupil's development of phonic skills for reading words and for spelling words.

Phonics for decoding (word reading)

In this section we begin by considering informal methods for monitoring students' development of phonics skills for decoding or reading unfamiliar words and finish with a consideration of some of the widely used formal methods used by specialists, such as learning support teachers and speech and language pathologists.

If you are already listening to your pupils read by means of running records and/ or informal reading inventories (as discussed earlier in relation to the assessment of listening comprehension skills), an extremely informative way to assess your pupils' mastery of phonics skills is to make note of their miscues (or oral-reading errors) as they read a passage or text. By examining the pupil's miscues and comparing them with a developmental phonics chart (e.g. Nicholson's [2006] Decoding Charts), you will be able to see which phonic elements the child has mastered and which elements are still posing challenges; for example, the student may have mastered initial and final consonants, simple consonant – short vowel – consonant (CVC) words (e.g. 'Sam' and 'dog'), as well as final consonant blends (e.g. /nd/ in 'found') but be having difficulty with words that include a 'silent e' (e.g. 'bone') and words containing vowel digraphs (e.g., /ou/ in 'found'). Your recording of the student's miscues would likely be as follows:

> ✓   ✓   ✓ bonny✓   ✓   ✓ foond✓
> Sam hid the bone but the dog found it.

The student's miscues tell you exactly which phonic elements the student still needs to learn and practice in order to be able to use phonics to decode unfamiliar words effectively and efficiently.

In the case of students whose decoding skills appear to be significantly weaker than might be expected for students of their age/year level, teachers will typically request a consultation with the school-based specialist teacher. In some cases, further assessment may be deemed necessary in order to obtain a fine-grained analysis of the student's decoding skills and abilities. If the student and parents agree to an assessment, there are a number of formal and standardised measures that a support teacher might choose to use. Some of the tests will require the student to read real words (decodable words from the English language) but some require the student to read 'non-words' (decodable pseudo-words). The latter are word forms that follow English phonics rules (e.g. 'litch') but do not constitute real words in the English language.

Formal tests that can be used to assess students' abilities to decode unfamiliar real words include the Word Reading subtest of Marie Clay's (2005) *An Observation Survey of Early Literacy Achievement*, as well as standardised measures such as the Word Reading subtest of the Wide Range Achievement Test (WRAT-4) (Wilkinson & Robertson 2007), the Word Identification subtest of the Woodcock Reading Mastery Test (WRMT-III) (Woodcock 2011) and the Burt Word Reading Test (BWRT) (Gilmore, Croft & Reid 1981), which was revised and standardised for use with children in New Zealand. Nicholson (2006) describes how to administer, score and interpret a child's performance on the BWRT as well as how to use the results to select suitable reading material for a student.

With regard to using non-word reading tests to assess students' phonic skills for decoding words, you may be very puzzled as to why anyone would ask a child to read a list of nonsense words. The rationale for this approach is that the reading of a carefully constructed list of non-words allows an examiner to assess purely phonic knowledge without the interference of any compensatory prior knowledge of a word, such as visual memory of the word or knowledge of any parts of the word (e.g. morphemes, the smallest units of meaning within a word) (McCutcheon, Green & Abbott 2008).

Formal non-word reading tests that specialist teachers may use to assess students' phonic decoding skills include the Bryant Test of Basic Decoding Skills (Bryant

1975). With Dr Dale Bryant's permission, Nicholson (2006) has made the Bryant Test of Basic Decoding Skills available in his handbook, where he has also provided detailed information about administering the test, analysing the results and designing follow-up practice activities.

More recent non-word tests that have been recommended by Colenbrander, Nickels and Kohnen (2011) from the ARC Centre of Excellence in Cognition and its Disorders (CCD) at Macquarie University in Australia include the Martin and Pratt Non-word Reading Test (Martin & Pratt 2001) which was developed and normed with Australian students aged 6–16 years of age; the Word Attack subtest of the Woodcock Reading Mastery Test (WRMT-III) (Woodcock 2011), which has a long history of use in many English-speaking countries; and the Test of Word Reading Efficiency (TOWRE) (Torgesen, Wagner & Rashotte 1999), which some support teachers in Australia use in their reading assessments. Colenbrander, Nickels and Kohnen (2011) reviewed commercially available non-word reading tests designed to assess primary school children's skills on the basis of reliability and validity, sufficient number and range of items, clear directions and ease of administration, provision of a pronunciation guide, a 'stopping' rule, and recent norms. They concluded that the three tests mentioned above fulfilled the highest number of their criteria for evaluation.

Let's turn now to the assessment of students' abilities to use their developing phonic knowledge to encode or spell unfamiliar words. As we did in the previous section, we will consider both informal and formal approaches to assessment as well as word lists that are comprised of real words and non-words.

Phonics for encoding (spelling words)

Although you may be required to use a specific spelling program, which has its own assessment program, when you begin teaching in the primary school years it is very important for you to have a good understanding of your pupils' developing abilities in relation to mastering phonics for spelling unfamiliar words. In this section we will restrict ourselves to discussing the importance of phonics (phoneme–grapheme correspondences) for spelling but you need to remember that there are many other skills – visual memory and knowledge of orthography (common spelling patterns such as -tion and -ought) and morphology (smallest units of meaning in words such as affixes) – that are needed in order for a student to become a good speller (Westwood 2008b). Learning to spell in the English language is extremely challenging because, as we discussed earlier, the English language is highly inconsistent in comparison with other alphabetic languages. English has 44 phonemes and approximately 1200 orthographic representations or spelling variations whereas German has 35 phonemes and 39 orthographic representations, Spanish 23 and 28, and Italian 25 and 33 respectively (Konza 2006).

Despite these differences in the numbers of phonemes and orthographic representations across languages, it is generally agreed that children develop their spelling skills in alphabetic languages across a number of stages or phases (Nicholson 2006; Westwood 2008b). It isn't easy, however, to analyse children's spelling errors and pinpoint the stage in which a student is operating (Kohnen, Nickels & Castles 2009). Nevertheless, stage models provide a valuable model for thinking about the development of children's spelling abilities. Nicholson (2006, p. 90) has described the stages as follows:

1. *Pre-phonemic* – children use random letters and marks to convey meaning.
2. *Semi-phonemic* – children use letters to represent some of the sounds in the words they want to write.
3. *Phonemic* – children use invented spelling to represent all of the sounds in the words they are writing.
4. *Transitional* – children's invented spelling of words begins to contain elements of conventional spelling.
5. *Conventional* – children are spelling most words correctly.

Experienced teachers can generally gain a sense of students' developmental levels and spelling abilities by observing their pupils as they write, analysing samples of their writing, and talking with individual pupils about their strategies and insights when spelling unfamiliar words (Westwood 2005). Until you have developed the necessary mental map of how children typically develop the ability to spell, however, you will likely find the support of some kind of specific developmental framework across the stages of great value. As noted in the section above on phonics for decoding unfamiliar words, you can use the framework from a quality phonics program or developmental charts such as those provided by Nicholson (2006) where the basic phonic elements needed for spelling or encoding words are presented in developmental order.

In the case of students who need additional support to strengthen their phonic skills for spelling, there are a number of measures that can be used by the specialist teacher or clinician to develop a fine-grained assessment of the student's skills. Such assessment will be necessary because writing samples cannot yield a complete picture of a student's phonic spelling skills in that students will be using words relevant to their chosen topics and likely avoiding words that they are uncertain about spelling correctly (Kohnen, Nickels & Castles 2009).

There are a number of formal tests that are designed for the general monitoring of students' progress in spelling but most – for example, the *Spelling* subtest of the Wide Range Achievement Test (WRAT-4) (Wilkinson & Robertson 2007) – have a limited set of words, which means that there are restrictions on the number of spelling subskills that can be assessed as well as the number of items that are appropriate for each developmental level. Accordingly, Kohnen and her colleagues (2009) recommend using either the British Spelling Test Series (BSTS) (Vincent & Crumpler

1997) or the Single Word Spelling Test (SWST) (Sacre & Masterson 2000), which assess a wide range of spelling skills and have different test forms for different ages of students.

In order to assess how well students are using phonics – making connections between phonemes and graphemes – Nicholson's (2006, pp. 90–100) informal Invented Spelling Test is a good choice because it allows the teacher or clinician to gauge on a four-point scale how well a student's response represents the underlying phonemic structure of the target words. Nicholson (2006) has provided clear directions for administering the test, using the results diagnostically, and developing follow-up practice activities.

With regard to formal assessment tools, Kohnen, Nickels and Castles (2009) recommend that non-word spelling tests be used. After reviewing commercially available non-word tests, these researchers noted that the only test without significant limitations in relation to the number of phoneme–grapheme correspondences assessed and the validity of the norms is the Queensland Inventory of Literacy (QUIL) (Dodd et al. 1996), which was normed with Australian children aged 6–16 years of age.

5 Fluency

The perfect opportunity for evaluating your pupils' reading fluency is when you are working individually with them to assess their reading comprehension skills by means of running records and informal reading inventories (which we will discuss in greater detail shortly in relation to reading comprehension). When conducting assessments with running records or inventories, it is easy to set a stopwatch running unobtrusively. When you know how long it took a pupil to read a passage, you can calculate *speed* (words per minute). When you count how many words were read correctly, you have an evaluation of *accuracy*. Together, these calculations yield a measure of *fluency* – that is, words read correctly per minute (Graves et al. 2011).

As each pupil reads, you should also note their behaviours as well as their errors. Did the pupil read so slowly and laboriously that meaning was lost? Did the pupil read so fast that words and lines were missed? Of course there are many other questions you can be asking and answering for yourself during a running record or inventory but we will turn to these in relation to comprehension.

There are numerous reading fluency charts in texts and on the Web but you can feel confident with Konza's estimation that by the end of Year 1, students should be reading about 60 words a minute; by the end of Year 2, about 90–100 words per minute, and in Years 3–6, 100–120 words per minute with less than three errors (Konza 2006). If you need a more accurate estimation of a student's reading fluency, perhaps to apply for additional time for a student on a 'high-stakes' examination, the Gray Oral Reading Test (GORT-5) provides an opportunity to assess fluency as well as decoding skills and oral reading comprehension (Wiederholt & Bryant 2012).

6   Sight words and sight vocabulary

As noted by Konza (2006), sight words (the high-frequency irregular words that must be learned visually) and sight vocabulary (the words a student has learned to recognise almost instantly) should not be confused. In the case of students whose reading lacks fluency, especially older primary students who are struggling with phonics, it can be extremely beneficial to have them focus on learning the most common sight words by means of visual memorisation. Similarly, the spelling of older primary students who are struggling with phonics can be strengthened by having them focus on learning to spell sight words.

Two of the most commonly used sight word lists are the Dolch Basic Sight Word lists and Fry's 300 high-frequency word list (Hill 2006). Most lists are readily available on the Web but be sure to consider the reliability of your source. It is very easy to use the lists to assess which words a student can recognise by sight (can the child say the word almost immediately without sounding out?) and to then have the student work on memorising the unknown words.

7   Reading comprehension

Most of what of what we want to know about our students' reading abilities is invisible (Barrentine 1999) and this is particularly true for reading comprehension. Nonetheless, there are many ways that we can begin to develop an understanding of how well our pupils are comprehending text and what strategies they are using to construct their own meaning.

One of the most efficient informal ways to assess a student's construction of meaning and use of reading strategies is to photocopy an unfamiliar text and have the pupil read the passage aloud while you follow along carefully making note of everything the pupil says and does, including any oral-reading errors (e.g. substitutions, omissions, insertions, repetitions, attempts, self-corrections, requests for help with words, and words supplied).

If the pupil has been able to read the text with reasonable accuracy, it would be useful to ask the pupil to retell the story (narrative text) or recall the information (expository text). Finally, you can ask the pupil a number of questions to further assess his or her understanding. Your questions should probe literal or factual comprehension (e.g. 'What was John riding?'), inferential comprehension (e.g. 'What do you think John will do next?') and critical or evaluative comprehension (e.g. 'Do you think it was a good idea for John to visit the old man?'). This procedure can be used with very simple one or two sentence texts (for emergent readers) to full passages (for more experienced readers).

With careful analysis this approach to assessment can yield valuable information about a pupil's level of development with respect to meaning making as well as the foundation skills of reading, namely, word-reading skills, fluency, and estimated reading level. In this section, we focus on attention to meaning, recall, and depth or comprehension because we considered word-reading skills and fluency earlier in this chapter.

Attention to meaning

In order to comprehend what they are reading, pupils have to learn to pay attention as they read. This sounds perfectly obvious, but in fact some young readers actually need to be convinced that they can do two things at the same time – that is, read aloud and comprehend. By analysing a pupil's behaviour while he or she reads, you will be able to tell whether the pupil is actively constructing meaning. For example, did the pupil use context clues to correct miscues? Did the miscues, omissions and/ or additions of words preserve or alter the meaning of the text? Did the pupil reread portions of the text to clarify meaning?

Recall

Many young students also find it difficult to recall what they have read, particularly if a lot of effort has been necessary in order to read the words correctly. As you listen to the pupil retell a story (narrative) or recall the information presented in an expository text, you can be asking questions such as: How well did the pupil recall the story or information? Was the retelling or recalling correctly sequenced? Did the pupil seem to have a general understanding of the text? Was the recall accurate and complete? Did the pupil use words and phrases from the text? Did the pupil seem to be con-necting the information to prior personal knowledge and experience? Students will sometimes need assistance to develop this skill. Allowing them a 'crutch' (e.g. turning the pages to check the illustrations) will help them to understand what is required in order to recall a narrative or the information conveyed in an expository text.

Depth of comprehension

Was the pupil able to answer factual questions based on information explicitly pre-sent in the text (i.e. literal comprehension)? Was the pupil able to read 'between the lines' and answer more abstract inferential questions (e.g. 'Why do you think John hid behind the bush?')? And finally, was the pupil able to answer higher-level criti-cal and/or evaluative questions (e.g. 'How well do you think the author conveyed his message about the dangers of mercury in the environment?')?

Estimated reading level

By examining how many errors a pupil makes when reading a specific text, you will be able to estimate whether the text is at an appropriate *independent* level for the pupil (e.g. the child is able to read the words with more than 95 per cent accuracy or less than four errors in 100 words), at an *instructional* level (90 per cent accuracy or 5–9 errors in 100 words) or at *frustration* level (less than 90 per cent accuracy or 10 plus errors in 100 words) (Konza 2006). It is important to have your pupils reading for pleasure as often as possible at the independent level. It is at this level that stu-dents will enjoy reading (likely unaware that they are practising their skills) and be motivated to continue reading (Allington 2012; Snow, Burns & Griffin 1998). Reading makes reading easier. Stanovich (1986) coined the term 'Matthew Effects' (from the Book of Matthew; essentially that the rich get richer while the poor get poorer) for this phenomenon; that is, those who read and write (and enjoy reading and writing) develop stronger skills while those who avoid these activities grow steadily weaker in comparison with their same-age peers (Stanovich 1986).

The relatively informal approach discussed above as a way to assess a pupil's reading comprehension skills and use of strategies is consistent with the methodology of running records (Clay 2000b), many informal reading inventories (e.g. the Informal Reading Inventory (Nicholson 2006) and the Qualitative Reading Inventory (Leslie & Caldwell 2010). We recommend that you, as a beginning teacher, gain experience using running records based on classroom-based reading materials or using a simple informal inventory such as that provided by Nicholson (2006) in his *Phonics Handbook*, because the texts and procedures will be largely familiar to your students and you will obtain useful information to guide your teaching.

If you find yourself teaching in a school where you have access to a purpose-built reading assessment program such as the PROBE 2 (Parkin & Parkin 2011), however, we recommend that you also gain experience using this assessment resource. The program was developed in New Zealand and has been used successfully by scores of teachers wanting more detailed information about their students' reading comprehension strengths and difficulties. The program provides clear guidelines for the student as well as the teacher and it has a number of optional elements, including methods and materials for assessing listening comprehension and also written comprehension, when group assessment is the only option.

Another purpose-built reading assessment program that you may encounter in your first years of teaching is the PM Benchmark Reading Assessment Resources (Smith, Nelley & Croft 2008). The program is used quite extensively in Australian and New Zealand classrooms and we recommend that you gain experience using this resource as well. The PM Benchmark kits contain a comprehensive teacher's resource book and procedures cards along with a set of student readers and assessment sheets. The program will provide you with an excellent scaffold to develop your knowledge and experience in assessing the reading comprehension skills of young readers.

After using some of the assessment methods and materials described above to guide your ongoing literacy instruction, you may find there are a still a few pupils in your class whose reading comprehension skills are a cause for continuing concern. At this time, it will be useful to consult with the child's parents and specialist staff (e.g. learning support teachers, guidance officers, and speech and language pathologists) to explore in greater depth what foundation skills need to be developed. Specialist staff may well choose to supplement your classroom observations, anecdotal records, and performance assessments with formal individualised standardised assessment. Three measures that they may use include the Neale Analysis of Reading Ability (NARA) (Neale 1999), the Gray Oral Reading Tests (GORT-5) (Wiederholt & Bryant

2012) and the York Assessment for Reading Comprehension (YARC) (Snowling et al. 2009). The NARA has a long history of use in Australia and New Zealand, but we have concerns about the results being reported as age equivalents and the validity of the norms given that they were constructed at least 13 years ago.

The GORT-5 is used, but perhaps more extensively in Canada, because the test yields a standard score for reading fluency (as well as comprehension) and this information can be used to support an application for a reader during high-stakes testing for students who have been previously identified as a having a 'learning disability,' a disability category that is not recognised yet in either Australia (Skues & Cunningham 2011) or New Zealand (Chapman, Tunmer & Allen 2003).

A recently developed instrument that also yields a fluency score in addition to information about a student's reading comprehension skills is the York Assessment for Reading Comprehension (YARC) (Snowling et al. 2009). The measure was developed by a group of researchers at the Centre for Reading and Language (CRL) at the University of York in the United Kingdom. The three versions of the YARC include: (a) early reading (ages 4–7), which assesses phonological awareness skills, letter sound knowledge and early word-reading skills; primary reading (ages 5–12), which assesses decoding skills, reading fluency and reading comprehension through passage reading; and (c) secondary reading (Years 7–11), which assesses single-word reading, reading fluency and reading comprehension through passage reading. The tests have been received well by practitioners in the United Kingdom (Martin 2011) and with the development of Australian editions by Psychological Assessments Australia (PAA) (these were published by GL Assessment in February 2012), we are likely to see increasing use of the instruments by teachers and reading specialists in Australia and New Zealand.

8 Written expression

Just as teaching your pupils to express their thinking in writing is a complex multidimensional process, so too is assessing their written work, especially if you are focusing on assessment *for* and *as* learning. But it is work that is well worthwhile because it will provide you with a window into how each of your pupils is developing insights into language and literacy (Hill 2006). But let's start simply, at the beginning.

When young children first begin to express their thinking in writing, they may not yet know how to form the letters of the alphabet, but their 'scribbles' across the page (left to right for English and the reverse for young children learning Arabic) convey their understanding that writing delivers a message. As you observe children develop their writing skills, you will see that they are beginning to learn the shapes of the letters, 'sound out' to spell new words (phonics), leave spaces between words (awareness of word boundaries) and spell those high-frequency irregular words (sight words) correctly.

As your pupils' writing skills develop, you will have even more to observe and learn about their use of written language. Hill (2006) developed early writing scoring sheets on the basis of the work of Marie Clay and others, which focus on the *written language* (use of letters, words and sentences), the *ideas* (what the pupil is communicating) and the use of *text conventions* (how well the pupil has placed the text on the page, used correct directionality, and used spacing, capital letters and punctuation). These scoring sheets are really a precursor to the writing rubrics that you will have seen in many writing texts and teacher-resource materials.

As your pupils become even more accomplished writers, we would like to suggest that you use rubrics, either ones that you take from relevant curriculum documents and resources or ones that you develop with your pupils. To illustrate how a curriculum document could be used, let's take a look at the new Australian national curriculum, 'English: Foundation to Year 10 Curriculum', which provides guidance for teaching and learning with respect to language, literature and literacy. Within the literacy strand for Year 2, there are elements and elaborations that provide an excellent basis for developing a rubric. For example, within 'Creating Texts ACELY1671', which states that students should be able to 'create short imaginative, informative and persuasive texts using growing knowledge of text structures and language features for familiar and some less familiar audiences, selecting print and multimodal elements appropriate to the audience and purpose' (ACARA 2012a), there are elaborations that could form the basis of items for your rubrics, such as:

• The sequence of ideas or events is obvious to the reader.

• Simple and compound sentences are used to express and combine ideas.

• The vocabulary is appropriate to the type and purpose of the text.

With regard to guidance from documents provided by the Ministry of Education in New Zealand, the National Standards for Reading and Writing (Ministry of Education 2009b) for Years 1–8 are an excellent resource for developing rubrics. For example, within the Writing Standards, it is expected that after three years at school, students will 'use their writing to think about, record, and communicate experiences, ideas, and information to meet specific learning purposes across the curriculum' (Ministry of Education 2009b). The document then provides a set of descriptors of the key characteristics of students' writing at this level, an annotated sample of student writing that illustrates the writing standard, and a link to the Literacy Learning Progressions (Ministry of Education 2010b). The progressions provide detailed information about the standards that you and your students will be aiming to meet; for example, it states:

> When students at this level create texts, they:
> • use planning strategies to organise ideas for writing;
> • revise and edit their writing for sense and impact and give their peers feedback on their writing.
> They draw on knowledge and skills that include:
> • using increasingly specific words and phrases that are appropriate to the content of the text;
> • using their visual memory to spell personal vocabulary and high-frequency words (Ministry of Education 2010b, p. 14).

In the next chapters (Chapters 13 and 14) you will be examining some examples of student writing from these documents in relation to both narrative and factual (or expository) writing.

With regard to developing rubrics for specific writing projects collaboratively with your pupils, you might find it useful to consider the work of Turley and Gallagher (2008). Although they are concerned with writing and rubrics at the secondary school and college levels, their arguments in favour of using rubrics as a shared tool are compelling for all students, even those in the early primary years. After considering the history of rubrics as well as some of the debate that has surrounded their use, particularly in relation to high-stakes testing, Turley and Gallagher (2008, p. 90) argue that rubrics can be important tools in a constructivist classroom in that they can:

- be co-developed with students, thus honouring students' input as writers
- be created after students have completed their first drafts, thus becoming guides rather than prescriptions for the writing task
- facilitate rich discussions with regard to evaluations by self and others
- be flexible and allow space for a student writer to include a 'wild card' or personal writing goal, thus enhancing student engagement with their writing and the writing of their peers.

Calfee and Miller (2007) describe an approach to designing rubrics that is based upon specific common features of writing (often referred to as the 'six traits plus one' approach popularised by Ruth Culham and Vicki Spandel (Tompkins 2012):

1. ideas (e.g. theme along with relevant details and anecdotes)
2. organisation (e.g. structure and sequence of ideas)
3. voice (e.g. sense that the writer is aware of audience and is speaking to the reader)
4. word choice (e.g. specific and rich vocabulary)
5. sentence fluency (e.g. range and flow of sentences)
6. conventions (e.g. spelling, punctuation and syntax)
7. presentation (e.g. layout and appearance of text).

These features will give you a very good place to start when designing writing activities and developing the rubrics for each task (see also Culham 2008 and Spandel 2008), perhaps collaboratively with your pupils.

In deciding upon what is important for the rubrics for a particular task with your pupils, you are giving your pupils rich opportunities to develop their understanding of the language of literacy (e.g. what is a paragraph?), learn what is valued in writing by others (e.g. clarity, a rich vocabulary, believable characters and a sense of the author's 'voice') and decide on what they value themselves (e.g. engaging in meaningful self-assessment). In the following chapters (Chapters 13 and 14), you will learn more about how to inspire and teach your pupils to be expressive writers and especially how to help them develop an engaging plot with scenes, episodes and believable characters with insights into their feelings, relationships and motivations in narrative texts (Wolf & Gearhart 1994) as well as structure, sequence, tone, cue words and transitional phrases in expository texts or factual writing (Tompkins 2012). At the end of each writing task, we hope you will invite your students to deposit their texts along with a copy of the rubric (perhaps annotated by the pupil, the teacher and several peers) in their personal performance portfolios. These portfolio submissions would provide rich concrete evidence of students' writing progress for student-led conferences.

With regard to consulting with specialists, particularly the learning support teacher and the speech and language pathologist, about any pupils who seem to be making limited progress in writing (despite additional support at school and at home), we would suggest sharing samples of the pupil's writing over time along with a brief description of the nature of the task and time taken to complete the task. A rich discussion focused on writing samples can be extremely informative and provides a valuable base for the planning of any additional assessment.

Standardised assessments of written language are problematic in a number of ways. They provide relatively limited information that is useful for planning instruction and the scoring of writing samples is challenging. Without detailed procedures and exemplars, it is difficult for two examiners to assess a writing sample and produce the same or a similar result (i.e. achieve satisfactory inter-rater reliability). Nonetheless, there may be times when a standardised assessment is useful – for example, when applying for a pupil to have additional time or access to a computer for a high-stakes assessment. In this case, the Test of Written Language (TOWL-4) (Hammill & Larsen 2009) can be very useful. The measure has two forms (A and B) and consists of seven subtests. The first five subtests assess conventional, linguistic, and conceptual aspects of writing – namely, vocabulary, spelling to dictation, punctuation, logical sentences (ability to edit and correct illogical sentences) and sentence combining, yielding an overall composite score for Contrived Writing. The final two subtests, conventions (spelling, punctuation and syntax) and story composition (vocabulary, plot, prose and character development) are based on a student's written response to one of two picture cards. This timed writing sample yields an overall composite score for Spontaneous Writing. Taken together, the Contrived and Spontaneous composite scores form an Overall Writing standard score and percentile rank based on the age of the student. The measure has adequate psychometric properties and can be a valuable addition to an individual assessment of a student who is experiencing significant difficulties with written expression (McCrimmon & Climie 2011) but it is a measure best utilised by specialist teachers and clinicians, with the results examined collaboratively with the pupil, the teacher and the parents in relation to samples of the pupil's writing, which have been collected over time and deposited in the pupil's writing performance portfolio.

Conclusion

This chapter has focused on the role of assessment during the primary school years. The chapter has reviewed assessment *for*, *as* and *of* learning. With regard to the latter, consideration has been given to the utility and purposes of standardised and high-stakes testing as well as the multiple levels of accountability for assessment results across the education sector. Although the chapter has touched upon your role in preparing your pupils for assessment *of* learning, greater emphasis has been placed on your involvement in assessment *for* and *as* learning in your daily work with your pupils and their parents. The chapter has also focused upon the importance of involving students in self-assessment, particularly through collaborative discussions based on performance portfolios. The chapter presented a model of the relationships among oral and written receptive and expressive language as a springboard for considering the complex interrelationships among the foundation skills for reading and writing. Finally, consideration was given to how a primary school teacher could assess and monitor a student's developing foundation skills and work with specialists when there were ongoing concerns about a student's progress and development. To conclude, learning to read and to write is not easy and many students need additional instruction and continuing support in order to begin mastering these complex processes. Not surprisingly, therefore, your role in orchestrating assessment *for* and *as* learning is equally complex and can be challenging. Lorri Neilsen, who wrote eloquently about teaching literacy in times of change (yes, there were changes in literacy practices in the 1990s and so will there be in 2090s), has likened your work as a teacher to that of a skilled craftsperson who must necessarily develop a wisdom of practice.

> Just as a carpenter measures informally but regularly, stopping to eyeball the structure in progress, or just as the cook adjusts seasoning while preparing the meal, expert teachers are now keeping written and mental records of what children do each day, adjusting their teaching according to what they see (Neilsen 1994, p. 120).

Reflective questions

1. How were your literacy skills assessed during your primary school years? Are similar methods used in schools today?

2. Do you remember having to read aloud to your teacher or another adult? How did this make you feel about yourself as a reader?

3. Do you remember taking weekly spelling tests? Did the weekly test help you to become a better speller?

4. What do you remember most about writing during your primary school years?

5. Do we teach and assess writing in the same way now?

Chapter 13

Reading and writing in the primary school: focus on narrative writing

Chapter objectives

1. To explain the structure of stories.
2. To explain how reading links to writing.
3. To explain how to instruct a pupil to write a story.

This chapter examines the research evidence on the powerful reciprocal relationship that exists between reading and writing development, the teacher's role in supporting pupils' emerging reading and writing abilities, ideas to inspire pupils to use reading as a springboard for writing, and the secrets of success in effective story writing.

Setting the scene

You are a teacher of a Year 1 class. Where do you start in teaching writing? Many teachers connect their teaching of writing to productive talk where the pupils talk together about a topic and generate ideas. Children and teacher talk together about a topic and this leads to writing. The following is an example where the teacher is sitting in front of the class and the class is sitting on the mat.

Example 13.1

A Year 1 class (five-year-olds) writing a story after oral discussion

Time: 9:30

Teacher: 'Today we are talking about "My family". Whose family?'

Class: 'My family!'

Teacher: 'Talk with the classmate sitting next to you about your family. Who is in your family? Share your ideas.'

Teacher gives a few minutes for discussion and then asks individual children to share with the class who is in his or her family.

Teacher models writing.

Teacher explains that she wants the class to write about their families. Teacher pins a big blank sheet of paper on the whiteboard. This acts as a template for a language experience lesson on writing.

Teacher suggests pupils start their writing as follows: 'I like my _____'.

Teacher asks children for the words they will write in their stories. Each child suggests some words. Teacher writes on whiteboard what they say, next to the language experience chart.

I have a
I like my
nana, cousin, mum, dog, baby, little sister, aunty, uncle

Teacher and class then read the chart together.

Transition to pupil writing.

Then the pupil's task is to write his or her own story about 'My family' in his or her writing book.

Teacher explains on the whiteboard how the children are to set out their writing:

My family

I have a

Instructions are for the children to write their stories and draw a picture of the people in their families.

Teacher readies each pupil's writing book as she gives the books out – she opens them on the right page and puts a mark where the pupil is to start. She asks each pupil to 'sit next to someone who won't talk to you'. She has to explain the instructions several times.

Teacher puts up the language experience chart on the whiteboard so everyone can see it and use it as a model for their writing:

My family

I have a

I like my

Teacher uses magnetic buttons to fix the chart to the board.

10:10 – Teacher asks the pupils to finish drawing pictures of their families and to start writing. She reminds them to write the heading 'My family'.

Teacher moves around the class. She reminds the pupils to put a finger between each word as they write.

10:30 – Children finish writing and wait in line for the teacher to mark their work. She writes a comment on each piece of work, such as 'Remember your finger spacing'. She ticks each letter written correctly and corrects words if spelled wrongly. If a pupil can't write, she writes for him or her (e.g. 'I like my friend'). She gives positive comments (e.g. 'Good try, Ali'), signs each story and puts a sticker on each piece of work.

10.30 – The class is back on the mat. Teacher tells the pupils to wash their hands and then go to play.

What are pupils interested in reading?

In a recent summer books study conducted by one of the authors of this book, a group of seven-year-olds were asked to select titles from a wide range of graded readers from one publisher, Sunshine Books. In fiction, they seemed to like to read stories that were funny, scary and exciting. In non-fiction, they chose factual texts that were exciting (e.g. killer whales), were mysterious, that related to their own lives (e.g. slumber party), featured things that were larger than life (e.g. Ancient Egypt, space), and showed things that they were curious about (e.g. natural resources, weather) and places far away.

The pupils were asked to select a mix of fiction and non-fiction titles. There was more **non-fiction** at the higher reading levels and some of the topics were complex (e.g. 'What is air?' and 'Natural resources'). These are not topics that pupils have learned about in their everyday experience and are more challenging than texts in junior primary. The most popular titles chosen are listed below. The selections give an idea of what texts pupils like to read.

> **Non-fiction:**
> text material that is not a story.

Fiction. *Monkey Messages, Forgetful Giraffe, My Sad Skeleton, Secret of Spooky House, Space Race, Crocodile, Crocodile, Monty Takes the Prize* (about a dog at a pet show), *Aunt Rosie's Sports Car, My Wonderful Aunt, Holiday Farm, Deep Trouble, Slam Dunk, Ice Cream Shop Window, Danger on Copper Mountain, Personal Trainer*

Non-fiction. *Exploring Space, I Love Killer Whales, Spiders, Gorilla Mountain, How the Sun Was Made, Places of Mystery, China's Treasure, Natural Resources, What is Air?, Ancient Egypt, Wild Weather, Slumber Party Organiser, Favourite Games around the World, Ancient Man of the Ice*

What do not-so-good readers like to read?

In another informal survey conducted by the same author, pupils who were not good readers were asked, 'What was the last book you read?' These were pupils in Years 2–6. The responses included *Captain Underpants, Oh Hogwash Sweet Pea, Three Little Pigs, A Cat and a Dog, Clifford, The Small Red Puppy, Ben 10, Clifford and the Big Storm, Super Fly Guy, The Amazing Adventures of Charlie Small, Airy Fairy, Angelina Ballerina.*

How do you hook your class into reading?

1. Let pupils choose the books they want to read

There is much agreement in research on student choice in reading that it is better to let good readers choose the books they want to read than impose books on them (Allington 2012; Guthrie & Humernick 2004), while poor readers need help to make sure the book is not too difficult (Forell 1985). On the other hand, some books are really interesting and the teacher can sell a book to pupils in the sense of sparking their interest if he or she 'markets' it by reading it aloud or explaining it to the class. You may remember an experience like that in your own schooling, such as a time when a replacement teacher spent a whole afternoon reading a book to your class and it sparked your interest in wanting to read that book, and others like it.

2. Give pupils access to books in different media

There are many ways to market books to pupils. Strategies include reading books aloud to the class, listening to audiotaped versions of books (many publishers produce audiotapes of their books) and watching the movie of the book. Movies involve reading when the movie has subtitles that pupils can read while watching the movie (e.g. *Alice in Wonderland, Fantastic Mr Fox, Charlotte's Web, Harry Potter, Lord of the Rings, The Hobbit*, various Shakespeare movies).

3.   Help struggling readers to make better book choices

Struggling readers can 'read' books indirectly through e-books, audiotaped books, and DVDs of the movies. These readers may not be able to decode books very well but by using other media the teacher can grow other aspects of language necessary for reading comprehension, such as vocabulary and general knowledge. Struggling readers tend to select books that are too difficult for them to read, possibly to hide the fact that they do not read very well, or they may choose on interest rather than readability. The teacher can get around this difficulty by asking strugglers to choose books within the reading level that they are at, or a little bit above that. This same strategy is important for the whole class in that all students are likely to make more progress in reading if they read books at their reading ability level and just above. Marketing books at the right levels for pupils in your class is very easy to do as most educational publishers list their books in reading levels.

Reading books to the class to create a community of readers

Many writers draw on their reading of other stories to help them with their own writing. They do not copy other ideas that they read about but the experience of reading books helps them to think about how to structure their own stories. They might also think of ways to write a story that is not the same but the story they read makes them think of a new story idea. One way to help your own pupils to read like a writer is to read to them and talk about how the writer has put the story together, developed the characters, and so on. Reading a story to your class is not as easy as it sounds. It is a good idea to practise your story-reading skills to make the story as exciting as possible.

Sometimes when pupils are asked if they like it when a teacher reads to them they'll answer they don't like it. They say the teacher is boring or the book is boring. You can market books to your class in a more effective way by reading them aloud, using strategies that capture the drama of the book. Here are some suggestions based on Mem Fox's popular book, *Reading Magic* (2001):

• Consider the culture, socio-economic background, age and interests of the class when selecting a book to read. If you are teaching in a diverse classroom, be sure to include books that draw on the pupils' cultural knowledge.

• Be sure to build vocabulary – explain the meanings of words pupils may not know when you read the book, or before reading the book.

- Make sure the class can see and hear you. Make sure no one is talking while you are reading. Ask the pupils to sit on the mat and move closer. If reading a picture book, check to see if the pupils can see the pictures. Another option is to use a 'big book' or present the text using an electronic whiteboard with a PDF copy so that everyone can see the text.

- Is the class comfortable? If it is a long chapter in the book, pupils can take a 'commercial break' and stretch.

- You may have read the story many times before but you must maintain your enthusiasm as if it were the first time you have read it yourself.

- The first line of the story has to be sensational! Try practising that first line at home. You will know immediately if you have grabbed the pupils. If they are sitting on the mat in front of you, they will start creeping forward to hear you better.

- Be as expressive as possible. A boring way of talking is a turn-off. We can all relate to this – for example, when you are on a plane and the safety instructions are read out and the flight attendant's voice has a bored and unenthusiastic tone. There is that annoying rise in tone at the end of every sentence. You just do not want to listen! It is the same when reading to your class. It is so important to vary your voice, emphasise some words that are of importance to the story (e.g. 'There once was a *baby* kitten'), not just the first or last word of every sentence.

- The eyes and voice are important, so make sure there is eye contact between you and the class. At the end of important parts of the story, at the end of each episode, as the suspense grows, you can stop for a few moments, pause, look around at the class, and then go on. Look at the group, widen your eyes, narrow them, show that your face is animated, that it is happy, sad, keen, surprised, make your body language OTT, that is, enthusiastic, move your head, jump with surprise, and so on.

- Make sure your voice is interesting, not cutesy saccharine or condescending. Make your voice do gymnastics: loud, soft, fast, slow, high, low. For example, use a slow voice for sad or scary parts, a fast voice for fast parts, a low voice for scary parts and a long pause for suspense parts. It is often good to read quickly – pupils have no problem with that. If you read too slowly, it can be boring.

- The last line has to be terrific, satisfying and complete. If you read it too fast, you can ruin the feeling. Read slowly and drag each word of the final line. For example: 'And – they – lived …'.

Why is it so hard to write stories?

Recent survey data on writing in Years 1–8 in New Zealand indicate many children struggle to achieve expectations in writing (Thomas & Ward 2010). A possible reason for problems in writing stories is a lack of knowledge about structure in story writing.

The 2002 National Assessment of Educational Progress (NAEP) (US Department of Education 2002) survey of writing illustrated this by comparing two student writing attempts. A narrative writing task for fourth graders was to write a story titled 'An Unusual Day'. The story was to be based on several imaginative illustrations shown to them. The NAEP report noted that children who wrote 'skilful' stories had a clear structure to their stories whereas those who wrote 'uneven' stories wrote lists of things they saw in the stimulus pictures.

For example, a skilful story showed structure right from the start: 'One morning I woke up to get my breakfast and I couldn't believe it!' (US Department of Education 2002, p. 15). In contrast, the uneven story started like this: 'When I got downstairs to the kitchen I saw clouds on my plate and a rainbow in my cup (US Department of Education 2002, p. 14).' The first sentence in the skilful writing example started with an immediate sense of a problem: 'I couldn't believe it!' The first sentence of the uneven piece of writing simply described what was in the picture with no sense of problem.

Do we make writing too complicated?

Reading is not the same as writing. Reading is a receptive activity and writing is a productive activity. Reading involves taking in someone else's ideas and writing is putting out your own ideas. Many people do not like to write letters because it is open-ended process and you have to choose the topic, the style of writing, the sequence of ideas, and so on. This is hard, which is why many of us would rather pick up the phone or send a text or email than write a letter. Texts and emails seem easier to write because they are usually shorter and less formal. They do not seem to have the same conventions applied to them as a letter. For example, you do not necessarily have to worry about **grammar**, punctuation or spelling. There is also a tendency to think that texts and emails are not real writing and often we are shocked when emails and texts (and even phone calls) are quoted or cited as evidence. We forget the rule that you should never say anything in an email, text, or phone conversation that you would not write in a real letter.

> **Grammar:** one of the considerations is whether the sentence structure is correct. For example, 'Pita hit' is not grammatically correct. You have to hit something.

The fact that most people do not like to write a letter but enjoy sending texts and emails, or talking on the phone, has relevance to teaching writing because you have to ask, why is this? We have already mentioned that the writer feels less restricted with a text or email in terms of spelling, and so on. Often you start to send a short text or email but end up sending a long one because you keep thinking of ideas. If we can teach writing that way, we may make it a lot easier for students to get their thoughts on paper.

Does process writing make the process too hard?

Thompson (2011) has observed that her students got bogged down in the process writing approach where they had to pre-write, draft, revise and publish. She was trained to teach that way and thought that this is what a 'good' teacher did, and that students had to produce a perfect product. But going through all the stages meant that it took her students weeks to produce a final product. Also, at each stage in the process students were writing the same thing again and again and not making any improvements in the quality of writing. According to Thompson (2011, p. 59): 'My most grievous error was confusing good writing with good grammar.' She decided to look at national exemplars of good writing to find out what made them so good. She realised that although the written products were often messy and grammatically incorrect and had spelling mistakes, they were interesting, exciting, and fun to read. They had substance and a genuine student voice. It occurred to her that as a teacher what she was doing was falling back on what teachers are good at, editing other people's work. Teachers spend most of their time in writing class correcting grammar and spelling, which they are good at, rather than helping students to find their own ideas and improve on them. She decided to move away from brainstorming, pre-writing and using graphic organisers to structure students' work, and encouraged them to find their own voice, start writing, discuss their ideas with others as they wrote, and let the story emerge.

Thompson (2011) came up with a checklist for her students to use when writing:

1. Stories need an interesting introduction.
2. Stories need ways to hook and hold onto the reader's attention.
3. Stories need figurative language, such as similes, metaphors and idioms.
4. Stories need interesting vocabulary – vivid and exciting words.
5. Stories need a beginning, middle and end.
6. Stories need sentence variety.
7. Stories need correct capitalisation, punctuation and spelling.

The combination of less stress on correctness, and more stress on writing interesting ideas and with one's own voice led to a dramatic improvement in the quantity and quality of writing. A sceptic may look at the checklist and say, 'Yeah, right – been there, done that, and it still does not work'. Or you might think, 'Yes, fine in theory and good in Year 1 when children are just starting to write, but to send home untidy and incorrect work in Year 3, even if it is Shakespearean in quality, will only bring a storm of parent protest about the incompetence of the classroom teacher.'

The reality, though, is that Thompson (2011) is right about process writing. It takes too long and it stifles creativity, even though it has noble aims and intentions. One of the authors of this book has often watched Year 3 children in small groups or on their own, sitting around the computer and revising their work, and it seems to take ages, and the final product never seems to appear. You think to yourself, 'Are they really writing or just rehashing ideas they thought of weeks ago?' On the other hand, this author has also been on the receiving end of performance review reports that say that students in her class have done a lot of writing but their teacher has not spent enough time editing and correcting their work. The problem is that if you spend a lot of time correcting and marking, then you are reluctant to have students continue writing because it means another 25 essays to mark each time they write. One way to avoid this issue is to have students read each other's work and give feedback. Then there is more time to write.

Looking at exemplars of writing: what is it that makes the writing effective?

The following pieces of writing were prepared in the context of New Zealand's National Standards in Reading and Writing and the Literacy Learning Progressions. In this chapter we look at stories written by Year 8 pupils (Ministry of Education 2007a, 2009b, 2010b).

In the example of writing at school entry below at left, we can see how the child has a sense that a story has words but he or she still has to learn the mechanics of writing and spelling in order to write more than this:

In the example below, from a pupil at the end of Year 1, the student writes a series of sentences and there is a basic plot. The writing has a sense of humour and it brings out some of the personality of one of the characters but it mainly describes the experience rather than creating a sense of action or excitement:

My gran has brown hair and comes in the pool with me and my boogie board. Sometimes she rings me and says there is a sheep on the lawn but she is only teasing.

In this example from a pupil at the end of Year 2 recounting an experience about a tupperware party, the writing has humour in that it says tupperware parties for adults are not like parties for kids. It also explains the difference between the two kinds of parties. It shows more complexity of writing than the Year 1 example but there is no development of character and there is no plot:

Tonight my mother is having a tupawer party. A tupawer party is not for children. A tupawer party goes like this. The adolts sit down and tok about plastic stuff in the kichin. It is not like a kids party.

My Aaron has [brown] ban hair and a green coat in the [pool] with me And my + [boogie board] Sometimes she ring me and she says it is a shep [shark] on the lan [lawn] but she is teasing.

Tonight my mother is havein the a tupawer party. A tupawer party is not for children. The a tupawer party goes like this. The adolts sit down and tok about plastic stuff in the kichin. It is not like a kids party.

In this example from Year 3, the pupil describes an experience of making a smoothie at school. It is a step up from the Year 2 example in that it has more detail, and introduces characters. It has a plot, beginning, middle and end. There is a sense of humour in the description about making the smoothies:

'Make a Smoothie!'

This morning I got to go to class space 14 to do a fun task. I don't normally go to class space 14 but when I walked in it was going to be fun because we were going to make our own smoothie. First we had to was [wash] our hands. I didn't wash my hand I just used hand senitiser. Next we all had to do some job I got to hand out bananas with Lauren we had to count the bananas then give it to everybody in class. Then the boys went first to choose thire smoothie. Nelson got a very dark smoothie. After that Rebecca did her smoothie it was funny because it splaterd every-where inside the magic bullet (blender). Finally it was my turn to blend my smoothie. The smoothie was very dark it was dark purple with little seeds. Then at the end we tidyed up the class. My smoothie tasted nice with all the berrys.

In this example, after four years at school, there is a definite change in the quality of writing. It is more exciting and funny. The writer has created a setting, characters, and a definite plot with a sense of suspense and a happy ending:

'The Ram'

'Maraea please go and feed your rabbit!' Mum called from the hallway. 'Okay' I said back and got a bucket to put some grass in for Aorha (my rabbit). So there I was getting grass for Aroha and as I was about to leave I saw a ram. It was approching me. I saw it stare at me a scary look like it was going to hurt me. I dropped the bucket and ran. I glanced back and it was chasing me. I was so close to the fence so I started climbing it. The ram caught my pants when I was almost over. I screamed as it pulled me to the ground. But it final let go so I jumped up, gabbed the buket, chuked it over the fence thon I climbed over the fence before the ram could get me. I lay on the grass relieved that I was safe. I looked in the buket nothing. 'Oh well' I said 'she'll just have to put up with no grass tonight'. As I walked back home I glanced back. I saw the ram. It was staring at me. I quickly turned away. I was safe.'

In this example, at the end of Year 5, the pupil has written a story about an experience of a flying fox. The story has some interesting qualities in that it describes the writer's emotions in more detail than in the Year 4 example, and it has a similar sense of anticipation and excitement, with a happy ending:

'My Big Challenge'

Slowly but steadily I climbed the stairs, One, two, three. I let my shaky legs guide me to my destination. Looking down I knew I couldn't do it! Ignoring the fact I was 50 feet from the ground, I pushed my feet to the edge. Click! That was the signal, I lowered myself so that I was level with the floor. OK go! The words echoed in my head like a bell. A second later I was half way down sliping and sliding like an eel. Touch down!

Summary

It is interesting to observe from these examples of student writing that correct spelling and punctuation is not insisted on under the National Standards. The exemplars mainly show differences in quality of writing. On the other hand, they also show that correctness in spelling and punctuation is noticeable and we have to avoid the tendency to rate the quality of writing according to correctness of spelling. All the examples are recounts of personal experiences, but how can we take the pupil into writing that goes beyond actual experiences, into more imaginative topic areas? Further on, we explain how pupils can use stories from different media as stepping stones to writing stories beyond their own experiences.

The reciprocal relationship between reading and writing

Many students struggle with writing even though they may do a lot of reading. What seems to happen is that they do not see clearly the links between reading and writing. This requires them mentally to stand back from the text and think about how the writer put it together. Teachers can show their pupils how the writer has put together a text and use this as a springboard to teach writing. Many writers build their stories on the shoulders of other writers; for example, how many different versions have you read of the 'three little pigs' story (O'Neill 2010; Trivizas 1993). The conventional story has been rewritten many times, from the wolf's point of view, and so on. Teachers can do the same thing with stories, showing pupils how to take the basic idea of the story and create something new and different. Every story has a problem – but many children do not know this basic feature of stories. Children enter school intuitively knowing a lot about stories. They have listened to stories, had stories read to them, watched DVDs, and viewed stories on television. Their whole life is a story. But there is much more for children to learn about stories once formal education begins.

Although they have an intuitive sense of stories, teachers need to make this awareness much more explicit. Young writers need to learn about the components of stories, how they are built. This is essential background for writing – the knowledge that stories have a setting, characters, a plot (consisting of one or more episodes) and a theme. Without this background knowledge children's writing will lack structure. Their efforts at writing stories will tend to be a list of disconnected sentences.

Juel (1988) reported a longitudinal study of the literacy development of children from first to fourth grade. In her study she found that poor writers lacked 'knowledge of story ideas (i.e. knowledge of story structures and the delivery of interesting story episodes)' (p. 442). At the end of fourth grade the poor writers in her study were writing simple descriptions rather than stories. They had yet to gain a formal sense of the structure of stories.

Ideas for writing stories come from a number of sources. Ideas, according to Wolf and Gearhart (1994), tend to come from books rather than 'people'. Juel (1988) also suggests that reading or listening to stories provides a rich source of ideas for writing stories. Steven Spielberg (cited in Juel 1988) wrote, 'Only a generation of readers will spawn a generation of writers.'

Teaching about the structure of stories

An important understanding to get across to students is the plot and how it works (see also Dymock & Nicholson 2010a). This is the foundation for any effective narrative writing that students will do. The plot is the heart of the story. It is where the action takes place. Young writers regard story writing as a linear process as they view stories as having a 'beginning, middle, and end'. As authors, they want to start at the beginning and continue writing until the story ends. This is fine but they often write a long story that lacks structure. It consists of 'and then, and then, and then –'. To stop this from happening, Martin Baynton (1995) suggests getting young writers to think about stories in terms of a problem. Baynton (1995) argues that every story has a problem. So, instead of asking students what their story is about, ask them what the problem will be about and whose problem it will be. Then the story structure 'falls into place' (p. 6).

What are stories?

Stories are **narrative** texts (see Dymock & Nicholson 2010a). Calfee and Drum (1986, p. 836) explain that 'stories generally tell "what happened". Who did what to whom and why'. Stories are more than simple lists of sentences or ideas. Stories have structure. There is more to a story than saying 'stories have a beginning, middle and an end'.

Narrative: means story.

There are many different types of stories known as story genre (Wolf & Gearhart 1994). Stories can be traditional literature (e.g. folktales, myths, fables and legends) or modern fantasy such as science fiction. Stories can be based in real times and places such as historical fiction (e.g. stories based on times gone by such as the Middle Ages, or the beginnings of colonisation of Australia and New Zealand) or contemporary realistic fiction (e.g. survival stories, stories dealing with death, sport or mystery). While there are many different types of stories, they share a common structure.

Story structure: every story has a problem and a set structure. The structure is characters, setting, plot and theme. The plot is made of four components: problem, reaction to the problem, action and outcome.

Narrative structure includes four components: characters, plot, setting and theme (Calfee & Patrick 1995; Dymock 2007; Dymock & Nicholson 2010a; Dymock & Nicholson 2012). Children as young as six are able to gain an understanding of these components as well as a sense of **story structure**. As one six-year-old put it (Calfee 1991, p. 178): 'What you have to do with a story is, you analyze it; you break it into parts. You figure out the characters, how they're the same and different. And the plot, how it begins with a problem and goes on until it is solved. Then you understand the story better, and you can even write your own.' A story tells the reader who (characters) did what to whom (plot) and when (setting). Stories usually also have a theme or message but it is not explicitly stated. The reader has to work it out. The characters in a story can be major or minor. They have features and personalities. The plot is made up of episodes. Each episode has four parts: a problem, reaction to the problem, action to solve the problem, and outcome (or solution to the problem). The setting explains where the story takes place, the time it takes place, and the mood of the place.

Story writing in Years 4–6: getting story ideas from television or the internet

Sometimes an idea for a story can come from a book, the internet or television (Dymock & Nicholson 2010a). For example, what if there were a news report on the internet or television that the local zoo is overcrowded and the animals are suffering because there is not enough space. This might trigger a possible story that pupils could write. You could start the story with a request from the zoo manager for families to adopt a zoo animal for a week until the zoo solves its overcrowding problem.

A possible structure for the story could be:

Problem: The zoo is overcrowded and they need people to look after some of their animals for a week or so.

Reaction: The family is worried about having to billet a large animal like a gorilla or elephant.

Action: The family decides to look after a gorilla but they have to cook food that the gorilla likes to eat, like banana cake, and decide where the gorilla will sleep, like in their tree house, and what TV programs the gorilla might like to watch, such as animal programs.

Outcome: The end of the story might be that the zoo comes to collect the gorilla but the family promises to visit their new friend at the zoo and not forget the gorilla.

Writing can result from reading

Students may have read 'School Dog's Big Mistake' (Simpson 2009), a story about a school dog who made a big mistake when the School Inspector came to the school carrying a strange black case. It was really a violin case, but it looked suspicious so the dog jumped on the Inspector and knocked him over. The story ends happily with the Inspector playing tunes to the children. See Figure 13.1 for a story web that shows the structure of the story.

The teacher asks the class to write a similar story. For example, what if a strange cat came to your school, and the teacher took it to the cat pound, but then a family from down the street came looking for their lost cat. Can your class write a story to solve this problem?

Using a quirky picture to generate ideas for writing

The teacher might use quirky illustrations that are not about anything in particular to stimulate creative writing (Dymock & Nicholson 2010a). Some good examples are in Byrne and Fielding-Barnsley (1991) and Fielding-Barnsley & Hay (2012) – see figure 13.2.

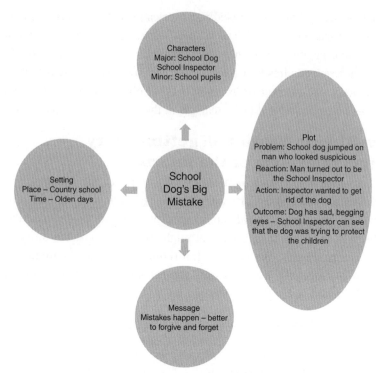

Figure 13.1 *'School Dog's Big Mistake' story web*

Figure 13.2 *'The Monster and the Mice'*

The picture in Figure 13.2 shows objects that start with the sound /m/ to teach the sound of the letter 'm' but the class can go beyond this and write a story. The teacher can talk with the pupils about how they could write a story about the image, asking about who the characters are (the monster, the mice) and the setting (in the kitchen) and the plot. The plot seems to involve baking and the class might be able to think of a number of possible plots. Here is an example of how you could approach this exercise.

The teacher asks the class to work in small groups to come up with different plots. Pupils can start by drawing up a structure for the story: characters, setting, plot and outcome. The teacher can instruct them: 'Try to help each other with ideas. One person can be the writer. Make sure that everyone in your group contributes at least one idea for the story. Then I want you to share your story with another group and get their feedback. I'll give each group a checklist of things to write about in your feedback.'

At the end of the writing lesson pupils in each group write feedback for another group and share it with that group. The checklist of things to comment on can include:

- Did the story have an interesting title?
- Did the story start with a problem?
- Did the story describe the characters, their personality and appearance?
- Did the story build up to a high point?
- Did the story have a good ending?

Two narrative plots are shown below.

Plot 1

Once ther was a monster. He wanted to have some porig but he dident have eney. Then the monster went for a walk to by some more. When he gpo home he said to the mice if they could help him but they said no way man. So he made it himself.

Plot 2

One day on a sunny morning the monster had to make his breakfast so he could be ready for work. He was going to make pancakes for himself and the cup cake for the three little mice. But there was a problem. They had made a big MESS! in the kicthen, everywhere in the kicthin. So the four of them cleaned up the kitchen and after they cleaned up the monster went to work and the three mice went to play outside, and the last mice closed the door and went off.

Conclusion

Pupils often do not know what makes a good story. They do not have a good sense of how to structure a story. They may know there are characters, a setting, a plot and a theme, but lack the ability to put the pieces together. It's like having the ingredients for a recipe but not knowing what to do with them.

Every interesting story starts with a problem that is somebody's problem. Helping children find the problem for the story is central to their ability to create narratives. Once students can state the problem, the rest of the story will fall into place. For example, a student might write: 'Ellen had a problem. She did not have enough money to go on the school trip.' Then the student can write how Ellen felt about the problem, what she did to solve the problem, and the outcome.

Students need to understand that every good story will have twists and turns and surprises along the way. The characters will have personalities and behaviours. The use of adjectives and other language features make them interesting and real. To help students to gain awareness of structure and ideas for writing, teachers can find interesting stories to read and then work with their students to deconstruct the way in which stories are written and encourage pupils to use the same structures in their own stories.

Reflective questions

1. Did you find it easy or hard to write a story when you were at school?

2. Did your teacher invite authors to your classroom to talk about writing? Would that have helped you?

3. Did anyone explain to you the structure of stories when you were at school – would it have helped you to write?

4. Reflect on one or two of the examples of pupil writing in this chapter. Do they have structure? Are there strategies that would make the writing more effective?

Part 4

Literacy learning in the senior primary school

Extending reading and writing in the senior primary school: focus on factual writing

Chapter objectives

1. To understand why factual reading and writing is more difficult than working with narrative texts.
2. To become familiar with successful strategies that will improve factual reading and writing in the senior primary school.
3. To be familiar with strategies teachers use to build vocabulary for reading and writing in the senior primary school.
4. To explain how to create and maintain positive attitudes to reading and writing.

This chapter moves from the discussion of reading and writing stories in the previous chapter to the reading and writing of factual works. These are not stories. The reading and writing of non-fiction, such as articles, reports and essays, is common in the senior primary school (Years 4–7). Pupils also encounter non-fiction in everyday reading material, such as magazines, newspapers, internet websites, Facebook, blogs, Twitter, and text messages on mobile phones.

What are the issues?

Survey data in New Zealand (Thomas & Ward 2010) indicate that students make rapid gains in reading and writing from Years 1 to 4 but this trend reverses after Year 4. The survey data used teacher ratings ('overall teacher judgement') of reading and writing in terms of whether children were at or above national standards, or below national standards. The survey sample was nationwide, made up of 3257 males and 3511 females.

In Year 4, when children are in the 8–9-year age range, 82 per cent of pupils scored at or above the standard in reading and 79 per cent of pupils scored at or above the standard in writing (see Figures 14.1 and 14.2 – and the appendix to this chapter). In contrast, in Year 8, 68 per cent were reading at or above the standard in reading and 52 per cent were at or above the standard in writing. These results indicate that schools were doing a much better job of teaching reading and writing in the junior primary years, and were better at teaching reading than writing.

Why is there a slide in reading and writing? In reading, what happens is that the first four years of school focus on building decoding skills. This is a good thing since they are essential for reading. The average Year 1 child when starting school is unable to read even a few words. Junior primary school teachers spend a great deal of time developing the skills of handwriting, alphabet knowledge, and decoding knowledge. In Years 1–4, this focus on skills pays off in terms of reading and writing.

Vocabulary: refers to the meanings we have for words. These meanings are stored in our mental dictionary and usually include a description of the meaning (e.g. a spider is a), a link to a higher-order meaning (a spider is an insect) and examples (daddy long legs, etc.)

After Year 4 these skills are still important but they are not the main skills that drive the reading boat forward. The texts children read in senior primary are not the familiar topics of junior primary but topics that are less familiar to pupils and require knowledge of ideas and **vocabulary** that are outside their immediate life experiences. Up to Year 4, students get a steady diet of fiction that they can easily relate to, but after Year 4 there is much more non-fiction, about places and things that are not in their everyday lives. The vocabulary and text topics are new and the student has to rely much more on cognitive skills such as background knowledge and depth of vocabulary. As seen in Figure 14.1 (over the page) and Tables 14.1 and

14.2 (p. 275), the percentage of students who are at and above the national standard in reading and writing keeps increasing through to Year 4, and then declines. This suggests that the content demands (general knowledge and vocabulary) become more difficult, and this makes it hard for students to maintain the gains they made in the early school years. As seen in Figure 14.1, general knowledge and vocabulary do not grow enough to maintain the gains made in the junior school.

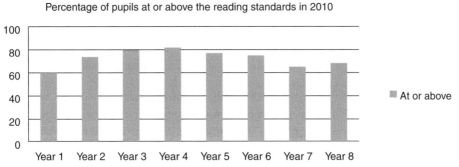

Percentage of pupils at or above the reading standards in 2010

Figure 14.1 *Percentage of students at or above the reading standards in 2010 (Thomas & Ward 2011)*

In writing, the situation for the student after Year 4 is even more challenging. To be a good writer, especially in the junior years of primary school, pupils need skills in spelling and handwriting. Unless spelling and handwriting are correct, writing is unreadable and incomprehensible so the teacher is unlikely to give a piece of writing a good grade. In the first four years of school teachers give a lot of attention to spelling and handwriting and pupils move forward very quickly. After the fourth year of school the demands of writing become more difficult. There is more factual writing (e.g. reports, research assignments on particular topics, and essay writing) than narrative writing. The factual writing tasks require strong general knowledge and vocabulary. In writing, students are expected to use interesting nouns and adjectives, to vary sentence length, to stop using strategies such as 'and then and then and then', and to find their own voice in writing.

Students can make gains in writing in the senior primary years but vocabulary build-up requires extensive reading and many pupils do not read enough to build their store of words. A good way to develop your 'voice' as a writer is to study the writing of others and this requires extensive reading. If you spend all your time playing computer games after school, or watching TV, or goofing off outside the house, and not reading, which seems to happen in many homes after school is out, then you lose the opportunity to read what writers have to say. Finally, writing factual texts is easier when pupils understand how professional writers structure their texts. Like an architect who designs houses, a good writer knows how to design a text, what to put in it and how to organise the ideas, so that it works. Like a builder, the good writer knows how to make the design happen, with strong foundations and frames that make the text tight and effective.

Designing and building texts in the senior primary school is different to junior primary because the texts are different. There is a lot more focus on non-fiction writing of reports and essays. This is so different to junior primary where students tend to write lots of stories. Most students have an intuitive understanding of stories. The nice thing about stories is that they all have the same structure – that is, there are characters, a setting and a problem to solve (Dymock 2007; Dymock & Nicholson 2012), but non-fiction is not like this. Students are often totally unaware of the many different structures of non-fiction texts (Dymock & Nicholson 2007). These structural features are not explicitly stated in texts and teachers need to point them out so that pupils have scaffolding to build their own written texts. The teacher asks questions about the meaning of the text but also asks questions about why it is an effective piece of writing.

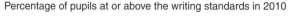

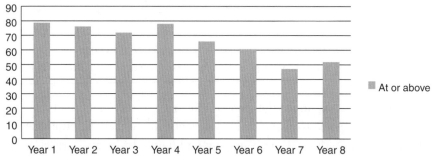

Percentage of pupils at or above the writing standards in 2010

Figure 14.2 *Percentage of students at or above the writing standards in 2010 (Thomas & Ward 2011)*

Factual text (also referred to as non-fiction): a difference between non-fiction and fiction (or stories) is that stories are not true whereas non-fiction is normally true. Also, non-fiction has a different structure. It is not a story structure, even though at times a non-fiction text may read like a story because there is a sequence of events, as in a historical article or a biography.

Challenges in teaching writing skills, especially for factual writing

In the senior primary and junior secondary schools, writing can be hard for students. There is more challenging reading and it is more factual. While writing narrative is also challenging in the senior primary school, factual writing is even more difficult in that it is not as intuitive as narrative writing. Students understand the nature of stories, that there is a single basic structure with a beginning, middle and end, and that they have characters and setting. In contrast, factual writing is not like that and there are multiple structures. One solution is to give students more practice in reading and writing both narrative and **factual texts**.

Duke (2000) studied 20 Grade 1 classrooms in the United States and found that teachers only spent four minutes of time on factual texts each day. In low socio-economic status schools, it was only two minutes of class time. Martin (1989) surveyed one kindergarten and one primary school in Australia and found that only 15 per cent of writing was factual.

There may be a bias among schools that junior primary school pupils are not ready to write factual texts, though there is no reason why this should be so. Some teachers are perhaps not comfortable teaching factual texts because they are less intuitive than narratives, and have different structural forms.

On the other hand, the following examples show that pupils can write factual texts even from Year 1. The examples show pupils' developing ability to write factual texts at higher levels of complexity.

What writing targets or 'standards' should we expect of pupils at each year of school?

The following writing examples are from New Zealand's National Standards for Reading and Writing (Ministry of Education 2009b, pp. 19–34) for Years 1–8. Interestingly, the standards do not include examples of narrative writing after Year 5.

When reading the writing examples, you will notice certain features of good writing, such as ideas, the hook, voice and the audience.

Example 14.1

Good writing

At the end of Year 1 this pupil wrote the following explanation to the question, 'I wonder why we have night and day?' The text has three sentences and it answers the question. There is an illustration to go with the text. It shows the orbit of the earth around the sun.

This pupil is in Year 1 yet can answer a question that took our society many thousands of years to discover. The pupil has ideas to write about. The pupil has her own voice. There is structure in that she answers the question. There is a sense of audience in that she explains the links between the earth, the sun, night and day.

The writing says: 'Day and night comes from the earth and the sun. And the earth orbits around the sun and the earth is round. When we face the sun it is day and when we face the moon it is night.'

I wonder why we have night and day?

Day and nit cae fom the Eof and the san. And the Eof ods ard the ean. the Eof eas ard. When we fae the ean it is day and when we fas the moon it is nit.

* * * * *

At the end of Year 2 this student wrote a factual text about the local river, the Waikato river. The class had been on a walk along the river and they had to write about ways to record information about the river. The student has mentioned two ways to do this, using maps and photos. She has used a title for the text and writes to an audience (e.g. uses the words 'people' and 'you').

MAPS
'People can find important places to go to and find there and so we do not get lost. It could lead you to something that belongs in the Waikato river. It might be a taniwha.'

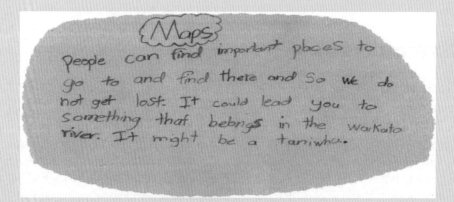

Maps

People can find important places to go to and find there and So we do not get lost. It could lead you to something that bebngs in the Waikato river. It might be a taniwha.

PHOTOS
'Photos tall you about the olden days of the Waikato river so we can see the changes of the river and the places a long the river.'

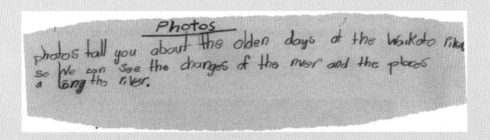

<u>Photos</u>
photos tall you about the olden days of the Waikato rike
so We can see the changes of the river and the places
a long the river.

* * * * *

At the end of Year 3 this student wrote a factual text about how to make a worm farm. The teacher organised a visit to the class by the Council's recycling officer and the pupil learned to make worm farms. The pupil used illustrations to support the text. The pupil used subheadings, like 'title', to give structure to the text. The pupil had a sense of audience, using expressions like 'Make sure you add'. The instructions followed a sequence, which helps the reader to know what to do next. There is even a little 'hook' at the end, to engage the audience, in the form of a short test. The text reads as follows:

STEPS
1. Get a big container with a hole in the bottem
2. Place a bucet under the hole
3. Put about 10 cm of shredded newspaper on the botom
4. Sprinkl some compost over top
5. Drip a little water over the compost to dampen it
6. Put in food scraps – not meat
7. Dariry fods, onions, garlic, citris
8. By some compost worms and put them in their new hom
9. Cover the container with something strong like carpet
10. Make sure you add food scraps ofen
TEST
Are the worm happy?

* * * * *

At the end of Year 5 this student wrote a factual text about jellyfish. The classroom was studying classification of animals. The pupil had a sense of structure, using subheadings like 'appearance', 'habitat' and 'food'. The student also had a sense of audience, using expressions like 'Guess what?' The pupil used easy explanations like 'That means ...' which is a mark of a good writer – to write clearly.

Here is the text that the pupil wrote:

Opening statement – Jellyfish are invertebrates, that means that they don't have any bones! Also they are cnidarians. As you all know, jellyfish have tentacles with a bunch of stinging cells. Guess what, the scientific name for the Antarctic jellyfish is Desmonema glaciale.

Appearance – All jellyfish are in a shape of a ball or a dome. They have transparent body's and in the water they look invisible to other animals. The Australian box jellyfish also known as the Sea … is around 25 cm across and 2 metres long … All jellyfish's tentacles trail along in the water, while they are moving

Habitat – Most jellyfish live in the …

Food – Compition is tough for the Antarctic jellyfish. It feeds on … Also the jellyfish paralyse their prey with their deadly tentacles before they try to eat it up

Conclusion – Most people know that the box jellyfish is one of the most deadliest animals on earth. Some beaches are closed during the jellyfish season!

* * * * *

By the end of Year 6, pupils are writing longer factual pieces with more complex structures. This student wrote a report about a science project for which a group of pupils were making a bottle submarine. The report is in draft form and is not complete. It is quite detailed and has subheadings and labels for each paragraph. The report follows a clear sequence. The first section explains what the group had to do. The next section explains how they went about it. Here is the text as the pupil wrote it:

First paragraph

In groups of 3 or 4 room 27 had aproximtly 3 weeks to build and design a prototype (submarine) that will explore the under water wourld and be airtight. It will also suspend in mid-water and when we are done we will test them in a tank of water.

2nd paragraph 'planning'

Each group started out with all of the group's ideas put into it. The group then all agreed on a disision and decided to build that decision. Each bottle had to have numerous details on it.

3rd paragraph 'our design'

Most of room 27's groups have tinfoil or bubble wrap to prevent it from sinking. Each group also has details such as perriscopes and plastic wings to help it float in mid-water and explore the under water world.

4th paragraph 'constructing'

At the moment my groups submarine looks a bit different from the design when we started. It has a layer of tinfoil to prevent it from leaking. It also has a straw perriscope.

5th paragraph – – – – – – Conclusion!!!!!!

In the end the groups model submarine did not work. The planning ended up a lot different to the design. The team work was not very good because people were getting distracted and some people wern't doing much work. The construction ended up haveing lots of weight on it. Most of the …

* * * * *

By the end of Year 8, students are writing a range of factual texts, from a science report to a social studies description to a piece of persuasive writing. This student had drafted out a speech on the topic of something you feel strongly about. The topic for this speech was television advertising. The text genre is persuasion and this means presenting a series of arguments. In a discussion essay, normally you need to give both sides of the argument (pros and cons) but in a speech of this kind the pupil only needs to give arguments to support her point of view.

As a piece of writing, it hits all the right notes. It has ideas, a distinctive voice, a sense of audience, and a hook to engage the audience ('Well, first of all …'). It also has a structure in that it makes assertions (e.g. advertisements are annoying) and then backs them up.

The speech works well because it is a topic that the audience is familiar with, the examples are from local television and the audience will know about them, the pupil shows emotion and feeling, e.g. 'That is what I call annoying' which is the right thing for a speech on this topic, and shows humour. The pupil uses audience-friendly expressions like rhetorical questions, 'Doesn't it blow your mind that …?' The writer also uses visual markers like capital letters to indicate where she wants to raise her voice during the speech. A transcription of the speech is below:

NO ADVERTISEMENTS

Well first of all I think that THE most irritating thing about advertisements is the time we waste watching them. I mean truth [be] told a normal t.v. programme would be around twenty minutes but if you include the advertisements then the time frame would stretch to thirty minutes … THAT! Is what I call annoying.

Advertisements are annoying theres no doubt about that especially when they continuously play the same advertisements over and over again. I [don't know] what is more annoying than when you have watched one of the most boring advertisements in your life and when it finishes you think, 'Thank God it's finished'. But suddenly it automatically plays again just like before. Also the volume of advertisements always seems to be double or even triple the volume of the actual television programme. Doesn't it blow your mind to think that they are trying to brainwash you with their pointless shows?

Ever woken up and turned on the tele only to find what's on are ads such as Thin Lizy girl make-up or Proactive face wash? Well I have and they seemed to be called infomercials. But to me they're just called non-relevant ads. The reason? Well it's just the fact that they don't stop shoving deals in your face! Such as the Thin Lizy ad, they say buy one, get one free. But wait! There's more! You'll also get this, this, and this. It just doesn't stop does it?

Racism is not OK and it shouldn't be used anywhere and anytime but did you know that some advertisements have got some in it? Yup you heard me some advertisement have got racism in it such as the 'thirty second spray and walk away'.

Strategies for teaching students how to read and write factual texts

Factual texts have different structures but they are easy to teach. There are three main kinds of factual text: descriptive, sequential and persuasive (Dymock & Nicholson 2007, 2012).

Descriptive (or 'recount') text

Descriptive texts tell the reader about the topic. Descriptions vary in the way the information is organised. Sometimes there is no organisation, as in a list, but usually the information has a structure – it could be basic, such as a 'web' about one topic, or a more complex presentation of information about multiple topics, such as the 'compare–contrast' and the 'hierarchy' structures.

List – where the text lays out information like a shopping list, such as a list of products made in a country, or a list of materials found in a rubbish dump. There is no clear linkage between the items of information. It is a list. In the example provided in Example 14.1 for the pupil at the end of Year 2, the student listed two strategies for recording information about the river.

Items found in a rubbish dump:
- old tyres
- garden rubbish
- broken furniture

Web structure – where the information in factual text is about one thing and is broken into categories. For example, the information in a text about Tasmanian Tigers might be in clusters of information, such as habitat, diet, descriptive features, and enemies. In the example provided in Example 14.1, the Year 5 student described jellyfish using a web structure with categories such as 'appearance'. The pupil in year 6 wrote a report that seemed to have a web structure with categories like 'planning' on the single topic of building a bottle submarine.

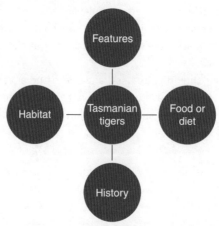

Compare–contrast structure – where the information is about more than one thing and there are direct comparisons and contrasts that can be made – for example, the similarities and differences between Auckland and Melbourne, such as location, population, product and weather. Or, the text might compare two different kinds of bird (colour, size, diet, habitat) or two different kinds of car (engine size, shape, comfort, safety, reliability). A variation of this structure is to diagram the comparison as a Venn diagram structure where two things are compared but the information is presented as two overlapping circles and the similarities between the two things are presented in the overlap.

Hierarchy structure – where information is described from a more general category to subcategories (e.g. in a high school there is the principal, then the deans, then the teaching subject areas, then the teachers, and finally the pupils).

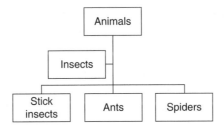

Sequence text

Sequence text presents information in a set order that you have to follow. It is a nice way to present procedures or time-related information, such as a history, a diary or a biography. It is also a good means of showing how one thing can cause another to happen, which is a sequence of A to B; or it can show a simple sequence, such as how a problem leads to a solution, where you start with the problem and finish with the solution.

Linear structure – where one thing happens after the other – for example, as is the case with making a cake, milking a cow and starting a computer. In the example provided in Example 14.1, the pupil in Year 3 used a linear structure to describe how to make a worm farm.

Cause–effect structure – where one event causes another event to happen – for example, an earthquake causes the ground to move, which then causes buildings to collapse and people to get hurt, and so on.

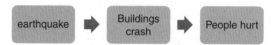

Problem–solution structure – where you state a problem and offer solutions. For example, an historic building may be located on land where a developer wants to build a supermarket. A possible solution is to find another location for the supermarket or move the historic building to another place, or build around the historic house, or if necessary, destroy the building.

Persuasive text

Normally a persuasive text gives information for and against an idea but sometimes the information may be one-sided, as in advertising, where the information about a product is usually positive, or in a submission or speech where the information may be negative (e.g. opposing an idea or action). In the example given in Example 14.1, the Year 8 pupil wrote a persuasive text titled 'No advertisements'.

Westby and Clauser (2006) argue that writers with the power to persuade are able to consider the audience, predict how well their ideas will be received, assess how strong their arguments are, appreciate the importance of negotiation, and understand the need for the audience to be convinced before agreeing. They argue that there are skills of persuasion, including being aware that the audience might disagree with you; that opinions will differ; that you can persuade them (they are not a fixed block of opinion), knowing what they think and what they are likely to accept, and knowing how to put your arguments in ways that they will accept or at least consider.

Persuasive writing is about arguments. Arguments have a claim (an assertion), a warrant (a principle you get from data) and data to back up the claim (Westby & Clauser 2006). For example, the claim may be that rainforests should not be cut down. One warrant to back up the claim is that cutting down forests will change the world's weather patterns. Data to back up the warrant show that we are already experiencing global warming (polar bears have no ice to walk on; icebergs are melting; there are droughts when there never used to be). Another warrant to back up the claim may be that we are losing important resources. Data to back up the warrant show that unique animals living in those forests will become extinct, and unique plants that might cure horrible diseases will be lost. A third warrant to back up the claim may be that we don't need to farm the land that once held forests. The data to back up the warrant shows that we can make farms more efficient and that we can cut down our consumption of farm products so as to reduce our obesity problem.

A persuasive speech or essay is well thought out; you state your position right up front (the claim), in the middle you present your arguments (the warrants and the data to support the warrants) and at the end of the essay you try to get the audience on side with a personal plea or a prediction or you simply sum up what you have said.

The difference between persuasive writing as it is taught in junior and senior primary school respectively is in terms of negotiation (Scott 2006). Younger writers are less likely to seek compromise. The rainforests must be saved at all costs! After Year 3, and through to Years 12 and 13, there is a bit more use of compromise in student writing. A more effective piece of persuasive writing uses more negotiation markers and counterarguments, and shows more of a sense of obligation (e.g. 'We should save the rainforests because it is a good thing to do'). It also shows more indicators of uncertainty (e.g. 'Maybe, surely'). And there is more a sense of accountability (e.g. 'My feeling is that …').

Writing in the classroom: some examples of turning mathematics problems into writing

Now that we have described different text structures, can we apply this to maths? Many maths problems can be turned into texts. Maths teachers can teach writing by asking students to turn the maths problems into real-life texts. Writing is important across the curriculum, and especially in maths. Students can often make maths problems easier if they turn them into a structure or story. When you look back over the structures we have described so far in the chapter, the best structure in Example 14.2 for item 1 is to draw a list (in picture form) of the three herds of cows with the four cows in each herd and then add the numbers in each herd. In item 2, if the students write a list of the 10 books (or the 10 dollars) they can then use their counting knowledge to figure out that the brother and sister each have five books, or that each packet costs five dollars. The teacher can discuss with students how 2x = 10 is a nice way to express the problem with numbers.

Example 14.2

1. Write a number problem such as 'What is 3 x 4?' on the whiteboard and ask the class to work in groups to find a real-world way to write the problem. For example, one group may write 'There are four cows in a herd and there are three herds. How many cows are there?' This can also lead to vocabulary discussion of 'grouping' terms such as 'gaggle', 'flock' and 'pod'.

2. Write the equation 2x = 10 on the whiteboard. Ask the class to write a real-world example of this problem and the answer for x because x stands for a number. One group may come up with 'I have 10 books on my bookshelf at home. My mum says I have twice as many books as my sister. How many books does my sister have?' Or the group might write a supermarket sign: 'Buy two packets of hot cross buns and pay only $10.' How much is one packet?

3. Show a sales table to the class. The students work in groups to make the sales table into a graph, and then write a series of quiz questions about the table and graph (see the examples below).

YEAR	RUNNING SHOES SOLD	WALKING SHOES SOLD
2007	600	300
2008	500	500
2009	400	700
2010	300	800
2011	400	900
2012	500	1400

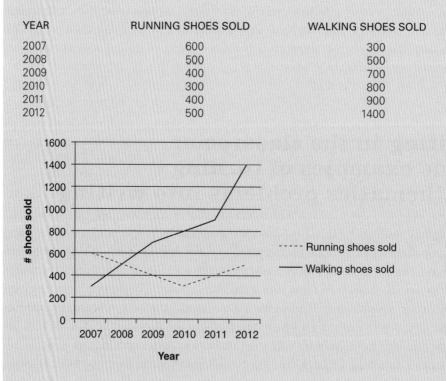

Questions

1. What is this graph about?
2. About how many pairs of running shoes were sold in 2007? (600)
3. During which year was the sale of walking shoes the lowest? (2007)
4. During which year was the sale of walking shoes about the same as the sale of running shoes? (2008)
5. What do you think affected sales between running and walking shoes between 2007 and 2012?

How can teachers build vocabulary for comprehension in the senior primary school?

Good readers have good vocabulary. The research on vocabulary shows that it is essential for reading comprehension, and that there is a major difference in vocabulary between middle-class homes and low-income homes, and pupils who are learning English as a new language even at school entry (Hart & Risley 1995; Nicholson 2003). In contrast to junior primary, where most texts use vocabulary that students often already understand, in senior primary it is very different. Having said that, it is amazing how many unusual words get used in so-called easy texts. These are words that can be discussed even in the senior school (see the vocabulary quiz in Example 14.3 on p. 268, taken from a book written for junior pupils).

Sometimes we are so focused on teaching the mechanics of decoding and spelling that we overlook that pupils might not know the meanings of the words we are reading to them. Research on the vocabulary of 'book language' tells us that writers tend to use more unusual words than in everyday speech (Nicholson & Dymock 2010). There are far more new words in book language than children will encounter talking to their friends or watching television. Writers like to use more interesting words than everyday words. For example, a writer might use 'leap' for 'jump' or 'thump' for 'tap' to make his or her writing more interesting but many pupils might not know the nuances of these alternates, especially if the pupils are from a minority culture or from disadvantaged backgrounds (Juel et al. 2003).

The good thing is that we have much research to indicate that vocabulary instruction is effective if we do it well (for reviews, see Nicholson & Dymock 2010; Beck, McKeown, Kucan 2002). A recommended way to attend to new vocabulary is to use the technique of 'anchored word instruction' (Juel et al. 2003, p. 16) where teachers select words from a book they are reading to the class, write the words on the whiteboard and discuss them with the class.

For example, in the book *Rosie's Walk* (Hutchins 1988), used in junior primary, Rosie the hen goes for a walk but a fox follows her. She walks past a mill, a pond and a haystack. These words might be familiar to some students but many others might not know them if they have not lived in the country. The teacher can write the words on cards, show the words to pupils and explain the meanings. When the words are written outside the book, pupils can focus on the spelling as well as the meaning and this helps to cement the meaning in memory (Nicholson & Dymock 2010). Research indicates that this anchored word study where pupils focus on meaning, spelling, and the sound of the word is far more effective than reading a book aloud or incidental discussion of words while reading aloud (Juel, Biancarosa & Deffes 2003).

Another strategy anchored to the text is to select out 10–20 interesting words from the text and write a quiz for the class to complete together with the teacher – or in groups. The point of difference of the quiz from a normal quiz on vocabulary is to write the quiz with the interest word presented in sentence context, as it occurred in the book, and give multi-choice options for the class to consider. The quizzes take a little bit of time to develop, though to save time we have had success in asking senior pupils who are good readers to work together to write class quizzes.

You can send quizzes home with advice to parents on how to help their child learn the words and practise using them – and include the answers! An example is shown below.

Example 14.3

***The Watchdog Who Wouldn't* by Elizabeth Best (Wendy Pye Publishing, 2002)**

In this story Dad buys a puppy for the family called Tick Tock. Dad wants Tick Tock to be a watchdog but the puppy is afraid of strangers. The children are worried because they think Dad might take the puppy back to the shop but Tick Tock makes them all proud.

Quiz

Here are some words from the story. See if you can write the **best** meaning for each word. In Question 1, the best answer is 'big stepping'.

1. Page 2 – 'Lizzie saw Dad <u>striding</u> down the drive'
   <u>Striding</u> means:
   • skipping
   • walking
   • big stepping
   • hopping.

2. Page 4 – 'Something warm and wet <u>flicked</u> across his eye'
   <u>Flicked</u> means:
   - scratched quickly
   - flew quickly
   - walked quickly
   - wiped quickly.
3. Page 6 – 'Where's our big, <u>fierce</u> watchdog?'
   <u>Fierce</u> means:
   - friendly
   - scary
   - furry
   - funny.
4. Page 8 – 'A little <u>mutt</u> of a puppy'
   <u>Mutt</u> means:
   - baby, a bit frightened
   - brother
   - bit
   - friend.
5. Page 10 – 'Dan asked his friend Jack to pretend to be a <u>burglar</u>'
   <u>Burglar</u> means:
   - cleaner
   - teacher
   - robber
   - police officer.

Quiz answers
- Yes, <u>striding</u> means walking with long steps.
- Yes, <u>flicked</u> means a quick, little wipe that just touches you.
- Yes, <u>fierce</u> means angry or scary.
- Yes, <u>mutt</u> means a puppy who is like a baby, a bit frightened of people and animals it does not know.
- Yes, <u>burglar</u> means thief or robber.

To summarise so far, vocabulary knowledge is extremely important for reading and writing. Although we think that texts in junior primary have easy vocabulary, there are often many words that are not familiar to pupils at all (e.g. in the above quiz, words such as 'striding', 'flicked' and 'mutt'). Vocabulary instruction that is 'anchored' to the text also gives the teacher an opportunity to allow students to become word detectives, to search out word meanings in the dictionary and thesaurus, either in hard copy or online, and to search out the meanings of words on the internet. The key message is that we should try to build vocabulary from the earliest stages, as part of an effective reading program. Pupils need to know how to decode words and know how they are spelled but also to be clear in their minds about what the words mean. There is no real value in knowing how to read a book with 100 per cent accuracy if it has words such as 'striding' or 'haystack' yet the pupil does not know what they mean.

Attitudes to reading

It probably seems obvious and not worth saying that teachers can inspire their class to love reading. On the other hand, teachers do not do as much of this as they think. Petscher (2010) reported that teachers do not spend much class time doing activities that will generate positive attitudes to reading. The same situation may also apply to writing.

Our experience as teachers suggests that as reading improves, attitudes to reading remain positive. As reading goes backwards, attitudes become more negative. A remarkable example of this was a four-year longitudinal study in the United States by Juel (1988). She followed the reading progress of 54 good and poor readers from Grades 1 to 4 and found evidence of negative attitudes among poor readers. The poor readers did much less after-school reading than did good readers. Reading had become an unpleasant activity for many of the poor readers, as was revealed by interview questions asked to the Grade 4 sample. In response to the question, 'Would you rather clean your room or read?', only 5 per cent of the good readers said they would rather clean their room, but 40 per cent of the poor readers said they'd rather clean their room. One poor reader said, 'I'd rather clean the mould around the bathtub than read' (p. 442). When asked the question, 'Do you like to read?', 26 of the 30 good readers said 'yes' but only 5 of the 24 poor readers said 'yes'. Several of the poor readers said they hated reading; most said it was boring.

The situation seems the same in this part of the world. To illustrate from our own data, here are comments from two 11-year-old New Zealand pupils when we asked them questions about their attitudes to reading (McGregor & Nicholson 2012). One was a very good reader and one was a poor reader, both from a low-socio-economic school. The responses show differences in attitudes to reading that may be more common than the research indicates.

Skilled reader:

Would you rather play with your friends or read? Read. I somehow feel that I want to read every book in the world, and that there isn't much time.

How often do you read at home by yourself? Every day. I love reading.
How good a reader do you feel yourself to be? Alright. I read books like *The Hobbit*, *Kingdom by the Sea*, etc. Most people my age don't.
How do you feel when you come to a new word while reading? Curious. I enjoy finding the meaning of words by putting them into context.
Can you remember the name of a book you read recently? *Kingdom by the Sea*.
Do you like to read? Yes. I like plots turned to words.
Do you like writing stories? Sort of. I like thinking of plots but I don't like writing them.

Struggling reader:

How good a reader do you feel yourself to be? Not good as aver pelple.
How do you feel when you come to a new word while reading? I feill fustratd.
Would you rather play with your friends or read? I would play then read.
How often do you read at home by yourself? Never because I ned help.
Can you remember the name of a book you read recently? *Show and Tell, Asralyun hidils* [*Australian Idols*].
Do you like to read? Yes but not that much.
Do you like writing stories? Yes but no it dusin min me [it doesn't worry me].

On the other hand, not all struggling readers are negative about reading. Stewart-Brown & Nicholson (2012) asked students who were below-average readers in Years 9 and 10 of high school this question: 'How will you feel about your reading next year?' Their answers varied a lot.

Positive responses:

A little nervous.
All right.
I will learn from my mistakes.
I will try to focus.

Not so positive responses:

Scared I will be mocked.
Shy because I might make a mistake but it is good to make mistakes.
I need to improve my reading.
People might put me down.
Shy. I might make mistakes.

Although experience in the classroom tells us that pupils are happier when they are reading texts they can cope with and understand, the picture is not totally clear. One recent meta-analysis concluded that when you average the results of many studies, there is a positive but weak link between reading achievement and reading attitudes.

Children get more positive about reading when they experience success in reading (Petscher 2010; Morgan & Fuchs 2007) but the relationship is also a weak one in that some studies get opposite results.

That is, there are studies where poor readers have negative attitudes to reading but other studies where poor readers are positive about reading, which could be the case in that you can like reading books even though you are not good at it yourself. Other studies have found that good readers can have negative attitudes to reading, especially at older ages, which suggests that good readers become bored as they get older. This could be due to the competition of other things such as peer group antipathy to reading, not wanting to appear a nerd, too much homework, the books get harder, and competition from other sources for the student's spare time (e.g. television, Facebook, texting, computer games).

Attitudes to writing

Good writers have positive attitudes to writing. There is also a link between reading books and writing, with the reading of books more helpful to pupils from disadvantaged backgrounds (Korat & Schiff 2005). We have argued in this chapter that books are a source of ideas for writing. They are also a source of coaching ideas for the teacher. This works well for fiction and non-fiction. Teachers can model a plan for writing after reading a story or article with the class. In this way, children generate ideas they will use for writing. The following responses from young writers indicate how important it is to prep students for writing. When pupils are not-so-positive, it is because they do not know what to write or how to write effectively. They will benefit from the model we used in this chapter – to generate ideas, have a hook, use a structure, have a sense of audience and find your own voice.

How do younger pupils feel about writing?

Here are some comments from younger pupils in answer to the question, 'Do you like writing?' (McGregor & Nicholson 2012).

Positive because of:

1. rewards – 'yes because sometimes I get a sticker' (Year 2)

2. spelling – 'so I can learn to spell more better' (Year 2)

3. ambition – 'yes because it's like practising to be an author which is what I'd like to be when I grow up' (Year 2)

4. freedom – 'yes because I like to express my feelings' (Year 4)

5. ideas – 'yes because I get ideas from books I have read' (Year 4).

Not-so-positive because of:

1. spelling – 'little bit because writing is hard and also you have to spell hard words' (Year 2)'; 'not that often I'm not good speller' (Year 2)

2. don't like writing – 'no because I don't like writing stories' (Year 2); 'no because when you make lots of mistakes you get in trouble for it' (Year 2); 'I don't like writing because I usually don't know what to write about. If I know what to write about I would write lots' (Year 4); 'no because it takes a long time to write and I don't know what to write about' (Year 4).

How do older pupils feel about writing?

Here are some comments from Year 9 and 10 pupils in answer to the question, 'How do you feel about writing for the teacher?' (Stewart-Brown & Nicholson 2012). They gave different answers.

Positive because of:

1. teacher feedback – 'she can see how good I write or how bad I write'; 'she can help me with things I did wrong'

2. feeling of accomplishment – 'proud – I like to write'; 'a good experience'; 'it helps me'; 'fun'.

Not-so-positive because of:

1. feeling of not knowing how to write – 'you might not know what to do'; 'not good'; 'confused'; 'I won't know how to spell most of the words'; 'boring'

2. obligatory nature of writing tasks – 'if my teacher wants me to write, I write'; 'or rit' (all right).

Conclusion

Research on literacy motivation suggests that teaching literacy is not a guarantee that students will like literacy experiences and engage with them. Even good readers and writers can get bored. Struggling readers and writers can be positive in attitude but that is more an indication of their resilience and strong self-esteem even though they are not doing well. It seems obvious that to like reading and writing you need to be good at it, so teaching students to improve their skill base is a direct way to improve their motivation.

Research on how to encourage a love of reading and writing suggests that the teacher can help students by creating an environment where such experiences are interesting and accessible. It may be that teachers are so busy teaching that they do not take out time to relax with a book and read to the class, or to model a writing task. This may seem to be wasting time, in that the teacher is only reading or modelling writing and not teaching, but it is very worthwhile because it can inspire pupils to read and write. We all remember times in our school lives when we were inspired – for example, that day when a substitute spent the afternoon reading a book to the class and everyone raced to the library to borrow the book, or asked their parents to buy the book. If you want your class to relax, listen and learn, read them a book. They love it.

There are many things a teacher can do to inspire a love of reading. For poor readers, this may mean finding ways to give them extra reading tuition, or making sure they are reading books that they can read, that are not too hard and that help them build their vocabulary and knowledge. You could also use talking books and DVDs with subtitles. For good readers, it may mean creating a real interest in books, sourcing books that they can read and will want to read, finding good stories and reading them to the class (with expression!), and giving them the opportunity to choose books they want to read.

Research on teaching writing in the senior primary school suggests that to develop factual writing skills, which is very common in senior primary, pupils can benefit from learning about the different factual genres. As discussed above, the three main factual genres are descriptive (recount), sequence and persuasive texts. Showing students how the factual genres differ from each other in structure and giving lots of practice in using the different structures to write factual texts will improve factual writing.

The teacher is a model to the class and if you as a teacher can demonstrate to the class the skills of effective reading and writing, and inspire them to believe that reading and writing are fun, then they will love reading and writing too.

Reflective questions

1. Do you remember what strategies you used for writing non-fiction texts when you were in primary school – such as reports and essays?

2. Did you teach yourself to write – or did you get coaching? What coaching was it?

3. Do you enjoy writing? What makes it fun (or not fun)?

Further reading

Fox, M. (2001). *Reading Magic*. Sydney: Pan Macmillan and New York: Harvest Original Harcourt.

Appendix

Table 14.1 *Reading by year level*

YEAR LEVEL	N	PERCENTAGES OF STUDENTS RATED			
		WELL BELOW	BELOW	AT	ABOVE
1	617	10	30	37	23
2	599	6	20	40	34
3	613	6	15	38	42
4	876	3	15	42	40
5	848	6	17	42	35
6	854	8	17	41	34
7	1128	12	23	29	36
8	1133	10	22	37	31

(Thomas & Ward 2011)

Table 14.2 *Writing by year level*

YEAR LEVEL	N	PERCENTAGES OF STUDENTS RATED			
		WELL BELOW	BELOW	AT	ABOVE
1	616	8	13	61	18
2	613	3	22	59	17
3	621	6	22	54	18
4	875	3	19	54	24
5	846	10	25	43	23
6	856	13	26	45	16
7	1128	17	36	34	13
8	1133	12	37	36	16

(Thomas & Ward 2011)

Chapter 15

Struggling readers: issues and solutions

Chapter objectives

1. To guide teachers in recognising pupils who may be at risk of developing reading difficulties.
2. To guide teachers in implementing suitable intervention with the assistance of families and providers for pupils with reading difficulties.

This chapter explores what happens when reading goes wrong. It investigates the origins of reading failure from the perspective of those who have lived the experience and covers the research literature associated with reading failure. This chapter also examines research evidence around 'Matthew effects' for pupils who get off to a slow start in reading, as well as issues of diagnosis of dyslexia and other reading-related disorders and the implications for educational practice. We discuss some of the recent moral panic around boys' literacy achievement and review the research evidence related to boys' achievement. The challenges for parents of pupils with reading difficulties are examined, along with the long-term implications for pupils with reading difficulties. Finally, the chapter reviews the roles of families, communities and agencies in supporting pupils with reading difficulties in the junior school and those with more persistent difficulties as they progress into the senior school.

The origins of reading failure

Pupils in our classrooms who demonstrate difficulties in learning to read are usually referred to as having a reading (or learning) difficulty or a reading (or learning) disability. It is important to understand these terms and also to appreciate the differences between them.

Learning difficulty or learning disability?

The terms **learning difficulty** and **learning disability** are not synonymous (Fletcher, Fuchs & Barnes 2007) even though in much of the literature they are referred to as being one and the same thing. Since the 1960s research into learning difficulties and disabilities has progressed from simple explanations 'to more complex explanations that link cognitive, neurobiological, and instructional factors' (Fletcher, Fuchs & Barnes 2007, p. 10). The most important difference between a learning difficulty and a learning disability is that a difficulty is usually short term and not neurobiological whereas a learning disability is exactly the opposite – that is, it is long term and neurobiological.

> **Learning difficulty:**
> involves a student having general difficulties in learning.

> **Learning disability:**
> concerns a smaller group of pupils with specific difficulties in learning.

A learning disability is a neurological disorder. In simple terms, a learning disability results from a difference in the way a person's brain is 'wired'. Pupils with learning disabilities are as smart as or smarter than their peers but they may have difficulty reading, writing, spelling, reasoning, recalling and/or organising information if left to figure things out by themselves or if taught in conventional ways.

To summarise, learning difficulties refers to pupils with general difficulties while learning disabilities refer to a smaller group of pupils with specific difficulties. Learning disabilities are sometimes referred to as 'specific learning difficulties' in some texts. Prevalence rates of learning difficulties have been reported as varying between 12 per cent and 30 per cent and for learning disabilities between 5 per cent and 6 per cent (Silver & Hagin 2002). Learning difficulties are short term and are not neurobiological so they are easier to remediate than learning disabilities. Can you think of reasons why learning might be difficult for some pupils?

Reflection 15.1

Think back to your childhood and try to remember when you might have found some things difficult to learn. Write them down together with possible reasons and see if there are any reasons that are not covered in the next section.

Possible reasons for learning difficulties and some solutions
1 Missed instruction due to illness

The illness may be temporary or long term. Long-term health problems such as asthma, diabetes and epilepsy, to name a few, may be common reasons for school absences. Consider, for example, the case of hearing deficits caused by glue ear (otitis media). This is particularly common in pupils who may not have access to good health care facilities – those in remote communities perhaps.

It is important to ensure that all pupils have their hearing tested before school entry. Be aware of pupils who are showing symptoms of hearing loss such as weeping ears, turning their heads in one direction or asking buddies to repeat instructions. Try to provide homework if there are long periods of absence.

The situation of difficulties with vision is similar to those pupils who might have hearing difficulties. We need to be careful, however, not to assume that because a child is demonstrating difficulties with learning to read, he or she must therefore have difficulties seeing the print. Problems with vision may interfere with reading but there are other reasons that you must consider. Make sure that you ask parents to have their child's vision tested if you suspect that it may be interfering with the child's reading. Be aware of signs of eye strain such as continual rubbing of the eyes, squinting at the board and frequent headaches.

2 Missed instruction due to transition between schools

Some pupils may have attended many schools and these may have been in other states or even other countries. Now that we have a national curriculum in Australia, we should not experience the same difficulties when pupils move interstate but some pupils may have missed vital parts of instruction due to transition from other countries. As a teacher, be sure to assess your pupils as soon as you can. To get a more complete picture, try to gain access to previous assessment and talk to the child's parents.

3 Inappropriate teaching and lack of catering to difference

It is very important to know your students and to cater to their differences. This is particularly important in the early years of education as this is when pupils are likely to form lifelong impressions about learning. Too often pupils experience frustration and failure in the early years (which can be through ineffective teaching) and this can in turn lead to low self-esteem (Elbaum & Vaughn 2003; Hay, Ashman & van Kraayenoord 1998).

4 Matthew effects – 'rich get richer and poor get poorer'

A slow start in reading may lead to what has been termed as **Matthew effects** (Stanovich 1986). This refers to a verse in the Bible where the rich become richer and the poor become poorer. The gap widens between good and poor readers as they progress through their schooling.

> **Matthew effects:** the achievement gap between good and poor readers, which widens as children progress through schooling. The term derives from the gospel according to St Matthew in the Bible in which the rich get richer and the poor get poorer.

As with all learning difficulties, the importance of direct and explicit teaching cannot be over emphasised (Swanson 1999). It is not appropriate to let these pupils 'grow out' of their learning difficulties. The pupils must be assisted to attend to instruction and to stay on task once instruction has been understood.

5 Curriculum and assessment

It is not always stated clearly that there will be a broad range of ability levels in a class. Sometimes it may be inappropriate to expect the same outcomes for all of your pupils. What is important is that regular assessment informs the teacher where there may be gaps in relation to what is expected in the curriculum. These skills must be covered either by specialist teachers or by informed teachers in the next grade. Many teachers will have the experience of teaching pupils in Year 2 who do not know their alphabet. It is clear that if a child misses out on this vital instruction, they will never learn to read. It may be that the child just learns a little more slowly than the rest of the pupils and may need more practice and perhaps a slightly different way of learning. In this context you may like to refer to the Orton-Gillingham approach to learning which includes a multisensory approach (see the 'Further reading' section for a reference).

6 The recent moral panic around boys' literacy achievement

While more boys are identified with reading problems (and popular opinion is that boys are more at risk than girls), the reality is that gender differences tend to be small. A study conducted by Limbrick, Wheldall and Madelaine (2010) on a sample of over one million students in Years 3, 5, 7 and 9 across Australia found that boys had significantly lower reading levels than girls but the effect sizes were small and decreased over time. More boys than girls are referred for reading difficulties but this is sometimes caused by problem behaviours that interfere with reading (Dahle,

Knivsberg & Andreassen 2011; Prochnow et al. 2001). As teachers we must be aware of the reciprocal nature of reading difficulties and behavioural disorders.

Socio-economic disadvantage related to reading and oral language difficulties

There is no doubt that socio-economic status (SES) will have a profound effect on a child's ability to learn at school (OECD 2001) but what is even more important is that as knowledgeable teachers we can turn this disadvantage around. The home environment can make a difference to learning. What is crucial is not to blame the child's background for his or her difficulties in learning to read but to understand the situation and to put effective measures in place to bridge the gap between home and school. Please refer to Chapter 6 for information on this topic.

One of the major difficulties that pupils from low SES homes have is that of poor oral language (Wasik, Bond & Hindman 2002). It was noted in an Australian study by Hay and Fielding-Barnsley (2009) that on school entry, one in three pupils from low SES homes were below their peers in vocabulary development. A study in the United States by Hart and Risley (1995) found that pupils from high SES homes heard 487 utterances per hour compared to 178 utterances per hour for pupils from low SES homes. This resulted in four-year-old pupils from high SES homes having heard 44 million utterances compared to those from low SES homes who had only heard 12 million utterances. Other differences include less exposure to books in the home (Fielding-Barnsley & Purdie 2003) and the language code used in a school environment may be vastly different to that used in the home.

Opposite is a picture of Jo and her son Alex reading together. Jo recorded all of Alex's spoken words up until the age of two years when he knew a total of 1031 words!

Teachers should model rich language whenever possible and give positive feedback when instances of improved language are noted either in speech or written work. Use opportunities to expand on pupils' language – for instance, during sharing time, as Example 15.1 illustrates.

Example 15.1

Michael: 'I gone to the beach with me dad.'
Teacher: 'Oh, you went to the beach, how exciting! What did you do at the beach?'
Michael: 'I went fishing.'
Teacher: 'Oh, what did you catch?'
Michael: 'Nuffin.'
Teacher: 'You didn't catch anything. That's a shame. Maybe you'll have better luck next time.'

Jo and her son Alex reading together

Reflection 15.2

Next time you have an opportunity to talk to a young child, try to expand on the conversation by introducing more descriptive language.

Another very effective and relatively easy way of introducing rich language is to read with your class. Notice that the term 'with' rather than 'to' is used. This is an important point and one that has been emphasised in research by Grover Whitehurst et al. (1994) in their model of shared-book reading. This is also referred to as 'dialogic reading' by many researchers in the field. Whitehurst coined the acronyms 'PEER' and 'CROWD' to help parents and teachers to use his methods efficiently.

PEER stands for:

Prompt the child to say something about the book.
Evaluate the child's response.
Expand the child's response.
Repeat the prompt to ensure understanding.

CROWD stands for:

Complete prompts. Leave a blank at the end of a sentence and ask the child to complete it. This is particularly useful for texts that rhyme.

Recall prompts. For example: 'Can you tell me what happened at the birthday party?'

Open-ended prompts. These are used with picture books. For example: 'Can you tell me what is happening in this picture?'

Wh prompts. This involves asking all the 'wh…' questions such as ' Why do you think that happened?' or 'What is the name of this?' to help develop new vocabulary.

Distancing prompts. For example, when reading a book about the beach, ask: 'Do you remember when you went to the beach? Did you see any of these?'

Pupils can jump ahead by several months in just a few weeks of dialogic reading (Whitehurst et al. 1994).

Reflection 15.3

Find a children's book and either practise the strategies listed or, if this is not possible, write a list of questions to accompany the book.

Emotional and behavioural disorders

It is very difficult to decide which comes first: the behaviours and associated emotions or the learning difficulties. A question you might ask parents of a child with reading difficulties is whether he or she has displayed behavioural difficulties before starting formal schooling or whether the behavioural difficulties emerged as a result of learning difficulties the child had when starting school. The answer is not always clear cut because, of course, other things happen at school apart from learning to read. There could be social issues or problems related to bullying, for example.

Emotional and behavioural disorder: a condition that manifests over a long period of time, is not appropriate behaviour for the child's age and is having a detrimental effect on the child's learning, which may be related to either emotional experiences or behavioural difficulties.

What we do know is that learning difficulties can certainly result in **emotional and behavioural disorders** (Farrell, Critchley & Mills 1999). We need to be on the alert for signs of emotional difficulties and behavioural disorders. Of course, it is much easier to see evidence of externalised behavioural problems but it is not so easy to ascertain whether a child may have emotional difficulties or internalised behavioural problems such as anxiety.

There are three things to bear in mind if you are concerned that a child may have an emotional and behavioural disorder: the condition manifests over a long period of time, it is not appropriate behaviour a for the child's age and it is having a detrimental effect on the child's learning (Gorman 2001).

The most important consideration is to include the family in any of your concerns. You should confer with the school counsellor who will know how to approach the family in a sensitive manner and discuss any similar problems that may be happening in the home.

In the classroom it is important to keep the child on task and to reward positive behaviours.

There are probably many more reasons for reading difficulties in the classroom. Some of these have been covered in more detail in other chapters: namely, pupils for whom English is not their first language, and pupils with attention problems and disabilities such as Asperger's Syndrome or High-Functioning Autism.

Reflection 15.4

Can you think of any reasons for children's learning difficulties that were not mentioned in this section?

Dyslexia – what is it and what can teachers do about it?

Who are the pupils who fall into the category of having **dyslexia**? It has been estimated that there may be as many as 10 per cent of pupils in Australian schools with a specific learning disability that includes dyslexia (Prior 1996) and between 6 and 8 per cent in the United Kingdom (Rose 2009). This means that in your class of approximately 30 pupils, there may be three pupils with dyslexia.

> **Dyslexia:** language-based learning disability of neurological origin.

A definition of dyslexia

'Dyslexia is a language-based learning disability of neurological origin. It primarily affects the skills involved in accurate and fluent word reading and spelling. It is frequently associated with difficulties in phonological processing. It occurs across the range of intellectual abilities with no distinct cut-off points. It is viewed as a lifelong disability that often does not respond as expected to best-practice, evidence-based classroom methods for teaching reading' (Dyslexia Working Party 2010). This definition was written by a group of experts who were called together by the Australian government to provide informed support for those pupils who have dyslexia (see also Tunmer & Greaney 2010; Nicholson 2008b). We will now 'unpack' the definition and relate it to our classrooms:

1 'Neurological origin'

The definition includes the term 'neurological'. What exactly does this mean? Basically it means that it involves the nervous system that is controlled by the brain. There is some very interesting research being done in this area and if you are interested in following this up, you might like to look at the book by Sousa (2001) which is listed in the 'Further reading' section. This fact is particularly important to understand as it relates to the best models of intervention and how they might overcome the neuro-logical origins of the disability.

2 'Accurate and fluent word reading'

The reason for these skills being part of the definition is that pupils with dyslexia may be able to decode text quite well but they will tend to demonstrate difficulty with accuracy and fluency. You might notice that these pupils tend to guess words from their first sound(s) and that their reading will be very laboured and slow. As you can well imagine, these reading behaviours will interfere with their understanding or comprehension of texts.

3 'Phonological processing'

This term refers to the ability to recognise and manipulate the sounds that make up spoken words – for example, the ability to recognise that words are composed of syllables, onsets and rimes, and smaller units of sound, called phonemes. While this topic has been covered in Chapter 8, it is important to add here that phonolog-ical awareness and phonological processing are not so much about being able to 'hear' the sounds in spoken words but about an 'awareness' of the sounds – that is, being conscious of the fact that words can begin or end with the same sound, for example. The ability to manipulate sounds depends upon this awareness. Try, for example, taking the /s/ sound away from the spoken word 'nest' and revealing the new word 'net' or exchanging the /n/ sound in 'nest' for /v/. Notice that you are not just 'hearing' the sounds when you do this. You do 'hear' the word initially but then you have to hold it in working memory while you manipulate the sounds. This is relatively easy for us but for someone with dyslexia it is difficult or sometimes even impossible.

4 'A range of intellectual abilities'

This fact should always be foremost in your mind if you suspect that one of your pupils may have a learning disability such as dyslexia. It is quite perplexing when a child appears to be very intelligent, or at least of normal intelligence, and yet seems to have terrible trouble in learning to read. As the definition states, intelligence really has nothing to do with dyslexia. In fact one way of diagnosing dyslexia is to measure a child's intelligence and his or her reading and if there is discrepancy, then dyslexia is a possible diagnosis. Dyslexia also appears on a continuum – a child may have quite a mild form or a more severe form. There are many forms of dyslexia but this will be up to a specialist to confirm.

5 'A lifelong disability'

This terminology is used in the current definition but it can be argued that it is not at all helpful. Yes, because it is a neurological problem it will always remain with the person but this does not mean that we cannot offer any hope to people with dyslexia. As we now know the brain is quite plastic, this means that a neurological deficit is not set in concrete. We know that we can help to create new neural pathways to compensate for those that are impaired. Exciting new research has demonstrated that an evidence-based phonological reading intervention activates the neural pathways that are known to be dysfunctional in pupils with reading disabilities (Shaywitz et al. 2004). However, even though advanced scientific methods are able to mediate reading disability, there are still noticeable difficulties, particularly with spelling in adult dyslexics.

Thoughts on diagnosis

Now that we understand the definition and how this may lead to a diagnosis of dyslexia, do we agree that a diagnosis may be useful? This is a contentious issue and to illustrate the debate further, some of the content from the study *Does a Diagnosis of Dyslexia Make a Difference?* (Gorell 2010) is presented here. These quotes by group of graduate students are provided below. These study participants were all university students at the time of the study:

Katie, diagnosed at age 16 years

Prior to my diagnosis I always thought I was just this dumb, dumb person who always lagged behind the class.

Sebastian, diagnosed at age 21 years

[The diagnosis] was quite liberating actually, yeah, I can remember sort of shedding a few tears because yeah …, it was quite relieving um … just to hear that it wasn't necessarily … ummm, you know my inabilities, it was, uh, there was some, you know, uh … functional problem there.

Nicole, diagnosed at age 41 years

I think that when you've grown up with a perception that you … will be … not much more than somebody who is a clerk, and that was instilled from a very early age … ummm …it's very difficult to overcome that and so, for me to do university is a big thing and I'm proving it not only to myself but I'm going to prove my mother wrong as well.

Olivia, diagnosed at age seven years

It [the diagnosis of dyslexia] didn't make a huge impact, it was just oh well … we will just put in place … other … mechanisms, it was no, there was no, you know, my father was dyslexic it was quite natural, it wasn't something that came as a great shock or a great blow, you just got on with it.

Reflection 15.5

Think about the quotes above and consider what is common to all four cases and what is different and why.

Best methods for teaching

There is some controversy regarding the best methods for teaching pupils with dyslexia, with some researchers suggesting that teaching targeting learning difficulties will be sufficient (Wheldall 2008). However, from what we know about dyslexia we can ascertain that it is a far more complex learning difficulty than learning difficulties caused by non-neurological issues. It is for these reasons that we can treat this group of pupils differently. All of the explicit and sequenced teaching that we implement for all learners will be of some assistance to those with more severe reading disabilities.

One of the main differences between a learning difficulty and dyslexia is that dyslexia affects pupils in a different manner. As we have discussed, these pupils are often very intelligent and even gifted in some areas such as art, music, drama and IT skills. As a result these pupils may become very frustrated with their inability to learn how to read. Even if the child does not have a diagnosis of dyslexia, we owe it to the child to explain why he or she may be experiencing problems. The easiest way to explain this to a young child is to say, 'You learn a little differently to other pupils but we will help you to find out how you learn best'.

We need to go back to the definition to help us decide on the best teaching for this group of pupils. Consider, first, the problems associated with accurate and fluent word reading. The best thing that we can do to improve these skills is to allow plenty of time for practice. Some pupils will find timed reading useful and this may be used to record improvements to develop self-motivation.

Poor spelling and phonemic awareness are associated with dyslexia and these skills should be incorporated into your teaching in an explicit manner. One way of teaching spelling and phonemic awareness is to utilise the methods advocated by Marcia Henry (2010) in her book *Unlocking Literacy*. By introducing morphology, the study of word formation, you can help children to learn about the derivation and structure of words. For example, the word 'tract' means to pull and this word forms a part of many other words that we know: tractor, extract, traction are just a few examples. Each time that a child comes across such a word, he or she will know how to spell the root word and also what it means. It is all about bringing words to life.

Positive aspects of dyslexia

Dyslexia can result in beneficial outcomes. There are some very famous people who have dyslexia. Did you know that both Richard Branson and Albert Einstein have/had dyslexia?

At the 'Happy Dyslexic' website (see the 'Further reading' section for the address), you can find examples and quotes from some of those successful people who had dyslexia or related learning problems. They are organised by activity. They are a living proof that dyslexia doesn't need to be a disadvantage, but on the contrary can become a strong advantage. These people may have become more resilient as a result of overcoming their disadvantages and consequently transferred this resilience into their professional lives.

It is impossible in this chapter to cover all of the teaching implications for pupils with dyslexia – please refer to the 'Further reading' section for other useful texts and websites.

Challenges for families and other concerned parties

'Learning in young pupils is socially mediated. Families, peers and teachers are all important' (Goswami & Bryant 2007, p. 20). While this is a broad statement about learning in general, the same sentiment has also been quoted by Snow, Burns and Griffin (1998) in their report on preventing reading difficulties in young pupils. They suggest that 'pupils need to have a caring adult to read to them and talk to them, preferably every day' (p. 143).

Most parents want to help their child overcome their reading difficulties but sometimes they are not sure how to go about it. This is where you as the teacher should work with the parents to give the best possible advice. Many parents may do exactly the opposite of what we know is good teaching practice in their efforts to help their child. Read the following example and then come up with your own scenario, including everything that you would hope a parent in your class might do to help his or her child.

Scenario 15.1

Seven-year-old Shane, who is struggling with his reading, arrives home from school after a pretty bad day. His best friend, Simon, called him 'dumb' and his teacher asked him to read out loud to the class.

Mum: 'Good day at school luv?'
Shane: 'All right, I 'spose.'
Mum: 'Did you bring your reader home?'
Shane: 'Yep.'
Mum: 'You read it to me while I get the tea.'
Shane: 'I'm going over to Simon's place.'
Mum: 'No, do your reading, you can see Simon tomorrow.'
Shane: 'I'm only doing a few pages.'
Mum: 'Hurry up.'

Shane: 'The fairy stood at the dock ...'

Mum: 'It's not fairy it's ferry.'

Shane: '... waiting to pick up the ummmm ...'

Mum: 'Hurry up, it's passengers.'

Shane: 'Everyone was very ... I don't know this word.'

Mum: 'You read that word yesterday – why can't you remember it? You'll never be as good as Simon if you don't try to remember the words.'

Shane: 'I hate you, I hate everyone. I'm going to my room.'

Obviously you can see where this parent is going wrong and you will be itching to tell her how to improve her home-reading sessions. The best way to assist parents, and this could be for all the parents in your class, is to demonstrate best practice. You could invite parents into your class during reading lessons or you could offer parent–teacher evenings. Ask yourself the following questions about the scenario above:

- Did the mother give her son quality time?
- Was the atmosphere relaxed?
- Did the mother read with the child as we have advocated for shared-book reading?
- Did the mother explain that reading needs to make sense?
- Did the mother give any hints or advice about how to read difficult words?
- Was Shane given any encouragement for what he did read correctly?

All of these points could be demonstrated by the teacher in a friendly and relaxed manner.

Do you think that there could have been other reasons for the difficulty that Shane encountered in reading his home reader? What about the level of difficulty of the reader?

There are three levels of difficulty:

- independent level where the child is able to read with a 97 per cent success rate
- instructional level at 90–95 per cent correct
- frustration level below 90 per cent correct.

In the scenario above, the book should have been at the independent level as the mother was not giving any instruction. As you will note, Shane made a mistake in every four words read; a rate of 75 per cent of words correct is at frustration level so no wonder Shane gave up. Imagine how much more useful it would be if the teacher sent home a reader at the independent level so that Shane could experience success and valuable practice.

Why do we always insist that the only way a parent can help his or her struggling reader is to make the child read more? There are many ways that we can help these parents to help their struggler. Think of all the games that we could recommend to parents. These do not need to be expensive games: they could be as simple as playing 'I Spy'. Think back to Chapter 8 and how this might help a child with poor phonemic awareness. A parent could read a more complex book with the child to improve vocabulary or watch and discuss TV programs together.

Reflection 15.6

Can you think of any other ways that a parent could help his or her child without resorting to something akin to Shane's experience?

One question that you may have been asking yourselves is 'What about the parents who don't come to the school?' Yes, there are parents who for one reason or another will find it difficult to come to the school. Unfortunately it is often these parents that we really need to help. Think about parents who come from low SES homes. They may not have transport, they may be single parents who do not have access to babysitters, they may have had bad experiences of school themselves and do not feel comfortable in a school environment. Some parents may be shift workers or work long hours. Whatever the reason, the teacher should be understanding when parents are unable to come to the school.

The last word on parental involvement in a child's education comes from The Sutton Trust. Its researchers' findings were that moderate gains of three months in improved learning were achieved with very moderate associated costs. The authors noted that the effects were larger for the primary and early childhood years. Again, communication with the parents relating to the classroom instruction was the most helpful aspect (Higgins, Kokotsaki & Coe 2011, p. 6).

Paraprofessionals helping pupils with reading difficulties

A paraprofessional in this instance is someone who is trained to assist a professional teacher but is not licensed to practice as a teacher. We can consider how we would assist parents to help their pupils at home and use the same strategies for our paraprofessionals. The important thing is that they are trained and not just left to their own devices. There is very little benefit for the child if the paraprofessionals are not trained (Allington & Baker 1999). The Sutton Trust noted that the impact of teaching assistants for regular primary pupils was almost nil and was also very costly (Higgins, Kokotsaki & Coe 2011, p.7).

Specialist teachers

We now have some highly trained and qualified specialist teachers in most of our schools. At the six-year-old level, many schools employ reading recovery teachers. For older pupils, schools employ other specialist teachers. For example, in Queensland they are known as Support Teachers in Literacy and Numeracy (STLaN). In New Zealand they are called Supplementary Learning Support Teachers (SLST). These teachers are extremely valuable and should be given every opportunity to assist both in the classroom and in withdrawal classes. The classroom teacher should always be open for discussion about pupils with reading difficulties and should welcome the specialist teacher into his or her classroom. If the specialist teacher considers that the child is falling significantly behind his or her cohort, then it may be wise to allow that child to have the valuable experience of one-on-one tutoring. The specialist teacher may also be able to help you with resources for teaching and assessment. The important point to consider is that the specialist teacher and the classroom teacher should work cooperatively, with the child's best interest as central to anything that they plan. Communication is the key to success when working with parents, families, paraprofessionals and specialist teachers (Fielding-Barnsley 2004).

Conclusion

Now that you are armed with a little more knowledge you are ready to teach all of the pupils in your class. All well-trained and prepared teachers should be able to cater for pupils who may find it difficult to learn how to read, but there will always be some pupils for whom you will need specialist advice and teaching. Remember that you are not alone in your class and do not be afraid to ask for advice from parents, teachers and the school counsellor.

Reflective questions

1. Think back to your childhood and the children you knew in school or in your family who had reading difficulties. What has become of them? Were they able to overcome the issues they faced in childhood?

2. What factors made a difference to these children's success or failure in literacy? Do you think the same issues apply today?

3. Identify three things you didn't know about struggling readers that you have learnt in this chapter which will make you think differently about practice in the future.

Further reading

Goodwin, V. and Thomson, B. (2004). *Making Dyslexia Work for You: A Self-help Guide*. London. David Fulton Publishers.

Happy Dyslexic. http://www.happydyslexic.com/node/4.

LD Online. 'What is a Learning Disability'. http://www.ldonline.org/ldbasics/whatisld.

Mykidssupport.com. 'Orton-Gillingham Approach: A Specialist Educator Explains'. http://www.mykidsupport.com/?q=node/208.

Riddick, B. (2010). *Living with Dyslexia: The Social and Emotional Consequences of Specific Learning Difficulties/Disabilities*. London: David Fulton.

Riddick, B., Wolfe, J. and Lumsdon, D. (2002). *Dyslexia: A Practical Guide for Teachers and Parents*. London: David Fulton.

Sousa, D.A. (2001). *How the Brain Learns: A Classroom Teacher's Guide*. 2nd edn. Thousand Oaks, CA: Corwin Press.

Chapter 16

Conclusion

Chapter objectives

1. To examine key principles for supporting children from emergent literacy to fluent reading and writing, using possible solutions to scenarios.
2. To review the notion of literacy for life and how parents, families, schools and communities all contribute to children's literacy acquisition.
3. To consider how teachers of the future can avoid the pitfalls of education of the past and provide greater equity of opportunity for the learners of the future.

This final chapter draws together the key findings of each chapter and provides an overall summary of the principles for supporting children to make the transition from emergent literacy to fluent reading and writing. This chapter stresses the notion of literacy for life and reiterates the need for readers to be lifelong readers and what a difference that makes to what and how children learn and with whom.

What is different about this book?

The first thing to say is that the book covers a wide range of ages, from early childhood through to the end of primary school, and covers both reading and writing, as well as diverse classrooms, assessment, and literacy difficulties. Many texts on literacy focus on either early childhood or primary education and do not include our strong focus on continuity of literacy learning and the importance of strong transitions between homes and early childhood or primary school settings. We have argued that literacy is determined by biology, development, opportunities, and social and cultural contexts. As we explained in our introduction, we have based our definitions of what constitutes literacy on explanations stemming from neuroscience, from sociocultural theory and from social practice definitions of literacy (Berninger & Richards 2002; NELP 2009; Stahl & Yaden 2004; Teale et al. 2009; Vygotsky 1978).

Within our explanations of literacy in early childhood and primary, it is also apparent that we see literacy as a process, rather than an event. In this world view, literacy is thus a lifelong process in which both children and adults 'use it or lose it'. Helping children develop a sense of self as a literate person, who uses literacy as a tool for navigating both school and life, is an important part of our message. Teachers and families play invaluable interwoven roles in supporting children's emerging identities as literate beings. Like all other aspects of personal identity, issues and challenges can present obstacles to a positive sense of self-worth, so it is imperative that teachers and families support each child's distinct pathway to literacy.

The second point of difference is that the book is not just about school. It tries to link the teacher's work to the community and to parents because all these groups are important if children are to succeed at school. Teachers will not be as effective as they might be if they work in silos, cut off from their community and from the parents of children in their class.

The third point of difference is that the book combines theory and practice. There is nothing more practical than a good theory. This book explains theories of learning to read and write but also shows how to put these into practical use. It explains what to do in teaching, not just why to do it.

What have we tried to explain in the book?

We hope the book has given you new insights into some of the issues that might arise when you start teaching. Do you remember back to the introduction to the book when we presented you with a number of scenarios? Now that you have read Chapters 1–15, how would you go about answering issues raised in each of the scenarios presented in Chapter 1? Take a few moments and think about them again. Remember we posed the following the questions:

- What do we know about the child described in the scenario?
- Are there any issues or challenges you would face as a teacher of this child?
- What do we know about the child's context and his or her family?
- Do the issues you identified pose any potential challenges for literacy acquisition?
- What might be some solutions to the issues described in the scenario?

Scenario 1.1: possible issues, challenges and solutions

You have a four-year-old boy in your early childhood classroom and you are wondering how well he will make the transition to school. Currently he spends most of his time outside in the sandpit, riding bikes or climbing things and seems to enjoy himself, but he rarely spends any time in the centre doing literacy-related activities and he wriggles constantly at mat session times and has to be told to pay attention.

1. *What do we know about the child described in the scenario?*

In this scenario we know we have a four-year-old boy in an early childhood centre who enjoys outdoor activities but squirms and wriggles at mat times when it is time for more formal literacy events. We also know that he has only about a year before he will go to school in New Zealand and possibly slightly more in Australia. Either way, time is of the essence!

2. *Are there any issues or challenges you would face as a teacher of this child?*

Potentially yes, but possibly no. It is important to gather more information about this child and find out if he has the emergent literacy knowledge and skills that predict literacy acquisition. For the teacher of this child, finding out why the child prefers to play in the sandpit is important, along with identifying if there are any literacy activities that he likes to do in the centre. Talking to the child about what interests him in terms of literacy is clearly an important first step towards creating meaningful literacy activities that will engage his attention. This child's development is something that you should be concerned about.

3. *What do we know about the child's context and his family?*

From this scenario, not much, so we cannot assume that the child lacks literacy knowledge and skills or doesn't engage with different forms of literacy in the home environment. We do know that he doesn't engage with the formal literacy program offered to him at mat times and we need to find out why. We also need to identify what opportunities for literacy the family environment offers.

Chapter 8 on the 'sound' foundations for literacy spells out some of the essential knowledge for success in early childhood. Children who like and enjoy literacy have had many home experiences of parents reading books to them on a regular basis and talking to them about books. They also have learned about letters of the alphabet and know about sounds in words, such as rhyme and alliteration. Children like this child may not have had such experiences, maybe because their parents work at night, or for some other reason. The message of our book is to find ways to include these children rather than to isolate or ignore them.

4. *Do the issues you identified pose any potential challenges for literacy acquisition?*

Yes, they do, if after we've talked to the child and talked to the family we identify that either there's a mismatch between what the home offers in terms of literacy or multiliteracies and the early childhood centre, or that the child is not engaging with literacy at home or in the centre and is potentially lacking emergent literacy knowledge.

Chapter 6 on diversity explains that we cannot assume that children will all have similar literacy knowledge when you teach them. Every child is different. The chapter points out that some children with behaviour problems during literacy time may lack literacy skills and we need to be alert to this, so that we can make adjustments. Such children very quickly decide that they are 'dumb' and become a nuisance in class or the early childhood setting. Too often, the teacher ends up spending half his or her time teaching the class and the other half of his or her time trying to keep one or two pupils on task because the pupils do not know what to do and are unable to do what the teacher wants.

This book offers solutions for such children. For example, you could make sure that if a child is having difficulties concentrating in group sessions, he or she sits close to you, so the child can interact more easily and you can keep him or her on task. Other suggestions include giving such children special responsibility, with scaffolding to help them. For example, the teacher might ask the boy in our scenario to point with his finger under each word while she points to each word from the top of the line while she reads aloud a big book to the class, or she might ask him questions that he can answer with a little help. Guidng his hand to the right place on the alphabet chart, she could, for example, ask him to identify certain letters. Obviously this strategy can be individualised to take account of the abilities of the child. The teacher uses praise to support the child's success and encourages everyone in the group to give positive feedback to each other. For example, another child might say to James about the story he wrote, 'You done a good story, James'.

5. *What might be some solutions to the issues described in the scenario?*

Any mismatch issues can be dealt with quite readily by reconsidering the literacy opportunities in the early childhood setting and making a greater effort to offer literacy experiences that will interest the child. It is probably very important to look at the format and content of the mat session in particular, if it is failing to keep the child's concentration and to aid comprehension. If the child has limited emergent literacy knowledge and skills, then a more concerted campaign to help the child develop the crucial predictors of literacy acquisition will be required. In this case, teachers would need to make time to read and play games with the child in a one-on-one approach that supported alphabet knowledge, phonological awareness, vocabulary and emergent writing.

Scenario 1.2: issues, challenges and solutions

You have a five-year-old girl in your new-entrant class who can clearly already read. When asked what she likes to read at home, she names books that most children are reading at the age of 10. Recent testing reveals that not only can she read the words in the chapter books she likes, but she also has excellent comprehension of what she is reading.

1. *What do we know about the child described in the scenario?*

In this scenario, we have a contrasting case of a five-year-old girl who can already read at a 10-year-old level. In Chapter 6 on diversity, we explained that some children in your class will be gifted. They may have come from a home and early childhood school environment that has been so supportive that they learned to read before starting school.

2. *Are there any issues or challenges you would face as a teacher of this child?*

In such cases, the teacher needs to find activities that will challenge these children yet still keep them involved as part of the class so that they are not seen as different. Find interesting but challenging stories for them to read. Ask them to write book reviews for you, suggest they use the internet to find interesting ideas for writing, and give them positive feedback about their work. These children may respond to leadership opportunities, such as being a 'buddy' or peer tutor for other children. Keep in mind that you need to train them in how to be helpful without being pushy.

3. *What do we know about the child's context and her family?*

Currently, not very much, so making time to talk to the child's family about the literacy activities in her home environment may provide clues as to why the child's literacy is well beyond the achievement of her classmates, as well as offering insights into how to keep this child motivated and interested. In this instance, building on the child's learning at home and in early childhood will be crucial to avoiding boredom.

4. *Do the issues you identified pose any potential challenges for literacy acquisition?*

As this book has suggested, literacy acquisition is not only related to cognitive skill, it is also related to developing identity and to self-esteem. As we've suggested, children who excel can face as many challenges as children who struggle, if they encounter teachers who are not willing or interested in supporting the child's growing literacy abilities. Sometimes these children will underachieve, in order to avoid unwanted attention. Sensitive teaching and meaningful, stimulating curriculum are crucial to this child's long-term interest and achievement in literacy.

5. *What might be some solutions to the issues described in the scenario?*

For this child, finding a way to keep her motivated and interested while children her own age are learning more fundamental aspects of literacy will be the challenge. Sometimes project approaches can work with such children, so that they have more in-depth research and writing to complete while other children have tuition in reading or writing; you'll be extending the child's knowledge and comprehension, as well as her multiliteracies abilities.

Scenario 1.3: issues, challenges and solutions

You have a six-year-old boy in your primary class who seems to be struggling with reading and is quite a long way behind the rest of the class, but the reasons why do not seem obvious. He has a large receptive and expressive vocabulary, he knows the alphabet, his parents are both highly educated and say that he has been read to every day since he was a baby.

1. *What do we know about the child described in the scenario?*

In this scenario we presented a child who may have dyslexia or something similar in that it is unusual for a child to have all the necessary prerequisites for learning to read such as a good oral vocabulary and know the letters of the alphabet.

2. *Are there any issues or challenges you would face as a teacher of this child?*

What the book has shown, especially Chapter 8 on 'sound' foundations and Chapter 15 on reading difficulties, is that some pupils have great difficulty in breaking words into phonemes, and this holds them back from learning to read and spell. Such pupils will benefit greatly from activities that help them to link sounds to letters for reading, and to break words into phonemes for spelling.

3. *What do we know about the child's context and his family?*

We know that this boy's parents have provided an ideal family literacy environment, in which the parents have spent time with the child engaged with story reading, so we can rule out that he hasn't had literacy experiences. We also know that the child's parents have supported his knowledge of alphabet and vocabulary, and the research we have presented suggests that the majority of children learn expressive vocabulary and knowledge of alphabet through ambient teaching in the home environment. If the child hadn't had these experiences, we would expect to see difficulties with alphabet knowledge and a lower vocabulary score.

4. *Do the issues you identified pose any potential challenges for literacy acquisition?*

It will be important for the teacher to identify with which aspects of literacy the child is struggling, so that some intervention can be put into place and as quickly as possible. At all costs we want to avoid the child beginning to sense that his literacy acquisition is any way different to that of other children. This issue is unlikely to be solved by giving the child 'the gift of time', as Chapter 3 explained.

5. *What might be some solutions to the issues described in the scenario?*

Diagnosis is the crucial first step with this child, so that the teachers and the family know what issues and challenges the child's literacy learning involves. Supporting this child's learning will be a joint endeavour between the home and the school and a strong partnership will be needed, so that consistency and effort are maximised.

Scenario 1.4: possible issues, challenges and solutions

There is a 10-year-old boy in your class who is well behind the rest of the class in reading achievement and you are finding it difficult to meet his needs as well as catering to the rest of the class. The boy regularly tells you he is 'dumb' at reading and is uncooperative and frequently disruptive when it is time for reading or writing activities in the class, both of which he finds difficult. He reads slowly, struggles with word recognition and spells with difficulty, suggesting that he is having difficulties with hearing phonemes in words. Although he did have 'Reading Recovery' at a previous school, he doesn't seem to have made much progress. More recently, other children have started to notice that he is finding reading and writing difficult and have made comments to him like 'it's easy' or 'you just need to follow the instructions', to which the boy has become both verbally and physically aggressive.

1. *What do we know about the child described in the scenario?*

As a teacher, you might want to put yourself in the place of the child. What if you were this child? You are 10 years of age and you still are struggling with reading and spelling words. You do not want to do what the teacher asks because you never get it right and you are easily distracted in class because you cannot read what the teacher is talking or writing about. You have been to special tutoring in Reading Recovery where you got taken out of class for literacy lessons but it did not work for you. Your classmates look down on you and you get angry with them. Your self-esteem is rock bottom. How can you get yourself out of this situation?

2. *Are there any issues or challenges you would face as a teacher of this child?*

If you were this child's teacher, what would you do? You do not want to write him off as a lost cause, just as you would not want to write off a gifted child who might also be totally out of kilter with the rest of the class and reading books that many adults would find difficult. You might remember back to this textbook and look for some ideas, especially in Chapters 14 and 15. This child is struggling with the code and is already 10 years old. Probably the best part of his day at school is eating lunch. How can you make your classroom a more positive learning and social environment for this child? This is your goal.

3. *What do we know about the child's context and his family?*

Chapter 6 told you that diversity in the classroom is a given. You will have extremely good readers and at the same time some who struggle. The class is not made up of 30 clones exactly alike in every way like this:

What is this child's family and home background like? The teacher needs to find out by inviting key members of the family to the classroom for afternoon tea, or talking with them at parent–teacher night, or visiting their home after work to talk with them. It is important that the teacher and parents are on the same page in terms of finding out why the child is struggling, and working together to help out.

In Chapters 3 and 4, we saw that reading difficulties sometimes pass down through families. In some families those looking after the child have very little education themselves and few books, and do not know how to help their child with reading. In other homes, the situation is the opposite. This means that children in your class will have very different levels of support at home.

Again, in other homes parents find that one of their children will shine in literacy while the other falters. Why is this? The explanation may be genetic. We know from twin studies that there are genetic reasons why some children have difficulties in reading and spelling. If one identical twin has reading problems, the other is likely to have them as well, even if they are brought up in different homes in different locations. There may be other complicating factors as well, such as problems with attention and sitting still. These factors are covered in Chapters 6 and 15.

The good news, though, is that brain imaging studies show that with effective instruction, struggling readers and writers can improve and also that they use different parts of the brain to do so. In other words, they learn to use their brain in more effective ways, in the same ways as their classmates, and can get back on track. The message from this research is that the teacher can make a difference, no matter what the family or home background.

4. *Do the issues you identified pose any potential challenges for literacy acquisition?*

There are two challenges. The first is the child's behaviour. The teacher can use a range of strategies to encourage the child to behave appropriately in class. A points system will involve giving points or a star for good behaviour. The child can gain points on a special card. The teacher can stamp the card at times when other students are not in the room, such as morning and lunch break, and at the end of the day. When the student achieves a certain number of points, the student earns a privilege such as leading the class into the room, or an opportunity to play a game, or a snack. The teacher can also make sure to praise for positive behaviour – for example, 'Thank you, Junior, for reading quietly'. Or, 'Thank you, Junior, for sharing your book with Dean'. Studies show that when the teacher increases praise and decreases reprimands, positive behaviour goes up.

The second challenge to literacy acquisition is the student's severe difficulty in reading and writing, even with simple words. Your challenge is to figure out what is going on. Your textbook says that many struggler readers have difficulty in hearing phonemes in words, and this keeps them at the back of the class year after year. Chapters 8, 9 and 10 explain how to assess progress and teach this skill. There is a chapter in the text on how to teach this skill. The textbook recommends teaching how to deconstruct the sounds in words, learning how to break spoken words into syllables, and syllables into phonemes – for example, rabbit = rab-bit = r-a-b-i-t. Once phoneme awareness is secure, the teacher can show the child how to read and spell words. Struggler readers respond better to explicit approaches such as phonics that teach strategies for breaking the code. For instance, they could be taught to break words into smaller meaningful parts and then decode the smaller parts (see Nicholson 2006). Struggler spellers also respond to spelling teaching that focuses on invented spelling. Invented spelling is where the child writes a letter for each phoneme. Invented spelling is a transitional strategy that encourages phonemic spelling, even if not 100 per cent correct (e.g. 'rabit' for 'rabbit').

5. *What might be some solutions to the issues described in the scenario?*

- Use a reward system with the child to encourage appropriate behaviour. The family can also help with this – for example, by keeping a reading log at home and awarding points for completed reading.

- Teach phonemic awareness.

- Teach the code – start with simple words and build up.

- Teach invented spelling.

- Reading practice is essential – make sure the child has lots of text to read that is interesting and at their reading level. Remember the old saying: 'Use it or lose it' – we get better at reading by reading.

- Writing practice is essential. Make sure the child writes something each day. Give rewards for the number of words he or she writes. Teach the child skills as in the textbook's writing chapter so that he or she understands simple things such as the structure of a story.

- Praise the child for appropriate behaviour – if you are not one to give praise easily, then lighten up for this child – he or she may not have heard praise very much before now!

- Enjoy the rewards of getting a child back on track in reading and spelling, and in behaviour.

These four scenarios all have 'answers' in this textbook. We have designed the book to be helpful in this way so that you can do more than just 'teach' but can also diagnose and help children who do not respond to regular teaching, or who are way ahead of the rest of the class. In other words, the book helps teachers to differentiate their teaching so as to cater for diversity. You will encounter many scenarios in your journey as a teacher, and we hope that you will always take the time to analyse what is going on. What we hope is also clear is that children's literacy learning is very dependent on what and how we learn through our centres, schools and families and that these fundamental relationships and the associated expectations of children will have longlasting effects.

Although our interpretation of the scenarios is obviously debatable, and we encourage you to do that, there are some key principles that are probably apparent in our analysis, which may be useful to you. These key principles are as follows:

1. *Know the child*. Each child is the unique result of biology, development and social context. You need to get to know how each and every child in your class learns and develops and know how to support diverse learners.

2. *Get to know the family*. It's important that you understand the literacy experiences and opportunities that children have had at home and build on these in your classroom. Children have diverse opportunities for literacy and their literacy outcomes can be determined by the goodness of fit or match between home and educational setting.

3. *Understand the research on how literacy is acquired.* There is an enormous body of evidence-based research on different aspects of literacy acquisition. Although challenging, your task as a teacher is to maintain currency with the evidence of literacy research.

4. *Aim for excellence in teaching.* The research evidence suggests that teachers who know about the unique abilities of the children in their classes understand the research literature on literacy and can translate theory and research into appropriate teaching practice are the most effective teachers of literacy. Note that this refers to both early childhood and primary school teachers.

5. *Plan for early intervention.* As previous chapters have suggested, the sooner teachers identify that children have any issues or challenges in their literacy learning, the more likely it is that solutions can be found and difficulties prevented.

6. *Work with families on issues, challenges and solutions.* Remember that the child's developmental pathway into literacy is a lifelong event and that you will play a small but important part. Always work in partnership with families, who will be the primary source of guidance and support to children as they become literate.

Concluding statement

Finally, we hope you have enjoyed the book as much as we have enjoyed writing it. Please send an email to c.j.mclachlan@massey.ac.nz if you have questions and give us your honest feedback. If we can help with your questions, we will do so. Best wishes for your future careers as teachers and teachers of literacy!

Reflective questions

1. So now you've read this text, what unanswered questions do you have about literacy and where do you think you might find answers to those questions?

2. What issues and challenges do you think will be the most prevalent in your role as an early childhood or primary teacher?

3. How significant do you think the role of the teacher and the parent is in children's developing literacy? Has your opinion on this changed since you started reading this book?

4. As a literacy teacher, what do you consider to be the most important things for you to recognise and respond to as a teacher of children in early childhood or primary? Does the age of the child make a difference to what you attend to?

5. As you go out on your journey as a teacher, what key principles will you apply to literacy teaching? Take a moment and list them now.

References

ACARA – see Australian Curriculum, Assessment and Reporting Authority.

Adams, M.J. (1990). *Beginning to Read: Thinking and Learning about Print*. Cambridge, MA: MIT Press.

Afflerbach, P., Parker, E.L., Armengol, R., Brooke, L.B., Carper, K.R., Cronin, S.M., Denman, A.C., Irwin, P., McGunnigle, J., Pardini T. and Kurtz, N.P. (1995). 'Teachers' Choices in Classroom Assessment'. *The Reading Teacher*, vol. 48, no. 7, pp. 622–4.

Alexander, R. (2009). *The Cambridge Primary Review*. http://www.primaryreview.org.uk. Accessed 13 June 2012.

Alexander, R., Rose, J. and Woodhead, C. (1992). *Curriculum Organisation and Classroom Practice in Primary Schools*. London: HMSO.

Allington, R. (2010). 'Recent Federal Education Policy in the United States'. In D. Wyse, R. Andrews and J.V. Hoffman (eds), *International Handbook of Educational Policy and Practice* (pp. 496–507). New York: Routledge.

Allington, R.L. (2012). *What Really Matters for Struggling Readers: Designing Research-Based Programs*. Boston, MA: Pearson.

Allington, R.L. and Baker, K. (1999). 'Best Practices in Literacy Instruction for Pupils with Special Needs'. In L.B. Gambrell, L.M. Morrow, S.B. Neuman and M. Pressley (eds), *Best Practices in Literacy Instruction* (pp. 292–310). New York: Guilford.

American Psychiatric Association (APA) (1993). *Diagnostic and Statistical Manual of Mental Disorders*. Washington, DC: Author.

Anderson, J. and Morrison, F. (2011). 'Learning from and within Immigrant and Refugee Families in a Family Literacy Program'. In P. Ruggiano Schmidt and A.M. Lazar (eds), *Practicing What We Teach: How Culturally Responsive Literacy Classrooms Make a Difference* (pp. 130–40). New York: Teachers College Press.

Anning, A., Cullen, J. and Fleer, M. (2008). *Early Childhood Education: Society and Culture*. 2nd edn. Los Angeles, CA: Sage.

Anthony, J.L. and Francis, D.J. (2005). 'Development of Phonological Awareness'. *Current Directions in Psychological Science*, vol. 14, pp. 255–9.

Ashton-Warner, S. (1986). *Teacher*. New York: Simon & Schuster.

Australian Curriculum, Assessment and Reporting Authority (ACARA). (2011). 'National Report on Schooling in Australia 2009'. Sydney, NSW: Author. http://www.acara.edu.au/reporting/national_report_on_schooling/national_report_on_schooling.html. Accessed 13 June 2012.

——(2012) 'The Australian Curriculum – Content Description ACELA1433'. http://www.australiancurriculum.edu.au/Curriculum/ContentDescription/ACELA1433. Accessed 13 June 2012.

——(2012a) 'The Australian Curriculum – Content Description ACELY1671'. http://www.australiancurriculum.edu.au/Curriculum/ContentDescription/ACELY1671. Accessed 13 June 2012.

——(2012b) 'The Australian Curriculum – Overview'. http://www.australiancurriculum.edu.au/Curriculum/Overview. Accessed 13 June 2012.

Australian Government, Department of Education, Employment and Workplace Relations (2012). 'Early Childhood Workforce Initiatives – National Quality Framework for Early Childhood Education and Care'. http://www.deewr.gov.au/earlychildhood/policy_agenda/quality/pages/home.aspx. Accessed 13 June 2012.

Bakhtin, M.M. (1981). *The Dialogic Imagination: Four Essays*. M. Holquist (ed.). C. Emerson and M. Holquist (trans.). Austin, TX: University of Texas Press.

Barrentine, S. (1999). 'Introduction'. In S. Barrentine (ed.), *Reading Assessment: Principles and Practices for Elementary Teachers* (pp. 1–7). Newark, DE: International Reading Association.

Bartram, A. (2010). 'Transition to School: Supporting School Yard Play'. *Every Child*, vol. 16, no. 3, pp. 10–11.

Baynton, M. (1995). 'Birth of a Book. A Difficult Labour from Conception to Delivery'. Paper presented at the 21st New Zealand Conference on Reading, Invercargill, NZ, May.

Bearne, E. (2009). 'Multimodality, Literacy and Texts: Developing a Discourse'. *Journal of Early Childhood Literacy*, vol. 9, no. 2, pp. 156–87.

Beauchat, K.A., Blamey, K. and Walpole, S. (2009). 'Building Preschool Children's Language and Literacy One Storybook at a Time'. *The Reading Teacher*, vol. 63, no. 1, pp. 26–39.

Beck, I., McKeown, M. and Kucan, L. (2002). *Bringing Words to Life: Robust Vocabulary Instruction*. New York: Guilford.

Benseman, J. and Sutton A. (2005). *Summative Evaluation of the Manukau Family Literacy Project*. Auckland, NZ: Uniservices, The University of Auckland.

Berninger, V.W. and Abbott, R.D. (2010). 'Listening Comprehension, Oral Expression, Reading Comprehension, and Written Expression: Related yet Unique Language Systems in Grades 1, 3, 5, and 7'. *Journal of Educational Psychology*, vol. 102, no. 3, pp. 635–51.

Berninger, V.W. and Richards, T.L. (2002). *Brain Literacy for Educators and Psychologists*. Amsterdam: Academic Press.

Berry, R. and Adamson, B. (2011). 'Assessment Reform Past, Present and Future'. In R. Berry and B. Adamson (eds), *Assessment Reform in Education – Education in the Asia-Pacific Region: Issues, Concerns and Prospects*, vol. 14 (pp. 3–14). Dordrecht: Springer.

Bertram, T. and Pascal, C. (2002). *Early Years Education: An International Perspective*. London: NFER.

Billings, E.S. (2009). '*El alfabetismo y las familias latinas*: A Critical Perspective on the Literacy Values and Practices of Latino Families with Young Children'. *Journal of Latinos and Education*, vol. 8. no. 4, pp. 252–69.

Bingham, G., Holbrook, T. and Meyers, L.E. (2010). 'Using Self-assessments in Elementary Classrooms'. *Phi Delta Kappan*, vol. 91, no. 5, pp. 59–61.

Bissex, G.L. (1980). *Gnys at Wrk: A Child Learns to Write and Read*. Cambridge, MA: Harvard University Press.

Blachowicz, C.L.Z. and Fisher, P.J. (2011). 'Best Practices in Vocabulary Instruction Revisited'. In L.M. Morrow and L.B. Gambrell (eds), *Best Practices in Literacy Instruction* (4th edn, pp. 224–49). New York: Guilford.

Blanton, W.E., Moorman, G.B., Hayes, B.A. and Warner, M. (2000). 'Effects of Participation in the Fifth Dimension on Far Transfer'. *Journal of Educational Computing Research*, vol. 16, pp. 371–96.

Blum, I.H., Koskinen, P.S., Bhartiya, P. and Hluboky, S. (2010). 'Thinking and Talking about Books: Using Prompts to Stimulate Discussion'. *The Reading Teacher*, vol. 63, no. 6, pp. 495–9.

Bond, M.A. and Wasik, B.A. (2009). 'Conversation Stations: Promoting Language Development in Young Children'. *Early Childhood Education Journal*, vol. 36, no. 6, pp. 467–73.

Borba, J.A. and Olvera, C.M. (2001). 'Student-Led Parent–Teacher Conferences'. *The Clearing House*, vol. 74, no. 6, pp. 333–6.

Boyer, N. and Ehri, L.C. (2011). 'Contribution of Phonemic Segmentation Instruction with Letters and Articulation Pictures to Word Reading and Spelling in Beginners'. *Scientific Studies of Reading*, vol. 15, no. 5, pp. 440–70.

Bredekamp, S. and Copple, C. (1997). *Developmentally Appropriate Practice in Early Childhood Education Programs*. Revised edn. Washington, DC: National Association for the Education of Young Children.

Briggs, F. and Potter G. (1995). *Teaching Children in the First Three Years of School*. Melbourne: Longman Cheshire.

Brooks, R. (2000). 'Self-esteem and Resilience: A Precious Gift for Our Children'. In *The Child Information and Resource Guide* (pp. 34–7). Landover, MD: CHADD.

Bryant (1975). *Bryant Test of Basic Decoding Skills*. New York: Teachers College Press.

Bus, A.G. and van Ijzendoorn, M.H. (1995). 'Mothers Reading to Their Three-Year-Olds: The Role of Mother–Child Attachment Security in Becoming Literate'. *Reading Research Quarterly*, vol. 30, pp. 998–1015.

Bus, A.G., van Ijzendoorn, M.H. and Pellegrini, A.D. (1995). 'Joint Book Reading Makes for Success in Learning to Read: A Meta-analysis of Intergenerational Transmission of Literacy'. *Review of Educational Research*, vol. 65, pp. 1–21.

Byrne, B. (1998). *The Foundation of Literacy: The Child's Acquisition of the Alphabetic Principle*. Hove, UK: Psychology Press.

Byrne, B. and Fielding-Barnsley, R. (1991). *Sound Foundations*. Sydney, NSW: Leyden Publications.

Byrne, B., Coventry, W.L., Olson, R.K., Wadsworth, S.J., Samuelsson, S. and Perrill, S.A. (2010). '"Teacher Effects" in Early Literacy Development: Evidence from a Study of Twins'. *Journal of Educational Psychology*, vol. 102, pp. 32–42.

Cairney, T. (2003). 'Literacy within Family Life'. In N. Hall, J. Larson and J. Marsh (eds), *Handbook of Early Childhood Literacy* (pp. 85–98). London and Thousand Oaks, CA: Sage.

Cairney, T. and Ruge, J. (1998). *Community Literacy Practices and Schooling: Towards Effective Support for Students*. Canberra, ACT: DEET.

Calfee, R.C. (1991). 'What Schools Can Do to Improve Literacy Instruction'. In B. Means, C. Chelemer and M.S. Knapp (eds), *Teaching Advanced Skills to At-Risk Students* (pp. 176–203). San Francisco: Jossey Bass.

Calfee, R.C. and Drum, P.A. (1986). 'Research on Teaching Reading'. In M. Wittrock (ed.), *Handbook of Research on Teaching* (pp. 804–49). New York: Macmillan.

Calfee, R.C. and Miller, R.G. (2007). 'Best Practices in Writing Assessment'. In S. Graham, C. A. MacArthur and J. Fitzgerald (eds), *Best Practices in Writing Instruction* (pp. 265–86. New York: Guilford.

Calfee, R.C. and Patrick, C.L. (1995). *Teach Our Children Well: Bringing K–12 Education into the 21st Century*. Stanford, CA: Stanford Alumni.

Care, E., Griffin, P., Thomas, A. and Pavlovic, M. (2007). *Early Years Assessment English*. Melbourne: Assessment Research Centre, University of Melbourne.

Carle, E. (1969). *The Very Hungry Caterpillar*. Philomel: Putnam.

Carnine, D.W. (1976). 'Similar Sound Separation and Cumulative Introduction in Learning Letter–Sound Correspondences'. *Journal of Educational Research*, vol. 69, no. 10, pp. 368–72.

Carr, M. (2001). *Assessment in Early Childhood Settings: Learning Stories*. London: Paul Chapman Publishing.

Carter, D.R., Chard, D.J. and Pool, J.L. (2009). 'A Family Strengths Approach to Early Language And Literacy Development'. *Early Childhood Education Journal*, vol. 36, pp. 519–26.

Casbergue, R., McGee, L.M. and Bedford, A. (2007). 'Characteristics of Classroom Environments Associated with Accelerated Literacy Development'. In L.M. Justice and C. Vukelich (eds), *Achieving Excellence in Preschool Literacy Instruction* (pp. 167–81). New York: Guilford Press.

Chapman, W., Tunmer, W.E. and Allen, R. (2003). 'Findings from the International Adult Literacy Survey on the Incidence and Correlates of Learning Disabilities in New Zealand: Is Something Rotten in the State of New Zealand?' *Dyslexia: An International Journal of Research and Practice*, vol. 9, no. 2, pp. 75–98.

Clark, B. (1983). *Growing up Gifted: Developing the Potential of Children at Home and School.* Columbus: Merrill.

Clay, M.M. (1966). 'Emergent Reading Behaviour'. Unpublished Doctoral Thesis, The University of Auckland.

——(1979). *Reading: The Patterning of Complex Behaviour.* Auckland, NZ: Heinemann.

——(1989). 'Concepts about Print in English and Other Languages'. *The Reading Teacher*, vol. 42, no. 4, pp. 268–76.

——(2000a). *Concepts about Print: What Have Children Learned about the Way We Print Language?* Portsmouth, NH: Heinemann.

——(2000b). *Running Records for Classroom Teachers.* Portsmouth, NH: Heinemann.

——(2005). *An Observation Survey of Early Literacy Achievement.* Portsmouth, NH: Heinemann.

Colenbrander, D., Nickels, L. and Kohnen, S. (2011). 'Nonword Reading Tests: Review of Available Resources'. *Australasian Journal of Special Education*, vol. 35, no. 2, pp. 237–72.

Coltheart, M. (1979). 'When Can Children Learn to Read – And When Should They Be Taught?' In T.G. Waller and G.E. MacKinnon (eds), *Reading Research Advances in Theory and Practice: Vol. 1* (pp. 1–30). San Diego, CA: Academic Press.

COMET (2012). 'Previous Programmes: Manukau Family Literacy Programme (MFLP)'. http://www.comet.org.nz/wawcs0143757/idDetails=165/Manukau-Family-Literacy-Programme-%28MFLP%29.html. Accessed 20 January 2012.

Commonwealth of Australia. (2009b). *Draft National Early Years Learning Framework.* Canberra, ACT: Author.

Cooper, P. and Ideus, K. (2000). *Attention Deficit/Hyperactivity Disorder: A Practical Guide for Teachers.* London: David Fulton Publishers.

Cope, B. and Kalantzis, M. (eds) (2000). *Multiliteracies: Literacy Learning and the Design of Social Futures.* London: Routledge.

Copple, C. and Bredekamp, S. (2009). *Developmentally Appropriate Practice in Early Childhood Programs: Serving Children from Birth through Age 8.* 3rd edn. Washington, DC: NAEYC.

Couglan, S. (2008). 'Is Five Too Soon to Start School? BBC News Online. http://news.bbc.co.uk/2/hi/7234578.stm. Accessed 13 June 2012.

Coulson, A. (2002). 'Delivering Education'. In E.P. Lazear (ed.), *Schools for the 21st Century* (pp. 105–46). San Francisco, CA: Hoover Institution Press.

Coyne, M.D., McCoach, D.B., Loftus, S., Zipoli, R. and Kapp, S. (2009). 'Direct Vocabulary Instruction in Kindergarten: Teaching for Breadth Versus Depth'. *The Elementary School Journal*, vol. 110, no. 1, pp. 1–18.

Crain-Thoreson, C. and Dale, P.S. (1992). 'Do Early Talkers Become Early Readers? Linguistic Precocity, Preschool Language, and Emergent Literacy'. *Developmental Psychology*, vol. 28, pp. 421–9.

Culham, R. (2008). *6 + 1 Traits of Writing: The Complete Guide for the Primary Grades*. New York: Scholastic.

Cunningham, A.E. and Stanovich, K.E. (1997). 'Early Reading Acquisition and its Relation to Reading Experience and Ability 10 Years Later'. *Developmental Psychology*, vol. 33, pp. 934–45.

Cunningham, A.E., Perry, K.E., Stanovich, K.E. and Stanovich, P.J. (2004). 'Disciplinary Knowledge of K–3 Teachers and Their Knowledge Calibration in the Domain of Early Literacy'. *Annals of Dyslexia*, vol. 54, no. 1, pp. 139–67.

Cunningham, A.E., Zibulsky, J. and Callahan, M.D. (2009) 'Starting Small: Building Preschool Teacher Knowledge that Supports Early Literacy Development'. *Reading and Writing*, vol. 22, pp. 487–510.

Cunningham, A.J. and Carroll, J.M. (2011). 'The Development of Early Literacy in Steiner- and Standard-educated Children'. *British Journal of Educational Psychology*, vol. 81, pp. 475–90.

Cunningham, P. (2007). 'High-poverty Schools that Beat the Odds'. *Reading Teacher*, vol. 60, no. 4, pp. 382–85.

Cunningham, P.M., Hall, D.P. and Defee, M. (1998). 'Nonability Grouped, Multilevel Instruction: Eight Years Later'. *Reading Teacher*, vol. 51, no. 8, pp. 652–65.

Dahlberg, G. and Moss, P. (2005). *Ethics and Politics in Early Childhood Education*. London: Routledge Falmer.

Dahlberg, G., Moss, P. and Pence, A. (2007). *Beyond Quality in Early Childhood Education and Care: Languages of Evaluation*. 2nd edn. London: Falmer.

Dahle, A.E., Knivsberg, A. and Andreassen, A.B. (2011). 'Coexisting Problem Behaviour in Severe Dyslexia'. *Journal of Research in Special Educational Needs*, vol. 11, no. 3, pp. 162–70.

Dalli, C., White, J., Rockel, J., Duhn, I., with Buchanan, E., Davidson, S., Ganly, S., Kus, L. and Wang, B. (2011). *Quality Early Childhood Education for Under-Two-Year-Olds: What Should it Look Like? A Literature Review*. Wellington, NZ: Ministry of Education.

Daniels, H. (2001). *Vygotsky and Pedagogy*. London: Routledge Falmer.

Davies, A. and Ritchie, D. (n.d.) *THRASS: Teaching Handwriting Reading and Spelling Skills*. Osbourne Park, Western Australia: THRASS.

Davies, D. (2001). *School Entry Assessment June 1997 – Dec 2000*. Report prepared for the Ministry of Education, Wellington, NZ.

De Temple, J.M, Dickinson, D.K. and Tabors, P.O. (2001). 'Extracts' in D.K. Dickinson and P.O. Tabors (eds), *Beginning Literacy with Language: Young Children Learning at Home and School* (pp. 31–51, 53–68). Baltimore: PH Brookes.

DEECD – see Department of Education and Early Childhood Development.

DEEWR – see Department of Education, Employment and Workplace Relations.

Department of Education. (1988). *Education to Be More*. Wellington, NZ: Government Printer.

Department of Education and Children's Services (2008). *Assessing for Learning and Development in the Early years Using Observation Scales: Reflect, Respect, Relate. A Resource Package for Educators*, Hindmarsh, South Australia: DECS.

Department of Education and Early Childhood Development (DEECD). (2009a). 'Prep to Year 10 Assessment – Assessment Advice'. http://www.education.vic.gov.au/studentlearning/assessment/preptoyear10/default.htm. Accessed 13 June 2012.

——(2009b). *Transition: A Positive Start to School*. Melbourne, Vic.: Author.

——(2009c). *Victorian Early Years Learning and Development Framework [VEYLDF]*. Melbourne, Vic.: Department of Education and Early Childhood Development and the Victorian Curriculum and Assessment Authority.

——(2011a). 'Transition to School – 2011 Follow-up Evaluation of the Transition: A Positive Start to School Initiative'. http://www.education.vic.gov.au/earlylearning/transitionschool/default.htm. Accessed 7 January 2012.

——(2011b). 'In the Classroom'. http://www.education.vic.gov.au/aboutschool/prepare/classroom.htm#12. Accessed 18 January 2012.

Department of Education, Employment and Workplace Relations (DEEWR) (2009a). *Belonging, Being and Becoming: The Early Years Learning Framework for Australia*. Canberra, Australia: Commonwealth of Australia.

——(2009b). *Supporting the Development of Young Children in Australia: 2009 – A Snapshot*. Canberra, Australia: Author.

Department of Education, Science and Training (DEST). (2002). *Raising the Standards: A Proposal for the Development of an ICT Competency Framework for Teachers*. Canberra, ACT: Commonwealth Department of Education, Science and Training.

——(2005). *National Inquiry into the Teaching of Reading: Report and Recommendations*. Canberra: Commonwealth of Australia.

DEST – see Department of Education, Science and Training.

Di Santo, A. and Berman, R. (2011). 'Beyond the Preschool Years: Children's Perceptions about Starting Kindergarten'. *Children and Society*. doi: 10.1111/j.1099–0860.2011.00360.x.

Dickie, J. and MacDonald, G. (2011). 'Literacy in Church and Family Sites through the Eyes of Samoan Children in New Zealand'. *Literacy*, vol. 45, no. 1, pp. 25–31.

Dockett, S. and Perry, B. (2006). *Starting School: A Handbook for Early Childhood Educators*. Castle Hill, NSW: Pademelon Press.

Dodd, B., Holm, A., Oerlemans, M. and McCormick, M. (1996). *Queensland Inventory of Literacy*. St Lucia, Australia: Department of Speech and Pathology, University of Queensland.

Ducke, N. (2004). 'The Case for Informational Text'. *Educational Leadership*, vol. 61, no. 6, pp. 40–4.

Duke, N.K. (2000). '3.6 Minutes per Day: The Scarcity of Informational Texts in First Grade'. *Reading Research Quarterly*, vol. 35, pp. 202–24.

Dunn, L.M. and Dunn, D.M. (2007). *Picture Vocabulary Test*. 4th edn. San Antonio, TX: Pearson.

Durrant, C. and Green, B. (2000). 'Literacy and New Technologies in School Education: Meeting the L(IT)Eracy Challenge'. *Australian Journal of Language and Literacy*, vol. 23, no. 2, pp. 89–108.

Dymock, S. (2007). 'Comprehension Strategy Instruction: Teaching Narrative Text Structure Awareness'. *The Reading Teacher*, vol. 6, pp. 161–7.

Dymock, S. and Nicholson, T. (2007). *Teaching Text Structure: The Key to Non-fiction Reading Success*. New York: Scholastic.

——(2010a). 'Every Story Has a Problem: How to Improve Student Narrative Writing in Grades K–3'. In B. Moss and D. Lapp (eds), *Teaching the Texts Children Need to Succeed in the Elementary Grades (2–6)* (pp. 26–44). New York: Guilford Press.

——(2010b). 'High 5!' Strategies to Enhance Comprehension of Expository Text'. *The Reading Teacher*, vol. 64, no. 3, pp. 166–80.

——(2012). *Reading Comprehension: The What, the How, the Why*. Wellington, NZ: NZCER Press.

Dyslexia Working Party (2010). *Helping People with Dyslexia: A National Agenda*. Report to the Hon Bill Shorten, Parliamentary Secretary for Disabilities and Pupils' Services.

http://www.rch.org.au/emplibrary/cah/dyslexia_a_national_action_agenda.pdf. Accessed 13 June 2012.

Earl, L.M. (2003). *Assessment as Learning: Using Classroom Assessment to Maximize Student Learning*. Thousand Oaks, CA: Corwin.

Early, D.M., Bryant, B., Pianta, R., Clifford, R., Burchinal, M., Ritchie, S., Howes, C., Barbarin, O. (2006). 'Are Teacher Education, Major, and Credentials Related to Classroom Quality and Children's Academic Gains in Pre-kindergarten?' *Early Childhood Research Quarterly*, vol. 21, pp. 174–95.

Education Review Office. (2011). *Literacy Teaching and Learning in Early Childhood*. Wellington, NZ: Author.

Education, Science and Arts Committee. (1991). *Standards of Reading in Primary Schools*. Third Report, vol. 1, pp. 261–8.

Egeland, B. Weinfeld, N., Hiester, M., Lawrence, C., Pierce, S., Chippendale, K. and Powell, J (1995). *Teaching Tasks Administration and Scoring Manual*. Minneapolis, MN: University of Minnesota Institute of Child Development.

Ehri, L.C. and Roberts, T. (2006). 'The Roots of Learning to Read and Write: Acquisition of Letters and Phonemic Awareness'. In D.K. Dickinson and S.B. Neuman (eds), *Handbook of Early Literacy Research* (vol. 2, pp. 113–34). New York: Guilford Press.

Ehri, L.C., Nunes, S.R., Stahl, S.A. and Willows, D.M. (2001). 'Systematic Phonics Instruction Helps Students Learn to Read: Evidence from the National Reading Panel's Meta-analysis'. *Review of Educational Research*, vol. 71, pp. 393–447.

Elbaum, B. and Vaughn, S. (2003). 'Self-concept and Students with Learning Disabilities'. In H.L. Swanson, K.R. Harris and S. Graham (eds), *Handbook of Learning Disabilities* (pp. 229–41). New York: Guilford Press.

Elley, W.B. (1992). *How in the World do Students Read? IEA Study of Reading Literacy*. The Hague: International Association for the Evaluation of Educational Achievement.

Elliott, A. (2005). 'Engaging with Literacy: Supporting Literacy Learning through Building Social Competence'. *Every Child*, vol.11, no. 4.

Engels, S. (1995). *The Stories Children Tell: Making Sense of the Narratives of Childhood*. New York: W.H. Freeman and Company.

Eun, B. (2010). 'From Learning to Development: A Sociocultural Approach to Instruction'. *Cambridge Journal of Education*, vol. 40, no. 4, pp. 401–18.

Evans, M.A. and Saint-Aubin, J. (2005). 'What Children are Looking at during Shared Storybook Reading: Evidence from Eye Movement Monitoring'. *Psychological Science*, vol. 16, no. 11, pp. 913–20.

Fabian, H. (2002). *Children Starting School: A Guide to Successful Transitions and Transfers for Teachers and Assistants*. London, UK: David Fulton Publishers.

Fabian H. and Dunlop, A. (2007). *Outcomes of Good Practice in Transition Process for Children Entering Primary School*. Paper commissioned for the *Education for All Global Monitoring Report 2007: Strong Foundations: Early Childhood Care and Education*. Paris, France: UNESCO.

Farr, R. (1999). 'Putting it All Together: Solving the Reading Assessment Puzzle'. In S.J. Barrentine (ed.), *Reading Assessment: Principles and Practices for Elementary Teachers* (pp. 44–56). Newark, DE: International Reading Association.

Farrell, P., Critchley, C. and Mills, C. (1999). 'The Educational Attainments of Pupils with Emotional and Behavioural Difficulties'. *British Journal of Special Education*, vol. 26, no. 1, pp. 50–3.

Ferreiro, E. (1986). 'The Interplay between Information and Assimilation in Beginning Literacy'. In W.H. Teale and E. Sulzby (eds), *Emergent Literacy: Writing and Reading* (pp. 15–49). Norwood, NJ: Ablex.

Fielding-Barnsley, R. (2004). 'Successful Learning Support Teachers in Inclusive Classrooms: Communication is the Key'. In B.J Bartlett, F.K. Bryer and R. Roebuck (eds), *Educating: Weaving Research into Practice* (vol. 2, pp. 32–43). Brisbane: Griffith University.

Fielding-Barnsley, R. and Hay, I. (2012). 'Profs Phonics 2'. iTunes, Apple Computers. http://itunes.apple.com/app/profs-skills based teaching/id496793198. Accessed 13 June 2012.

Fielding-Barnsley, R. and Purdie, N. (2003). 'Early Intervention in the Home for Children at Risk of Reading Failure'. *Support for Learning: A Journal of The National Association for Special Education Needs*, vol. 18, pp. 73–8.

Firth, I. (1972). 'Components of Reading Disability'. Unpublished PhD Thesis, University of New South Wales.

Fisher, J.P. and Glenister, J.M. (1992). *The Hundred Pictures Naming Test*. Hawthorne, Vic.: ACER.

Fitzpatrick, M. D., Grissmer, D. and Hastedt, S. (2009). 'What a Difference a Day Makes: Estimating Daily Learning Gains during Kindergarten and First Grade Using a Natural Experiment'. *Economics of Education Review*, vol. 30, pp. 269–79.

Fletcher, J.M., Fuchs, L.S. and Barnes, M.A. (2007). *Learning Disabilities: From Identification to Intervention*. New York: Guilford Press.

Fletcher-Flinn, C.M. and Thompson, G.B. (2000). 'Learning to Read with Underdeveloped Phonemic Awareness but Lexicalised Phonological Recoding: A Case Study of a 3-Year-Old'. *Cognition*, vol. 74, pp. 177–208.

——(2004). 'A Mechanism of Implicit Lexicalised Phonological Recoding Used Concurrently with Underdeveloped Explicit Letter-Sound Skills in Both Precocious and Normal Development'. *Cognition*, vol. 90, pp. 303–35.

Forell, E.R. (1985). 'The Case for Conservative Reader Placement'. *Reading Teacher*, vol. 38, no. 9, pp. 857–62.

Fox, M. (2001). *Reading Magic*. Sydney, Pan Macmillan and New York: Harvest Original Harcourt.

——(2002). Speech presented at the New Zealand Reading Association Conference, Christchurch, July.

Freebody, P. (2007). *Literacy Education in School: Research Perspectives from the Past, for the Future. Australian Education Review*, no. 52. Camberwell, Vic.: Australian Council for Educational Research.

Freeman, L. and Bochner, S. (2008). 'Bridging the Gaps: Improving Literacy Outcomes for Indigenous Students'. *Australasian Journal of Early Childhood*, vol. 33, no. 4.

Freire, P. (1972). *Pedagogy of the Oppressed*. Translated from Portuguese into English by Myra Bergman Ramos. London: Sheed and Ward.

Freire, P. and Macedo, D. (2000). *Pedagogy of the Oppressed*. New York: Continuum.

Fry, E.B. and Kress, J.E. (2006). *The Reading Teacher's Book of Lists*. 5th edn. San Francisco: Jossey-Bass.

Gallimore, R. and Tharp, R. (1990). 'Teaching Mind in Society: Teaching, Schooling and Literate Discourse'. In L.C. Moll (ed.), *Vygotsky and Education: Instructional Implications and Applications of Sociohistorical Psychology*. Cambridge, UK: Cambridge University Press.

Gee, J.P. (1996). *Social Linguistics and Literacies: Ideology in Discourses*. 2nd edn. London: Taylor & Francis.

——(2004). *Situated Language and Learning: A Critique of Traditional Schooling*. Routledge: London.

Georgiou, G., Parrila, R. and Liao, C.H. (2008). 'Rapid Naming Speed and Reading across Languages that Vary in Orthographic Consistency'. *Reading and Writing: An Interdisciplinary Journal*, vol. 21, pp. 885–903.

Gilmore, A., Croft, C. and Reid, N. (1981). *Burt Word Reading Test – New Zealand Revision*. Wellington, NZ.

Glasson, T. (2009). *Improving Student Achievement: A Practical Guide to Assessment for Learning*. Carlton South, Vic.: Curriculum Corporation.

Golbeck, S.L. (2001). 'Instructional Models for Early Childhood: In Search of a Child-regulated/ Teacher-guided Pedagogy'. In S.L. Golbeck (ed.), *Psychological Perspectives in Early Childhood Education* (pp. 3–34). Mahwah, NJ: Lawrence Erlbaum Associates.

Gordon, J., O'Toole, L. and Whitman, C.V. (2008). 'A Sense of Belonging as Part of Children's Well-being'. *Early Childhood Matters*, vol. 111, pp. 7–12.

Gorell, L. (2010). 'Does a Diagnosis Make a Difference?' Unpublished Honours Thesis. University of Tasmania.

Gorman, J.C. (2001). *Emotional Disorders And Learning Disabilities: Interactions and Interventions*. Thousand Oaks, CA: Corwin Press.

Goswami, U. and Bryant, P. (2007). *Children's Cognitive Development and Learning*. Primary Review Research Briefings Survey 2/1a, Cambridge, UK: University of Cambridge Faculty of Education.

Goswami, U. and Ziegler, J.C. (2006). 'Becoming Literate in Different Languages: Similar Problems, Different Solutions'. *Developmental Science*, vol. 9, no. 5, pp. 429–53.

Gough, P.B. and Lee, C.H. (2007). 'A Step toward Early Phonemic Awareness. The Effects of Turtle Talk Training'. *Psychologia*, vol. 50, pp. 54–66.

Graves, M.F., Juel, C., Graves, B.B. and Dewitz, P. (2011) *Teaching Reading in the 21st Century: Motivating All Learners*. Boston, MA: Pearson.

Greaney, K.T. (2011). 'The Multiple Cues or "Searchlights" Word Reading Theory: Implications for Reading Recovery'. *Perspectives on Language and Literacy*, vol. 37, no. 4, pp. 15–19.

Gregory, E. and Kenner, C. (2003). 'The Out-of-School Schooling of Literacy'. In N. Hall, J. Larson and J. Marsh (eds), *Handbook of Early Childhood Literacy* (pp. 75–84). Thousand Oaks, CA: Sage.

Gunning, T. (2006). *Assessing and Correcting Reading and Writing Difficulties*. Boston, MA: Pearson/Allyn & Bacon.

Gutek, G.L. (2011). *Historical and Philosophical Foundations of Education: A Biographical Introduction*. 5th edn. Upper Saddle River, NJ: Pearson.

Guthrie, J.T. and Humenick, N.M. (2004). 'Motivating Students to Read: Evidence for Classroom Practices that Increase Motivation and Achievement'. In P. McCardle and V. Chhabra (eds), *The Voice of Evidence in Reading Research* (pp. 329–54). Baltimore: Paul Brookes.

Hales, B. (2006), 'Using Old Favourites to Support Australia's Current Literacy Needs'. *Practically Primary*, vol. 11, no. 2, pp. 45–7.

Halliday, M. (1978). *Language As a Social Semiotic: The Social Interpretation of Language and Meaning*. London: Edward Arnold.

Hamer, J. and Adams, P. (2003). *The New Zealand Early Childhood Literacy Handbook: Practical Literacy Ideas for Early Childhood Centres*. Palmerston North: Dunmore Press.

Hammill, D.D. and Larsen, S.C. (2009) *Test of Written Language*. 4th edn. Austin, TX: Pro-Ed.

Hanlen, W. (2010). *Aboriginal Students: Cultural Insights for Teaching Literacy*. http//:www. curriculumsupport.education.nsw.gov.au/literacy/assets/pdf/packages/ab_studs_cult.pdf. Accessed 20 January 2012.

Hannon, P. (2007). 'Commentary: Play, Learning and Teaching'. In K.A. Roskos and J.F. Christie (eds), *Play and Literacy in Early Childhood: Research from Multiple Perspectives* (2nd edn, pp. 201–14). New York: Lawrence Erlbaum Associates.

Harms, T., Clifford, R.M. and Cryer, D. (1998). *Early Childhood Environmental Rating Scale*. Revised edn. New York: Teachers College Press.

Harp, B. and Brewer, J.A. (2000). 'Assessing Reading and Writing in the Early years'. In D.S. Strickland and L.M. Morrow (eds). *Beginning Reading and Writing* (pp. 154–67). New York: Teachers College Press/International Reading Association.

Harris, J., Michnick Golinkoff, R. and Hirsh-Pasek, K. (2011). 'Lessons from the Crib for the Classroom: How Children Really Learn Vocabulary'. In S.B. Neuman and D.K. Dickinson (eds), *Handbook of Early Literacy Research* (vol. 3, pp. 49–65). New York: Guilford Press.

Harrison, C., Lee, L., O'Rourke, M. and Yelland, N. (2009). 'Maximising the Moment from Preschool to School: The Place of Multiliteracies and ICT in the Transition to School'. *International Journal of Learning*, vol. 16, no. 11, pp. 465–74.

Harste, J.C., Woodward, V.A. and Burke, C.L. (1984). *Language Stories and Literacy Lessons*. Portsmouth, NH: Heinemann.

Hart, B.H. and Risley, T.R. (1995). *Meaningful Differences in the Everyday Experiences of Young American Pupils*. Baltimore, MD: Paul H. Brookes.

Hattie, J. (2009). *Visible Learning: A Synthesis of over 800 Meta-analyses Relating to Achievement*. London: Routledge.

Hay, I. and Fielding-Barnsley, R. (2009). 'Competencies that Underpin Pupils' Transition into Early Literacy'. *Australian Journal of Language and Literacy*, vol. 32, pp. 148–62.

Hay, I., Ashman, A. and van Kraayenoord, C. (1998). 'The Educational Characteristics of Students With High or Low Self-concept'. *Psychology in the Schools*, vol. 35, pp. 391–400.

Hay, I., Elias, G., Fielding-Barnsley, R., Homel, R. and Frieberg, K. (2007). 'Language Delays, Reading Delays and Learning Difficulties: Interactive Elements Requiring Multidimensional Programming'. *Journal of Learning Disabilities*, vol. 40, no. 5, pp. 400–9.

Heacox, D. (2002). *Differentiating Instruction in the Regular Classroom: How to Teach and Reach All Learners, Grades 3–12*. Minneapolis, MN: Free Spirit Publishing.

Healy, A. (ed.) (2008). *Multiliteracies and Diversity in Education: New Pedagogies for Expanding Landscapes*. Melbourne: Oxford University Press.

Heath, S.B. (1983). *Ways with Words: Language, Life, and Work in Communities and Classrooms*. Cambridge, UK: Cambridge University Press.

Henderson, S.J., Jackson, N.E. and Mukumal, R.A. (1993). 'Early Development of Language and Literacy Skills of an Extremely Precocious Reader'. *Gifted Child Quarterly*, vol. 37, pp. 78–83.

Henry, M.K. (2010). *Unlocking Literacy: Effective Decoding and Spelling Instruction*. 2nd edn. Baltimore, MD: Paul H. Brookes.

Higgins, S., Kokotsaki, D. and Coe, R. (2011). *The Sutton Trust. Toolkit of Strategies to Improve Learning: Summary for Schools Spending the Pupil Premium*. Durham: CEM Centre, Durham University.

Hill, S. (2005). *Mapping Multiliteracies: Children in the New Millennium: Report of the Research Project 2000–2004*. Adelaide: University of South Australia.

——(2006). *Developing Early Literacy: Assessment and Teaching*. Prahran, Vic.: Eleanor Curtain.

——(2010). 'The Millennium Generation: Teachers-Researchers Exploring New Forms of Literacy'. *Journal of Early Childhood Literacy*, vol. 10, no. 3, pp. 314–40.

Hill, S. and Mulhearn, G. (2007). 'Children of the New Millennium: Research and Professional Learning into Practice'. *Journal of Australian Research in Early Childhood Education*, vol. 14, no. 1, pp. 57–67.

Hill, S., Comber, B., Louden, W. and Rivalland, J. (2002). *100 Children Turn 10: A Longitudinal Study of Literacy Development from the Year Prior to School to the First Four Years of School*. Canberra, ACT: Commonwealth of Australia.

Howes, C., Burchinal, M., Pianta, R., Bryant, D., Early, D., Clifford, R. and Barbarin, O. (2008). 'Ready to Learn? Children's Pre-academic Achievement in Pre-kindergarten Programs'. *Early Childhood Research Quarterly*, vol. 23, pp. 27–50.

Huey, E.B. (1908/1968). *The Psychology and Pedagogy of Reading*. Boston, MA: reprinted by MIT Press.

Hume, L. (2007). *Clancy the Courageous Cow*. New York: Greenwillow Books.

Hutchins, P. (1998). *Rosie's Walk*. London: Bodley Head.

Ibabe, I. and Jauregizar, J. (2010). 'Online Self-assessment with Feedback and Metacognitive Knowledge'. *Higher Education: The International Journal of Higher Education and Educational Planning*, vol. 59, no. 2, pp. 243–58.

Jackson, N.E. (1988). 'Precocious Reading Ability: What Does it Mean?' *Gifted Child Quarterly*, vol. 32, pp. 200–4.

——(1992). 'Precocious Reading of English: Origins, Structure, and Predictive Significance'. In P.S. Klein and A.J. Tannenbaum (eds), *To Be Young and Gifted* (pp. 171–203). Norwood, NJ: Ablex.

Jalongo, M.R., Fennimore, B.S. and Stamp, L.N. (2004). 'The Acquisition of Literacy: Reframing Definitions, Paradigms, Ideologies and Practices'. In O.N. Saracho and B. Spodek (eds), *Contemporary Perspectives on Language Policy and Literacy Instruction in Early Childhood Education* (pp. 57–110). Greenwich, CN: Information Age Publishing.

John-Steiner, V. and Mahn, H. (1996). 'Sociocultural Approaches to Learning and Development: A Vygotskian Framework'. *Educational Psychologist*, vol. 31. nos. 3/4, pp. 191–206.

Johns, K. (2010). 'What Bugs You about Teaching Reading?'. *Educating Young Children – Learning and Teaching in the Early Childhood Years*, vol. 16, no. 3, pp. 29–33.

Jolly Learning (2012). 'Teaching Literacy with Jolly Phonics'. http://jollylearning.co.uk/ overview-about-jolly-phonics. Accessed 13 June 2012.

Juel, C. (1988). 'Learning to Read and Write: A Longitudinal Study of 54 Children from First through Fourth Grades'. *Journal of Educational Psychology*, vol. 80, pp. 437–47.

Juel, C., Biancarosa, G., Coker, D. and Deffes, R. (2003). 'Walking with Rosie: A Cautionary Tale of Early Reading Instruction'. *Educational Leadership*, vol. 60, pp. 12–18.

Justice, L.M. and Ezell, H.K. (2004). 'Print Referencing: An Emergent Literacy Enhancement Strategy and its Clinical Applications'. *Language, Speech and Hearing Services in Schools*, vol. 35, pp. 185–93.

Justice, L.M. and Pullen, P.C. (2003). 'Promising Interventions for Promoting Emergent Literacy Skills: Three Evidence-Based Approaches'. *Topics in Early Childhood Special Education*, vol. 23, no. 3, pp. 99–113.

Justice, L.M., Kaderavek, J.N., Fan, X., Sofka, A. and Hunt, A. (2009). 'Accelerating Preschoolers' Early Literacy Development through Classroom-Based Teacher–Child Storybook Reading and Explicit Print Referencing'. *Language, Speech and Hearing Services in Schools*, vol. 40, pp. 67–85.

Kalantzis, M. and Cope, B. (2005). *Learning by Design*. Melbourne: Victorian Schools Innovation Commission.

Kane, R. (2005). *Initial Teacher Education: Policy and Practice. Final Report*. Wellington, NZ: Ministry of Education.

Kendeou, P., Lynch, J., van den Broek, P., Espin, C.A. White, M.J. and Kremer, K.E. (2005). 'Developing Successful Readers: Building Early Comprehension Skills through Television Viewing And Listening'. *Early Childhood Education Journal*, vol. 33, no. 2, pp. 91–8.

Kern, M.L. and Friedman, H. S. (2009). 'Early Educational Milestones as Predictors of Lifelong Academic Achievement, Midlife Adjustment, and Longevity'. *Journal of Applied Developmental Psychology*, vol. 30, pp. 419–30.

Kintsch, W., Mandel, T.S. and Kozminsky, E. (1977). 'Summarising Scrambled Stories', *Memory and Cognition*, vol. 5, pp. 547–52.

Kirby, J.R., Georgiou, G.K., Martinussen, R. and Parrila, R. (2010). 'Naming Speed and Reading: From Prediction to Instruction'. *Reading Research Quarterly*, vol. 45(3), 341–62.

Klenowski, V. (2011). 'Assessment Reform and Educational Change in Australia'. In R. Berry and B. Anderson (eds), *Assessment Reform in Education* (pp. 63–74). Dordrecht: Netherlands: Springer. doi: 10.1007/978–94–007–0729–0_5.

Knobel, M. and Lankshear, C. (2003). 'Researching Young Children's Out-of-School Literacy Practices'. In N. Hall, J. Larson and J. Marsh (eds), *Handbook of Early Childhood Literacy* (pp. 51–65). London and Thousand Oaks, CA: Sage.

Kohnen, S., Nickels and Castles, A. (2009). 'Assessing Spelling Skills and Strategies: A Critique of Available Resources'. *Australian Journal of Learning Difficulties*, vol. 14, no. 1, pp. 113–50.

Konza, D. (2006). *Teaching Children with Reading Difficulties*. 2nd edn. South Melbourne, Vic.: Thomson.

——(2011a). *Research into Practice. Phonics*. (Series 1, 1.3). Adelaide: Government of South Australia Department of Education and Children's Services. http://www.decd.sa.gov.au/literacy/files/links/UtRP_1_3_v2.pdf. Accessed 13 June 2012.

——(2011b). *Research into Practice. Phonological Awareness*. (Series 1, 1.2). Adelaide: Government of South Australia Department of Education and Children's Services. http://www.decd.sa.gov.au/literacy/files/links/UtRP_1_2_v2.pdf. Accessed 13 June 2012.

——(2011c). *Research into Practice. Vocabulary*. (Series 1, 1.4). Adelaide: Government of South Australia Department of Education and Children's Services. http://www.decd.sa.gov.au/literacy/files/links/UtRP_1_2_v2.pdf. Accessed 13 June 2012.

Korat, O. and Schiff, R. (2005). 'Do Children Who Read More Books Know "What is Good Writing" Better than Children Who Read Less? A Comparison between Grade Levels and SES Groups'. *Journal of Literacy Research*, vol. 37, no. 3, pp. 289–324.

Kostons, D., van Gog, T. and Paas, F. (2010). 'Training Self-assessment and Task-selection Skills: A Cognitive Approach to Improving Self-regulated Learning'. *Learning and Instruction*, vol. 22, no. 2, pp. 121–32.

Lareau, A. (2000). *Home Advantage: Social Class and Parental Intervention in Elementary Education*. 2nd edn. Lanham, MD: Rowman & Littlefield.

Larsen, S., Hammill, D. and Moats, L. (1999). *Test of Written Spelling (TWS-4)*. Austin, TX: Pro-Ed.

Lee, L. and O'Rourke, M. (2006). 'Information and Communication Technologies: Transforming Views of Literacies in Early Childhood Settings'. *Early Years*, vol. 26, no. 1, pp. 49–62.

Leslie, L. and Caldwell, J.S. (2010). *Qualitative Reading Inventory*. 5th edn. Boston, MA: Allyn & Bacon.

Levine, M. (2002). *A Mind at a Time*. New York: Simon & Schuster.

Lieberman, E. (1985). 'Name Writing and the Preschool Child'. Unpublished Doctoral Dissertation. University of Arizona, Tucson.

Li-Grining, C, Votruba-Drzal, E, Maldonado-Carreño, C and Haas, K. (2010). 'Children's Early Approaches to Learning and Academic Trajectories through Fifth Grade'. *Developmental Psychology*, vol. 46, no. 5, pp. 1062–77.

Limbrick, L., Wheldall, K. and Madelaine, A. (2010). Estimating Gender Ratios of Poor Reading Using Large Scale Assessments'. *Australian Journal of Education*, vol. 54, no. 2, pp. 190–22.

Lippman, L., Moore, K. and McIntosh, H. (2011). 'Positive Indicators of Child Well-being: A Conceptual Framework, Measures, and Methodological Issues'. *Applied Research in Quality of Life*, vol. 6, no. 4, pp. 425–49.

Liu, S. (2000). 'Friendships, Attitudes toward Reading, and Reading Achievement'. Unpublished Dissertation. The University of Auckland.

Lonigan, C.J., Burgess, S.R. and Anthony, J.L. (2000). 'Development of Emergent Literacy and Early Reading Skills in Preschool Children: Evidence from a Latent-Variable Longitudinal Study'. *Developmental Psychology*, vol. 36, pp. 596–613.

Love, A., Burns, M.S. and Buell, M.J. (2007). 'Writing: Empowering Literacy'. *Young Children*, January, pp. 12–19.

Luke, A. (1997). 'Critical Literacy and the Question of Normativity'. In S. Muspratt, A. Luke and P. Freebody P (eds), *Constructing Critical Literacies: Teaching and Learning Procedure*. St Leonards: Allen & Unwin.

Luke, A. and Freebody, P. (1999). 'A Map of Possible Practices: Further Notes on the Four Resources Model'. *Practically Primary*, vol. 4, no, 22, pp. 5–8.

——(1999). 'Further Notes on the Four Resources Model'. *Reading Online*. http://www.readingonline.org/past/past_index.asp?HREF=/research/lukefreebody.html. Accessed 18 June 2012.

Luke, A. and Grieshaber, S.J. (2003). 'New Adventures in the Politics of Literacy: An Introduction'. *Journal of Early Childhood Literacy*, vol. 4, no. 1, pp. 5–9.

Luria, A. (1973). *The Working Brain: An Introduction to Neuropsychology*. New York: Basic Books.

Makin, L., Hayden, J., Holland, A., Arthur, L., Beecher, B., Jones Diaz, C. and McNaught, M. (1999). *Mapping Literacy Practices in Early Childhood Services*. Report prepared for NSW Department of Community Services and NSW Department Education and Training, Sydney, NSW.

Makin, L., Jones Diaz, C. and McLachlan, C. (eds). (2007). *Literacies in Childhood: Changing Views, Challenging Practice*. 2nd edn. Sydney, NSW: MacLennan & Petty/Elsevier.

Mandler, J.M. and Johnson, N.S. (1977). 'Remembrance of Things Parsed: Story Structure and Recall'. *Cognitive Psychology*, vol. 9, pp. 111–51.

Margetts, K. (2000). 'Establishing Valid Measures of Children's Adjustment to the First Year of Schooling'. *Post-Script*, vol. 1, no. 1, pp. 33–48.

——(2002). 'Planning Transition Programs'. In H. Fabian and A. Dunlop (eds), *Transitions in the Early Years – Debating Continuity and Progression in the Early Years* (pp. 111–22). London: Routledge Falmer.

Marsh, J. (2005a). 'Cultural Icons: Popular Culture, Media and New Technologies in Early Childhood'. *Every Child*, vol. 11, no. 4, pp. 14–15.

——(2005b). 'Ritual, Performance and Identity Construction: Young Children's Engagement with Popular Cultural and Media Texts'. In J. Marsh (ed.), *Popular Culture, New Media and Digital Literacy in Early Childhood* (pp. 28–50). London: RoutledgeFalmer.

——(2007). 'Mind the Gap: Continuities and Discontinuities in Young Children's Textual Experiences at Home and at School'. In R. Openshaw and J. Soler (eds), *Reading across International Boundaries: History, Policy and Politics* (pp. 171–86). Charlotte, NC: Information Age Publishing.

Martello, J. (2007). 'Many Roads through Many Modes: Becoming Literate in Childhood'. In L. Makin, C. Jones Díaz and C. McLachlan, C. (eds), *Literacies in Childhood: Changing Views, Challenging Practice* (pp. 89–103). 2nd ed. Marrickville, NSW: MacLennan & Petty/Elsevier.

Martin, C. (2011). 'Review of the York Assessment of Reading for Comprehension (YARC)'. *Educational Psychology in Practice*, vol. 27, no. 4, pp. 437–9.

Martin, F. and Pratt (2001). *Martin and Pratt Nonword Reading Test*. Camberwell, Vic.: ACER Press.

Martin, J.R. (1989). *Factual Writing: Exploring and Challenging Social Reality*. Oxford: Oxford University Press.

Mashburn, A.J. (2008). 'Evidence for Creating, Expanding, Designing and Improving High Quality Preschool Programs'. In L.M. Justice and C. Vukelich (eds), *Achieving Excellence in Preschool Literacy instruction* (pp. 5–24). New York: Guilford Press.

May, H. (2005). *School Beginnings: A Nineteenth Century Colonial Story*. Wellington, NZ: NZCER Press.

——(2011). *I Am Five and I Go to School: Early Years Schooling in New Zealand 1900–2010*. Dunedin, NZ: Otago University Press.

McCrimmon, A.W. and Climie, E.A. (2011). 'Test Review: Test of Written Language – 4th Edition'. *Journal of Psychoeducational Assessment*, vol. 29, no. 6, pp. 592–6.

McCutcheon, D., Green, L. and Abbott, R.D. (2008). 'Children's Morphological Knowledge: Links to Literacy'. *Reading Psychology*, vol. 29, pp. 289–314.

MCEETYA – see Ministerial Council on Education, Employment, Training and Youth Affairs.

McGinty, C.S., Lonigan, C.J. and Kim, Y. (2011). 'Contributions of Emergent Literacy Skills to Name Writing, Letter Writing, and Spelling in Preschool'. *Early Childhood Research Quarterly*, vol. 26, pp. 465–74.

McGregor, S. and Nicholson, T. (2012). 'A Survey of Reading, Attitudes to Reading and Strengths and Weaknesses'. Unpublished Manuscript, Massey University, Auckland, NZ.

McKay, M.F., Fletcher-Flinn, C.M. and Thompson, G.B. (2004). 'New Theory for Understanding Reading and Reading Disabilities'. *Australian Journal of Learning Disabilities*, vol. 9, no. 2, pp. 3–7.

McLachlan, C. (2008). 'Early Literacy and the Transition to School: Issues for Early Childhood and Primary Educators'. *NZ Research in Early Childhood Education*, vol. 11, pp. 105–18.

——(2010). 'What Do Teachers Need to Know and Do about Literacy in the Early Childhood Context: Exploring Evidence'. http://www.hekupu.ac.nz/index.php?type=journal&issue=13&journal=243. Accessed 13 June 2012.

McLachlan, C. and Arrow, A. (2011). 'Literacy in the Early Years in New Zealand: Policies, Politics and Pressing Reasons for Change'. *Literacy*, vol. 45, no. 3, pp. 141–8.

McNaughton, S. (1995). *The Patterns of Emergent Literacy*. Oxford: Oxford University Press.

——(2002). *Meeting of Minds*. Wellington, NZ: Learning Media.

Meiers, M. and Khoo, S. (2006). 'Literacy in the First Three Years of School: A Longitudinal Investigation'. *Australian Journal of Language and* Literacy, vol. 29, no. 3, pp. 252–67.

Meiers, M., Khoo, S., Rowe, K., Sephanou, A., Anderson, P. and Nolan, K. (2006). *Growth in Literacy and Numeracy in the First Three Years of School*. Camberwell, Vic.: Australian Council Education Research.

Menet, F., Eakin, J., Stuart, M. and Rafferty, H. (2000). 'Month of Birth and Effect on Literacy, Behaviour and Referral to Psychological Service'. *Educational Psychology in Practice*, vol. 16, no. 2, pp. 225–34.

Ministerial Council on Education, Employment, Training and Youth Affairs (MCEETYA) (2008). *Melbourne Declaration on Educational Goals for Young Australians*. Melbourne: Author. http://www.mceecdya.edu.au/verve/_resources/National_Declaration_on_the_Educational_Goals_for_Young_Australians.pdf. Accessed 13 June 2012.

Ministry of Education (1985). *Reading in Junior Classes*. Wellington, NZ: Learning Media.

——(1996) *Te Whāriki: He Whāriki Mātauranga mō ngā Mokopuna o Aotearoa: Early Childhood Curriculum*. Wellington, NZ: Learning Media.

——(1997). *Quality in Action*. Wellington, NZ: Learning Media.

——(1998). *Quality Journey*. Wellington, NZ: Learning Media.

——(1999). *Report of the Literacy Task Force*. Wellington: Ministry of Education. Available from http://www.minedu.govt.nz/NZEducation/EducationPolicies/Schools/ResearchAndStatistics/LiteracyResearch/ReportoftheLiteracyTaskforce.aspx. Accessed 13 June 2012.

——(2004). *Kei Tua o te Pae. Early Childhood Assessment Exemplars*. Wellington, NZ: Learning Media.

——(2007a). *Draft – Literacy Learning Progressions. Meeting the Reading and Writing Demands of the Curriculum*. Wellington, NZ: Learning Media.

——(2007b). *The New Zealand Curriculum*. Wellington, NZ: Learning Media.

——(2007c). 'Self-review Guidelines for Early Childhood Education'. http://www.lead.ece.govt.nz/LeadHome/ManagementInformation/GoverningAndManaging/SelfReviewGuidelinesForEarlyChildhoodEducation.aspx. Accessed 18 January 2010.

——(2008). 'Centre-Based ECE Services'. http://www.lead.ece.govt.nz/ServiceTypes/CentreBasedECEServices.aspx. Accessed 18 January 2010.

——(2009a). *Te Kòrero, te Titiro, me te Pànui-Tuhi/Oral, Visual and Written Literacy* (Book 17). Wellington, NZ: Learning Media. http://www.educate.ece.govt.nz/~/media/Educate/Files/Reference%20Downloads/ex/ECEBk17/ECEBk17Full.pdf. Accessed 13 June 2012.

——(2009b). *The New Zealand Curriculum Reading and Writing Standards for Years 1–8*. Wellington, NZ: Learning Media.

——(2010a). 'Assessment for Learning'. Wellington, NZ: Author. http://www.educate.ece.govt.nz/learning/curriculumAndLearning/Assessmentforlearning.asp. Accessed 13 June 2012.

——(2010b). *The Literacy Learning Progressions. Meeting the Reading and Writing Demands of the Curriculum*. Wellington, NZ: Learning Media. Available from http://literacyprogressions.tki.org.nz.

Misra, M., Katzir, T., Wolf, M. and Poldrack, R.A. (2004). 'Neural Systems for Rapid Automatized Naming in Skilled Readers: Unraveling the RAN–Reading Relationship'. *Scientific Studies of Reading*, vol. 8, no. 3, pp. 241–56.

Moats, L.C. (2000). *Speech to Print: Language Essentials for Teachers*. Baltimore, MD: Paul H. Brookes.

Moats, L.C. and Foorman, B. (2003). 'Measuring Teachers' Content Knowledge of Language and Reading'. *Annals of Dyslexia*, vol. 53, pp. 23–45.

Moll, L. and Greenberg, J. (1990). 'Creating Zones of Possibilities: Combining Social Contexts'. In L. Moll (ed.), *Vygotsky and Education: Instructional Implications and Applications of Sociohistorical Pyschology* (pp. 319–48). New York: Cambridge University Press.

Moll, L.C. (ed.) (1990), *Vygotsky and Education: Instructional Implications and Applications of Sociohistorical Psychology*. Cambridge, UK: Cambridge University Press.

Moll, L., Manti, A., Neff, D. and Gonzalez, N. (1992). 'Funds of Knowledge for Teaching: Using a Qualitative Approach to Connect Homes and Classrooms'. *Theory into Practice*, vol. 31, no. 2, pp. 367–76.

Montgomery, W. (2001). 'Creative Culturally Responsive, Inclusive Classrooms'. *Teaching Exceptional Children*, vol. 33, no. 4, pp. 40–7.

Moody, A.K., Justice, L.M. and Cabell, S.Q. (2010). 'Electronic versus Traditional Storybooks: Relative Influence on Preschool Children's Engagement and Communication'. *Journal of Early Childhood Literacy*, vol. 10, no. 3, pp. 294–313.

Morgan, P., & Fuchs, D. (2007). 'Is There a Bidirectional Relationship between Children's Reading Skills and Reading?' *Exceptional Children*, vol 73, no. 3, pp. 165–83.

Morgana, A., Nutbrown, C. and Hannon, P. (2009). 'Fathers' Involvement in Young Children's Literacy Development: Implications for Family Literacy Programmes'. *British Educational Research Journal*, vol. 35, no. 2, pp. 167–85.

Morphett, M.V. and Washburne, C. (1931). 'When Should Children Begin to Read'? *Elementary School Journal*, vol. 31, pp. 496–503.

Morrow, L.M. (2005a). 'Language and Literacy in Preschools: Current Issues and Concerns'. *Literacy Teaching and Learning*, vol. 9, no. 1, pp. 7–19.

——(2005b). *Literacy Development in the Early Years: Helping Children Read and Write*. Boston, MA: Allyn & Bacon.

——(2007). *Developing Literacy in Pre-school*. New York: Guilford.

——(2009). *Literacy Development in the Early Years: Helping Children Read and Write*. 6th edn. Boston, MA: Pearson.

——(2012). *Literacy Development in the Early Years: Helping Children Read and Write*. Boston, MA: Pearson.

Morrow, L.M. and Schickendanz, J.A. (2006). 'The Relationship between Socio Dramatic Play and Literacy Development'. In D.K. Dickenson and S.B. Neuman (eds), *Handbook of Early Literacy Research* (vol. 2, pp. 269–80). New York: Guilford.

Mullis, I.V.S., Martin, M.O., Kennedy, A.M. and Foy, P. (2007). *IEA's Progress in International Reading Literacy Study in Primary School in 40 Countries*. Chestnut Hill, MA: TIMSS and PIRLS International Study Center, Boston College.

Multiliteracy Project, The (2012). http://www.multiliteracies.ca/index.php. Accessed 20 January 2012.

Munns, G. and Woodward, H. (2006). 'Student Engagement and Student Self-assessment: The REAL Framework'. *Assessment in Education: Principles, Policy and Practice*, vol. 13, no. 2, pp. 193–213.

Murdoch, K. (2002). *Practical Literacy Programming*. Newtown, NSW: Primary English Teaching Association.

National Association for the Education of Young Children (2009). *Where We Stand on Learning to Read and Write: NAEYC and IRA*. Washington, DC: Author. http://www.naeyc.org/files/naeyc/file/positions/WWSSLearningToReadAndWriteEnglish.pdf. Accessed 13 June 2012.

National Early Literacy Panel (NELP) (2009). *Developing Early Literacy: Report of the National Early Literacy Panel*. Washington, DC: National Institute for Literacy.

National Institute of Child Health and Development (2000). *Report of the National Reading Panel: Teaching Children to Read: An Evidence-Based Assessment of the Scientific Literature on Reading and its Implications for Reading Instruction*. Washington, DC: Author.

NationMaster (2012). http://www.nationmaster.com/graph/edu_ele_sch_sta_age_yea-elementary-school-starting-age-years. Accessed 13 June 2012.

Neale, M.D. (1999). *Neale Analysis of Reading Ability*. 3rd edn. Camberwell, Vic.: ACER Press.

Neilsen, L. (1994). *A Stone in My Shoe: Teaching Literacy in Times of Change*. Winnipeg, Canada: Peguis.

NELP – see National Early Literacy Panel.

Neuman, S.B. (2007). 'Social Contexts for Literacy Development: A Family Literacy Program'. In K.A. Roskos and J.F. Christie (eds), *Play and Literacy in Early Childhood: Research from Multiple Perspectives* (2nd edn, pp. 151–68). New York: Lawrence Erlbaum Associates.

Neuman, S.B. and Dwyer, J. (2009). 'Missing in Action: Vocabulary Instruction in Pre-K'. *The Reading Teacher*, vol. 62, no. 5, pp. 384–92.

Neuman, S. and Roskos, K. (1990). 'The Influence of Literacy Enriched Play Settings on Preschoolers' Engagement with Written Language'. *Annual Yearbook of the National Reading Conference*, vol. 39, pp. 179–87.

Neuman, S.B and Roskos, K. (with T. Wright and J. Lenhart) (2007). *Nurturing Knowledge: Building a Foundation for School Success by Linking Early Literacy to Math, Science, Art and Social Studies*. New York: Scholastic.

Neuman, S.B., Copple, C. and Bredekamp, S. (2000). *Learning to Read and Write: Developmentally Appropriate Practices for Young Children*. Washington, DC: National Association for the Education of Young Children.

Neuman, S.B., Newman, E.H. and Dwyer, J. (2011). 'Educational Effects of a Vocabulary Intervention on Preschooler's Word Knowledge and Conceptual Development: A Cluster Randomised Trial'. *Reading Research Quarterly*, vol. 46, no. 3, pp. 249–72.

New London Group. (1996). 'A Pedagogy of Multiliteracies'. *Harvard Review*, vol. 66, no. 1, pp. 145–66.

New Media Consortium. (2005). 'NMC Horizon Report 2005 – Higher Education'. http://www.nmc.org/publications/horizon-report-2005-higher-ed-edition. Accessed 11 January 2012.

New Zealand Government (1998). *Education (Early Childhood Centre) Regulations*. Wellington, NZ: Government Printer.

——(2008). *Education (Early Childhood Services) Regulations 2008*. http://www.legislation.govt.nz/regulation/public/2008/0204/latest/DLM1412501.html. Accessed 18 January 2010.

NICHD – see National Institute of Child Health and Development.

Nicholson, T. (1999). 'Literacy, Family and Society'. In G.B. Thompson and T. Nicholson (eds), *Learning to Read: Beyond Phonics and Whole Language* (pp. 1–22). New York: Teachers College Press.

——(2000). *Reading the Writing on the Wall: Debates, Challenges and Opportunities in the Teaching of Reading*. Melbourne: Thomson.

——(2003). 'Risk Factors in Learning to Read, and What to Do about Them'. In B. Foorman (ed.), *Preventing and Remediating Reading Difficulties: Bringing Science to Scale* (pp. 165–96). Timonium, MD: York Press.

——(2005) *At the Cutting Edge: The Importance of Phonemic Awareness in Learning to Read and Spell*. Wellington, NZ: NZCER Press.

——(2006). *Phonics Handbook*. Berkshire, England: Wiley.

——(2008a). 'Achieving Equity for Maori Children in Reading by 2020'. *New Zealand Annual Review of Education*, vol. 18, pp. 159–182.

——(2008b). 'Dyslexia – Researchers in Denial'. *Learning Difficulties Australia Bulletin*, vol. 40 (nos. 3–4), pp. 10–11.

——(2011). 'At the Chalkface: A Morning Visit to a Grade 1 Classroom in Chicago'. *Reading Forum NZ*, vol. 26, no.2, pp. 16–20.

Nicholson, T. and Dymock, S.J. (2010). *Teaching Reading Vocabulary*. Wellington, NZ: NZCER Press.

——(2011). 'Matthew Effects and Reading Interventions'. *Perspectives on Language and Literacy*, vol. 37, no. 4, pp. 28–33.

Nicholson, T. and Tunmer, W.E. (2011). 'Reading: The Great Debate'. In C. Rubie-Davies (ed.), *Educational Psychology: Concepts, Research, and Challenges* (pp. 36–50). London: Routledge.

Nicholson, T., McIntosh, S.A. and Ell, F. (2000). 'A Longitudinal Study of Reading Development of Children from Different Socioeconomic Backgrounds from Ages Five to Ten Years'. Unpublished Manuscript, The University of Auckland.

Noel Foulin, J. (2005). 'Why is Letter-Name Knowledge Such a Good Predictor of Learning to Read'? *Reading and Writing*, vol. 18, pp. 129–55.

O'Brien, J. (1987). 'Tales'. *School Journal*, vol. 1, no. 3, pp. 16–22. Wellington, NZ: Learning Media.

OECD – see Organisation for Economic Cooperation and Development.

Ohi, S. (2007). 'Teacher's Professional Knowledge and the Teaching of Reading in the Early Years'. *Australian Journal of Teacher Education*, vol. 32, no. 2, pp. 1–14.

Olson, D.R. (2009). 'Literacy, Literacy Policy, and the School'. In D. Olson and N. Torrance (eds), *The Cambridge Handbook of Literacy* (pp. 566–76). Cambridge, UK: Cambridge University Press.

O'Neill, K. (2010). 'Once upon Today: Teaching for Social Justice with Postmodern Picture Books'. *Children's Literature in Education*, vol. 41, pp. 40–51.

Organisation for Economic Cooperation and Development. (2001). *Knowledge and Skills for Life*. Paris: Author.

Parkin, C. and Parkin, C. (2011). *PROBE 2 Reading Comprehension Assessment*. Upper Hutt, NZ: Triune Initiatives.

Pearson, P.D. and Hiebert, E.H. (2010). 'National Reports in Literacy: Building A Scientific Base for Practice and Policy'. *Educational Researcher*, vol. 39, pp. 286–94.

Peters, S. (2010). *Literature Review: Transition from Early Childhood Education to School. Report to the Ministry of Education, New Zealand*. http://www.educationcounts.govt.nz/publications/ece/literature-review-transition-from-early-childhood-education-to-school/executive-summary. Accessed 20 January 2012.

Petscher, Y. (2010). 'A Meta-analysis of the Relationship between Student Attitudes towards Reading and Achievement in Reading'. *Journal of Research in Reading*, vol. 33, no. 4, pp. 335–55.

Phillips, B.M., Clancy-Menchetti, J. and Lonigan, C. (2008). 'Successful Phonological Awareness Instruction with Preschool Children'. *Topics in Early Childhood Special Education*, vol. 28, no. 1, pp. 3–17.

Phillips, G., McNaughton, S. and MacDonald, S. (2001). *Picking up the Pace: Effective Literacy Interventions for Accelerated Progress over the Transition into Decile 1 Schools*. Auckland, NZ: The Child Literacy Foundation and Woolf Fisher Research Centre.

Piaget, J. (1962). *The Language and Thought of the Child*. London: Routledge & Kegan Paul.

Piasta, S.B. and Wagner, R.K. (2010). 'Developing Early Literacy Skills: A Meta-analysis of Alphabet Learning and Instruction'. *Reading Research Quarterly*, vol. 45, no. 1, pp. 8–38.

Piasta, S.B., Justice, L.B., McGinty, A.S., Kaderavek, J. (2012). 'Increasing Young Children's Contact with Print during Shared Reading: Longitudinal Effects on Literacy Achievement'. *Child Development Perspectives*, vol. 83, no. 3, pp. 810–20.

Piasta, S.B., Purpura, D.J. and Wagner, R.K. (2010). 'Fostering Alphabet Knowledge Development: A Comparison of Two Instructional Approaches'. *Reading and Writing*, vol. 23, pp. 607–26.

Prensky, M. (2001). 'Digital Natives, Digital Immigrants'. *On the Horizon*, vol. 9, no. 5, pp. 1–2.

Pressley, M. (2006). *Reading Instruction that Works: The Case for Balanced Teaching*. 3rd edn. New York: Guilford Press.

Prior, M. (1996). *Understanding Specific Learning Difficulties*. London: Psychology Press.

Prochnow, J.E., Tunmer, W.E, Chapman, J.W. and Greaney, K.T. (2001). 'A Longitudinal Study of Literacy Achievement and Gender'. *New Zealand Journal of Educational Studies*, vol. 36, no. 2, pp. 221–36.

Puranik, C.S., Lonigan, C.J. and Kim, Y. (2011). 'Contributions of Emergent Literacy Skills to Name Writing, Letter Writing, and Spelling in Pre-school Children'. *Early Childhood Research Quarterly*, vol. 26, pp. 465–74.

Raban, B. and Nolan, A. (2005). 'Reading Practices Experienced by Preschool Children in Areas of Disadvantage'. *Journal of Early Childhood Research*, vol. 3, no. 3, pp. 289–98.

Read, C. (1971). 'Preschool Children's Knowledge of English Phonology'. *Harvard Educational Review*, vol. 41, pp. 1–34.

——(1975). *Children's Categorization of Speech Sounds in English*. Urbana, IL: National Council of Teachers of English.

Ritter, A. (2006). 'Do Informal Reading Inventories and Standardized Reading Tests Produce Similar Results? A Comparative Study between New Zealand and the United States of America'. Master's Thesis, The University of Auckland, Auckland.

Robb, M.B., Richert, R.A. and Wartella, E.A. (2009). 'Just a Talking Book? Word Learning from Watching Baby Videos'. *British Journal of Developmental Psychology*, vol. 27, pp. 27–45.

Roberts, S., Djonov, E. and Torr, J. (2008). '"The Mouse is Not a Toy": Young Children's Interactions with E-games'. *Australian Journal of Language and Literacy*, vol. 31, no. 3, pp. 242–59.

Robertson, V. and Salter, W. (2007). *The Phonological Awareness Test*. 2nd edn. East Moline, IL: LinguiSystems.

Rogoff, B. (1990). *Apprenticeship in Thinking: Cognitive Development in Social Context*. New York: Oxford University Press.

Rose, J. (2006). *Independent Review of the Teaching of Early Reading: Final Report*. Nottingham, UK: Department for Education and Skills.

——(2009). *Identifying and Teaching Pupils and Young People with Dyslexia and Literacy Difficulties*. London: Department of Pupils, Schools and Families.

Rowe, D.W. (2008). 'Social Contracts for Writing: Negotiating Shared Understandings about Text in the Preschool Years'. *Reading Research Quarterly*, vol. 43, no. 1, pp. 66–95.

Rowe, D.W. and Neitzel, C. (2010). 'Interest and Agency in 2- and 3-Year-Olds' Participation in Emergent Writing'. *Reading Research Quarterly*, vol. 45, no. 2, pp. 169–97.

Sacre, L. and Masterson, J. (2000). *Single Word Spelling Test*. Nfer-Nelson.

Saracho, O.N. and Spodek, B. (2010). 'Parents and Children Engaging in Storybook Reading'. *Early Child Development and Care*, vol. 180, no. 10, pp. 1379–89.

Sarra, C. (2007). 'The Role of Schools in Shaping Behaviour'. Cape York Leadership Institute Address, 26 June.

Savage, R. and Frederickson, N. (2005). 'Evidence of a Highly Specific Relationship between Rapid Automatic Naming of Digits and Text-reading Speed'. *Brain and Language*, vol. 93, pp. 152–9.

Schneider, W., Kuspert, P., Roth, E., Vise, M. and Marx, H. (1997). 'Short- and Long-term Effects of Training Phonological Awareness in Kindergarten: Evidence from Two German Studies'. *Journal of Experimental Child Pyschology*, vol. 66, no. 3, pp. 311–40.

Scott, C. (2006). 'Learning to Write'. In H.W. Catts and A.G. Kamhi (eds), *Language and Reading Disabilities* (pp. 233–73). Boston, MA: Pearson.

Scott, D. (2008). *Critical Essays on Major Curriculum Theorists*. London: Routledge.

Sénéchal, M. (2006). 'Testing the Home Literacy Model: Parental Involvement in Kindergarten is Differentially Related to Grade 4 Reading Comprehension, Fluency, Spelling, and Reading for Pleasure'. *Scientific Studies of Reading*, vol. 10, pp. 59–87.

——(2011). 'Relations between Home Literacy and Child Outcomes'. In S.B. Neuman and D.K. Dickinson (eds), *Handbook of Early Literacy Research: Volume 3* (pp. 175–88). New York: Guilford Press.

Sharp, C., George, N., Sargent, C., O'Donnell, S. and Heron, M. (2009). *International Thematic Probe: The Influence of Relative Age on Learner Attainment and Development*. London: NFER.

Shaywitz, B.A., Shaywitz, S.E., Blachman, B.A., Pugh, K.R., Fulbright, R.K., Skudlarski, P., Einar Mencl, W., Constable, R.T., Holahan, J.M., Marchione, K.E., Fletcher, J.M., Reid Lyon, G., Gore, J.C. (2004). 'Development of Left Occipitotemporal Systems for Skilled Reading in Pupils after a Phonologically Based Intervention. *Biological Psychiatry*, vol. 55, no. 9, pp. 926–33.

Shields, M.K. and Behrman, R.E. (2000). 'Children and Computer Technology: Analysis and Recommendations'. *The Future of Children*, vol. 10, no. 2, pp. 4–30.

Silver, A.A. and Hagin, R.A. (2002). *Disorders of Learning in Childhood*. 2nd edn. New York: Wiley.

Silverman, R. and Crandell, J.B. (2010). 'Vocabulary Practices in Prekindergarten and Kindergarten Classrooms'. *Reading Research Quarterly*, vol. 45, no. 3, pp. 318–40.

Simpson, G. (2009). 'School dog's big mistake'. *Countdown*, 94(1), pp. 16–20.

Siraj-Blatchford, I., Sammons, P., Taggart, B., Sylva, K. and Melhuish, E. (2006). 'Educational Research and Evidence Based Policy: The Mixed-Method Approach of The EPPE Project'. *Evaluation and Research in Education*, vol. 19, no. 2, pp. 63–82.

Skues, J.L. and Cunningham, E.G. (2011). 'A Contemporary Review of the Definition, Prevalence, Identification and Support of Learning Disabilities in Australian Schools'. *Australian Journal of Learning Difficulties*, vol. 16, no. 2, pp. 159–80.

Smith, A., Grima, G., Gaffney, M., Powell, K., Masses, L. and Barnett, S. (2000). *Strategic Research Initiative Literature Review: Early Childhood Education. Report to the Ministry of Education*. Dunedin, NZ: Childrenz Issues Centre.

Smith, A., Nelley, E. and Croft, D. (2008) *PM Benchmark 1: Reading Assessment Resource*. South Melbourne, Vic.: Nelson/Cengage.

Snow, C. E., Burns, M. S. and Griffin, G. (eds) (1998). *Preventing Reading Difficulties in Young Children*. Washington, DC: National Academy Press.

Snowling, M.J., Stothard, S.E., Clarke, P., Bowyer-Crane, C., Harrington, A., Truelove, E., Nation, K. and Hulme, C. (2009). *York Assessment of Reading for Comprehension*. GL Assessment.

Soler, J. and Openshaw, R. (2009). '"To Be or Bot to Be?" The Politics of Teaching Phonics in England and New Zealand'. In J. Soler, F. Fletcher-Campbell and G. Reid (eds), *Understanding Difficulties in Reading Development: Issues and Concepts* (pp. 161–75). Thousand Oaks, CA: Sage.

Spandel, V. (2008). *Creating Writers through 6-trait Assessment and Instruction*. 5th edn. Upper Saddle River, NJ: Pearson.

Spedding, S., Harkins, J., Makin, L. and Whiteman, P. (2007). *Investigating Children's Early Literacy Learning in Family and Community Contexts: Review of the Related Literature*. Adelaide, SA: Department of Education and Children's Services.

Spencer, L.H. and Hanley, J.R. (2003). 'Effects of Orthographic Transparency on Reading and Phoneme Awareness in Children Learning to Read in Wales'. *British Journal of Psychology*, vol. 94, pp. 1–28.

——(2004). 'Learning a Transparent Orthography at Five Years Old: Reading Development of Children during Their First Year of Formal Reading Instruction in Wales'. *Journal of Research in Reading*, vol. 27, no. 1, pp. 1–14.

Stahl, S.A. and Nagy, W.E. (2006). *Teaching Word Meanings*. Mahwah, NJ: Erlbaum.

Stahl, S.A. and Yaden, D.B. (2004). 'The Development of Literacy in Preschool and Primary Grades: Work by the Centre for the Improvement of Early Reading Achievement'. *Elementary School Journal*, vol. 105, no. 2, pp. 141–65.

Stainthorp, R. and Hughes, D. (2004a). 'An Illustrative Case Study of Precocious Reading Ability'. *Gifted Child Quarterly*, vol. 48, pp. 107–120.

——(2004b). 'What Happens to Precocious Readers' Performance by the Age of Eleven?'. *Journal of Research in Reading*, vol. 27, pp. 357–72.

Stanovich, K. (1986). 'Matthew Effects in Reading: Some Consequences of Individual Differences in the Acquisition of Literacy'. *Reading Research Quarterly*, vol. 21, no. 4, pp. 360–407.

——(2000). *Progress in Understanding Reading: Scientific Foundations and New Frontiers*. New York: Guilford Press.

Stewart-Brown, B. and Nicholson, T (2012). 'A Pilot Study of Cross-age Tutoring of Reading in a Secondary School: Seniors Tutoring Juniors'. Unpublished Manuscript, College of Education, Massey University, Albany, NZ.

Stuart, M. (2005). 'Phonemic Analysis and Reading Development: Some Current Issues'. *Journal of Research in Reading*, vol. 28, pp. 39–49.

Sulzby, E. (1985). 'Children's Emergent Reading of Favorite Story Books'. *Reading Research Quarterly*, vol. 20, pp. 458–81.

Swanson, H.L. (1999). *Interventions for Students with Learning Disabilities: Meta Analysis of Treatment Outcomes*. New York: Guilford Press.

Tabors, O. and Snow, C. (2001). 'Young Bilingual Children and Early Literacy Development'. In S.B. Neuman and D.K. Dickinson (eds), *Handbook of Early Literacy Research*. New York: Guilford Press.

Tagoilelagi-Leota, F., McNaughton, S., MacDonald, S. and Ferry, S. (2005). 'Bilingual and Biliteracy Development over the Transition to School'. *International Journal of Bilingual Education and Bilingualism*, vol. 8, no. 5, pp. 455–79.

Tangen, D. and Fielding-Barnsley, R. (2007). 'Environmental Education in a Culturally Diverse School'. *Australian Journal of Environmental Education*, vol. 23, pp. 23–30.

Taylor, D. (1983). *Family Literacy: Young Children Learning to Read and Write*. Portsmouth, NH: Heinemann.

Taylor, D. and Dorsey-Gaines, C. (1988). *Growing up Literate: Learning From Inner City Families*. Portsmouth, NH: Heinemann.

'Teaching Baby to Read'. (1966), *Time*, 8 December, pp. 52–3.

Teale, W.H. (1984). 'Reading to Young Children: Its Significance in the Process of Literacy Development'. In H. Goelman, A. Oberg and F. Smith (eds), *Awakening to Literacy* (pp. 110–21). Exeter, NH: Heinemann Educational Books.

Teale, W., Hoffman, J., Paciga, K., Lisy, J.G., Richardson, S. and Berkel, C. (2009). 'Early Literacy: Then and Now'. In J.V. Hoffman and Y.M. Goodman (eds), *Changing Literacies for Changing Times: An Historical Perspective on the Future of Reading Research, Public Policy and Classroom Practices* (pp. 76–97). London: Routledge.

Thomas, G. and Ward, J. (2010). *National Standards: School Sample Reporting and Evaluation Project 2010*. Wellington, NZ: Ministry of Education. http://www.educationcounts.govt.nz/publications/schooling/national-standards-school-sample-monitoring-and-evaluation-project-2010. Accessed 13 June 2012.

Thompson, C.L. (2011). 'A Dose of Writing Reality. Helping Students Become Better Writers'. *Phi Delta Kappan*, vol. 92, no. 7, pp. 57–61.

Thompson, G.B. (1993). 'Reading Instruction for the Initial Years in New Zealand Schools'. In G.B. Thompson, W.E. Tunmer and T. Nicholson (eds), *Reading Acquisition Processes* (pp. 148–54). Clevedon, England: Multilingual Matters.

Thomson, P. (2002). *Schooling the Rustbelt Kids: Making the Difference in Changing Times*. Crows Nest, NSW: Allen & Unwin.

Tizard, B. and Hughes, M. (1994). *Young Children Learning: Talking and Thinking at Home and at School*. Hammersmith, London: Fontana.

Tomlinson, C.A. (2001). *The Differentiated Classroom: Responding to the Needs of All Learners*. Alexandria, VA: Association for Curriculum Development.

Tompkins, G.E. (2010). *Literacy for the 21st Century: A Balanced Approach*. 5th edn. Sydney, NSW: Allyn & Bacon.

——(2012). *Teaching Writing: Balancing Process and Product*. Boston, MA: Pearson.

Torgesen, J.K. and Bryant, B. (1994). *Test of Phonological Awareness*. Austin, TX: Pro-Ed.

Torgesen, J.K., Wagner, R.K. and Rashotte, C.A. (1999). *Test of Word Reading Efficiency*. Austin, TX: Pro-Ed.

Treiman, R. and Rodriguez, K. (1999). 'Young Children Use Letter Names in Learning to Read Words'. *Psychological Science*, vol. 10, pp. 334–8.

Trivizas, E. (1993). *The Three Little Wolves and the Big Bad Pig*. London: Egmont.

Tse, L. (2011). 'Can Phonics and Big Book Shared Reading in Combination Work Better than on Their Own?'. Unpublished Doctoral Thesis, Massey University, Auckland. NZ.

Tuinstra, C. and Hiatt-Michael, D. (2004). 'Student-Led Parent Conferences in Middle Schools'. *School Community Journal*, vol. 14, no. 1, pp. 59–80.

Tunmer, W.E. and Greaney, K. (2010). 'Defining Dyslexia'. *Journal of Learning Disabilities*, vol. 43, no. 3, pp. 229–43.

Tunmer, W.E. and Nicholson, T. (2011). 'The Development and Teaching of Word Recognition Skill'. In M.L. Kamil, P.D. Pearson, E.B. Moje and P.B. Afflerbach (eds), *Handbook of Reading Research* (vol. 4, pp. 405–31). New York: Routledge.

Tunmer, W.E., Chapman, J.W. and Prochnow, J.E. (2006). 'Literate Cultural Capital at School Entry Predicts Later Reading Achievement: A Seven Year Longitudinal Study'. *New Zealand Journal of Educational Studies*, vol. 41, 183–204.

Turbill, J. (2002). 'The Four Ages of Reading Philosophy and Pedagogy: A Framework for Examining Theory and Practice'. *Reading Online*, vol. 5, no. 6. http://www.readingonline.org/international/inter_index.asp?HREF=turbill4/index.html. Accessed 13 June 2012.

Turley, E.D. and Gallagher, C.W. (2008). 'On the "Uses" of Rubrics: Reframing the Great Rubric Debate'. *The English Journal*, vol. 97, no. 4, pp. 87–92.

Unsworth, L. (2001). *Teaching Multiliteracies across the Curriculum: Changing Contexts of Text and Image in Classroom Practice*. Buckingham, UK: Open University Press.

US Department of Education. (2002). *The Nation's Report Card: Writing 2002*. http://nces. ed.gov/pubsearch/pubsinfo.asp?pubid=2003529. Accessed 13 June 2012.

Vincent, D. and Crumpler, M. (1997). *British Spelling Tests Series*. Windsor, UK: Nfer Nelson.

Vizyak, L. (1999). 'Student Portfolios: Building Self-reflection in a First-grade Classroom'. In S.J. Barrentine (ed.), *Reading Assessment: Principles and Practices for Elementary Teachers* (pp. 135–8). Newark, DE: International Reading Association.

Vukelich, C. and Edwards, N. (1988). 'The Role of Context and As-written Orthography in Kindergarteners' Word Recognition'. *National Reading Conference Yearbook*, vol. 37, pp. 85–93.

Vygotsky, L.S. (1978). *Mind in Society: The Development of Higher Psychological Processes*. M. Cole, V. John-Steiner, S. Scribner and E. Souberman (eds). Cambridge, MA: Harvard University Press.

——(1998). *The Collected Works of L.S. Vygotsky*, vol. 5. R.W. Rieber (ed.) (trans. M.H. Hall), New York: Kluwer Academic/Plenum Publishers.

Vygotsky, L. and Luria, A. (1930). *Essays in the History Of Behaviour: Ape, Primitive, Child*. Moscow and Leningrad: Gosudarstvennoe Izdatel'stvo.

Wagner, R., Torgesen, J. and Rashotte, C. (1999). *The Comprehensive Test of Phonological Processing*. Austin, TX: Pro-Ed.

Wasik, B.A. and Hindman, A.H. (2010). 'Understanding the Home Language and Literacy Environments of Head Start Families: Testing the Family Literacy Survey and Interpreting its Findings'. *National Head Start Association Dialog*, vol. 13, no. 2, pp. 71–91.

Wasik, B.A., Bond, M.A. and Hindman, A. (2002). 'Creating Opportunities for Discourse: Language and Literacy Development in Economically Disadvantaged Pupils'. In O.N. Saracho and B. Spodek (eds), *Contemporary Perspectives in Literacy in Early Childhood Education* (pp. 53–76). Greenwich, CT: IAP.

——(2006). 'The Effects of Language and Literacy Intervention on Head Start Children and Teachers'. *Journal of Educational Psychology*, vol. 98, no. 1, pp. 63–74.

Welsch, J.G., Sullivan, A. and Justice, L.M. (2003). 'That's My Letter! What Pre-schoolers' Name Writing Representations Tell Us about Emergent Literacy Knowledge'. *Journal of Literacy Research*, vol. 35, pp. 757–75.

Westby, C. and Clauser, P. (2006). 'The Write Stuff for Writing'. In H.W. Catts and A.G. Kamhi (eds), *Language and Reading Disabilities*. Boston, MA: Pearson.

Westcott, K., Perry, B., Jones, K. and Dockett, S. (2003). 'Parents' Transition to School'. *Australian Research in Early Childhood Education*, vol. 10, no. 2, pp. 26–38.

Westwood, P. (2001). *Reading and Learning Difficulties: Approaches to Teaching and Assessment*. Camberwell, Vic.: ACER Press.

——(2005). *Spelling: Approaches to Teaching and Assessment*. Camberwell, Vic.: ACER Press.

——(2008a). *Learning Difficulties*. Camberwell, Vic.: ACER Press.

——(2008b). *What Teachers Need to Know about Spelling*. Camberwell, Vic.: ACER Press.

——(2009). 'Arguing the Case for a Simple View of Literacy Assessment'. *Australian Journal of Learning Difficulties*, vol.14, no.1, pp. 3–15.

Wheldall, K. (2008). 'Effective Instruction for Socially Disadvantaged Low-progress Readers: The Schoolwise Program'. *Australian Journal of Learning Difficulties*, vol. 14, no. 2, pp. 151–70.

Whitehurst, G.J. and Lonigan, C.J. (1998). 'Child Development and Emergent Literacy'. *Child Development*, vol. 69, pp. 848–72.

Whitehurst, G.J., Epstein, J.N., Angell, A.L., Payne, A.C., Crone, D.A. and Fischel, J.E. (1994). 'Outcomes of an Emergent Literacy Intervention in Head Start'. *Journal of Educational Psychology*, vol. 88, no. 4, pp. 542–55.

Wiederholt, J.L. and Bryant, B.R. (2012). *Gray Oral Reading Tests*, 5th edn. Austin, TX: Pro-Ed.

Wilkinson, G.S. and Robertson, G.J. (2007). *Wide Range Achievement Test (WRAT-4)*. Austin, TX: Pro-Ed.

Williams, K.T. (2007). *Expressive Vocabulary Test*. 2nd edn. Circle Pines, MN: American Guidance Service.

Wing, L. and Gould, J. (1979). 'Severe Impairments of Social Interaction and Associated Abnormalities in Children: Epidemiology and Classification'. *Journal of Autism and Childhood Schizophrenia*, vol. 9, pp. 11–29.

Wolf, S.A. and Gearhart, M. (1994). 'Writing What You Read: Assessment as a Learning Event'. *Language Arts*, vol. 71, no. 6, pp. 425–44.

Wong Fillmore, L. and Snow, C. (2000). *What Teachers Need to Know about Language*. ERIC Clearinghouse for Language and Linguistics. http://www.utpa.edu/dept/curr_ins/faculty_folders/guerrero_m/docs/links/FillmoreSnow2000.pdf. Accessed 20 January 2012.

Wood, D.J., Bruner, J.S. and Ross, G. (1976). 'The Role of Tutoring in Problem Solving'. *Journal of Child Psychiatry and Psychology*, vol. 17, no. 2, pp. 89–100.

Woodcock, R.W. (2011). *Woodcock Reading Mastery Tests – R/NU*. Revised edn, normative update). Circle Pines, MN: American Guidance Service.

Yaden, D. and Templeton, S. (eds) (1986). *Metalinguistic Awareness and Beginning Literacy: Conceptualising What it Means to Read and Write*. Portsmouth, NH: Heinemann.

Yamada-Rice, D. (2010). 'Beyond Words: An Enquiry into Children's Home Visual Communication Practices'. *Journal of Early Childhood Literacy*, vol. 10, no. 3, pp. 341–63.

Yelland, N. (2006). 'New Technologies and Young Children: Technology in Early Childhood Education'. *Teacher Learning Network*, vol. 13, no. 3, pp. 10–13.

Yopp, H. K. (1995). 'A Test for Assessing Phonemic Awareness in Young Children'. *The Reading Teacher*, vol. 49, no. 1, pp, 20–9.

Zajicek-Farber, M. (2010). 'The Contributions of Parenting and Postnatal Depression on Emergent Language of Children in Low-income Families'. *Journal Child Family Studies*, vol. 19, pp. 257–69.

Zammit, K. (2010). 'The New Learning Environments Framework: Scaffolding the Development of Multiliterate Students'. *Pedagogies: An International Journal*, vol. 5, no. 4, pp. 325–37.

Zeece, P.D. and Wallace, B.M. (2009). 'Books and Good Stuff: A Strategy for Building School to Home Literacy Connections'. *Early Childhood Education Journal*, vol. 37, pp. 35–42.

Zevenbergen, R. and Logan, H. (2008). 'Computer Use by Preschool Children. Rethinking Practice as Digital Natives Come to Preschool'. *Australian Journal of Early Childhood*, vol. 33, no. 1), pp. 37–44.

Index